"THE BIG MUDDLE STARTED BEFORE I
WAS BORN. IT WENT ON, GETTING
WORSE . . .
WHEN I WAS GROWN UP IN YEARS, I
GOT A VAGUE IDEA THERE WAS A BIG
SPLIT IN ME BETWEEN MY HEAD AND
MY HEART. I SEEMED TO GO AROUND
THINKING BIG THOUGHTS IN MY
HEAD QUITE CUT OFF FROM THE LIFE
IN MY HEART."

—Mary Barnes

For thirty years Mary Barnes was a schizophrenic.

In 1965 she found two psychiatrists, R.D. Laing and
Joseph Berke.

This is the story of her resurrection.

MARY BARNES

*Two Accounts of a
Journey Through Madness*

Mary Barnes
and
Joseph Berke

BALLANTINE BOOKS • NEW YORK

My writing is for My Mother and My Father,
My Brother
and My Sisters.
Mary Barnes

For Ronald Laing and John Thompson.
Joseph Berke

Library of Congress Catalog Card Number: 76-187704

ISBN 0-345-27527-6

This edition published by arrangement with Harcourt Brace Jovanovich, Inc.

Manufactured in the United States of America

First Ballantine Books Edition: April 1973
Second printing: May 1978

Acknowledgements

I wish to thank Mother Michael for her ever-present help. Others, more actively involved with the work at Kingsley Hall, I wish specially to mention. Firstly, Dr. Ronald Laing, through whom I came here. The other past and present members of the Philadelphia Association; Dr. David Cooper, Dr. Aaron Esterson, Joan Cunnold, Sidney Briskin, Ben Churchill, Dr. Hugh Crawford, Raymond Wilkinson, and Clancy Segal. Also Dr. St. Blaize Maloney and Dr. Kennedy of the Langham Clinic. Mr. Sidney Russell, of the Trustees of Kingsley Hall, do I warmly thank. Also Muriel and Doris Lester, the Founders of Kingsley Hall, both of whom died during the time of this book.

The American doctors who came over here to help with the work of the Philadelphia Association I specially acknowledge. Firstly, Dr. Joseph Berke, who was the first to come and who has so particularly helped me. Secondly, Dr. Leon Redler, who came next, then Dr. Morty Schatzman and Dr. Jerome Liss. To Noel and Paul am I specially indebted; Noel Cobb, Doctor of Psychology, and Paul Zeal.

For the physical help I have been given, I thank Dr. Bernard Taylor of Bow, the General District Nurses, and the Matron and Staff of St. Andrew's Hospital, Bow. The Officers of the Bow Social Security Office. Jesse Watkins for all his help, particularly with my painting and sculpture. For other encouragement I have had with my painting I acknowledge specially Mr. Pitchforth, teacher at Cass College School of Art, the help of Felix Topolski, artist, Harry Trevor, artist, Jutta Werner, artist, and David Annesley, artist. Also Jeannette Jackson, Chairman, and members of the committee and staff of the Camden Arts Centre, Harry Kloss, exhibitions officer, Shirley Pountney, publicity officer, of the Tower Hamlets Arts Group, and Anne and John Gillie, Inez and

Geoffrey Branson of the Calouste Gulbenkian Gallery, New-castle-on-Tyne.

For the time before Kingsley Hall, I wish specially to re-member Mr. James Robertson of the Tavistock Child De-velopment Research Unit, through whom I reached Ronnie, and the late Dr. Theodor A. (Alfons) Werner, through whom I was got out of a chronic ward of St. Bernard's Mental Hospital. My debt to him is enormous.

Many others helped me, some, matrons, who gave me jobs, knowing or unknowing, of my past.

Those to whom, in the past, I could "tell more" I feel special warmth; my University Tutor, Dr. Bernard Miles, and the then Warden of my Hall of Residence, Margaret Beaton.

All the people, past and present, of Kingsley Hall, I re-member. Very specially do I thank Michael Dempsey for all his help in the publication of this book. Also Muriel Eden, who typed some of this manuscript, Charlotte Victoria, who very kindly typed the rest, and Rhiannon Gooding, who helped with the editing of the manuscript.

Above all, I acknowledge the pain, the suffering, of my own family.

                                        Mary Barnes

In writing our accounts we have extensively quoted our-selves, each other and many of the people who were in-volved in the events described. Primarily, we have relied on our memories to recall what was said at various times. We have also sought to refresh our memories by referring to a few of the written records of conversations at Kingsley Hall and by asking people what they said, or might have said on specific occasions.

We have tried to be as honest and accurate as possible in attributing quotes. We do realize that distortions may have occurred due to lack of total recall. This we very much re-gret. However we are certain that the use of quotations in our narratives has greatly enhanced our ability to recreate the "feel" of our relationships and to bring the reader more fully into the picture.

                            Mary Barnes and Joseph Berke

I would like to acknowledge my indebtedness to Ronald Laing for many of the concepts which I discuss and illustrate throughout my account. I refer, most particularly, to the awareness that psychosis may be a state of reality, cyclic in nature, by which the self renews itself; and to the awareness that a person may function at several levels of regression at the same time.

Joseph Berke

Part 1

My life up to the age of forty-two years by
Mary Barnes

Madness

Much of me was twisted and buried, and turned in upon itself, as a tangled skein of wool, to which the end had been lost.

The big muddle started before I was born. It went on, getting worse. My Mother and I battled with feelings. My Father was in it, then my Brother barged in. My two sisters came and the mess got bigger.

When I was grown up in years, I got a vague idea there was a big split in me between my head and my heart. I seemed to go around thinking big thoughts in my head quite cut off from the life in my heart.

In 1953, when I was for one year in Saint Bernard's Mental Hospital, I got put in a padded cell. I felt so bad, I lay without moving or eating, or making water or shits. They didn't let me die, they tube fed me. I wanted to be looked after. I didn't know then, I do now, that what I was trying to do was to get back inside my Mother, to be re-born, to come up again, straight, and clear of all the mess.

Dr. Theodor A. Werner, an analyst, got me out of Saint Bernard's. That was not the place for me to go down and up again. Dr. R. D. Laing, Ronnie, got the place for that. He told me when he got the place that it was where Gandhi had stayed when he was in London.

I looked up about Gandhi in the library and went to where I reckoned the place was. It was early spring, 1965. When I got near there, it was dark and raining, and I heard a gang of boys shouting. I was afraid and desolate and lost. I did not know I was nearly there, and I turned back.

I went again, in the light, and then I saw the blue plaque that said Gandhi had stayed there. I had found the "place."

Over the door was written "Kingsley Hall."

3

Chapter One

*My abnormally nice family—my early childhood—
the lost "not here" feeling—the coming of Ruth*

My family was abnormally nice. Friends, relations and neighbours thought that we all lived happily together. Mother and
Father were devoted parents. My brothers, sisters and myself thrived.

Mum and Dad were always considerate and polite to each
other. Mum might say, "Daddy, please could you get me my
tablets, I've got a migraine coming on. You're going all
blurred." Father lightheartedly would suggest, "Well, dear, you
want to take more water with it." (Mother never drank anything alcoholic. It made her feel sick.) Smiling, taking the
tablets, she said, "Thank you dear. It's time you gave me
that pullover to wash. It smells."

They never shouted. The air was cold yet a storm was
always brewing.

Life was like ice, brittle ice. The whole family wanted this
ice to melt, wanted to be loved. But we feared if the ice
broke we would all be drowned. Violence and anger lurked
beneath the pleasantries. On the surface, we were a kind
family. Physically we were well cared for, good food, lots of
milk, fruit and eggs, clean clothes and a big enough house.
Deep down we were torn up with hatred and strife, destroying, killing each other. Our love was sour. Every family
has jealousies and envy. My Mother's view of our world
didn't seem to take this into account.

My brother and I were born in Portsmouth. There we had
a semi-detached house with a small garden and a green-
house adjoining the dining-room.

On Tuesday Mother would stand ironing in the living-room. My brother Peter would be close by, sitting on his pot. I too would be there, often grumpy, frowning and sulky. Mother forced me to help take care of Peter. This was the only way I could please her. Really I wanted to kill him. It was hell having to be a little brother's mother at two and a half. Later when Peter was in a state of breakdown and madness he turned away and was repelled by me. Now I know how he feels my past hate, all the times I wanted to murder him while pretending to be "nice." Peter's inside knows all about my nastiness.

When I was five years old we moved to a bigger semi-detached house with a long garden. It was in the country about twenty miles from London, in those days a rural area. Father would give us a half-penny for collecting horse manure from the road for the rose bushes. In the garden Father made two wells, there was a big "bottom shed" with lots of spiders that Peter was afraid of, and plum trees and apple trees, and we each had our own little bit of garden.

Father did electrical work in a laboratory and came home to dinner on his bike. Nowadays such a family as ours would have a car. At that time a car was a rarity. Only the wealthy and the local doctor could afford one. The greengrocer and the milkman had a cart and horse, but the baker and the butcher had vans. Lighting was by gas that hissed and glowed. The Front Room was preserved for Sundays. Goods were delivered, the post came before eight o'clock, a farthing would buy a "gob stopper" and for a penny you could get two sugar mice. We knew children who never went away for holidays, had never seen the sea. At Christmas and also in the summer for my Father's two weeks holiday, the family travelled to Portsmouth, to Nannie's, the house of my Mother's mother.

My Father's mother, Granny Barnes, came every summer to stay with us for two weeks. In the dining-room, Granny would survey the sideboard, a polished piece of furniture like an open dresser. Its cupboards and shelves were well-filled with all the silver, prizes and trophies my Father had won in races and other athletic sports. There were flat dishes and deep dishes, a cake-stand, a tray, a salad bowl, a cruet.

"Kit," Granny would announce, "I'll clean the silver."

"Oh, yes, all right, Granny," my Mother would say. She could never be bothered to clean "all that silver." Granny worked hard, proceeding to the cutlery, including the fish-knives and forks. Mother would declare she tasted plate powder in the spoons.

On November 5th (Guy Fawkes Day) we had a huge bonfire with a "guy" and fireworks. Christmas Eve we hung a black stocking at the rail of our bed. Some children put up pillowcases. Mother told us that was greedy. We believed in Father Christmas and wrote our lists for him, even when we no longer believed. Weeks before Christmas Father would disappear into his shed. Then Father Christmas would bring me a doll's bed, a scooter, a bicycle, a train you sat in for Peter.

Whoever came to stay with us was usually taken on a trip down the river in the punt, which is a flat shallow boat propelled along by means of a long pole. The river was only a few steps from the house. I wanted to paddle my feet over the side of the punt. In the summer, all the family went swimming. The swims began before breakfast and continued till evening, especially before meals. Mother always wanted us to keep clear of her. She liked a smooth patch alone, to swim in with no interference. My Father romped with us in the water. Then we stood drying ourselves, dripping wet on the kitchen tiles. As Father wrung out the bathing costumes, Mother mopped the floor, and we all set to on a big meal.

Mother endured. She used to get ill and rest in bed. Father was so strong. To Mother his hand would make pushing-down movements. "Calm down, calm down. What are you worried about? There's no need for you to get upset." Nothing stopped Father. At seventy-six he still plays tennis and drives a car at a furious speed.

Outwardly robust as Father, inwardly we longed for the "weakness" of Mother. She kept herself back, in the dark. "Mary, you go on out, with the others. I'd only be in the way." I violently loved my Mother and wanted her to cuddle me. She was nearer "true," less "off the mark" than my Father. My sister Dorothy used to say, "I want just to be a plain woman, like my Mum." And indeed Mother was delighted to see herself as "just a plain woman." She never used

make-up, was never really happy about her clothes, and
always kept her hair short, in a fringe. I, too, grew up
feeling ashamed to look in the mirror, to use make-up, to
be nice, good-looking, attractive.

Unlike my mother I didn't want to pride myself on being
"a plain woman." Yet it felt so shameful to be anything
else. If only I'd been born a boy. Then I'd get married.
Girls had to wait to be asked, so my Mother reminded me.
This used to worry me. How would I know? Will a man
just tell me "I want you to marry me?" When does he give
you the ring?

When my brother broke down, the reason seemed a complete mystery. Father said, "It's his age." He was sixteen.
Mother felt it was her fault, grieved and was sad, but
absolutely believed what the doctors said. My parents were
told Peter had a disease, *dementia praecox*, that he would
gradually get worse, dying in a vegetable-like state in a
mental hospital. Mother hoped he wouldn't live long, she felt
dreadful seeing him suffer. He was caught, stuck in his anger.
No one knew he was angry. Incredible as that seems to me
today it really was the truth. We didn't know and there was
no one able to tell us. The emotional life of the family was
killing him, breaking his heart. Peter, struck speechless with
anger, just got more and more isolated. The rest of the family
were considered sane. He was mad. We were all a seething
mass of wrath, covered by a film of pretence, a spider's
web in which we were all caught.

The tangle of the emotions of my family was so intense
that automatically one member struggling free must be
killed, annihilated, rather than the grip be loosened. Such was
the fear of truth. Madness was a step on the way to truth.
It was the only way.

Peter was instinctively seeking freedom. I too came to go
that way. The route my parents had barricaded and barred.
The step into the dark, to the torment of torn emotions.
Through the years backwards and forwards the tensions increased and burst. As bubbles exploding across the world is
the anger of my family concentrated and released, again and
again.

In the end may there be nothing between us but love.
May all be shattered into God, split into the light of heaven.

I was born at home, before I was ready, feet first, without fingernails, but with lots of black hair. My Mother had been in labour three days and I was at first thought to be dead but I responded to a slap and breathed and cried. Unable to suck, I was fed by means of a pipette for three weeks. My Mother had no milk and I was never put to the breast.

For two and a half years I was at home with my Mother. Then, don't know why, I was sent away, to my Granny's for two weeks. When I got home, there he was, a boy. He was put into the cot. My cot with wooden rails. He was different from me. Mother was always holding him and bathing him. I felt pushed out. I wanted my Mother to do to me all the things she did to him. I wouldn't talk. I was so angry, I wanted to suck all day, and find another mother and run away.

Some time later Mother took me to the doctor because I wouldn't talk. I couldn't, I wanted to sit in the warm water and have my mother do everything for me. The doctor asked me to open my mouth. I was frightened, I wanted to fly away. The doctor let me go, my Mother took me home. When I did start to talk I knew what the words meant, but no one else did except my Mother. She came to understand some words, but tried to make me talk her way. I was not really interested, wanted something of my own. Alone in my own queer language, I came to chatter away to myself.

Mother always took my shits and water straightaway into the lav. She got me so clean, so soon. I wanted all my shits with me, in the bed, all over me, wet and warm. It was what I had made, and I wanted to keep it, nice and safe so I shouldn't be left lost and empty.

If strangers were about I was shy and hid behind my Mother. It was such a relief to get home, if we went out anywhere. I liked to see my Mother in the house. I was so frightened of getting lost. Sometimes my body would seem to swell up as if I had gone away. It would become all "clumpy" and swollen. This went on all through my childhood. The "clumpy" feeling is a bit like having pins and needles. It feels rather as a spaceman seems to walk. Things got worse as I grew older, and I walked in my sleep.

Afraid to be ill, I told my Mother lies. Mother would say, "What's the matter, why aren't you eating your breakfast?

Hold your head up, look at me, I believe you *have* got a sore throat. Mary, is your throat sore?"

"It's all right."

"Come here. Stand up. Open your mouth. You *have* got a sore throat. Don't contradict me. Go and sit by the fire."

Later I went to school. It was very hard to talk with the children. They chased me and bashed me about, also they would force me to say words, but if I did the children laughed and laughed at me.

I hated school. I hated my Mother. I hated myself. All my time was spent hanging about, dodging other children. Other children were strange beings. As if I was on the moon looking at different creatures. They weren't like me. They were unknowable, unknown. Had I got inside them I would have been safe from being a strange object outside. How to hide, so I didn't show, so they wouldn't see me, that was the problem.

In the class I wished I could disappear in my desk so no one would see me. Any time the teacher might ask me a question. I wouldn't be able to answer. Everyone would look round and if I tried to say anything they would laugh because I couldn't speak like them. It was miserable knowing I could get caught any time. School was very dangerous. The teacher always called my name, it was near the beginning of the register, and I was always there, never late. I couldn't say the word, "Present." You had to answer that word. When I tried it sounded something like "Prewick"—without the "r." I never could say "r's." If I shut my eyes, I was still there, in all the strain and trouble.

One day, after dinner, I just couldn't go back to school. I was sitting on the dumpy step in the sun with Peter—he didn't have to go to school. Mother said, "It's time for school." I didn't move. "Mary come on, it's school time." I sat still.

"Come on, hurry up, you'll be late. What's the matter? Answer when I speak to you."

Father heard.

"Mary, do as your Mother tells you."

I put my head down. Mother tried again. "Mary stand up. I'll brush your hair. Don't you *want* to go to school?"

I can't move; Mother gets violent.

"If you don't get up, I shall take you to school. You have got to go."

I can't move. Mother gets hold of me. I scream and hit and kick. But she put me in the pushchair and wheeled me to the school, right outside my classroom she brought me. She put me in the class and left. It was late, after the register, I fought the teacher to run away. Angry, I forgot everything. Usually I was too scared to move. Now I punched the teacher. In the end I just cried and cried and wanted to die. I felt so bad. The teacher had completely overcome me. She made me sit with a girl I knew, at the back, but I sobbed and sobbed.

Most things at school worried me, I fretted over sums and sat in terror when it was drawing lesson. I could never use a ruler. Once the teacher caught a boy drawing a line for me and another time I was caught copying a girl's drawing of a flower. There was a flower on each desk that we were supposed to copy. I felt a criminal when found out. Mother had told me it was a dreadful thing to do, to copy.

When it was singing lesson I pretended to sing, and there again I was caught. The teacher one day came round to listen at each pupil's mouth. Nothing was coming out of mine in the way of sound. My Mother said I was not musical, had no voice, was no good at handwork, nor sums. At dancing I was like a baby elephant. At composition I was better. I could do that, and got to like reading, soon becoming absorbed in school stories. How marvellous it must be to go to boarding school and come home for the "hols." I was always lost in a book, curled up in a chair, screwing my hair up. Mother always cut my hair short, much as I longed for ribbons and long hair, but I had to have a fringe, same as my Mother. Father cut her hair. He also cut mine. I hated having it cut. Later when other girls put bands round their hair I wanted one. Mother told me, "You don't want your brains tied up."

Sometimes Peter and I would both be naughty. One Saturday morning we were so bad, Mother told us, "I can't stay with such naughty children. I am going away." She put her hat and coat on. We heard the back-gate latch click shut. She had gone. Suddenly we really seemed to realize it. We were both sitting crying on the dumpy step between the kitchen and dining-room. In terror I shrieked; Peter screamed. I got hold of him. "Peter, Peter, it's all right. Daddy will come home from work and look after us." It was agony. I tried to comfort us both. Then Mother came back. We were dead quiet. Mother reminded us, "That's better. I can't love naughty children."

Later I read God loved sinners. I decided to adhere to God. Mother was out. God was in. I didn't then know that God was in Mother.

At breakfast Mother often said all her dreams aloud. She dreamt a lot. "Last night I was back at College, Gus, my girl friend, was going swimming. We were then on a boat. Then I was flying in the air. What a lot of silly rubbish. It was night, I was being chased and couldn't run, a big tiger was after me. I woke with a start. Did I wake you, Daddy? Eat up that egg, Mary. Peter, hurry up, it's nearly time for school. Where was I? Oh, yes, I couldn't run away, well, then I was in a hospital, all my teeth were pulled out. Then, Mary, you were there, we were by the sea. You were drowning. I couldn't get to you. Then a shark ate you up. Come on, Mary, it's time you were getting ready for school. Goodbye, dear—that was a peck, Daddy was in a hurry. What, Peter? Did I dream about you? Not last night, I was all over the place. I ate beautiful strawberries. Then we got lost in a wood, Gus from College was with me. There were a lot of geese cackling. There's the paper. What? Read *Tiny Tots?* Well, just one story, about Snowdrop. Sit quiet and don't interrupt, it's nearly time for school."

Mother was always concerned that we should eat all the dinner she gave us. I often didn't want it. She would persist in trying to shovel it in. "Just one more spoonful, one for uncle, two for aunty. Look at all the nice gravy and the greens that Mummy cooked. Make you grow big and strong. See the bottom of the plate. What's the matter, don't you like the pretty picture? Look, Peter has eaten all his, off the tick-tock plate. You should be ashamed, big girl like you, being fed, come on, hold the spoon."

"Don't want it."

"What, what did you say?"

Father said, "Come on Mary, clear that plate, it's all good food."

"Can't."

"Now, don't argue."

Mother is getting weary, "All right, if you *really* can't, but take that plate out to the kitchen."

Father, "Now *look* what you're doing, hold your head up, you see, that's not looking what you're doing."

Mother, "Get a cloth and wipe it up, the *floor*-cloth. All that nice gravy. I was going to put that in a stew for you tomorrow."

Exhausted, I would then have to tackle pudding. We always had pudding, and on Mondays it was rice. I really couldn't eat it. Every week it came. Sometimes Mother let me go to the pantry for a piece of cake but that almost made it worse. I was ashamed eating the cake. Mother would be doing the dinner all morning. I used to feel cross about that because Mother was with the dinner instead of with me. Then Mother got angry if sometimes I rebelled against dinners. If I ate because Mother wanted me to, even if I didn't want it, this was goodness. If I didn't eat it because I didn't want it, this was naughty. My Mother always wanted me to eat it all. She was angry, I was naughty, if I didn't.

Once when Father took us out we had Welsh Rarebit, cheese on toast, in a teashop. Enthusiastically I told Mother about this delicious food that she didn't make. "Couldn't we have it at home?" Mother was very cross. I couldn't understand why or how it was. I felt "naughty," ashamed. Now I see how Mother sensed our eating other people's food as a betrayal of herself.

Sometimes it was difficult to leave off "picking" myself. Mother would tell me, "Mary, stop picking your nose. You make it sore inside. Let me see that finger. It's going septic. You'll have to put it in hot water. Haven't I told you to stop picking your nails? What's the matter with your foot? You haven't touched that toe, I hope."

"It hurts."

"Of course it hurts. You won't leave it alone. Just as soon as it gets better you start picking again. Do you *like* having septic toes? What? Stop muttering. Speak up. You'll get round-shouldered. Stand up."

"I just have to do it before I go to sleep."

"Tonight I'm coming up when you're in bed and I'm cutting all your toenails."

Every Saturday night Peter and I were washed together in
the big bath. My Father usually bathed us, as Mother found
it too exhausting. I loved this, but didn't like it at all when
we got bigger we were separated. I had to bath alone and
Peter went to sleep in the end bedroom. Up till then we had
been very used to seeing each other naked. Often I would be
scratching myself, as my Father tickled me between my legs,
and Peter would be playing with his little cock. To us there
was nothing "wrong" about it. Mother, might say to Father,
"Don't excite her so, it's nearly her bedtime, she'll never get
to sleep." I loved Daddy to tickle me under my arms, on
my tummy and specially between my legs. Then I would
scream with delight. Sometimes I would stand rubbing my
legs together, particularly when holding on to the pram,
waiting for Mother to stop talking to someone else's mother
and move on. Mother might say, "Mary, stop fidgeting."
Within our family we never thought it was "wrong" to
scratch and tickle and rub ourselves. Peter and I used to rub
our noses together. Instinctively, at school and in company,
I knew not to hold up my dress and "tickle" myself. Mother
thought that wasn't very nice.

Although my Mother was dead against us reading in bed or
having sweets in bed or making noise, we did manage to do
some things we wanted. Sunday mornings we often got into
each other's beds. Worming under the bedclothes to come out
at the bottom, head first, we called going underground. It was
rather like being born. Coming out of the dark, into the light.
A favourite game was "Monkey, Monkey, Monkey Man."
We had a puppet monkey doll that was hollow, without legs.
In the game Peter was Monkey Man. I would sing, "Monkey,
Monkey, Monkey man, one foot up and one foot down, both
feet up and no feet down." The last two lines could be
varied, such as, "both feet up, no feet down, one foot up, no
feet up, both feet down." I would yell it, and scream with
delight as Peter bounced up and down on his bed, or mine,
trying to keep his feet down or up as I shouted. We got
breathless, excited, as faster and faster we played. Once
Father came in, angry, with his slipper. There was dead
silence. I cried, in bed. Peter went right away, dumb and
silent in his bed. He couldn't come down to breakfast.

In our bedroom I had Elizabeth and Marigold in a doll's

bed and Peter had Dinah, his rag doll, in his bed. When I grew up my little girl was going to be called Marigold. A frequent question of mine was, "Mother, how will I know what man wants to marry me? How did *you* know?" Again Mother would tell me how she met my Father at a church Bible study group. Then he went away to the war, came back, asked her to marry him. At first she said "no" (I felt sorry for Father). Then she said "yes." I was relieved.

At night Mother stayed with us while, kneeling, we said our prayers, "Jesus, tender shepherd, hear us," "Our Father," and "Visit, we beseech Thee." Then in bed she would kiss us "Goodnight, God bless," and close the door. A little red light, "the micky light," was left on. We often called, "Say it *once* more, once *more*." "Now I've called 'God bless' *three* times—that's *enough*. Go to sleep!" Thursday evening Father was out playing badminton. I always waited to hear him come in before going to sleep, then it was "safe."

As I got older and washed myself alone in the bathroom, Father would call up the stairs, "Mary, whatever are you doing—have you gone to sleep in there? Hurry up."

"I'm washing my feet." With one foot in the washbowl in the warm water I would get stuck in a dream. Mother called it "dilly-dallying."

Unlike me, Peter was considered very good with his hands. My Mother kept his drawings. Some she sent to her mother, our Nannie. Many she showed to other people. I was jealous about this, but as Peter got to school and was excellent at all subjects, I could have eaten him with anger and jealousy. To be a boy, to be chosen. He was chosen to be Australia, with a little girl, not me, on Empire Day. My Mother got a school photograph of them. People thought what a beautiful boy Peter was. He had fair hair. Especially at school, I was very shy. What with having to run and dodge because of my talking, and feeling bad because I wasn't much good at anything, I got like a mouse in a panic, never able to nibble enough holes to hide in. Sitting exposed in a desk was agony. At home I could be wild and noisy. Mother would get alarmed that I might be "showing off." "Whatever would your teacher say if she saw you *now*, the way you behave at *home*." The one thing I always got good for at school was "Conduct." I hardly breathed in class, never mind spoke to another child. Oh to dance and sing and draw, and to be seen, in safety.

Mother said I had no patience. "Do that carefully, keep within the lines, colour that blue, and the other pink, take your time. You see, you rush, look, Peter is still doing his. You have gone outside the lines." I was bursting to crash through lines.

"Mary be quiet, don't tear about so, walk nicely. Now, you've torn that again. Other children don't get into the state *you* do. Calm down. I can't understand you, I really can't."

Always I found it so difficult to be what Mother considered good. It seemed impossible. Like eating worms when you weren't a bird.

"Just look at you, whatever would Gwen's mother say if she saw her like that? Wherever do you get it all from? Where have you been? Don't come into the house. I don't like you going there alone. Those shoes are ruined. Mud on that skirt too. What, you lost your way? Well you shouldn't go. I've no patience with you, Mary, none at all. It isn't as if you haven't been told. You just don't *do* as you have been told."

Sometimes, after tea, Mother would try to make me say words after her, to teach me to talk. I hated this. I was so tired of it all. I wanted to shine, but I felt all the polish was being rubbed off. Mother would quote: "Be good, sweet maid, and let who can be clever." Not everyone, Mother would say, can do well. You have to accept how you are. As long as you keep trying and do your best, and be *content,* realizing you cannot *make* yourself clever, that's all that matters. That's your trouble, you are never *content.* Mother was sucking me dry, but then telling me I had no juice.

She assured me that in the future I would be very grateful to my mother for not "spoiling" me. It seemed there were great dangers in doing "just as you liked." A favourite phrase of Mother's was, "and don't think *you* can do *just* as you like." I would dare on occasions to wistfully mention such matters as that "Flo had long hair," "Edie was allowed out to play," "Some children had fried things." Mother would get very cross and suppose I thought her a bad mother and wonder how perhaps I might like to go and live with some-one else's mother.

Especially when the pamphlet about the poor in the East End of London came, was I reminded to really think about my many blessings; good food, warmth, clean, whole cloth-ing. I quite forgot I wanted more sweets and fried eggs and a fire in my bedroom and pretty clothes and long hair with a ribbon. In fact, I used to look at the pictures of "rat-infested rooms" and "Father unemployed" and spindly-legged children in tatters, and weep for shame that I could ever complain to my Mother.

All the time, I was forgetting and forgetting about myself and Mary Barnes was getting buried and buried in a great big hard shell.

I can remember, as a child, and all through my life, having very strange feelings. I would seem to go away, right away from everything and everywhere. I didn't belong anywhere. I would jolt myself back, perhaps by touching something. But then the thing did not want to be touched. It was as if I was lost in the air, as a ghost or dissolved, everything would seem to leave me. I was empty and not there, not anywhere. If someone spoke with me, it didn't seem to be me. It was "just a thing"—I had gone. Sometimes it was quite difficult to come back because familiar things didn't seem the same. The air had changed and everything was alien as if I was on the moon and was just something—anything, not a person, me. There was a feeling of deadness, of being in a blind alley. My soul was musty, like a cobweb in the dust.

I don't know how I ever really came back. I didn't exactly want to, yet I was afraid, being strange and out of myself. Later, this feeling seemed to take me back into the womb, right back into the womb of the world.

As I got older one of my great delights was to go into an old church, alone, to pray. Occasionally Mother had taken me to church, to evensong. The old stones, the feel, the smell of the wood, fascinated me. But all the other people seemed "too much." Being alone in a church gave me a sense of distinctness.

It seemed I had to be physically alone to be separate, to live, that being in a crowd was to be lost. Like my Mother,

I "hated crowds." Yet later still, crowds attracted me, especially at a fair or circus or in a market; to be part of the throng was to be alive.

When I was eight years old my sister Ruth was born. I was talking clearly, though outside my home I said very little. Mother had taught me words, but the "voice" wasn't my own.

Mother always said she liked us best as little babies. It seemed we were then as dolls more easily to her. I didn't know where babies came from, yet I felt something was on the way. Mother was very upset during the time of Ruth's coming. She later told me, "I wanted another baby. I got bad itching between my legs. It was terrible. I couldn't sleep. The doctor wanted to take the baby away. I said no. I *want* this baby. I was desperate. One night I was in bed, I came downstairs, I was going to put my head in the gas oven. I stood in the kitchen. There were pears on the table. I sat down and ate pear after pear." This must have been about September, when the pears were ripe. Ruth was born in December. Mother had no milk.

About this time I played with my shits. In bed I used to put my fingers into my bottom and dig out pieces of hard shit. These I would squeeze in my fingers. It frightened me but was so fascinating and interesting I just had to do it even though it seemed a very dangerous secret. Even Peter didn't know. Always this used to happen while I was hidden under the bedclothes. I felt nice. It delighted me and I put it away softly, safely under the mattress.

One morning I was in the garden. Mother was making the beds. As usual, she was singing one of her favourite hymns, "For all the Saints who from their labours rest." Suddenly it was quiet. Mother called out of the window, "Mary."

"What is it? I'm playing."

"I want you. Come upstairs." She sounded very serious. Terrified, I went into my bedroom. It was like being in a dream, a dreadful nightmare. I hardly knew I was walking up the stairs. I felt not there, like a ghost.

Mother was towering above me. She had the mattress turned up. I was all falling to pieces. "What is this? Mary, whatever have you been doing? Turn round. Come here. What is it?"

I whispered, "I don't know."

Mother said, "You must *never* do such a thing again." I hung my head. "You can go now. Go on. Never let me see such a thing again. I can't think what's come over you." I felt cold. It seemed this was a very *serious* naughty thing. Mother was calm and collected. I felt so ashamed. Dismissed I crept down the stairs. I was all over the place. I couldn't seem to play, I felt lost, apart. I wanted something, I didn't know what.

Much later on, at times on the lav, I got out my shits. But the matter was never mentioned again in any way.

I used to look at my bed. My shits had been hidden under the mattress, the hard flock mattress on the black iron bedstead. That bed had housed my shit. For years that was my bed, until I left home, and always on return in that bed I slept. Eventually, taken apart, the bed and the mattress went with all my things to the convent. There it stayed for years until Mother Michael sent all my things to Kingsley Hall.

Then I slept in it again. Joe put it up, with the same hard mattress, in the flat. Then it went down to the basement because I wanted a divan bed like the other people. Two years later I hauled it up, with the mattress. The black iron was painted yellow and blue. Standing on it I painted my walls and the Children of Israel going through the Red Sea. Then wanting again to sleep on the floor I put the mattress and all the parts of the bed back down in the basement. Francis found it and now he sleeps on it in his room in Kingsley Hall.

I still have my pot, the enamel chamber that was always under Peter's bed. For years we both pissed in that. It was after Mother cut her hand on a china chamber she got us the enamel pot. Once in my sleep, dreaming I was on my pot, I wet the bed. When I told Mother the truth she did not seem to believe me. I felt hopeless, as if what I said could never be true.

Mother was very strict about cleanliness inside as well as out. Once she washed my brother's mouth out with soap and water because he said a swear word, "bloody." I looked on in horror, she was holding him over the sink and he was screaming and struggling to get away. I knew quite a few swear words. If Mother heard us say "OK" we got told off. We couldn't go play in the street because of what we might "pick up." Bad words, bad habits, and dirty things in our hair.

Eventually, Mother let Peter go and he drank from his special mug. If anyone else used it, it was, he said, "fum-mi-ant-son." He meant contaminated for him. Usually Peter was very controlled, being able to save his money and make his sweets last. I was a greedy gobbler and having crunched up my own, would look to Peter for some of his, or moan to Mother for more. This I never got.

Every Saturday morning we went to "Granny Dawson's," a little shop in a cottage opposite our house, to spend our weekly penny. Mother warned us, "Now don't buy *rubbish*." Peter often spent his penny on a bar of Nestlés milk chocolate. "Look what Peter has got. Mary, that's rubbish. That's not wrapped, you don't know where it's been. You don't know what that's made of." "It's only sweets." I liked different things, a farthing each. I got four, sherbert, gob sucker, coconut candy and a sugar mouse.

One of Mother's biggest complaints was that I would "keep on"; I would not rest content when she said *no*. Mother was always saying "no" and I was always "keeping on." "Mary, that's enough. I said no, and no means no, and if you start whining I shall get a headache. There you go. My head's bursting. I shall have to go and lay down. Now get off me. *Go away*." Isolated, overcome, and unable to cope, I would feel everything was on top of me. Mother used to say sometimes, "I just feel flattened out."

Sometimes I would take Peter off, away from Mother. Maybe down the garden. Amongst the fruit trees we couldn't be seen. One morning in hushed whispers, in the shed we concocted mixtures of powders. We were trying to make gunpowder. Father had all sorts of things in jars and bottles. Like him, we put our noses in and smelt. Only we didn't know what was what. We had a box of matches. I kept striking lights and giving Peter new stuff to try. Nothing caught, we got absorbed in testing things to see if they would burn. We didn't hear Mother, she opened the shed door and caught us, red-handed.

"Whatever are you doing? Mary, what have you got there. Give me those matches. *Both* of you, come into the kitchen. *Who* said you could play in the shed? *Who* said you could touch Daddy's things? Peter, what were you doing at the bench?"

"She told me to."

"What, you do as she tells you? Haven't you got a mind of your own? What did you tell him? Answer me, Mary."

"We were just trying to make gunpowder."

"Haven't I told you children you are not to touch matches. Don't you know the dangers of fire? What would have happened if I hadn't come? The whole house might have been burnt to the ground. You both might have been burnt to death. Do you know how painful it is to be burnt? It would have served you right. You were asking for trouble. Peter, you are a 'silly' to do as she tells you. Mary, you should know better. I am ashamed of you both. Father will have to be told about this. Now get something *useful* to do and just be thankful you are not *both* in *hospital* with bad burns."

We knew we had been "getting up to mischief." In a sense, Mother expected this of us. I would hear her say to people it was normal to be naughty, it showed we were healthy. Sometimes I could bash Peter one for telling on me. But it was nothing to what I felt later when I had two young sisters and my Mother specially called upon me to "set a good example." By this time I was wanting to run really wild. I was so jealous I could have killed them. I wanted all my Mother's attention and to be looked after as a baby and I wanted to be a boy and have all my brother had that I didn't have. The moment they said, "Well, he's a boy," I would have the most terrible anger, and when my body got fat and it got periods and breasts I hated all that. I wouldn't wear a brassière and I demanded to know why didn't boys have "it," periods. My mother told me boys had a different body than girls. The blood that came every month was the blood meant for a baby. If I ever had a baby then I would not have periods for nine months. I must not be surprised if I saw blood one day when I went to the lavatory. I was about the age for it to happen. It would come once a month.

My Mother would give me something to wear. I was so frightened. I daren't speak of it. I looked at other girls and wondered if they got "it"—periods. I didn't ask them. Then I realized what it was all about, girls "not being well," being excused swimming or gym. I was more angry than ever and frightened of my sex. I felt so ashamed. I wanted to be a boy. I had no idea of how a boy might like me because I was a girl.

As a very little girl I had been attracted to a certain boy who made me laugh. He made funny faces. I wanted to go and play with him. His mother had invited me. I told my Mother.

"No, Mary, you cannot go."

"Why not?"

"Look, when I say no I mean no. Don't ask questions."

"But his mother *asked* me."

"I don't know his mother."

"You've *seen* her. He's a clean boy, he has no brothers and sisters. I want to see where he lives."

"Mary, I don't want you to go. The answer is *no.*"

"He rides me on his bike."

"That's *very* dangerous. I don't like you to be with him. There's girls you can play with."

"But I like him. Can he come here, to play with me?"

"*No.*"

"But *why?* Edie's brother comes, when she comes to play."

"That's *different.* Now don't start, I won't have that whining."

"He's a funny boy. He's in my class."

"Now just attend to your lessons in school. You're not there to look at him. You need to work hard. Now go away and get something to *do.* Don't get sulky."

I felt that my Mother felt there was something queer about Teddy. I just liked him. His house was up a long drive, off the road. I was so curious to see it. I knew my Mother didn't like "only" children. She said they were spoilt. Yet I felt somehow there was something else about Teddy that made my Mother so forbidding. I didn't ask my Mother again if I could go to play with a boy. I felt it was wrong.

When I was twelve and Peter was ten, Father took us on holiday to a Youth Hostel. The first night I was quite dismayed when I realized I had to sleep in a women's dormitory, away from Father and Peter.

About the time I got periods, at thirteen and a half years, Mother told me, I had asked, where babies came from. She explained when my Father loved her something passed between them and that started the baby. I knew how my brother passed his water, but I had no idea that it was *that* that went *inside* the Mother so she could have a baby, *if* they loved each other. Also I had been told that *God* sent the baby.

I didn't know what went where, or what was passed. One day in the kitchen when I saw my Mother and Father embrace each other I told Peter, "Go to the other side!" He did. I thought we would see what passed and how. Mother turned round and demanded to know whatever we were doing. I got all confused, trying to say that we were trying to see. Mother told me to go away and stop being silly. I wanted to know.

My Father never spoke to me of such things. When I was a little girl he used to tickle and tickle me between my legs. I loved it and would scream with delight. Also to put my head into the thick black hair on his chest was a great joy and a comfort. When I was laughing with being tickled, Mother would tell Father to stop exciting me. I would also often romp with my Father, as well as with my brother. We would fight and wrestle and roll on the floor. A wild romping game Peter and I had was "cat and mouse." Under the table was the hole of the mouse. Whoever was the cat, waited to pounce. We played it on the floor, crashing against table and chairs, often begging one more minute's play, when Mother's head started to ache.

I never knew then, in words, yet I must have felt the strain of how my Mother was. I remember my Father used to make a pressing-down movement with his hand as he told my Mother not to "get upset." He used to warn us not to "upset our Mother." Mother could never really let my Father love her. As I got older she told me she could never imagine how anyone could enjoy making love. She wanted to be married to have babies. Before she got married she thought you only "got together like that" when you wanted a baby, or rather every time you got together like that you got a

baby. Mother did not enjoy having a baby. She hated it.
She would tell us, "You don't know what mothers endure
to have children. Some mothers only have one child. How
would you like it if you had no brother or sisters."

"Why didn't you have any milk to feed us?"

"Some mothers just don't. It's a terrible pain having a
child. There's no other pain like it. Then you forget it.
This is how a mother is made, or she could never have
another child, if the memory of the birth pains stayed with
her."

"Some mothers die having babies?"

"Oh yes, you can die having a baby. I was very ill, in
great pain, Mary, when you were born."

"*I* was nearly dead."

"Yes, but they didn't use instruments on me, for fear of
killing you. I had to push you out. It took three days. I had
a lot of pain."

"But you wanted me?"

"Oh yes, I wanted you very much, I *love* babies."

"Oh."

I was puzzled.

At this time I read a lot. "Come on, put that book down
and help your Mother," my Father would say. Down the
garden on the swing I made up stories myself. In my
imagination, on the swing, I started an organization called
a Chain of Friends. People from all the world belonged to it,
to be friends, and love each other. I went alone for long
walks. I tried to console myself. All the time I was so jealous
and angry. I was a girl, and there was my brother, a boy.
He passed the scholarship and went to the grammar school.
There was I still in the elementary school struggling with
sums and getting punched in the back because my sewing
got all screwed up and dirty. There was he, learning French
and getting "educated." That's what I wanted, and to go to
college, to be a "student." I felt wretched and I despised
myself. I knew my Mother was disappointed in me. When I
had failed the scholarship she had come to see the teacher
about me. Although I was never, as my brother, top of the
class, I had wistfully imagined because I so wanted to go
to the grammar school, that I might somehow pass the
examination.

Mother was always telling us how she had passed the exam that I failed, and gone to the grammar school and then to college. I knew all about Mother's student days. How she acted in plays, principal parts, sang in concerts, her voice was admired, her paintings were framed. She did so well in all her examinations. There were all her books in the front room, with prize labels in them. She loved teaching, the tinest children. Eventually, I got to a technical school.

Chapter Two

Through adolescence—into nursing and the
sacrifice of my brother—despair and rebellion—
some time with my brother

When I was thirteen years old my sister Dorothy was born.

One night while asleep I suddenly felt a violent panic. Getting out of bed I knelt on the floor, begging and begging God not to let my Mother die. Crying, I told God that if she died I would have to stay home to cook the dinner and look after my sister, but I really wanted to stay on at school. Please could my Mother stay?

A nurse came in to get sheets.

"What is the matter? What's happening?"

"Get into bed. Go to sleep."

"Oh, God, God, don't let her die, God don't let her die, don't let, don't let her die please, don't—please, please, God."

Different voices, where was Father's? What was he saying? "I'll go now, to the chemists." All the lights were on. The front door opened. It was slammed. Cars started and stopped. Frightened and cold, worried and bewildered I lay awake. I knew so little about babies. Mother was ill, somehow I seemed responsible, to have caused it.

Morning came. They told me to be very quiet. Mother was still alive. "You have a baby sister. Now get off to school."

At dinner-time there was a lady we had to call Miss somebody. She came every day to get the food and clear up. Mother was still very ill. Father looked serious and silent. We were taken (I hardly dared breathe) to see the

26

baby and I looked for my Mother. She smiled and looked very far away. Very subdued, we crept down the stairs, "God, don't let her die, please don't" went over and over again inside me. There was no possibility of naughtiness. It seemed that one wrong move and Mother would be in the grave.

Mother survived. There was the baby sister, Dorothy, to be loved, admired and perhaps even to be held. Naughtiness came upon me. The strain was intense. God had saved Mother. How could one be jealous and angry, naughty to God, when Mother was still alive. More than ever I wanted Mother all to myself, to be cuddled, and comforted, nursed and fed. But Mother, more exhausted than ever, had another baby to look after and Father demanded she be helped, especially by me, the eldest.

Dorothy had a birth mark on one hand and swelling on her head and had to be taken every few weeks to the hospital. This made me more jealous than ever, the concern for her, and me having to stay at school for dinner. It seems just when I wanted so much to be carried I had to carry a lot more.

Mother told me how she nearly died. "There was the face of Aunty Nina, you remember her before she died? She smiled. She looked happy. Going towards her, she stopped me. 'Go back, it's not time for you yet.'" Someone said, "three minutes, it's back, her pulse, here.' I stayed. Never doubt about life after death. It was so vivid. I was not dreaming. What happened was, they couldn't get my after-birth away. The baby, Mary, grows through a spongy mass that comes away after the baby is born. Dorothy came. They waited, but nothing else came away. It was stuck to me. The nurse got a doctor and he got the specialist, and then they got a lady doctor. She had a smaller hand and she pulled it out of me."

"Did it hurt?"

"Yes."

"And it bled?"

"Yes, a lot. They took blood from Daddy's arm and put it into me."

"You were *very* ill?"

"Yes, I went away, I died and I came back."

"How did you die?"

"My heart stopped beating."

"How did you know?"

"I felt it stop."

"Then you saw Aunty Nina?"

"Yes, she told me it wasn't time for me. I was happy, at peace. I came back."

"I was praying you wouldn't die."

"Well, I didn't."

"No."

I was deeply impressed by Mother's experience. It was at about this time that I really started to talk to myself, to God, to be always praying about things. Often I had spoken aloud to myself, imagining all sorts of companions when alone. Later my perpetual friend, especially on a journey, was always an imaginary daughter. She was told where we were going, how, and why. Her name was frequently Marion, and eventually in my mind a storybook was made about her. Sometimes, most secretly, I tried to write stories. There was a feeling of shame about this activity, something that I had wanted to do.

Dorothy was fed on a bottle. Mother had no milk.

Friday afternoons I would come home with a plant in a pot or a bunch of flowers for Mother. To get to the technical school I went by train and bus, so I was entrusted with money, which all got spent. This school prepared pupils to work in offices or shops. I was not keen. When I told a teacher my idea about becoming a nurse, she said, "What, a *nurse?*" as if I was crazy. Never, as a child, had I played at being a nurse. My dolls were not bandaged, and they only got put to bed to sleep at night. Within me there was a great fear of illness. Nurses and doctors were wonderful people who must be "right," but I was terrified of them.

The sight of blood scared me. When I cut my finger trying to cut the bread for tea, I ran down the garden to hide under the trees in the raspberry canes. It was a deep cut, the bone showed and I held it together. Oh, why ever hadn't I obeyed Mother. "Mary, when you get in before me, you may lay the table for tea but do *not* cut the bread and butter." Mother was still out shopping. I had so wanted the tea to be completely ready. Oh dear, oh dear, how to hide my finger. If anyone else hurt themselves I would turn away.

It seemed to become a nurse might somehow be a solution to all this horror. To wear a white cap, to do good, to live away from home, all seemed very attractive. Also to have textbooks and study, that was to "get on," to be "someone," to get "somewhere."

My cousin John, who had been to Cambridge, was a journalist. If only I had passed the eleven-plus, the "scholarship" as we called it. Mother was so angry and disappointed about this. Hadn't I liked composition at school, wanted to write, to be a journalist? Such thoughts were put out of my mind in a grim determination for nursing.

My father took me to another technical school where they had a pre-nursing course. Mother was doubtful. The Headmistress of this other school said she usually only took girls from a grammar school, but she would give me a chance. I resolved to work hard.

A year before the war all the family had a holiday together by the sea. At first, when Father suggested going away, Mother was, as always with such a thought, very gloomy. We told her, "Mother, it's a question of going on *holiday*, not to prison." Father rented a bungalow. Ruth remembers it as the last time we were together as a family. Mother, who rarely enjoyed going out, seemed on this holiday to get some relief. In bed we could hear the sea. We ran on the sand dunes. We swam in the sea. It was shallow and safe. Dorothy was toddling. She lay naked in the sea. We played with the sand, romping and rolling with Father. We watched the fishermen with their nets. It was far from a town. On the beach there were seldom any other people. Mother seemed happy. Life was all sun and sand and sea, and us playing. Peter and me, Ruth and Dorothy, Mother and Father. There seemed room for us all. We hoped to go there again. But next year war had broken out. I forgot the baby I wanted to be.

The day the war started, Father was sent away, out on the North Sea on minesweepers, and I was sent away, to school, as an evacuee. This was the beginning of the physical split-up of our family. Mother was left with my brother and sisters. Sometimes Father came home during the school holidays. He was in the Home Guard and used to get us on the kitchen floor, practising unarmed combat.

Battered about as I felt, mad and angry and often homesick, it was not me but my brother who then broke down.

After a year as an evacuee doing a pre-nursing course, I entered a hospital near my home as a probationer nurse. I was then seventeen years old. Mother would say, "I don't want to keep you tied to me. You are free to go where you please." Father reminded us, "You have to learn to stand on your own feet, to be independent."

During my first year of training I had three weeks holiday which I spend walking on the Yorkshire moors with my Father and brother. It was spring. The wild daffodils were out in the dales. It was a great relief to be away from the strain of the hospital. The thought of going back with a haunting nightmare. Pretending to love nursing, I really hated it. Everyone found nursing "hard." But, if you "stuck it out," then people admired you for being "a nurse." What "a nurse" appeared to be, to me, was not to my liking. However, when I was "pulled apart" and I was always having "strips torn off me," I got to pretending I didn't care and I laughed and got hard. The only people who seemed nice to me were the patients. Against those in authority I inwardly, and sometimes outwardly, rebelled. I got eaten up with anger. I hated being sucked into the nursing machine.

My brother—I last seemed to see him as a real person on that holiday on the moors—just got pulled apart, and never to this day has he got together. Unlike me, at this time, Peter could not push his feelings down and sit, as it were, on top of a volcano and smile and pretend he was quite happy and very well. Mother coped, as she always did, by getting physically ill and so being looked after.

It was Peter, more true than the rest of the family, who showed the madness. He was at a technical college doing an advanced electrical engineering course. My Father had, against advice, moved Peter from the grammar school. Father had been through the First World War and subsequent unemployment depression, and feared that Peter might not be able to get a good job with an academic education. Peter, always in the top three of an "A" form at the grammar school, was very good at all subjects and liked the grammar school, which was mixed, boys and girls. Peter has recently told me he didn't want to go to the technical school because it was only boys.

One day he just could not go to school to sit an examination, his headmaster said he would have easily passed. He stayed in bed. He could not talk about it. No one understood. Father got severe and said "He's all right—it's his age," and later that he should go and "get a job." Mother got physical aches and pains. My sisters, especially Ruth, avoided Peter. She was aware that Peter never stayed in a room if she entered it. I remember how Peter used to take Ruth with him to watch trains. This had made me jealous. Ruth was "our" baby. We used to fight over her. Later Mother "kept out of his way," as she put it. She feared Peter might hit her as she felt he hated her.

I felt great sympathy for Peter. I wanted to help him. Sometimes I stayed near him and spoke gently to him, sensing that he quite understood, though he never answered. He seemed so lost and unhappy. He incarnated all the anger I felt but couldn't feel, anyway not then. Later, in the only way I knew how, in a very baby way I expressed anger and then I was "mad" and silent and trying to avoid living. In Peter I was seeing what I wanted to be and it moved me towards him.

Three or four years later Peter was certified insane. There was no one to help him, no understanding. He was himself reading Freud, painting with oils and studying Yoga. I did not realize how angry and guilty I felt about Peter's state or all Mother's illnesses. I always felt impelled to try to help them.

On my first day in hospital I was given a uniform to put on and sent to a ward and called "Nurse." For a month I was thrown about in chaos. Then I landed in the Preliminary Training School. The other four or five nurses who started with me left, saying they weren't going to be "kicked around any more." Everything was such a mystery, bewildering and obscure. Everyone was always in a hurry and very busy. To know what to do or what you were supposed to be doing was quite something. I was expected to look busy and get on. Get on where, or with what, I was never certain. The

hospital seemed a big machine geared at high pitch, grinding
everything up that entered its mouth. But I tried not to be
swallowed by it. Tidying a bed, I looked at the patient,
"Nurse, hurry up there, you haven't all day to tidy those
beds. Make the patient comfortable and come into the office."

We had lectures about making patients comforable, different ways to put pillows, folds on sheets, how to make
a bed, neatness, tidiness. We lifted, we turned. I wanted to
listen; I felt there was something in what patients said they
wanted. Despite the most strenuous efforts, patients seemed
anything but comfortable. This bothered me. It seemed so
cruel to be put in a bed and tidied and washed, like the ward
being brushed and dusted. They didn't know a thing about the
operation or the illness or the medicine or if they were going
to die. I was like them, I didn't know what was happening
to me and trying to help them, I found out a bit. The bit I
found out wasn't quite in keeping with the rest.

"Take your time, drink slowly. There's no need to talk."

"Nurse, Nurse Barnes, hurry up with those special diets. He
can take that himself. I won't have you sitting on patients'
beds. Take this prescription to the dispensary."

"Yes, Sister."

It was hopeless to argue. The more truth you knew and the
more you let it show, the worse it was for you, and the
patients. In the beginning all my torment was bursting out of
me. Never on time, untidy, curious, frightened and sometimes
trying to hide, I got a bad reputation, I was inefficient, lazy,
careless. Called to the Matron's office I stood, hands behind
my back:

"Nurse, what is the meaning of this? Another bad report.
Nurse, I asked you a question, answer me."

"I really think if something is worth doing it is worth
doing well. I don't seem to be doing anything well, perhaps
I had better leave."

"Nurse, get back to your ward."

"Yes, Matron."

Crying in the sluice, I got more confused than ever. I so
wanted to be a nurse, a good nurse, to really help people
when they felt sick and had pains. I loved them. I meant
to help, to be kind and gentle. I couldn't tell people off,
or worry about the beds; they were dying, they didn't know

what they wanted, but sometimes they wanted me and I was torn away.

In my first year my despair was so black I wanted to kill myself. Somehow I dragged through. The doctors seemed nice, but so distant. Later as I got more senior I realized they too played the game. If you didn't join in you got labelled a bad patient or an inefficient nurse. I later got very interested in bad patients and inefficient nurses. The patients didn't seem to have time to die, or to pass their water, or to eat their dinner. The machine worked at high speed. Admissions, discharges, operations and deaths. Numbers of nurses in training, wastage, examination results. An efficient nurse looked smart, answered crisply, was never late, kept patients in order, beds tidy, and devoted herself to becoming part of the pattern. The machine had an indelible stamp. Four years and she was a nurse. The stamp never washed out. Never an "efficient nurse," I survived, and without leaving and without killing myself. Often in a dull state of misery or desperate despair, I don't know how I survived, but I did. Towards the end, I was exhausted, very tired and thin.

I now realize my destructive suicidal despair was bound up with my denial of my body. As I grew up I loathed my breasts, avoided boys, denied to myself that I wanted a boyfriend, forgot what the friendship of boys was like. I'd wanted to be a boy. I pretended to be feminine but couldn't feel or admit my desire for a man. Eventually, without conscious longings for love, I decided I wanted to have a baby.

It seemed in Russia women with babies and no husbands were quite accepted. I wondered about going there and made some inquiries. It was just after the war. The fact that Russia was a communist country didn't worry me. That then all seemed right to me. Also I wanted to go to Russia because I read in a nursing journal that there you could carry on studying from being a nurse to become a doctor. I felt ashamed that I wanted to be a doctor. I know this shame was bound up with the enormous guilt I had in connection with my desire to be a boy. Anything masculine in myself must be hidden, buried in secret, hardly admitted.

All these seemingly "wicked" ideas were fermenting within

me. To get to Russia, to study medicine, to have a baby. Fantastic, I must be crazy, so I told myself, it seemed too dangerous to tell anyone else. I drifted into midwifery and, wondering about working on the continent with the United Nations Relief Organization, went, I think on their advice, to work as a District Nurse. By this time, perhaps because of my shame and fear, I turned away from my own real inner desires and settled, in a sort of compromising mediocre way, to be content just to travel, and to get married in order to have a baby. I decided to become an Army Nursing Sister.

By the time I was ready to enter the Army, my brother was very sick mentally. He was at home, isolated in his room. He could not bear to be near my Mother or with Ruth. I wanted very much to help him, to be with him.

Mother had been in hospital. She had been bleeding from her womb and the doctor thought she might have cancer. A dilatation and curettage revealed that she hadn't. However, she was tired and strained and when Father and Ruth and Dorothy wanted her to go with them for a holiday by the sea, she agreed to go. I assured them I would be all right staying alone at home with Peter. They left.

Speaking with Peter was difficult.

"I've made some supper. Would you like something to eat? Have some soup."

Peter walked away. Stayed alone in his room. Sometimes he came alone to the kitchen for food. Food left on the table he would sometimes eat, if there was no one else in the dining-room. He looked cross and tense.

One night, while I was in bed, my bedside lamp on, Peter walked into the room. Standing above me he said, "I have come to sleep with you, I want to come into bed with you."

"No, Peter, we are not children any more."

He turned and slammed out of the room. He could have killed me. My muscles froze. There was banging about in his room. What to do? Go to him, try to calm him. No. Keep away. Get downstairs. He might come back. Creeping downstairs to the kitchen I sat numb. There was still noise upstairs. Be quiet, have a drink. The tap, the gas, everything seemed to sound so loud. Warm milk, it brought me to life. The shivering started, it wouldn't stop, my teeth chattered.

Oh God, God, don't *let* him come after me. Where to go, the doors are all open. Nothing locks in the house. It's dark. The outside lavatory. It latches. Could he break the door. Sit against it. Get together. Keep quiet.

Oh God, what has happened. Where to go?

Creep back into the house. It's quieter.

Slowly, steal upstairs. Get some clothes. Dress in the kitchen. It was getting light. Tell the neighbours? No. Go to Aunt's? No. Three days before the family got back. Go to them? No. Go away, somewhere for three days? No. Stay with Peter. How? Alone? Impossible. Too risky. Couldn't go to bed. No. Not another night alone. Not me, alone. Not him alone. Who, who would stay with me? My friend in the library. She often stayed. Peter ignored her. She let him be.

Yes, that's it, ask Jessica. No need to say exactly. Simply say, "please come, for the last three nights, before the family return."

It's morning, quite light. Not a sound upstairs. Go out. Take a walk. Calm down. She will come. Peter was in his room all day. We have a meal. We go to bed, in my room. Everything is quiet, Jessica is in Ruth's bed. We slept, all night.

My parents and sisters returned. We talked about the holiday. Mother sensed Peter hated her. She was afraid he might hit her, or my young sisters. The atmosphere of the whole house was taut, like a tightrope. Nothing broke. As always there was with me the fear of "upsetting" Mother. Deciding to speak to Father, I went down the garden. He was weeding the onions.

"When you were away, three nights ago, Peter came into my room. He wanted to sleep with me. Somehow I was not altogether surprised, don't know why. It was very frightening. Angry, he went away. He didn't touch me. I'd kept still, lying down, and said quietly that we were no longer children."

"Don't tell your Mother." Father often did speak to me of Mother and she used to speak to me about Father. I was jammed between them. Mother seldom went out and when

Father took me out, especially if we took "the children," Ruth and Dorothy, I would be mistaken for his wife. This, at the time, feeling old for my years, quite pleased me.

About Peter Father would only say, "Oh, he'll be all right. It's his age." Mother feared there was something very wrong. Living in the house, the fright of that night upon me, I was quite certain Peter would not be all right.

Some days later—it was washing day. We were rinsing the clothes.

"Mary, you notice Peter is still the same?"

"Yes."

"What can be the matter? If only we knew, we could help him."

"Yes."

Long pause, rinsing, washing. Shall I tell her. Yes. No.

"Mary, do you think Peter might harm the children?"

"He wanted to sleep with me."

"What?"

"When you were all away, one night he came to my room. He didn't touch me. But he was very angry. You know how he is, with you."

"Yes. Why didn't you tell me?"

"Father said not to. In case you would worry."

"I'm glad you told me."

"So am I. It was something that happened to me. I'll tell Father I've disobeyed him. Shall I go to the doctor about Peter?"

"You could ask your Father."

Father was sorry. "It worries Mother. Yes, dear, go to the doctor."

Alone at the doctor's. It was the lady doctor.

"You know my family? It's about my brother, Peter. He doesn't talk. Nor eat with us. He wanted to sleep with me."

"When? How?"

The doctor explained that Peter was mentally ill. He must go to hospital. An ambulance would come for him the next day.

I told Mother and Father. Nothing more was said. No one told Peter. Joe, when I first told him, noticed this at once. The fact that no one spoke to Peter. He didn't know about me going to the doctor. We were afraid to talk to Peter. I thought he might punch me in the breast. Mother, sensing his hate, kept out of his way. She was fearful that he might hurt Ruth and Dorothy. Father seemed very far, mentally, from Peter.

The ambulance came. I opened the door. The men said, "Where is he?" I pointed upstairs to Peter's room. They carried a strait jacket. Mother was shut in the dining-room with my young sisters. Peter walked out with the men. There was no violence. He just went. I saw the ambulance go away. My heart went out of me. He was lost and gone. It was the end, forever, and the murder was mine. Alone, in the front room, stone cold, it seemed no heat of any fire would touch me.

Mother sent the children out, to play. We got the dinner. Father came home. "He's gone?" "Yes."

Some days later I went to see Peter, in a locked ward. All he wanted was his pen. This I brought him.

Before going into the Army, overseas, I saw Peter once more. With my Father, we went to where they had moved him, to a big mental hospital with high walls and long tiled corridors. We knew then that Peter was schizophrenic, *dementia praecox* they called it. I asked to see the doctor. It seemed there was little hope for Peter. Was it really true? He still seemed Peter to me. Changed, but he was Peter. I couldn't accept it, that he was a mad person, locked up. Peter, my brother whom I had wanted to help. They had given him insulin and electric shocks. Because he spoke a little my Father thought he seemed better. He stood there by the white tiles, alone and lost. I looked back and saw him, how he was standing. The deepest sadness hit me. Unable to cry, I seemed to die.

Recently, at Kingsley Hall, Peter told me, "You know, that night I was not going to commit incest, to put my penis into you. I just wanted to feel your body, to fondle your breasts."

If only we could then have helped Peter to know in words the violent feelings that terrified him. But we were all the same, speechless with anger between our minds and our bodies. We slew Peter to preserve our shells. Of course, had we understood, been the sort of family that more truly lived its feelings, it would not, could not, have so happened.

I was terrified of my own sexual feelings, yet immensely attracted to my brother. It seems now, in the way I had not been surprised at his intrusion, that unconsciously I had seduced him to my room, to my bed. In a breakdown state, below words, he was very susceptible and responsive to the truth not only in himself but in others. He was functioning at that level, less divided than me, replying totally to what my inner depth was saying. So terrible our ignorance and what was done to Peter.

Unaware that I was seducing and then castrating Peter, I was alarmed to near panic. Had I then been able to know my own feelings it would have been quite possible, without seducing Peter, to relieve his state. It would not have hurt me to let him touch my breasts and gentle speech would have softened his anger. My terror increased his fear.

Chapter Three

The coming of religious faith—breaking down— recovering

When I was twenty-two the Army stationed me abroad, first to Egypt and then to Palestine. Peter remained locked up in a mental hospital.

Ken, who was in the Army education corps, was the man that I really came to love. He teased me, "You're the proper little sister. You are shy, so am I." Always he was in my mind. It was such a happiness, knowing him. His black hair and fine face attracted me and he certainly had charm. To be his wife, to have his child, became a very strong desire. He was going to Oxford, to finish studying for the Anglican priesthood. That he could prefer God to me was a blow I had not reckoned on. In those days, vaguely Christian as I was, the idea of a vicar not having a wife was foreign to me.

We more or less parted but it was not until my return from home leave, after Ken had departed, that I really felt the depth of my misery. Now I know that had I married and had children I would inevitably, twisted as I was then, have done unto my children as my Mother did to me, and given my husband hell, because of all my guilt.

It was difficult looking for another boyfriend. Wanting to marry and have children determined me not to let the sadness overwhelm me. However, nothing ever came of any other attractions. It was not that I never went out with boys, but somehow nothing ever developed. At this time I tended to be rather opposite to my Mother, to do things almost simply because she didn't. I used make-up, smoked, wore earrings, liked travelling, didn't consider myself "ordinary." Mother always used to stress we were a very *ordinary* family. She had never made a journey alone, without my Father, always used Palmolive soap, and sent to Pontings for our shoes and sheets.

Much later, in working free from my Mother, I would often catch myself going according to Mother's ways, a thing in itself I would previously externally have avoided. Not so my brother, who at the age of forty-two still shops at Pontings and uses Palmolive soap.

One thing that seemed quite distinct from Mother was the matter of religious faith. Careful to "discard" Mother, I was yet anxious to retain "God." Mother had never been insistent about us going to church or Sunday school. Going out with Ken had caused me to fairly frequently go to a church service and I got confirmed in the Church of England. I was now twenty-four years old.

In my nursing work there was love and compassion, and visiting the shrines of the Holy Land was a very moving experience. One weekend, in Egypt, some friends with whom I was staying invited me to Mass. This was my first contact with the Catholic Faith. Later, when in charge of an officers' ward, a doctor who was in torment with a skin disease told more about the Faith. His faith seemed so deep. It really was the core of his life. Alone, I, visited the German Catholic church in the adjoining P.O.W. Hospital. Something, undeniable, indefinable, attracted me.

Back in England, nursing in a tuberculosis hospital, there was a girl, Anne, who was near death for three months. Medically speaking, she hadn't a chance. She knew this, and though wanting to live, was quite prepared to die. She was a Catholic. The way she was, how she accepted her state, impressed me. She didn't die. But this was almost incidental in comparison to how she was. Being with her so much, as a Sister there was always greater freedom to devote time to people who were very ill, I seemed to get through her something of the Catholic Faith.

Going to a priest was not easy, because of my past prejudices and pride. I was very proud. Oh dear, this "foreign" church, they could at least have laid on an English priest for me. This man's accent wasn't right—how could I learn from him. Somehow I got to quite desperately praying for Faith.

People say, "What brought you into the church?" Quite simply the Grace of God. Why me, to be given so much, the pearl of great price. Many know about it, but to have it is what matters. It is a mystery. The Faith is a mystery. Why I, not you, have that Faith is a mystery. Being received into the Church, into the mystical Body of Christ was the most important event in my life. It happened on the eighth of December 1949. I was twenty-six years old.

Making confession and receiving Communion bound me into the Body of Christ. That same Body that carried the Cross to Calvary had I received into myself.

My Mother was curious.

A year later she became a Catholic.

About this time I met a man through the Catholic Introductions Bureau. I had written to the Bureau because I so wanted to marry to have a baby, and it seemed such a sure sound way of being able to marry a Catholic. By now there was in my imaginative feeling some longing to be loved by a man, to be wanted and to want, for my own sake, irrespective of a baby.

The man I met I just couldn't love. He didn't seem to understand why. He was about my own age, secure, in a high salaried civil service post. He just did not attract me. I felt he never would, and something in me simply refused to merely marry a man, a penis and two or three thousand pounds a year.

I told him, "You are just not the man for me." He could not seem to believe me, being quite crazy to marry me. I just did not love him, could not desire to be *his* wife. Eventually he believed me when I told him, "Anyway, I'm not sure now that I'm wanting marriage, because I have got desires toward being a nun."

It seemed I had to go to God, to give myself to God, to be the "bride of Christ." That I must suffer a physical deprivation, make sacrifice, in order to gain through my Faith the wholeness that lay buried within me, was not within my reckoning. The immediate results of my desires at this time were to "run after God" as if God were a man with a penis. I was always in a hurry, frantic to get somewhere. On holiday with a friend I would fly into furious tempers, exploding with rage, if a bus was late, a café closed, or if we couldn't get somewhere on time. I was always on my knees, praying, at Mass, going to confession. I wanted to be a saint. My head was busy working out how. It seemed you just had to let God make a saint of you. "Well, God, here's me. Get on with it. Tell me what to do." I got very demanding of God.

Such matters as spiritual guidance, purification, confrontation of the evil in myself, were just not in my vision of things. The living, surging whirlpool that was me was held back, hidden deep below dead ground. Mercifully, I broke down, went mad. There was no question of me hiding under a habit, a false divided self. It was my quest for God, for myself, that brought me to this point. Desiring to become a nun I had started visting Carmelite convents, when on holiday in Spain and France. Then I went at once to the Spanish Father who had received me into the Church. He took me at first to a nursing order where the novice mistress advised me to go to a Carmelite convent. When we got to such a convent, we found them in the middle of moving to Wales. The Mother Prioress suggested I come later to stay with them in Wales.

I did, and my Mother came to stay for a week. My Father was quite cross and grieved at the idea of me going to a convent. My Mother had let me be. In Wales my Mother was concerned because it seemed I could not bear her near me. Wanting to hit her made me only able to very coldly kiss her. The Mother Prioress seemed warm and loving. Telling her about my brother didn't seem to put her off me at all. She said I could enter the convent. I was there about five months.

Much later the Mother Prioress told me, "I was not at all aware of the strain between you and your Mother. I thought you were most considerate to your Mother." It always bothered me that I couldn't really love, be in harmony with, my Mother.

Soon after arriving at the convent, on the eighth of December 1951, I was for a few weeks sent out to care for a lady physically and mentally ill. As Mother Michael advised me, I got this lady to the Catholic Home that I was myself later sent to. The Mother Superior of this Home subsequently told me she thought on first seeing me, that it seemed as if I was like the patient I was then bringing her.

Back at the convent, a small pimple on my knee became a big boil and for a short time I was in bed on penicillin with a high temperature. Then what happened was that I had gone down into a dumb-struck state. Trying to keep up with the others brought me to a standstill. A great cloud seemed to come over me. I was quite unable to express any feeling in words.

I seemed able to *do* things and then couldn't. Sister Angela showed me how to make altar breads. One day everything seemed wrong. She had to help me a lot. It was difficult to move. I was quite unaware of my own state. Mother Michael suggested I go to the Catholic Home to help. I knew the sisters there had had breakdowns.

Once there, I still felt dreadful, cut off, unable to contact anyone. My speech seemed to have gone. Sitting alone sometimes in the chapel, where I would say long prayers of my own, then just sit, brought little relief. Wandering about the garden, playing with the earth, rather than weeding. Sitting watching people, seemed more within my scope. Any sort of order to do this or that, especially washing up or any sort of housework, got me caught, unable to move. Left alone, talking to myself, pleasing myself, was, in a sense, my only relief. Sometimes the Mother Superior sent for me. She would say, "How are you?" "All right." Then there was silence, nothing more. To me other people there were sick.

When they took me to London to have E.C.T. I decided I must be sick, and wanted to go in a taxi, not a bus. My trust was in them. My knowledge of the dangers of electric shocks and how some people "punished" other people by so-called "treatment" was then completely beyond me. This was in 1952.

Back in a few days with the community, things seemed much as before. Alone, out of touch with other people, going my own ways, speaking very little, wanting to explode yet hardly knowing it, life was a horrible ghostly dream, unreal and distant. The spell was broken by the appearance of my Father. He came to take me home. The Mother Superior advised me to live at home, doing part-time nursing work.

My inclinations were not towards being at home and

nursing. However, in my mind, "they" understood, "they" knew, therefore "they" must be obeyed. The results were disastrous. I was unable to sleep. A local doctor gave me sleeping tablets, then later, sent me as a voluntary patient to the mental hospital.

They put me in a side room on the admission ward. The ward was locked. They physically examined me, took my temperature and wanted a specimen of my water. All this made me think that I was ill and that they would make me better. Then they moved me to the Villa, a new part of the hospital. Here we were also locked in, which gave me the impression that people were afraid we might kill ourselves.

Being at first allowed to go home on a Sunday, I brought back some flowers for one of the sisters. As she was off duty I had to go to the Nurses' Home to take them to her. She told me, "You should not be here." Quite quickly the lost feeling came upon me. It made me stuck, unable to speak, or move my body. As a tiny child I had picked flowers for my Mother. Always on Monday mornings Mother had cut me a bunch of flowers to take to school to the teacher.

They gave me insulin and pushed me about to keep me moving. Then I got electric shocks and was put in a padded cell. Though aware of people and things, everyone, everything, seemed unreal, out of contact with me.

A sister came to take off some of my water. My tummy was full. She seemed cross. I wondered why, because I liked her, and wanted her to take off my water. Somtimes when I was fed it got too difficult to eat. Then they tube-fed me.

It was terrible to be touched. Noise disturbed me. Light was blinding. It was agony if they left the light on. The pads on the chronic ward, where they moved me to, had black walls. The only relief was to be alone in the dark, curled up, like a baby in the womb. In those days I knew of no such connection. It was terrible to be moved and much as I liked to be in the water, when they came to get me to the bath I struggled to be left where I was.

Lying in the water with my eyes shut was a relief, but it was always too short. Forced out, struggling, rushed back to bed, in a big check thing that would not tear, I would be quite lost and hopeless. It was dead misery, too bad for tears. Light was like a blinding pain going into me and I sheltered from it under the blanket.

Once a nurse tried to cut my nails. The touch was such that I tried to bite her. Sometimes they gave me paraldehyde. It was medicine, they were treating me.

On one occasion they dressed me to go outside, but I didn't want to go, so they pushed me. It was cold and dismal an asphalt squre surrounded by high brick walls. We were supposed to walk round for exercise. A nurse, she was young and kind, stood with me and held my arm. They took me back inside the ward and put me to bed. When standing I would hold myself still and stiff, to keep together, so as not to lose everything and go away. Moving was dangerous. Sleep blotted out. Not to wake made it easier. Someone said I was on suicide caution. Although aware, if the door of the pads was opened I didn't move or open my eyes.

It was a chronic ward. It seemed they couldn't cure me. Always to be there, mad. In a despairing way I accepted it, wanting only to lie still in the dark, in the pads.

Then one day a nurse came in to me. She gently said, "Would you come with me to see another doctor. He is visiting the hospital, his name is Dr. Werner." Something seemed to stir in me. Letting the nurse move me, I slowly came out of the pads.

She had some papers. Half in a sort of dream I followed her. We went through corridors. She unlocked doors. Barefoot, with ragged hair, wrapped in a big check thing, I padded after her. We got to a little room where there was an old man with white hair.

Somehow, secretly I saw this. It was too much to really look out. He said my name. "Mary." Something moved inside me. He didn't have a white coat on. He was sitting, smoking cigarettes. He had big glasses. Standing there seemed safer. He cared for me. He wanted to help me. Without words, he touched something inside me. As I inwardly moved towards him he touched me with his hand.

He saw us out, the nurse and me. Silently, we went back to the ward, to the pads, the nurse locked me in. The pads were not the same. Nothing there was ever the same again.

That tiny bit of me that was not punishing me to death, but that wanted to live, Dr. Werner had got hold of. He gripped it and he strengthened it. He strengthened that tiny part so much that I got out of that hospital. We didn't have discussions. I hadn't got words. He used very few.

"You are better?" "I hear you helped the nurses." Later, "Perhaps you can go home for a weekend." "I will see your parents with you." Later still, "Get a nursing job. There's no need to say anything about this. You are all right."

His few minutes of tremendous ability changed my life. From the pads, to a small locked room with a barred window, from there, off the chronic ward, back to the Villa.

Once they sent me flowers and home-churned butter from the convent. I showed them to a young nurse and she started to read the accompanying letter to me, which was a great delight. The ward sister saw us; "Give her that, she can read it herself." Everything went dead, far away. I was in a daze, didn't know why.

As I "recovered," the only possible way out of the mental hospital, I worked a lot on the ward, cleaning lavatories and sluices, mending sheets instead of tearing them, going to the coal yard for buckets of coal for the night nurses' fire, washing down walls. I got half a crown a week and a septic finger with a high temperature. Put to bed on penicillin I was terrified to stay there in case I got "bad" again. But by now I could see the hospital gates; I was working my way out. Out for a weekend, out to stay, back into nursing.

The nursing job I got was that of a night sister. Dr. Werner had said goodbye to me. In the circumstances at that time there was no more he could do. Without drugs, just with the use of himself, he had got me out of hospital, back into nursing.

Sometimes I went home. It was always the same; excitement, joy in going home, then misery, deadness.

"What's the matter?" Mother would say.

"It's just that you seem on top of me."

"I suppose you think I'm possessive?"

"Oh, no, no, Mother."

We both felt bad. In fear I'd instinctively denied the truth. We weren't getting anywhere.

Mother states a fact. "You seem not to like me near you, yet you don't like it if I ignore you—I can't get *right* with you."

"I like coming home—but every time it's the same. I can't explain it."

"Well, Mary, I do my *best*."

"Yes, I *know*." Oh dear, life was so weary.

At times I felt quite fantastic. Within months of the pads I would suddenly feel, "What am I? Where am I?" I was in a uniform, stiff, starched. Held up, buoyed up. A patient asks my advice. I reply, "I'm a nurse." A doctor tells me, "Get her into an oxygen tent." The Matron wants the report. A child is bleeding from where her tonsils were. I'm a nurse. I'm a nurse.

"Sister, I can't sleep. Check the drug. Show me the phial."

What nurse?

"She's gone."

"Quietly, I'll help you. Pull the screens closer."

Death, it's all a breath, life. Oh God, where am I? What am I? Hold me, keep me. She's gone. She spoke, an hour ago. She's gone. Gone away. Her flesh is cold. Death. Where am I? What am I?

It's getting light, I drink, I eat, I move. Listen, there's a bird. I breathe, deep. I'm here. It's a hopsital. I'm a sister, I'm not in the pads. Where am I? What am I? Where am I going? What am I doing? The blood's running out. Check the group. Feel his pulse. It's hot, he's sweating. The blood is flowing. I walk away. Out into the day. I'm in the air. The air is all around me. It's cool. I'm in a pool floating, in the air. In a bath. Water, water. I walk in a shop. My feet are on the grass. It is light. It's spring. Where am I? *Who* am I?

Alone, I run on the grass. I fling off my shoes. My feet are wet. Oh, God, oh God, I dance, I kick stones, I fling sticks. I run. I bend, I twist. Breathless, I sit. I gasp in the sun. Where am I? What am I?

I go back, into the hospital. I am afraid. I am lost. I am angry. I feel a great weight pushing me down flat into the ground. The laundry is there. I must do my hair. Make up a new cap. I feel stale. I sleep. I eat. Where am I? What am I? I must think, I must think. I go to the church. A boyfriend comes with me. Dr. Werner said I might marry. I've been ill. I must try to keep well. I wanted to be a nun.

I want to bare my soul—to get to heaven—to be a saint. I must do as I'm told.

Yes, Matron, No, Matron. I must think. I must think, I'll marry this boy. I'm not really keen. The priest tells him go, find someone else. The boy wanted me, without my Faith. This couldn't be. Where am I? What am I? What can I do? My belt holds me in. The buckle is big. I bear it and grin. I'm smashing inside. I'm twisting. I'm tearing. What can I do? Where can I go?

I read of a course. Teaching, why not. Two years away. Thinking, reading, writing. References, my past. Back at the hospital, I tell the Matron. I need a grant. No, I must stay as a Night Sister. She cannot ask for money for me.

"Sister, I do not consider you suitable. You are too quiet, too reserved, to teach."

"But Matron, I have been accepted by the University. I am entitled to a grant."

"Not through me. I will not ask the hospital committee."

I am sweating inside and cold with fear. I apply, above her head. I get it. I go.

Chapter Four

*Studying and religious teaching—reaching Ronnie
—at the Richmond Fellowship Hostel—living in
the divide*

For two years I worked and played as a student. It seemed
the terror lifted, that even if "they" knew about you they
still accepted you. We had dances, I had my bike there. I
went to lots of student meetings. Exam times, I swotted it
all up and poured it all out. My tutor liked me, and I liked
him. Once at a teaching practice, I lost my way and dried
up. It was all about blood, I had some slides. I got in a
panic. My tutor asked the students questions. Such was his
skill, they never knew.

"Did we answer his questions all right—do you think he
thought you had taught us?" they asked me. So unlike hospital ways. My tutor only ever criticized in a helpful way—
and that only in private. I dreaded going back to hospital.
I felt on edge. As if I was on a ledge and might fall over.
But I felt freer than I did in a hospital. It was a relief to
meet many people and to talk at last about thoughts. My
ideas were acceptable. I felt I belonged there. At times I
would feel "dead" and distant. Looking back I realize I
must then have been angry, perhaps because I felt the lack
of a boy-friend. Other girls had boy-friends. They were getting degrees. They were getting husbands. They would have
babies. Dr. Werner had advised me to get married and not
go too much to church. Dr. Werner understood what I
was doing. Such understanding was not then possible for me.

I wondered about the one unmarried man on the course
I was on. No, I thought, no, I definitely couldn't. The other

49

boys, on all the courses, like the girls, were all much younger in years than me. I loved the company, but I felt the gap. I wasn't getting what the other girls had. At the time, when I felt far away, sad, dissatisfied and strained; I put it all down to my recent past. I had been ill mentally. I must get better. Get on. Progress. Go somewhere. Somehow, I was not really ambitious. I just wanted to "be", to live. I hardly knew it. I put all my desires and energies into Nursing Education. How I wanted to teach student nurses. The sort of nursing school I wanted to start. My tutor was in great sympathy. Yet somehow, I was not quite "with it". It was all there, as sound and sensible as I could make it. But I was somewhere else. I was away—apart from it all. This big heap of ideas. It was me. Yet it wasn't me. I was not really in my thinking and all the time I was trying to force myself into my thinking. Like physically trying to pull at my heart and stuff it into my head. I couldn't. I went to Norway on a study tour. I wrote about it. It was published. I had asked a lot of people a lot of questions.

Someone, somewhere told me, in Oslo, "Go to the Dominican church and look at those paintings on the walls, the work of a French Jesuit." I did. There, I moved, I moved to God. No questions. No words. Dim light. The very powerful paintings. A red glow. The Blessed Sacrament. I was still. I had what I wanted.

Again, the race was on. The scramble of exams.

I got mine.

I went off to a nursing school job. In three months I left it. I got another. I got battered about with my "ideas". I got accepted by the National Catholic University in Washington. I was going for a year to get an MA in Administration, in Nursing Education. Then the American Embassy refused me a visa on account of my mental history.

I tried to get a waiver. Dr. Werner's filling in the forms reminded me that I had been his star patient. He was very angry because of all the trouble and so was I. But again I was refused. I got another teaching job. Waiting to know about the waiver, I was helping at a home for Mentally Handicapped Children. My parents were just moving to South Africa. My Mother was in bed with a bad vaccination reaction. I took her food. I can remember how I hated her.

I must have been angry. I felt like throwing the food at her. I could not bear her near me. I just could not then tell my parents about my change of plans. That I had been refused a visa. I felt it must be written all over me. Mad person. Not safe to be let into America. I felt not fit to live, and quite terrified anew that people would "find out about me". Eventually I told my parents. There was little comment. They were too busy sorting themselves out from a house they had lived in for thirty-three years.

In order to get accepted by the American University I had done a lot of extra-mural London University lectures in philosophy and psychology. One of the psychology lecturers had, at my invitation, come to the Nursing School where I taught to give some psychology lectures to the student nurses. After a lecture one day we somehow got into the subject of masturbation. She was a Catholic and said it was sinful. On inquiring exactly what it was, and on being told it was to physically excite oneself sexually, I then asked do I do it?

"I often scratch myself between my legs. I've always done it. My Mother used to tell me my Father excited me when he tickled me here."

Cecily assured me that I was masturbating and that it was sinful. I realized, having been quite ignorant, that I had not been in a state of sin, but that now, knowing it was wrong, I must not do it.

For the time being all was well. I rather wondered how I came to be so ignorant, but it was such a usual thing for me. I'd always done it so never sort of noticed it. Now sometimes when going to confession I decided I had masturbated. It was a bit difficult. Cecily had said, "You could scratch yourself if it itched."

In 1962, after my parents had been in South Africa for three years, I went to see them, and my sister Ruth and her children, whom I had never seen before. My Mother would say to me, in great anguish, "What have I done to you? What have I *done* to you? I feel you can't bear me near you."

I begged her to believe me, "I don't *mean* to feel like this. I can't help it. Something comes over me. In my will

I don't hate you. I love you. Please, can't you accept it, the same as I have to. I have to keep away from you when I'm like this."

My Mother would cry. Often I also cried. It was agony. I so longed to be with my Mother, in peace, to enjoy her company. My Father, not able to understand, would reprimand me for bad behaviour towards my Mother. Mother seemed better able to understand. When she seemed to beat herself, I would tell her, "You tried to do your best for us; whatever happened was *not* your fault. I *don't* blame you. Stop blaming yourself."

My Mother was caught and so was I. We wanted to help each other. Neither of us knew how. Although I was sure the trouble lay in the childhood my Mother had, and in turn how she had been with her children. I could only tell my Mother this truth. It was difficult to leave it at that. My whole being was rearing to get free. I was like a butterfly fluttering in a net. Not until I was released did I really know how caught I'd been. The net was so big. The flutter so violent, a panic of movement, like a moth on the window-pane, unable to make open my own way. The physical presence of my Mother stirred me as nothing else could. Alone with my parents, especially when on a touring holiday, I felt very strained and tense, afraid I would hit my Mother.

One night, it was wet and dark, we got to a hut in a tourist camp. There were three bunks. I took the highest, my Mother the lowest. My anger was swollen to bursting. How to hold it, what to do, my Mother was so physically near.

I paced about outside. The eucalyptus trees were dripping rain. It was pitch dark, deserted, lonely, but how to face my parents, the night with them, in that hut. My Father called:

"Mary, are you there?"

"Coming." Oh God, don't let me touch her, don't let me kill my Mother.

It was no good, I couldn't hide my anger. My mood broke through. Mother questioned, "Mary, what's the matter with you?"

"Oh don't start!"

My Father intervened, "Now don't be rude to your Mother."

There were no words, I couldn't "explain". Somehow I forced myself into my bunk, held the bedclothes, made myself stay there. It seemed I was very near to being put in a mental hospital. How could I keep up the exterior "wellness"? How not to break. The ultimate relief of being in a bunk on a ship returning to England was enormous. I was *not* in a mental hospital. Somehow I had got by—just.

Except for six weeks with my sister, I had been six months in the house of my parents. I'd gone out, meeting people, making friends, trying to keep going. My face didn't show my soul. People said, why ever don't you stay with your parents? Do you *have* to go back? I most certainly did.

Returning to England I went to stay at the convent in Wales. The Mother Prioress advised me, as she had done before, to get analytical help. I could not, no analyst would take me on. Why, I did not then know.

My brother came to stay a night at the convent. I learnt that Peter had become a Catholic, and that some time ago he had wanted to enter a contemplative monastery. Since my leaving home to go into the Army, I had seen very little of Peter. For years with great difficulty he had kept out of a mental hospital. Sometimes he came home to rest. Usually no one knew where he was or even if he was still alive. At the time of my return to England, my sister Dorothy had just left on an overland trip to the Far East, from which she went to Australia, and Peter was working in an hotel in London. For eighteen months Peter had been washing up in the kitchen of this hotel. He was very depressed and feared that he would commit suicide. He wanted me to get a job and a flat and he would come and live with me.

It was all very disturbing. I told Peter about my own mental illness and that I thought we both needed help. I thought that we could live together within a psychotherapeutic community. The only place I knew of would not consider us. The Catholic community where I had previously stayed was now only for priests and nuns. Soon after this Peter wrote saying he was in a mental hospital.

I visited him, it was very worrying. Peter was then in a

part of the hospital in which he could only stay for three months. Then if he didn't leave, he would be sent to the chronic part of the hospital. His doctor asked if Peter could come with me. I said no. I knew Peter needed very skilled help and that I did also. I told Peter what we both needed was psychoanalysis and that I thought we should both go to the same analyst, as we came from the same family. Peter said, he thought his mind was clear. I felt Peter did not understand. I did not feel I could talk to Peter's doctor. I was not keen on mental hospitals, but I wondered whatever did Peter's doctor think, suggesting Peter just be sent out to "carry on". Didn't he realize Peter needed very skilled help? I had been reading a lot of psychological books. Everything I could find anywhere about schizophrenics having analytical psychotherapeutic help. I read and read. I got books about the life of Freud. I realized his daughter, Anna Freud, was still alive, living in London. I found out where. Perhaps she would help. I wrote to her about myself. I imagined she would see me and then she would have Peter and me to live in her house with her. Then we would both have somewhere together safe, to stay, and she would analyse us and make us better. I felt surely, she would know. I thought out all I wanted to say to her and waited for her to reply to my letter.

When her letter came, I was afraid to open it, as if I had done some wicked thing. She wrote, in effect, "You had better leave well alone. Your previous psychotherapist did not recommend analysis for you. You have your profession and I would advise you to continue in your nursing work in which you have done quite well." Her whole letter was considerate and kind. Yet I was shattered. Everything seemed to fall from me. I had told her about Dr. Werner and my time in the mental hospital. I wanted her to know all about me before seeing me. Then when I went to see her, I planned to tell her all the rest of my idea, about Peter and me coming to live with her. I also thought the nuns' parents might also come and be helped by Anna Freud.

After this idea was smashed I got worse. Quite in a panic, I was trying to think of other places, appear as usual, and look after the nuns' parents. Things were beginning to seem unreal. I wondered about the Cassell hospital. Peter agreed to come there with me. He got his best suit out of the store. I had a letter. The hospital doctor would see me. They would not consider looking at Peter. At once I turned it down. I knew I was sick, but at that time, I felt I just could not leave Peter. I knew the convent were praying for us. I was imploring heaven for help.

Then I remembered James Robertson. I knew him through the wonderful films he had made, *Two Year Old Goes to Hospital* and *Going to Hospital with Mother*. I had often shown these films to student nurses and James Robertson had come and helped me with student discussions. He was very kind. I decided, I have nothing to lose. I am going to write him of my past and tell him about my brother, and ask for help. This I did; through those films, the work of James Robertson, I reached Ronnie.

James Robertson replied to my letter. He wrote he knew of no place where Peter and I could both stay and get help, but that Dr. Ronald Laing would see us both.

That was it. I was satisfied. Here, at last, was a doctor, a psychoanalyst, who would see us both. I went at once to Peter. I showed him the letter. Yes, he would come. He would meet me there. His hospital doctor was quite angry, telling me Dr. Laing's treatment would do him no good. By this time I had read *The Divided Self*. I was in no doubt that Dr. Laing understood about schizophrenics.

I imagined Ronnie. I imagined his office. His secretary would show me in. He would be standing by a desk. He would turn towards me. He was dark and wore a dark suit. He was not very young. Rather staid. Quiet. Professional. He stood by a flat desk, on the far side of his office. He was medium height, if anything a bit short. He was not fat, but he was solid. So, in my mind I saw Ronnie. His hair was rather dark. The desk was brown. There was a fireplace. I had to rather make a couch come into the picture. Analysts had a couch. I would lie on his. I would go often. I was going to have analysis. He would cure me. Get me right. Make me better. I would tell him all my thoughts. Just how they came, everything in my mind, I would say. I'd read all about it, how you have to tell everything. I thought hard of all the things in my life. Everything I felt ashamed of or frightened of I must tell. Everything I was angry about and all my jealousy I didn't think of. I didn't know, in that way, in my head that I was jealous and angry. I tried to read a bit more about analysis. Somehow I couldn't read any more. Everything seemed to wander away from me.

At last the day came to see Ronnie. I got there, to Wimpole Street. I was in very good time. I rang the bell, a lady opened the door, Peter was not there. The waiting-room was empty. I sat down. There were magazines. I didn't want to look at them. Walking round the room I very closely inspected everything, touching very carefully, for fear anything should break. Then I sat down, in the same place, facing the window, wrapped in my black velvet coat, watching for Peter.

My thoughts wandered, schizophrenics, my clothes, a mauve and green skirt, they—schizophrenics—dressed "in bizarre ways" the books said. Would Peter *come?* Oh God, get him here, *get* him—*please* don't let anything stop it now. I get up. I can't see far out. I sit down, back on the sofa, facing the window, I decide. There is nothing I can do. If he doesn't come, he doesn't. I must think what I am going to say. I'm sitting up straight, I can't lean back. I'm holding myself together, I'm afraid of my life. I'm wrapped in my coat, I'm looking out. I feel the moments, I'm here. He's an analyst. He can help us. James Robertson knows. He's an analyst. I like him. He knew this man was the person to help me. Over and over inside me I'm saying, Laing, Laing, Ronald David Laing, Doctor Laing.

I see Peter. He sees the house, yet walks by. He comes back. Slowly, he walks up the steps, rings the bell. He is shown in. He sits down.

"Hello Peter."

"Hello."

He looks very clean and brushed. He sits up, stiff on the edge of a chair.

"You got here all right?"

"Yes," says Peter.

We wait. It's silent.

The door opens. He stands, supple, like a young boy. Dark hair, black suit. He bends towards us, hand on the door.

"Er, I'm Dr. Laing," he says. I want to laugh. He is young

and warm and human. I like him. I feel myself coming back. My insides seemed to have left me. He moves easy. He's able. He laughs. "How can we do this?" he says. He's looking at Peter. He will see Peter first.

They go. Again, I am alone in the room. It seems a long time. They come back. Peter smiles. His face is soft and warm. I feel his life. I see something I had almost forgotten Peter ever had, a spark of life, love. Peter was dead, cold, and gone away. Just then he came back. I saw him. I felt him.

Then I followed Ronnie into his office. He offered me a seat. I sat down. He sat at his desk. It was near the door. He sat on a swivel chair, swung towards me. I liked his desk. It was a roll top one. Open with all the papers showing. His couch was grey—to the side of me. I wanted to lie on that, I felt stuck. I couldn't talk. He offered me a cigarette. I took it. He lit it. It was a menthol one. I felt queer. What was the matter. Why this—this sort of cigarette. I put it out. I started to talk. He got me off Peter, on to myself.

"I hated it, I hated it," I said about a hospital teaching job. "My Mother says Peter is herself intensified."

"Who said that?"

I say again: "My Mother said it." I tell him of my time in the mental hospital. "I was a bad patient." In a whisper, "I played up." "I want analysis, I want to get right." He reminds me I am a nurse. He knows of a place where Peter and I could go. A hostel, a Richmond Fellowship hostel. Perhaps I could help there.

I assure him, no, no, I *need* help myself. In the Catholic community I didn't know I was sick, now I do know. He says he will arrange for me to go to the Richmond Fellowship hostel. I feel he is going to help me. He sees me out. We pick up Peter on the way. I am full of hope for the future.

At the station, I drink warm milk.

I get there. I had been lost and all falling apart inside. I had left Peter. Inside the house I come away, more. This is where I have come to have treatment. They are to do with Ronnie. I remember the Catholic place. I didn't talk there. That's where I went wrong. Now I will talk fully, about myself—so they can help me. Everything I think, I will say aloud. All my thoughts I will speak all the time. Allison, the social worker, took me into her room. I tell her how I've been. About seeing Ronnie. The mental hospital —how I was then. I tell her I'm having analysis. I tell her I will trust her. I will tell her everything. I tell her about writing to Anna Freud, and how I imagined I might have gone there. Allison shows me to my room. She helps me put clothes in the cupboard. It's a big room with four beds. Mine is near the door. I lie on it. Allison takes me down to tea. We have it off a trolley in the sitting-room. A girl called Margee comes up to me. She's heard I'm a nurse. I move away. I don't want her leaning on me. She lies on the floor. I want to lie on the floor. I do. Someone else comes. She's helping there. I know at once. She must be one of the therapists. Like Allison. They are to do with Ronnie. I talk to her. Would I like to walk outside? Yes, I say, but not far. I tell her of the Catholic Home. I worked there. That was wrong. I didn't talk. I know now, I understand, I have to rest a lot. I have to talk. I'm having analysis. I talked all the time she was walking outside with me.

Soon it was supper time. I was still talking, saying my thoughts. I didn't eat much. I went to bed. They showed me the wash place. I didn't wash much. I lay in the bath. I didn't lock the door. Everything must be open. The next day was Sunday. I went to church early. Then I settled down to another day of "treatment". I said my thoughts, Allison told me Elly, Elly Jansen, the head one, was coming back to the house and would see me the next day.

I sat around. I thought as well as talking all my thoughts I would write to Ronnie. He also must know all my thoughts. Everything I would write him. In this house they spoke of him. They called him Ronnie. So did I, now, to myself. They would take me to see him again. Elly came. I liked her. She was the head therapist of the house. If she noticed me, if she spoke with me, then everything must be well. I must open myself up—that's how people were for analysis. I had read about it. The analyst got inside you and helped you. I was opening myself up, for Ronnie. I must rest. I must get everything out of myself. I must be empty. Make room for the treatment. I wrote and wrote. Every day— all about everything. I sent it all to Ronnie. I went out to post it. Otherwise I was mostly in the sitting-room. On the sofa, writing. Or on the floor, lying on my stomach. That's how Margee lay. She was having analysis. Ronnie would send for me. They would take me. When I was ready. They would tell Ronnie about me. He would know when to see me. He might come and see me. I must just trust them. Elly told me not to interrupt a meeting. I feel I must. It's the only right thing to do. She means really I should do so. I do, she tells me to sit on a stool in the dining-room. I do. I am being punished, that's right. That's how it's meant to be. I'm having treatment.

I'm naked in the bath, shouting and throwing water about. Edward, he was a helper, a therapist, comes to help me. I make a big noise. Dressed, I go downstairs with him. I like him. Allison gets me a certificate from a doctor who calls. I knew this would happen. I am starting my treatment. Allison helps me to know what to wear. I don't dress when I first get up in the morning. I take some food to eat in bed. Someone had breakfast in bed. I want it in bed. Allison brings me some food in bed. Elly takes me to another house, where the person in charge has been a Sister Tutor. I talk to Elly and the therapists in this house about my time in the mental hospital. They want me to live there. I beg Elly, "No."

She takes me home. I feel I love Elly. She has put her arms around me. Later I shout, "I'm being pushed out. It's not fair. Why should he push me out. Why do boys get the best of it. I'm only a girl." When Elly is speaking to Ronnie on the telephone she calls me to say hello to him.

I'm put in a room to sleep alone, downstairs. It's really a games' room. It's a big room. I like it. I feel I'm being a good patient. They are treating me. Elly smiles at me. Other patients go out. They can't understand about the treatment. I stay indoors and rest myself—except for going to post the writing to Ronnie.

Lots and lots I wrote to Ronnie. When I went to the

lavatory I never shut the door. Once I held out my knickers
in the dining-room. I must show them—like my body. I said
it's not right—I have vaginal discharge.

I was always smelling my clothes and my body. I did
more and more just as I felt and if I was told not to do
something, then I knew I must do it. They understood. This
was a therapy place. I was having treatments. I was quite
up "in the air". If they had told me, we don't understand
all this behaviour, I wouldn't have believed them. They were
under Ronnie. This was all my treatment. I liked it there.
I "blew up". I went wild.

Then about mid-day one day, Elly said to me I was being taken to see Ronnie and afterwards I would go to her
other house. So Allison put my things in the bag. I didn't
want any lunch. I felt it must be all right. Ronnie has ordered this. I felt I was being rewarded for all my efforts
to co-operate with the treatment. I was excited. I was being
taken to see Ronnie. Allison took me in her car. I felt I
must make the most of the remaining time. I talked as
much thought as I possibly could all the way to Ronnie's.

Ronnie met us at the door. It wasn't his office. It was
the Tavistock place. He took me downstairs. I felt this was
better here—he was seeing me more "unofficially". I felt I
had done very well. I rushed in. I was all over the place.
Ronnie sat me down. Allison was there with my things. At
first she waited outside. There was a big tall man there. He
was dark with glasses and a beard in a dark suit. I liked
him. Ronnie asked if he could stay in the room. I quite
agreed.

At first I was left where Ronnie sat me. I saw the room.
I looked over the desk, my chair was at the side of the
desk. There were some Catholic leaflets on the desk and
lots of papers. The room was underground, below the street.

Ronnie came and sat at the desk, very near me. He told
me I couldn't stay at the Richmond Fellowship Hostel. They
couldn't help me. I was stunned. I had *no* idea.

"You have to leave."

He called Allison in and she left my bag.

Ronnie asked me, "Do you know where you can go?"

"No, would you know where to go?"

"No, I don't think so. I have no hospital beds."

"I don't want to go to a mental hospital."

I am down below him, on the floor. He sits above me. I am frightened and whispering. "I *want* analysis." He holds me. I feel he loves me.

"You need analysis twenty-four hours out of twenty-four. You will be like a child and cannot be around like that. You would only get locked up—in a mental hospital. What there is of you is very frail. You can't lie on a couch to have analysis and get up and carry on." I feel he has told me the truth.

"In one year's time I will have a place and there you can stay and have treatment."

"Will there be pads in the place you are getting?"

"Yes, sort of."

I am glad. I feel relieved. Then Ronnie asked me, "Can you hold it for a year, not go down into your mad state?"

I said, "Yes, I want to . . . I *will* have a place in that place, and a place for Peter?"

"Yes, when I get a place, there will be a place there for you and a place for Peter."

I breathed, I felt relief. I felt I understood. I felt satisfied. I trusted him. He sat me back on the chair. He went out of the room. I was alone. I was quite quiet and at peace. He came back. He thought with me where I could go. I couldn't live in the office with them for a year. I felt so safe there. I didn't feel I could live in a house with a family. Marion, Ronnie's secretary, rang up some Catholic hostels. Then Ronnie said, "Would you go down to the convent, to Mother Michael?"

I said, "Yes, she'll have me."

Ronnie went to ring her. The tall big doctor was still there. Ronnie called me to the phone. I spoke with Mother Michael. "Hullo, Mary. Have you got any money?"

"Yes, Mother."

She had told Ronnie I could come. So it was arranged. I had somewhere to go. I have been about two hours with Ronnie, and the big tall dark man. I was out of it, the mad state, I was quiet. I didn't feel at all that I was being pushed out. I felt I was being really cared for and most of all I knew I was understood. Everything seemed quite right.

Ronnie went. The tall doctor saw me into the next room

and Marion, Ronnie's secretary, gave me some food and tea.
He had told her to. I had an egg and bread and butter and
a mug of tea. She asked would I like more tea. I said yes.
There was no more milk. I felt strange. My nice feeling
changed. What was wrong. I felt all wrong, I felt stuck.

Ronnie had ordered a mini car to take me to the station.
The car came. The big doctor, who told me his name was
Dr. Berke, went then. I had my bag. I got to the station
and took the train to Hereford. I understood I had been in
a mad state. Because they had nowhere yet where I could
stay in it to come through it, they had got me out of it.
I must stay out of it for one year.

I slept in Hereford Station. Early in the morning I got the
bus to the convent. I arrived in time for Mass. Mother Michael
assured me everything was in the hands of God. They would
start at once praying for Ronnie and the place he was getting. I could be alone as much as I liked. She sent me out
some beautiful books of paintings. It was September 1963.
As usual I just went to the Turn three times a day for food
and otherwise I stayed quietly in the Hermitage.

I wrote out an account of my life for Ronnie. I thought
it would help him to help me. I thought hard about how to
get back to London, where I would get help in preparation
for going to "the place". The place where I would "go down"
and grow up again. Mother Michael understood about this.
She knew about the madness of schizophrenics but she also
used to say to me, "Mary, I always feel schizophrenics have
got *something* 'extra' to other people." Being a deeply spiritual, suffering person she had great love and understanding.
The nuns inside were much with me in prayer, at that time
particularly, on the matter of my getting back to London.

I had my Youth Hostel card with me and I thought I might
be able to get a job helping in a London Youth Hostel. So
I did. I stayed there for over a year.

The work at the hostel was mainly cleaning and cooking.
We worked different shifts, sometimes until late at night.
But after a time I was put in charge of the kitchen and
my work then finished after the evening meal had been
served. We cooked hundreds of breakfasts and suppers a
day.

Soon after I arrived at the hostel, during my free time in the day, I went back to the Tavistock place, under the ground, from where Ronnie had seen me off to the convent. Down the stairs I spoke to someone, "I have come to see Ronnie." They said, "Wait here," showing me into a room.

In the next room I could hear Ronnie. A little man came in. He looked quite nice. He smiled, picked up a briefcase and went out. I wanted Ronnie. I waited. Ronnie came. He took me into the office. Book on the chair. Exactly where I had been before and he sat at the desk in his same place. I told him what I had come to tell him. I had a job, here was my address. I understood, I had to wait a year for him to get the place. What did he think, would I "hold it" best alone, or should I have help, to keep it up a bit but not to go into it before he got the place.

Ronnie said, "How do you feel?"

"I feel I could do with some help. But I don't *know*— I'm asking *you*. *You* know. Will you see me?"

Ronnie saw he would arrange for me to be seen by another doctor.

"Who? Do you really know him? Does he work with you? Does he understand all you know? Will he be able—as you —to help me towards the place?" I was very worried and I realize now how I must have been very angry. I wanted Ronnie.

Ronnie assured me this other doctor was in close touch with him and was well able to help me. "Where would I go to him?"

"In the same place in Wimpole Street where you first came to see me."

"All right."

Ronnie arranged it. The first time I had to go I rang the bell and was waiting on the doorstep when the little man I had seen at the other place came along. "Are you Mary Barnes?"

"Yes."

"I'm Doctor Esterson."

Once a week for one hour I got help and relief in his office. His office was on the second floor of the building. Ronnie's was on the ground. Dr. Esterson took me up the stairs. The next time I came he came downstairs to the waiting-room for me. Then when I came again, the receptionist lady said would I go up to Dr. Esterson. He couldn't come down, he had a bad back. I didn't believe her. I felt all wrong. I felt I couldn't move. Dr. Esterson came out to the top of the stairs and called for me to come up. I went. I told him, "You haven't got a bad back—not really." He said, yes, he had—the other doctor had just been in to him. True, there was another man on the stairs. I still felt very queer. Something was wrong. I got on the couch. I took my shoes off. He looked all right. He was sitting in his usual place—to the side of me. There was the small picture near the fireplace—Leonardo da Vinci's *Head of Christ*, and there in front of me was the big picture of Vincent Van Gogh's *Boats*. I liked those paintings, and his big blue chair. I sat on that, the first time he saw me. I was very frightened. I kept twining my hands about all the time I talked. I was holding my arms out and twisting my hands in the air, like branches, and twining my fingers. I had on my black coat. I was telling him, "and Ronnie says he will have a place in a year. I want to have analysis. I'm having a place in that place. I'm going down to before I was born—to come up again straight. I have to keep my feelings up now. But I mustn't go down—before Ronnie gets the place. Will you help me? Do you *know* about me?"

He said he had been told something about me. I wanted to be sure—quite certain, he knew. I tell him where I am —where I've been, about the mental hospital. He tells me he will see me again—I can come in the morning, on my day off.

The next time I take my coat off. "I want to lie down— on there." I look from the chair where I was to the couch. It is blue. I like blue very much. He said "Yes." I take my shoes off. I lie down.

Always, after that, I lay on his couch. Sometimes I got off it and hit him. He let me. I felt angry. He helped me. Then I felt more at ease. More together. I wouldn't have to so hold myself together. I loosened my grip on myself.

All the time at this hostel I was outwardly sane and inwardly getting nearer and nearer into insanity. At times I felt quite out of touch with myself, unreal and lost. Touching my body, masturbating, playing with my shit, wetting the bed, gave me more "together feelings". I often terribly feared the inrush of others. I kept myself apart, physically alone. Mentally, I was quite alone. I had to cope from one Wednesday to the next. I was living in the "space". Or rather existing in it. I was tormented between a dead state and a mad living being. The former I *had* to stay in; the latter I was nearly dropping into. The force of my being was demanding release into its truer, mad state. It was a time of terrible strain. Most of the time, when not working, I lay on my bed. For quite a time I was sharing a room.

When I masturbated, wet the bed, played with my shit in the bath, I was terrified of getting caught. Once I tasted, ate a bit of my shit. Dr. Esterson had told me, if I didn't keep together, somehow, and landed in a mental hospital, he could no longer help me. The danger of going right down into the mad state was very real, and I was well aware of it. Yet at times the effort and agony were so great that I could hardly keep from sinking down into myself, into all the mess of my mad twists. Usually I only went out twice a week. To Dr. Esterson, on my day off, and to Mass on Sunday. Otherwise, when I was not working, I remained in bed.

At the doctor's I used to get stuck. Once I felt I just couldn't move my body. I was on the floor in the passage near Ronnie's office. Somehow his secretary got me on my feet and out of the building. I knew if I didn't move, Dr. Esterson would have to get the ambulance, as he told me, and put me in hospital. Yet the thought of another week alone was so much. I just didn't know how to keep together. I used to feel sick, unable to eat; I lived mostly on milk.

There was no news of a place. Dr. Esterson advised a nursing job. I got all the forms, then threw them away, telling Dr. Esterson, "You don't really *mean* me to do it." I was in a mad state. He understood and steered me through it. I felt I only half knew what I was doing. I was so "inside myself" that everything else, everything outside me, was blurred and unreal.

Then, one Sunday, after Mass, I went running up to Ronnie's. I remember, before I went out early that morning I had found a lot of milk gone sour and we had had to throw it away. I was afraid. Again, down in my mad state, I was only half aware of the outside world. I seemed in a cloud, as if my feet were in the air, as if everything was veiled and hidden from me. I felt out of touch, unreal. I wanted to be safe, in with Ronnie's family, to live with his children. Because I wanted it, because I went there, I thought it could be.

Ronnie was out, his wife got me out of it. She literally saved me, that day. I got back late to the hostel. The next day I went to Dr. Esterson, and Ronnie also helped me, when walking along the road. He assured me it wouldn't be mad, to go to my aunt's for a week. I was upset in my stomach, so for that reason, I was at once allowed a week's leave at the hostel.

My relatives took me in, but rather wondered why I needed to go to a psychotherapist. I was in *no* doubt of my need. It always amazed me when I was so sick how I ever got by. Despite my efforts to the contrary, I used to think surely they must see a bit that I am so sick. I felt I was bleeding to death inside. It was as if my arm was pouring blood and no one took any notice. I was in an unreal state. I wondered why they didn't see me, how I *was*. It seemed they saw a normal person. I used to feel they felt I was "like them". I knew I wasn't.

Eventually, when I was leaving the hostel, the warden's wife told me, "Mary, we shall miss you, you have been such a rock." I left the hostel to go into a hospital teaching job. This second time Dr. Esterson advised it, I went through with it. There was still no news of a place. The Matron took me on in ignorance of my state. She looked at my age, counted up the years, and said I had nineteen years to do before I retired. I felt the end. I wanted to curl up and die. Yet I felt I so needed that job I couldn't lessen my chances in any way by confiding in the Matron. I had been advised to stay much alone, and keep quiet, and not talk to anyone about my insides. This was Dr. Esterson's very sound advice. The Richmond Fellowship hostel were very welcoming to me on my day off when I was first at the Youth Hostel, but Dr. Esterson warned me of the dangers to myself of such a place. Feeling very "accepted" I might easily have slipped there into the mad state despite my past knowledge and memories of what had happened there. I stayed clear of them.

About this time I seemed to get into a very bad state with masturbation. All the time I had been going to Dr. Aaron Esterson I'd been masturbating. It just wouldn't seem to stop, though I went to confession about it, and resolved to stop it. Sometimes I got orgasm. It seemed to help me in that it relieved the tension in me, enabled me to feel myself. In church it seemed I was opening myself to God. Masturbation tortured me. My mental state at the time was very bad and I agreed with Aaron's idea that in certain circumstances it may be right to do a lesser sin to avoid a greater evil. I needed therapy, I wanted therapy. I didn't want to disintegrate into such a state that I would be taken into a mental hospital. I didn't want drugs. Sin to me as a whole was a "state of the alienation of the self". I was engaged in therapy to get me whole. So far as was humanely seeable there was no other means to my wholeness except through analytical psychotherapy.

Some time before, I had heard E. O'Doherty, Professor of Psychology, University College, Dublin, tell a group of nuns and lay people at a Psychology Conference that he would send a nun to a non-Catholic psychiatrist—in fact he had done so, because the non-Catholic happened to be the better psychiatrist. He assured us the questions must always be which is the better man at his job—rather than is he a Catholic psychiatrist or not. Some Catholic friends of mine, a married couple, who had both had psychotherapy, assured me, "Mary, you must have help, there is no equivalent Catholic help available, therefore you have no question—no problem."

Looking back now I wonder how ever I could, in the desperate state I was in, not only "be so choosy" but really jeopardise my whole future, slay my chances of ever getting whole, by holding out, in a sense, using as a resistance, my plea, "I'm a Catholic, it's a sin for me, stop me masturbating."

During this period I was suicidal. It was the time of existing in "The Divide", the worst time I have ever known. All my feeling was towards Aaron, whom I trusted. I didn't want to leave him but when a priest thought it was wrong for me to go to a doctor who didn't consider masturbation sinful then in my will I decided I must stop going to Dr. Esterson. I did and got very bad. I have since realized I was very angry with the priest, but wouldn't let myself feel it as he was a priest. Even now my feelings are always carefully reserved and contained before priests and nuns.

I had been going to Aaron for over a year. Ronnie had said there would be a place in a year. I had not expected to be working at the hostel for more than a year. It was now late October, 1964. I must have been very angry. My state in August when I'd run to Ronnie's home had been quite desperate.

Sid (Sid Briskin, a social worker who helped Ronnie) had interviewed me in Aaron's office.

"Mary, I'll read you a list of jobs, of things you might do, instead of being at the hostel till we get a place. You tell me to stop, when I say what you might like."

Sid got to, "Helping in a house, living in with a family."

"Stop."

"Sid, that's what I want, to be with a family."

"Well, all right, I might know of a family. I'll see."

That was a possibility, but still I felt so dead, so exhausted, begged Aaron, "What about a bed in a psychiatric ward of a general hospital. I want you to put me to bed somewhere." Never had I so wanted to be held and carried —yet instinctively, in my worst moments I somehow saved myself from kind and well-meaning non-understanding "help." Once along Wimpole Street I was creeping, moaning away, by some railings. An elderly lady put her arm around me. "What's the matter, come with me." I gasped, held on to myself, shook my head, walked on. I hardly realized how dangerous it could be to collapse in the street. An ambulance, hospital, it could so easily happen.

Aaron reminded me, "Mary, I have no beds anywhere. You cannot be under me in a hospital." I dragged on. It was a terrible time. I feel now that my then unrecognized anger at Aaron for not producing a place, as well as the masturbation muddle, influenced me towards my dangerous crazy move away from him, my therapist. It wasn't Aaron's fault they hadn't got a place. They were all searching very hard.

The year had been so difficult. To me it seemed so cruel that I had to wait longer.

My Father wrote to me that my Mother was very ill and going to be operated upon by a neurosurgeon to relieve the pain of a swollen blood vessel behind her eye. He added, they had been told Mother might die or survive paralysed, or it might be successful. Mother had decided, because the pain was so bad, to have the operation. I knew I was in no state to go to my parents. I wanted to go more to Aaron, told my Father so and that I was suicidal, and he sent me thirty pounds. I was so bad, one Wednesday evening I rang up Aaron's office and then went to Wimpole Street in a taxi to collect some tablets from Ronnie's secretary. Aaron kept me on them, *Largactil,* for some weeks. I didn't feel they made any difference. I just knew I was very very bad.

Having left Aaron I went to Mother Michael, who told me, "We must prefer to die, rather than commit sin." She advised me to go to Dr. Elkisch, a Catholic analyst. He told me, "Look here, I have a religious brother, a patient, who masturbates every day of his life. I've forbidden him to go to confession about it." Dr. Elkisch also told me, "It's not sinful to have vaginal imaginings." I imagined my vagina was being medically examined, probably as an instinctive inhibition to the sinful imagining of a man putting his penis into me.

But I still thought, "However can a doctor tell anyone what or what not to say in confession?" My confusion, my disturbance, my agony, was very great. All the time it seemed I would just "fall apart". The anxiety of this time was enormous. I went to see a priest, who had been connected with a Catholic psychotherapy group. He told me, "If you have sexual intercourse with a man that is sinful if you are not properly married to him, but it's not against the natural law. Masturbation is against the natural law. It is a lesser evil to have intercourse with a man." The Father did not seem to think it would help if he were to see Dr. Esterson, who had assured me he would see a priest on my behalf.

This put me in a worse stew, because it made me feel I must be in a state of perpetual mortal sin. Being near physical suicide, in desperate despair, I was in no mood to get a boyfriend. In any case, I reasoned, whatever sin state I am in—if I slept with a man, it's still a sin and what seemed worse to my mind, I would be involving someone else, a cause of their sin. Fortunately I was so isolated that I never seriously tried to find a man to do what the priest seemed to be trying to tell me was a "lesser sin".

In the most vicious grip of the torment, the problem, insofar as I could see it from the outside (mostly I felt inside so bad I couldn't see anything) was like this, I must prefer to die rather than commit sin. Masturbation was sin. I felt I wanted to kill myself physically, commit suicide. This was sin, I must *not* do it, somehow I *must* stay physically alive—impossible though it seemed at times.

I must not make excuses for myself—I'm mad—I'm schizophrenic, therefore I can masturbate. Somehow I must not sin at *all*—this meant refraining from masturbating as well as from killing myself. I did not, God alone knows how, attempt to take my own life. I could not, I just could not, stop masturbating.

Mother Michael thought, come what may, I must at all costs still go to Ronnie's place—if and when he got it. On this I was quite determined and begged Ronnie, meanwhile, "Please, if you know a Catholic analyst who understands about your work, get me to him." Ronnie did. He literally saved me just as I was about to go to Banstead hospital to be with Peter. My idea had been to train as a psychiatric nurse. Such was the illusive state I was getting into within two months of leaving Aaron.

All the time my feeling was urging me to go to Aaron. I longed for his help, but my will, my thought was saying, you mustn't sin, he doesn't know it's sin, a priest, a Carmelite Father, has told you to change your doctor. I realize now, because outwardly I appeared "normal" the priest quite likely had no idea of my inner desperate, quite suicidal state.

When Ronnie saw me I told him, "I want to go to the place but I don't want to lose my Faith."

He said, "There's no need for that."

Ronnie sent me to Dr. St. Blaize Maloney who was a Catholic analyst at the Langham clinic. When he saw me, he said, "I want to hear nothing about it. Look at you now, masturbating with your hair." So that was it. I still masturbated. But he was a Catholic analyst. I'd done all I could. I must confess it and stop it. This I did—for four years—until it stopped. Much involved in prayer, as well as masturbation, I had been rescued from the immediate terrible dangerous mess by Ronnie.

It was Christmas and I went to the convent in Wales. There was snow, it was dark; they had other guests, and I had to go to the town to sleep out at a pub. It started to snow again. I was bitterly cold, alone, desolate, feeling so bad, utterly spent. It seemed all the struggle, the utter weariness of all my resistance, the masturbation of the past few months, was upon me. Exhausted, I wanted just to lie down in the snow to die, to end it all. The snow was thick and deep, tiring to walk through, inviting to lie in.

On New Year's Day, I said to Sister Angela, a nun, who worked in the kitchen, "I just don't know how I am going to go on. I fear I shall commit suicide or go to a mental hospital." Peter all this time was in a chronic ward of his mental hospital.

Sister Angela remarked, "You never *really* know. This *could* be the best year of your life."

Within seven *months* from this time Ronnie had found the place. It was actually Sid Briskin, a social worker, and friend of Ronnie's, who discovered the building.

I was saved. I had been on the brink of the pit. Mother Michael assured me of great prayer for myself and for all that would be where I was at last going.

Part 2

How I came to meet Mary Barnes by Joseph Berke

Chapter Five

How I came to meet Mary Barnes

Mary Barnes is a vibrant, engaging, enraging, charismatic baby girl, little girl, bobby soxer and woman. In the past she found it hard to be but one of these at a time, although she was possessed of an extraordinary ability to move among any and all positions very quickly. Today Mary is very much together, much more so than most people who have not had the opportunity, or who have not dared, to enter into the profound experiences described in this book and in her paintings.

Although trained as a nurse, and later as a teacher of nurses, Mary eventually took up a second career as a hospitalized schizophrenic. Specifically because she wished to give up both of these professions, and come to terms with herself as a woman, she eventually created the situation by which we met, and I assisted her project of emotional disintegration and resurrection.

God knows how Mary allowed herself to unwind, as she did. And I often look back with disbelief on how entangled I got in her process of unwinding. But our relationship, even when most trying, has always proved to be mutually beneficial. If Mary has had someone to help her cut through the spiderwebs of her soul, I have received expert teaching on how and why a person can manage to tie her life into knots and then forget where the last strand begins. More spectacularly, I have seen confirmed before my very eyes the need for a radical re-thinking of the question of "mental illness".

Long before I ever heard of Mary Barnes, I had begun to realize that what is commonly called "mental illness" is not an "illness" or "sickness" (according to the prevailing medical-psychiatric use of the term), but an example of emotional suffering brought about by a disturbance in a whole field of social relationships, in the first place, the family. In other words, "mental illness" reflects what is happening in a disturbed and disturbing group of people, especially when internalized in and by a single person. More often than not, a person diagnosed as "mentally ill" is the emotional scapegoat for the turmoil in his or her family or associates, and may, in fact, be the "sanest" member of this group. The disturbance may express itself slowly or rapidly, quietly or explosively, immediately or after many years.

In medical school I had been taught that the gravest form of "mental illness" was something called "schizophrenia". I say "something" because I could never match the definition of this "illness" with the reality of the people who were supposed to manifest it. So, I shall begin my contribution to this book by telling you how I began to understand that "schizophrenia" is a career, not an illness. This career always involves at least two professionals, a patient and a psychiatrist. More often than not it is launched with the aid and encouragement of one's immediate family. Furthermore, the experiences that occur in the person labelled "schizophrenic", and are commonly subsumed under the term "psychosis", are not at all unintelligible, that is, crazy. They simply occur at a different order of reality, akin to a waking dream. The social invalidation of such experiences by calling them "sick" or "mad" is a basic interpersonal manoeuvre among peoples in Western cultures where dreams and dream-like states are not considered a valid vehicle for conveying reality, no matter how much truth they may express.

During my first years of training I discovered that I was more fascinated by the totality of my patients' lives than by the particular diseases that happened to inhabit them. Blood tests did not turn me on. Too bad for me. My professors and fellow students studied serum chemistries with an obscene passion.

I felt trapped between my naïve self-image as a future GP and the "scientific" mannerisms of contemporary medicine. Psychiatry seemed an honourable alternative. Here was one discipline where it was still fashionable to talk to the patient, or so it seemed. On closer examination it became obvious that the reverse was true. Both the interview and treatment situations were carefully structured to prevent any genuine exchange between patient and therapist. The hospital ward was a factory farm designed to label, process and dispose of the human fodder fed into it.

Grist for the mill was the battery of clinical signs and symptoms which determined whether so and so should be shoved down the psychosis, neurosis, psychopathy or organic brain damage slots. Yet, the clinical picture was rarely clear cut. It could vary enormously, and especially in regard to the first three categories (the functional nervous disorders). What mattered was who was doing the examination; where it was taking place—hospital, home, police station, street, elsewhere; and the patient's perception of his or her situation.

Those who could elicit the manifestations of this or that disease were said to be blessed with clinical acumen. As students we struggled to gain this peculiar blessing. We forced ourselves to see what we were supposed to see, even when we didn't see it. And then we forced ourselves to forget that we often did not see what we said we saw. I was pretty good at this game.

What disturbed me was that I never gained the ability to treat my patients purely as objects to be studied, and then discarded. As is said in England, many were good blokes. And they all managed to convey something of themselves, as people, rather than as categorizations. This remained annoyingly obvious with patients who had been tagged "schizophrenic". I never found it too difficult to pick up what they would say about themselves and the way they were being treated, although sometimes I had to listen on their terms, not my own. But the very fact of intelligible communication between them and me ran totally contrary to their having been defined as "schizophrenics". After all, to be "schizophrenic" is to be crazy, and to be crazy is to be unintelligible; at least that's what the textbooks implied, if not actually stated.

To add to my confusion, very few of my classmates or teachers agreed that my patients' "productions", that is, what they said or did, were meaningful other than as signs and symptoms of a progressive, debilitating illness. What if my conversing with the "crazies" was a sign of craziness in me!

Fortunately, I met Dr. John Thompson, one person who could appreciate my dilemma and help me to deal with it. He did this by simply confirming my understanding of the situation with my patients, and also by teaching me how to communicate even more effectively with people who have entered that waking dream state known as psychosis.

How strange and wonderful that John Thompson, a handsome, silver haired Scotsman, a friend of poets, writers, artists, philosophers, men of thought and action all over the world, and himself a poet as well as psychiatrist, should finish his life as Professor at the same New York medical school where I happened to be a student. John Thompson's presence was the lone reminder of the need for human dignity and compassion amid the purveyors of egos and ids, neurohumors and EEGs in our department of psychiatry.

Unlike the rest of the staff, Dr. Thompson did not talk down to patients or students. Nor did he categorize people, or what they said or did, according to what was nosologically fashionable. What John did do, and what he taught me and others who would listen to him, was always to try to observe another person from *his* or *her* social and experiential reference points. This means that one cannot assume a knowledge of another's interpersonal field, nor prejudge peculiar behaviour as "sick". What is peculiar in one situation may well be "normal" in another, as I later found out time and time again in the course of visiting the families of my patients. Secondly, the psychiatrist cannot assume that his inner experience and that of his patients is similar, or even related. For that matter, he cannot even assume that when he perceives a difference between the two, his world is "better" or "saner". Every patient is entitled to a fresh and unbiased study of his or her experiential world. And to do this is to shed some light on that complexity which is the life of another human being.

Space and time were the two parameters of the phenomenal world which John Thompson considered of prime importance in orienting oneself to another's version of reality. For example, how could you meet Mrs. Smith if she lived in past time and you in future time, and neither realized this?

Or how could you converse with Mr. Brown if your minute was his second, or vice versa? And was Miss Grant's anxiety upon entering your office really crazy, or might it be due to the fact that the 8 x 12 cubicle which you felt was reasonably sized, if only a trifle small, was experienced by her as so tiny that she didn't even have room to expand her chest?

And when the Mrs. Smiths, Mr. Browns and/or Miss Grants began to appreciate that you were endeavouring to meet them on their terms, the transformation of the relationship, and the change in their attitude to themselves, was nothing short of phenomenal. Patients, who but a second before had been manifesting the most bizarre behaviour, became calm and collected. Often they proceeded to talk to Dr. Thompson or myself in a quite rational way, explaining what had been disturbing them, and asking for help from such and such a nurse, parent, doctor, demon or what have you.

Now a disease is a disease. You don't have a disease in the presence of one person and not in the presence of another. No cancer that I have ever heard of disappears when Dr. X arrives and reappears when he leaves or someone else arrives. No tumour, infection, endocrinopathy, etc. does likewise. That the signs and symptoms of severe "mental illness" changed according to whom the patient was with made me suspect that "illness" was not a sufficient explanation for the personal states and interpersonal situations with which I was becoming increasingly familiar. And given John Thompson's facility for communicating with so called incommunicable "chronic catatonics" or other "hopeless backward cases", I realized that the onus of "craziness" or "unintelligibility" did not necessarily lie in the minds of the patients. True, these people may manifest peculiar mannerisms in the course of their attempts to communicate something about themselves, but then it is not the job of the psychiatrist to moralize about the right or wrong of another's life style. Rather the psychiatrist best functions as a communications expert. He has to be conversant with many styles of communicating, both to enable him to talk with another person and, more importantly to enable him to listen, no matter how idiosyncratic the language. During my clinical years it became clear to me that most psychiatrists are not only not experts in communication, but are not at all interested in what their patients have to tell them. The concept of "unintelligibility" is therefore a clever ploy for masking the true nature of their operations. Quite simply many psychiatrists attribute *their own non-attempts at communication* to someone else, usually a patient or prospective patient, while, at the same time, denying that this is what they are doing. *This disturbance in communication* is then seen as a sign of the patient's "illness" for which he must be "treated". Should the patient still try to comment on what he thinks is going on, his "productions" are passed off as "unintelligible".

R. D. Laing gives a blow by blow description of this common practice as applied by the "Father" of modern psychiatry, Emil Kraepelin, to an eighteen year old boy, in the first chapter of *The Divided Self.** Dr. Laing's unusually perceptive discussion of this teenager's predicament as well as his keen understanding of the life experience of people diagnosed as "schizoid" or "schizophrenic" further verified the possibility of coming to terms with the language of people whom our culture would consider "mad".

Students of psychology no longer need remain linguistic philistines, beholden to a "science" which treats any language but its own as an unintelligible bastardization of its own, and worse yet, a grave sign of mental derangement in anyone who speaks it. The words and movements of the "madman" are not a bastardization of any tongue, rather they are a unique event to which one can learn to respond.

I discovered *The Divided Self* in the Bronx shop of an obnoxious purveyor of medical texts. It was the fall of 1962 and I had gone prowling for a book, any book, to rouse me out of the doldrums of surgery at a VA (Veterans Administration) hospital. The title attracted me, and also the pretty picture of the author on the back cover, another Scotsman, and from Glasgow of all places. What a mind blower when I opened the pages and found that amid the key phrases of "existential-phenomenology", "ontological insecurity", "false self" and "true self", Ronald Laing had explained my own

The Divided Self by R. D. Laing. Published in the UK by Tavistock Publications and in the USA by Quadrangle Books.

experience to me better than anyone I had ever read, and far better than I could then interpret it myself. More important, his characterizations did not remain literary cadavers, but came to life, jumped out of the book, reminded me of oh so many people I had known as friends and teachers and patients.

As soon as I had finished reading *The Divided Self* I showed it to John Thompson who was also very impressed with it.

"John," I said, "why don't you put your thoughts on to paper as Laing has done?"

John didn't answer but just smiled. Later he indicated that he was satisfied to "do his thing" with the spoken word and silence. Writing was a sacred occasion, reserved for his poetry. Somehow this answer did not completely satisfy me.

Weeks went by. I wrote to Dr. Laing at the Tavistock Institute in London, expressing my appreciation for his work. I also stated that I would very much like the opportunity to meet him and, if possible, work with him.

At about this time I had to decide what I was going to do during a six month senior elective period. One thing I knew. I wanted to travel far away from New York, preferably to Europe. So I proposed to study with Dr. Laing. The school accepted my project after I had got the backing of John Thompson. All that mattered was to hear from Dr. Laing.

The snows came. Huge drifts made even my five minute walk to the hospital an arctic passage. Still no word from Dr. Laing. In need of an alternative project, I wrote to Dr. Maxwell Jones, a pioneer in the development of the Therapeutic Community, to see if I could get a post in the hospital he had just taken over near Edinburgh. I liked what Dr. Jones had accomplished at the Henderson Hospital near London, having transferred a psychiatric unit into something more like a hip community.

Max Jones (everyone called him Max, he insisted) replied affirmatively. Things were beginning to move. Then I got my long awaited letter from Dr. Laing, "Do stop by when you are in London." Fine.

Summer 1963. Off to Scotland. I was privileged to participate in the initial stages of developing a sophisticated social milieu out of a rustic, sheep encrusted mental hospital. The summer passed. I moved to London. I was looking forward to my meeting with Dr. Laing.

On the appointed day I took the underground to Bond Street, got lost at Wimpole Street, walked on through Harley Street, doctors' row, and over to Hallam Street where I was expected at noon. I found the correct address, number 66, but to my discomfort, couldn't find the door. There was none. The likeliest candidate had a few crates stacked behind it. Workmen in a nearby house were equally mystified.

"Sorry mate," they chortled as I paced back and forth in front of the building wondering how the hell to get in. I couldn't even rap on a window because the house was separated from the sidewalk by a black iron fence followed by a gap of several feet which dropped down precipitously into bowels of the building. Dustbins took up much of the space at the bottom of this moat-like hole.

It was getting late. Nobody left the building and no one else tried to enter it. The thought crossed my mind that this situation was some sort of metaphysical joke. A thin smile, echoing this idea, broke the tension I felt.

At last I noticed a narrow stairwell leading from the sidewalk down into the hole. Was this the only way in? And what about the need to maintain a correct professional façade? For all I knew Laing might be one of those "dignified types", who would not appreciate my determination to keep the appointment with him. Nevertheless, I decided to risk impaling myself on some iron spokes by climbing over the fence and on to the stairs. Fortunately this proved unnecessary. There existed a gate through the fence at the head of the stairwell. It was open. Gingerly I began my descent into the basement. Cursing as I stumbled over an orangepeel, I went to the window of a room in which I could see some people talking.

Tap tap tap. They look up. A dark haired medium-built man ambled over and opened the window.

Resisting the urge to shout, "Dr. Laing, I presume?", I said, "Hello, I have a noon appointment with Dr. Laing, but have had some difficulty finding the way to his office."

The man replied, "Ah yes, I am Dr. Laing. Go upstairs and I will let you in."

Having gone to all the trouble of traipsing down the hole, at this point, I was both glad to find him and a bit peeved that he did not just invite me to climb through the window. However, I quickly went up the stairs and waited outside till Dr. Laing emerged through the front entrance of the building.

"Sneaky!" I thought, and walked in.

Two basement rooms at Hallam Street provided Dr. Laing with space for a secretary, files, and meetings with others engaged with him in studying patterns of communication in the families of people who had been diagnosed as schizophrenic. Noon provided the occasion for the doctor to take a break from his busy practice a few blocks away at Wimpole Street and lunch with his colleague Dr. Aaron Esterson, or his secretary, assorted research assistants and visitors like myself.

After the usual banter about "pushy Americans getting into the strangest places" and some effusive praise on my part for *The Divided Self,* we seemed to hit it off, and I was added to the Hallam Street gang. My job for the next few months would be to soak up communications theory, familiarize myself with hundreds of hours of taped interviews without falling asleep, visit the odd home, and think about the structure of family life in Western culture along with Laing and the others.

On that first day I also suggested that people call me "Joe" and that I do likewise. Immediately Dr. Laing gave a snort, raised his eyebrows, winked at Dr. Esterson, and nodded. So from then on they were "Ronnie" and "Aaron" to me and I "Joe" to them.

Listening to the many interviews of parents, sibs, grandparents, uncles, aunts, cousins, etc. and in different combinations (such as Mother, Father and child, or Mother and child, or Grandmother, Mother and child), made it clear that the one family member who happened to have been diagnosed schizophrenic or neurotic or whatever was not necessarily the most disturbed person in the family. Often he or she was the least disturbed member of the entire group.

This conclusion was reconfirmed by actually visiting the homes of such people and seeing, firsthand, how they got on with each other. In all cases where one or more family members had been labelled "schizophrenic" a unique pattern of communication could be made out. People did not talk to each other, but at each other, and tangentially, not directly. There was a continual shifting of position. It was difficult to follow who was talking about what, because the issues always seemed to be shifting, and it was extremely rare to find two people actually talking about the same issue at the same time. Parents seemed impervious to the point of view of their children, and vice versa, but to a lesser extent. And most infuriatingly, what people said was often contradicted by the way they said it (tone of voice and/or facial and bodily movements). These aberrations in communication particularly centred about issues such as personal autonomy and sexual activity. People seemed bound up in such a hot house of guilt and rage that the power politics of a Medici were small stuff in comparison to the intrigues, backbiting and murderous onslaughts of "those quiet Joneses down the block". And this is the point. To the casual observer such families may be paragons of moral and civil rectitude. But once their façade is brushed aside, generations of "shit" come pouring out.

One particular feature of such families and an essential weapon in the hands of parents bent on destroying the autonomy of their kids (and later on, vice versa) is known as double binding. Double binding is a means for putting another in a strait-jacket of guilt and anxiety in order to prevent him from doing something which you have already told him it is OK to do. It is a marvellous tool for driving someone mad. A good example would be the situation where you and I were together and I took out a gun and screamed at you to "sit down or I shall shoot you dead". If you then proceeded to comply with my order, I would immediately shout "Stand up or I shall shoot you dead." And if you looked confused and didn't know what to do I would say, "If you don't sit/stand by the time I count three I will shoot you dead, and I shall also kill you if you try to point out that my orders are impossible to carry out."

The following is a common variation of the above situation as it commonly occurs in the context of the family: Momma goes out shopping leaving three-year-old Leo with Daddy. As she returns and opens the door, Leo runs over to greet his mother. Whereupon the woman involuntarily freezes. Leo sees this and stops. Whereupon his mother says, "Leo baby, what's the matter, don't you love your Mommy? Come and give me a big kiss."

If baby Leo ignores his first perception and runs up to the woman again, she freezes and takes his kiss in an off-hand angry way. If baby Leo refuses to budge, she scolds him for being a bad boy. Because of his age or inexperience Leo can't comment on what is happening, or if he does, either his mother or father scolds him for being naughty, "Don't talk to your mother/father that way or you will be punished." The net result is that Baby Leo is reduced to an impotent rage whereupon he is sent to bed for being bad.

Comment: The poor kid never had a chance! Nor do millions like him. It was hard work listening to these "crazy" families in action. Mind you, the "craziness" did not consist in these families being unintelligible, for it was always possible to relate the behaviour or internal experience of any family member, no matter how weird, to the overall operations of the group. Ronnie and Aaron did this very well in their book, *Sanity, Madness and the Family** which details the inner workings of eleven families, each of which with one son or daughter diagnosed "schizophrenic". It was hard work having to share in these people's emotional morass. After an hour at the tape recorder, my muscles would almost become paralytic. This happened with the others too. On some occasions our research discussions ended up with us dancing around the room.

During the course of the summer I increasingly admired Ronnie's skill as a battlefield tactitian, whether in the home,

**Sanity, Madness and the Family* by R. D. Laing and A. Esterson. Published in the UK by Tavistock Publications (Paperback by Penguin Books) and in the USA by Basic Books.

Subsequently, Dr. Esterson has greatly extended the analysis begun in *Sanity, Madness and the Family* by focusing on one of the eleven families and studying the transactions on the level of fantasy that occurred among its members. Under the title, *Leaves of Spring,* this superbly informative work has been published by Tavistock Publications in the UK and by Barnes and Noble in the USA.

with Mr. and Mrs. X, or in a hospital situation with Dr. Y. He could hold his own with the best operators—parent, patient, or psychiatrist. We all knew, of course, that the mental hospital was simply an institutionalized extension of the family living room, or maybe bedroom, but with the hospital staff, the parent surrogates, having a more varied and powerful armamentarium—forced withdrawal (ninety day order), tranquillizers, electric shock—to use against the "sinner". What wasn't clear was the extent to which the hospital damaged a person who had entered psychosis by preventing him from totally disintegrating and then spontaneously re-integrating his personality at his own speed. Ronnie felt that psychosis was potentially a healing experience for a person who had the proper "life support" to go through it. The mental hospital cannot provide such support, because it functions as an agency of social repression. It's "proper" function as an "asylum" from the pressures of the external world has been lost to the collective conscience of the backward taxpayer.

So Ronnie and his friends and colleagues very much wanted to get a house in which they could live and personally provide an efficient life support system for one or two people who would be undergoing a psychosis "trip". In this way they hoped to learn about the entirety of the psychotic experience, not just the disintegrative phase. They also wanted to see whether psychosis was our culture's means of archetypal renewal of the inner self. The ceremonials of many other cultures, by no means primitive, provided a great deal of evidence that this view was correct.

At odd times throughout the fall one or another of us would go off with Ronnie to look at this house or that house which most assuredly was "the" house we all sought for the new community. But it was not to be found for another year. Then Kingsley Hall would be its name.

About mid-September, and just before I had to go back to the States to finish my formal medical training, I met Mary Barnes for the first time. After the meeting, I never dreamed that within two years the end result of Mary's relationship with Ronnie, and my own, would lead both of us to live at "the" place, Kingsley Hall, where I would help her go through a most profound emotional death-rebirth experience.

What most intrigued me about Mary on this occasion was her metamorphosis from an extremely disturbed "catatonic" to that of a slightly eccentric, quite communicative and cheerful middle-aged woman; and all within the space of a couple of hours. When she first came into the office, Mary was very dishevelled, was whimpering incoherently, and, after sitting down, kept her head stiffly between her legs. Ronnie talked to her slowly, telling her confidently that he would be getting a place soon and that she should hold on. While doing so, he allowed Mary to rest her head on his lap. Gradually she became less rigid, stopped whimpering, and began to talk quietly with him. Later still she accepted some warm milk from Ronnie's secretary and waited for arrangements to be made for her to catch a train to the convent where she had previously stayed. I nodded, "Goodbye," as she left the office and walked confidently to the taxi which whisked her off to the railway station. After she had gone, Ronnie said that he hoped he would be able to get a house for the proposed community where, in Mary's own words, she could "go down". But nearly two years had to pass before Mary was firmly ensconced in Kingsley Hall and "doing her thing".

After this London experience, it was quite a come-down to have to fit back in the old hospital routine, especially when I could see better than ever, that psychiatric treatment, even in our "most advanced" wards, was essentially oppressive, rather than emotionally liberating. But what if "nuts" *were* just "nuts" and all the departmental stuffed shirts with their ego theories, or id theories, or even biochemical theories were really on to something? These doubts vanished after an encounter between a young Puerto Rican girl and a senior psychiatrist which I was privileged to observe. The incident illustrates much of what is confusing and oppressive in the relationship between a person labelled "psychiatrist" and another labelled "patient". However, before I describe what happened, it is important to convey to you some background information about the structure of the psychiatric ward in which the encounter took place.

About the early 60s it became very fashionable in liberal departments of psychiatry to try to treat patients by means of a conscious manipulation of the social environment of the ward. This new approach was a direct follow on from the success of Maxwell Jones's work with "therapeutic communities". The idea was that the rigid staff-patient relationship should be de-emphasized, if not broken down. Patients should have a say in how the ward was run, they should wear their own clothes, do much of the work of the ward themselves, and determine who got admitted as patients (and in radical circles, who got admitted as staff). Most importantly there should be a running dialogue between all levels of the staff and patients in order to sort out feelings and help people get on with the day to day operation of the ward. This was the most important aspect of the programme. An honest but brutally truthful account of ongoing events on the part of all concerned would lead to "sick" egos being replaced by "well" ones. Presumably the patients would refrain from taking over the administration of the hospital, but with heads held high, and rosy cheeks, they would clamour to take outside work, get married, and live the rest of their lives as upstanding citizens.

In practice, the programme depended on the personality of the psychiatrist in charge. At best, people like Max felt sure enough of themselves to allow the staff and patients a large measure of self determination. They then got on with their daily lives as best they could, and with the knowledge that all the rules of interpersonal behaviour were open to question and that definite channels of communications existed among all concerned. A community had been created.

At worst, the programme degenerated into organized brain washing. Patients were supposed to talk honestly about their feelings, and were often punished for what they said, but the staff was under no pressure to do so. Power remained in the hands of the administrator, although everyone would be told that the group was free and open. Minor trappings of therapeutic community life, like men and women patients meeting together, and being allowed to wear their own clothes, substituted for the basic issues of personal autonomy and sexual identity.

Unfortunately, 99-44/100% of the programmes that laboured under the aegis of "therapeutic community" were of this latter variety. Such was also true of my hospital, where the daily indoctrination about the importance of group meetings and everyone talking freely of what's on his or her mind clashed with the fact that the door to the ward was not even open. Patients could not leave for a Coca-Cola if they wanted to do so. Ah yes, this exercise in social deception was sugar-coated by the fact that patients could mingle fairly freely during the day. But always a nurse's aide stood at the door to the stairwell down the hall to prevent unauthorized personnel from slipping away.

In the mornings patients and staff gathered together for a two hour interrogation of the patients by the staff. It was called a "group discussion". This title was a perverse joke, but few questioned the nature of the meeting. The brighter patients were cowed by the power of the doctors to prescribe tranquillizers for "acting out".

One night I happened to be passing by the hospital's emergency room when a pretty Puerto Rican teenager, not unlike one of the dancers from *West Side Story,* came bouncing through the doors followed by an elderly woman, most certainly her mother, and several police. The girl seemed unconcerned and she proceeded to glide about the room, but her mother was very agitated. She explained that that evening her daughter had suddenly burst out laughing and then begun to dance about their apartment. This had been going on for several hours. The girl, let's call her Angela Rivera, had refused to talk or sit down. Neighbours told the distraught woman that her daughter had "gone loco". So the police were called.

In the emergency room the *mother's hysteria* quickly infected the nurses and interns. They seemed to vie with each other to see who could sedate *Angela* first, and prepare her for shipment upstairs to the admitting ward. No one tried to communicate with her. One doctor did take a rudimentary history from the mother, however.

Here was an interesting situation. Angela was being admitted to the psych-ward because of her mother's hysteria. I decided to follow Angela's progress as a patient. Next step was to attend the morning meeting of her ward at which time she would be "presented".

I got to the recreation room just as the day's discussion was about to start. A couple of dozen patients, recognizable by their street attire, sat uneasily amid a like number of nurses, nurses' aides, medical students, residents and the chief ward psychiatrist. The latter, a diminutive man in a dark business suit and bow tie, stood close by a pile of charts, the patients' records. Looking around I noticed Angela. She too stood, swaying to the rhythm of people's voices, and seemingly not taking any notice of the others present till her name was mentioned and "The Chief" began a staccato run-down on her mental state. Perking up her ears, she began to prance about the room, slowly at first, then faster and faster, as if moving to the strains of Ravel's *Bolero*. Her eyes glistened, it was obvious she was quite enjoying her impromptu dance.

For a moment, it looked like the others were going to join in. The patients smiled and started to clap their hands. A nurse's aide or two made a motion to get up and join the dance. Then, booming across the room, came the voice of the bow-tied psychiatrist, "Miss Rivera, you are disturbing the meeting. The *Group* would like you to sit down."

Angela continued to dance about. A nurse's aide sat down. Several patients lost their smiles and stopped clapping. Otherwise silence.

"Miss Rivera, don't you hear *us*, the *Group* is asking you to sit down."

No change.

"Miss Rivera, if you don't sit down immediately, the *Group* is going to send you back to your room."

No change.

Addressing two nurse's aides, the doctor continued, "The *Group* has decided that Miss Rivera should not be allowed to disrupt *our* discussion. Would you please escort her back to her room."

After hesitating a few seconds, the nurse's aides got up and proceeded to drag the Puerto Rican girl back to her room. She did not go voluntarily. Before the meeting was resumed, a senior resident piped up, "This is an example of what happens when we do not carry out the Group's decisions."

More to the point, this incident is a prototypical example

of the misuse of interpersonal power ploys on the part of the psychiatrist to control the behaviour and experience of people who find themselves in the position of patient. Angela Rivera did nothing, in the above situation, which justified her being dragged out of the room. She had not disrupted the group. In fact, both patients and those staff who were sufficiently awake were quite enjoying her performance. It was the chief psychiatrist who was the disruptive influence, because he felt his position of authority and control was being undermined by Angela's dancing. Behind his benevolent bow tie, there lurked an anxious tyrant. The unfortunate effect of this man's need to perpetuate his dominant position was to undo Angela's attempt to communicate something about herself, to further confuse her about where she was and what was happening to her, and to return the assembled men and women to their usual state of apathy. Here was another medico-psychiatric triumph.

But why did the group submit so quickly to the doctor? Was it just habit, or fear of losing a job, or fear of "treatment", or fear of Angela's aliveness, spontaneity and sexual provocativeness? Was it this they were putting down, and in themselves? We shall never know, for Angela was not allowed a repeat performance. Within days one highly tranquillized girl was shipped off to a state mental hospital, affectionately known in the trade as the "bin".

What is obvious in this scenario is that the identities of the case were by no means identical with the roles they played. In other circumstances the psychiatrist could well have been the patient, or criminal, or jailer, or field marshal. Angela could have been the psychiatrist, or nurse, or dance therapist, or, as in some Japanese hospitals, the state courtesan. No doubt the identities of individual members of the chorus could also have been regrouped.

What isn't obvious is whether the chief psychiatrist (and his lackeys) was evil, or simply out of touch with himself. If he did what he did in full knowledge and anticipation of the damage that Angela would sustain, notwithstanding the continued demoralization of patients and staff, then the psychiatrist can be considered evil. On the other hand, if he was unaware of the effects of his actions on Angela and the group, unaware of their feelings, and *unaware of his unaware-*

ness, then the psychiatrist can be said to be perceptually unsound. The man's interpersonal destructiveness consisted of perpetrating in others the very condition of unawareness from which he, himself, suffered.

During the ensuing year I was privileged to witness variations of the foregoing drama over and over. Far too often the brutality and sadism with which patients were treated by both doctors and hospital staff were even more odious than that which Angela was forced to undergo. Consequently, I resolved that I would never put myself in the position of being expected to or forced to relate to others as my psychiatrist mentors. In the first place the answer was to *stop* —*stop* projecting one's own disturbance into others, *stop* perpetrating one's own ignorance in others, and *stop* acting towards others as task-master for some agency of institutionalized brutality.

Secondly, I needed to refine my understanding of the complex changes in consciousness and behaviour so blithely glossed over by the medical profession as "illness" and to explore new ways of dealing with people who enter into such states.

It was easy to keep the first resolution. As regards the second, it was my extraordinary good fortune to be invited back to London by Dr. Laing and his group to participate in the founding of the Kingsley Hall community.

Part 3

Kingsley Hall — the "down" years by Mary Barnes

Chapter Six

The first five months and the coming of Joe

The first time I came to Kingsley Hall was a Saturday morning. Clancy Segal met me outside the front door. We came upstairs, on to the roof. I felt horrible. "Suppose I get bad, I might throw myself over."

We went down into the kitchen.

Gwen, one of the people then still living in the building, offered me coffee. I accepted. We went on into the big room where Frank was. He said, "Hello." We saw Barbara—she was nice. I told Clancy about Peter, my brother, walking how he walked. Clancy replied, "You want to get him out of there, the big institution hospital." Coming down to the Hall we looked in at the Chapel.

"That's where I'm going to say my prayers in the morning."

Clancy took me across the Hall into what was then still the Library, now the Meditation Room. We went up to the Flat. This really suited me. In the one empty bedroom, I said this is where I'm coming, this is my room.

Clancy explained to me that Sid, Mr. Briskin, who had found the building was in charge of the allocation of rooms.

"Why not ring him?" he suggested. I did, telling Sid I had a week's holiday, and would spend it there. Sid agreed to my coming. My happiness and excitement was terrific. I was thrilled with Kingsley Hall. It was a beautiful place. Everything in it delighted me. I rang Mother Michael to send all my boxes up from Presteigne, as quickly as possible.

The next day, Whit Sunday, I went on a parish pilgrimage to Walsingham, to specially beg the help of the Mother of God. Then I moved in, bringing my stuff bit by bit every night from the hospital. Some local boys helped me with a big load. We dumped it in the bedroom. My boxes came. I got out my big enamel pot. I watered in it. I shut the curtains of my room. A black counterpane went over the empty bed. Finding cushions, I covered these in black and put them on the floor. A wall I painted black. A picture of Saint Therese of Lisieux was put on top of the chest of drawers. The bed I slept in was always getting covered in things. Books, clothes, make-up, crockery, scarfs, flowers were all over the floor. The drawers were open. What was put in them got turned over and scattered out every time I wanted something. Everything was getting lost. Always untidy, this was the biggest mess I had ever known.

Sid looked in. "Don't you want any light?"

"No, I want the curtains drawn."

"What's that?"

"Oh, my pot. I'm going to empty it."

In the Hall, my boxes, six big trunks, were spilling all over the floor.

"They can go down in the basement."

"No, no, Sid, they must stay there."

Dennis, one of the people still living in the house, forces open locks for me. All my things revealed, unearthed, are crowded into the flat. The Cubs carried a lot up, they met in the Hall with their mistress. She had a whistle and yelled commands. They scooted around. I sat on the floor, digging out all my things, old bits of silver from my parents' home went into the flat kitchen.

Another room was empty. Dr. Esterson came to stay. He got morning tea out of the silver. When a third room was empty, Sid thought of having an office in the flat. This pleased me, quickly I looked around to make it "office-like". Blotter, pens, a paper weight. That was Sid's. Here was I, in the big bedroom. Opposite, was Dr. Esterson's room. Downstairs was Ronnie.

The first Saturday I was in Kingsley Hall Ronnie was there. He shows me the Box, made by John Latham.

"It's in the basement. You can get in it." We try it, it's beautiful. A big wooden box. You bend down to go in the opening. There's coloured lights inside. They go on and off. All different colours. Wires and books on a wall, and it has a floor. It's super. Stay in the box and you really go places. I want to try it. John has to come to fix it up a bit more. I really want experience of the box.

Some elderly lady, a friend of Dr. Esterson's, has turned up. She's talking about chairs and furnishings. She doesn't understand, I'm not interested, Ronnie has shown me the BOX.

Then the P.A.* came to have a meeting.

"Ronnie, why can't I come, you're going. Clancy thought I could go."

Ronnie suggested, "Suppose you come down in the middle, with some tea, then you can see everyone."

"All right."

"You'll be having it in there, in your room, for *privacy?*"

"Oh no, out here in the Hall."

Ronnie moves his big table out.

Taking down the tea, I see them all sitting in the middle of the Hall. David, Dr. Cooper, offers me a cigarette. He's nice. I have tea with them. I've made sandwiches without crusts. Chocolate biscuits also I gave. There was quite a lot left.

They were a long time meeting. I go to have a look.

"Do you want any supper? I'm having some."

Ronnie smiles, very nice, "No," shaking his head.

I get on with my things in the flat.

There's my sister's ironing board in the kitchen. Her boxes, which she had left in London, have just arrived. She's in Australia, but I thought I'd better be getting some of her things here. I want all my family. My brother I try to get. First I visit him, walking him on the common outside the hospital. The next week he comes for a day, then he comes for the weekend, after that, I go to bed. He came no more.

Why Ronnie didn't write to my parents to get them over I could not understand. Very cross, I was ringing up Ronnie to get them. This was the place for us, a schizophrenic family. The whole family must be there, to help me, to help Ronnie help me, and to get right themselves.

Somehow I didn't seem to get a chance to seriously discuss

*The Philadelphia Association.

matters with Ronnie and Sid. Everything was moving so
fast. One thing I must tell them was how to control me,
so I wouldn't go mad. Such was my panic. In fear, I had
gone quite blind as to why I was really at Kingsley Hall.

Ronnie asked me to write out my "ideas". This is what I
gave him.

"I organize and I fight; I don't mean to be bossy, I hate
being bossed myself. I like to please myself. I like other
people to please themselves. However, I think you have to
have some law and order in any community and I like
sanity and common sense, not madness. Through personal
past experience of 'funny business' and Ronnie will tell you
what I mean by that, I am very wary of it. I can only
live 'ordinary'. That's not to say I don't want to understand
interpersonal relations. I see my way of understanding what
is happening by two means (A) through my own individual analysis and (B) through group discussions with someone in the chair who is competent to interpret, i.e. Ronnie.
I want to contribute to Ronnie's presentation of it. I want
to be on TV and in books and I want to show people around
and take part in weekly seminars with outsiders during the
winter. In order not to regress 'out of hand'. I need *security*
and *independence*. I consider having to 'pretend' is not helpful to me. Wearing a stiff collar and black stockings and a
cap involves me in a 'set up' I don't agree with. I think I
will learn to be myself better and in time help others if I
don't have to dress up every day. I want to work here as
well as live here, full time. I want to help Sid with secre-
tarial work and show people round. I want to work as a
nurse if the need arises e.g. someone has the flu—I have
them up in the flat and give them tablets and hot milk or
penicillin injections, etc. If someone is very bad and wants
to come and Ronnie thinks so then they sleep in my room
—or in my bed. For this real need sort of thing I sleep on
the floor and give all I've got in me. But to be 'sat on'
and pushed around when I can see no good in it for me—
nor anyone else i.e. for the community, as a whole, no.
That muddles me, makes me insecure and leads me to madness, Sid is inclined to 'mess me about' like this. I want the
flat and Sid can have his office there, the end room. (The

room next to the bathroom is for anyone sick or for a particular guest, e.g. my Father if he comes over to work about the house this summer.) I don't want my brother up here, not to sleep unless Ronnie says so. So far as I can see it wouldn't be good for either of us to be so close. I want to see Allan and his wife and child settled in—together. In the big room next to the kitchen. I would like to help his wife into the main kitchen but not to get involved there. The run of that kitchen and the housekeeping I see as her right and concern as the caretaker's wife. I would like sometimes to come down to the dining-room opposite the kitchen for a meal, e.g. weekend lunch, an evening meal. Otherwise I would like to be free to arrange my own eating and entertaining in the flat. Payment for any communal meals I ate would be direct in accordance with what the meal was worth.

FINANCE

My present salary is about £1400 a year. My main expense is analysis, now six guineas a week and it could rise higher for more sessions. If I reckon the rent of the flat at £5 per week and you give me £15 a week then my salary is actually £20 a week.

If your financial state is such (and I want the facts) that this salary is quite beyond you, then I suggest less but an 'expenses' account. For example I buy wine, cigars to entertain professional people, I have the fare to Scotland (end of July when going to Ronnie's lectures). Or if your finances are much better than I imagine I have my suggested salary plus an expense account. The immediate need is to get the house in order, the dining-room arranged our own community in firstly Allan and his wife and child and in the best place with regard to their function in the community."

In my mind, at this time, I, not Ronnie, was running Kingsley Hall.

"Dr. Esterson hasn't got a front door key. Barbara, could you please give him one?"

Dr. Esterson is standing just behind me. Barbara issues him one.

Every day I visited Ronnie's room, leaving food, noticing what he had eaten, and how he had left everything else. Ronnie knew, but to me, it was "secret" activity, or someone else might have changed his sheets or brushed his shoes.

One evening in the Games Room, Dr. Esterson said to me and Gwen, "If you had unlimited money how would you have this room?" My choice was velvet curtains with a thick carpet, to make everything quiet, soft and warm.

"Dr. Esterson, want a game of table tennis?"

"No."

I went queer, rather dead feeling. Didn't know why. Later I got to saying, "Give me a game of table tennis. Please play with me."

One night a week the local Beatle boys came in to practise,

"Hello Mary."

"Hello Alex."

They sorted themselves out in the Games Room, with wires, flex—yards of it—and a microphone, drums and all sorts of things to smash and clash. The thing I loved was something on a stick that you shook and it made a noise. I danced with two of these. Backwards, forwards, shaking, shaking my body, the things, with the music. Arms and shoulders free, a black counterpane falling from my naked body. The noise was stupendous, the room shook with it. The boys sang. I sang. Everything clashed and banged. Rose up, bent down, all part of the beat of the drums, of the sway of the music. Joined with the boys, lost in the beat, breathless, exhausted, I would fall to the ground. Then up again, on, on, on. My body just couldn't twist enough.

Then it was over. The boys were packing up. Alone, silent. The impact of the silence. By this time as soon as I got home, I shed my clothes, lying naked in bed or sometimes squatting with the black counterpane around me, on the kitchen floor.

Going out in the mornings I would forget to put on make-up and arrive at the hospital all in a mess. Somehow I got changed. Rushed through the day and hurried home, particularly wanting to steal, on the way, some orange flowers growing outside the church.

Twice a week I had therapy, and all the fights about that

at the hospital because I had to have time off, further aroused my feelings: I was in a storm of temper and panic. Everything had to be controlled, organized. We must have table mats, the caretakers on the middle floor, next to the kitchen, me in the flat, in command.

Coming home from therapy, I was especially wild. Shouting up the stairs, kicking my red shoes off, flinging my clothes about, I would run, down, down, to the Box. This was my biggest delight, the Box. I sat still in there. Bringing blankets and my quilt down from my boxes, I lay, cuddled in with my things. Then I watered. This worried me, suppose the Box was damaged. It might not "work". I was "going somewhere" in the Box. It was to give me experiences— out of this world. The lights came on and off. You watched them. I went upstairs, wrapped in some bedding. There was a meeting. In a whisper: "Ronnie, I have watered in the Box."

"You have watered in the Box."

I nodded.

Ronnie was quite nice and smiling. Not cross. It seemed it was all right. I went back to the Box, feeling nice.

From then it took Sid just about another three weeks to get me to bed. I was in a fever of activity, never giving myself freedom or rest. Trying to get a job nearer home, I was involved with three different applications. Enlightenment came. It was one evening, at my typewriter, in the flat. In comes Sid. An interruption. What does he want? As if there wasn't enough to do, organizing everything here, work at the hospital, this writing to be done. Sid sits himself down. In no hurry, as if there was all the time in the world.

"Mary, what a nice typewriter."

"It's a Hermes."

"Beautiful small type."

"That's an article, a case history, it's got to be done tonight."

Sid sits back, lights a cigarette.

"That last interview, the job is nearer home, it seems they might have me."

Sid sits further back, quiet, thoughtful like. There's the typewriter, the window, the street, outside, outside.

I'm going away, my voice is weak, faint.

"Sid, Sid, I've come here to have a breakdown."

"Have a cigarette."

"It's cold."

"Hold still, I'll light it. Mary love, you've had a break-down. Look what you went through that time with Dr. Esterson, when you were at the Youth Hostel."

"Yes but but I've come here to go down and come up again."

Everything was slow, disjointed. "Mary, I've got to go."

His chair was empty. Sid had gone. I was here, not there. But was I, here, all here? Touched myself. Sat like a statue. Still. Cold. Remembering. Ronnie said he would get a place. For me to go down and come up again. Be as a child. Go mad. Re-grow. It had happened, the truth had come back.

I changed the paper in my typewriter. Three times.

"I do not wish to continue with my application. I am now otherwise engaged."

A fourth sheet:

"I wish to give one month's notice of leaving." Four times my name. Four envelopes, sealed. The lid on the typewriter. To bed. Sleep.

Only a week of that notice was worked.

Meanwhile, Sid was most concerned. "Mary, what have you done? You've no job."

"Sid, you know what I'm here for. I can't work outside, it's too much. I'm going in, in, mad." Everything was going away.

"Sit down." What, you want to see Ronnie? He'll be here, on Sunday, you can see him up here in the flat. I keep re-membering, telling myself over and over again, so I won't forget. I tell Ronnie. He understands.

"I'll see Sid about getting you on to National Assistance."

I'm so scared. But glad. I feel I'm getting somewhere. Dennis helps me move my things down into the room opposite the kitchen, on the middle floor. It's more inside the building. I have to get down, inside. By now, very aware that I was "going mad," I was in terror of losing control at the hospital. The last week of work was a nightmare of two worlds, the inner and the outer. The outer was becoming woolly, vague, distant. The inner was a force that could not be resisted.

One afternoon, I seemed to burst with anxiety. My pulse

was one hundred and ninety. While I was sitting, breathless, exhausted in the Practical Room, the students came. In a whisper, my voice was far away.

"I am very tired. Let's just sit, quietly together. Tell me—" They did the talking, I could not move to demonstrate. Relaxing, my breath came back. I got home. The next day, I was up again: violently "on top," around the wards, in the lecture room, the "efficient" teacher, "bang on." That was it. At home that night, I careered around the place, shouting, painting. With a tin of black paint I shouted on the walls. The Hall, the Games Room, the corridors, the Flat. Every picture the same. Black, black, black, suck, suck, suck. All in black. Everything black. Naked except for black, the black counterpane. This flung off, naked, I played table tennis with Clancy. Then I went for the tin of paint. Dennis got hold of me. Clancy was there. Then I'm in the kitchen, eating, sitting on the floor. We go upstairs to the Flat. There's music, loud music, way into the night.

Next morning, how to dress? Everything was lost. What to put on? How to put it on? It was getting late. My stockings were falling. My hair was down.

On the floor I sat, what to do? Nothing, nothing. The Matron. Frozen. Struck with terror. I lay on the floor. What would happen. Mad, going down. Oh God, God, I get to the phone.

"The Matron?"

"She's not on duty yet."

"Who? the Night Sister?"

"A message?"

"Yes, say, say I'm not coming in—they know."

Silence. Dead silence. That's right. Home, stay at home. Sid, ring Sid.

"Mary, it doesn't sound like anything physical. Go to bed. I'm coming over."

Relief. Sid—God—Bed.

Exhausted, in my room, on the floor. My bed. A blanket. Pull some clothes off. Naked. In the blankets. It's cold. My teeth chatter. I'm shivering all over. I can't stop it. Stay still, still.

Sid came. I knew to stay where I was. He put an apple to my mouth. I bite it. He had a bit. He gave me another bite. That was easier. Sid goes. Sleep. Cold. The night. The next day. Therapy, therapy, I must go to therapy. How? Get a car. Someone gets a car.

Suck, suck. In the chemists, get a bottle. In the waiting room, ask for some milk. Suck the bottle. Not long to wait. Get me a car. Home. Naked. Bed. Next time, Anna dressed me—only my skirt and jumper.

"Nothing under?"

"No, no, Anna."

"No ribbon on your hair?"

"No, no, bare, down."

"All right."

"Is the bottle full, warm milk?"

"Yes."

I put it here, in the back of my Teddy, with my ball.

The car comes, Wait, Suck, Play ball. Lay with my Teddy. Therapy. The car. Home. Clothes off. Wet the bed. Cuddle Teddy. The first doll; black, Susannah, that I had bought myself I had pulled to bits, limb by limb and then I pulled her head off. Then I asked Ronnie to get me a doll. He said "You want a doll?"

"Yes, to play with." He got me a black one, Topsy, and my Teddy. Teddy's back opened to hold things; he had a big pink bow and jingly bells in his ears. I took him in the Box. We sit down there, alone in the dark, or watching the lights, when Allan turned the Box on.

In my room I lay on the floor in blankets that I wet and wet. Feeling very bad, lying still in the warm wet, I would go to sleep. Also, after playing with my shits, I would sleep with it on me. When Ronnie came I showed him my painting in shit on the wall. A sperm, an ovum, a breast. The Cross—Eternity for ever. Birth—Suck—Suffer—Space—Eternity.

I told Ronnie "I could put my shit all over you, you would still love me."

Once, covered in shits, I crawled up to the Flat. Bent over at the door I heard Allan say "Look up, there are several people here." Slowly, I unbent and seeing a girl, whispered "Will you bath me?" "I would, but I'm not sure how." Allan took me to the bath. He washed it all away, and out of my hair. Then warm and relieved, he put me back to bed.

Once, when I was full of milk, Sid came.

"Hullo, Mary, would you like your bottle? I'll feed you."

"Mm, er, er—"

"What you want, Mary, is salt, you need salt."

Suck, suck, all of it, all the salt. I loved Sid. He went. Then I was queer. Bad terrible. Didn't know what was the matter. At this time, I was still unsettled, getting up at times to crawl to the kitchen and sit on the floor, sometimes asking to be fed. Ronnie gave me a sup of his tea. It was very weak and milky.

Once, Lili, a local lady, who then still helped in the house, fed me from a cup. Her hand was trembling. I was kneeling up naked, in bed.

Sid got me properly off sick, under the local doctor, Dr. Bernard Taylor. He came to see me. "Dr. Taylor, before I was in a mental hospital. Now I'm going down to come up again, here. You know about me? My brother, he is in a mental hospital. Mary Garvey knows me." Mary, who had just come to live in the house, was feeding me with a boiled egg, in the kitchen. From a chair she was bending down to me, on the floor. Mary offered Dr. Taylor a cup of tea. But he had to be quickly on his way.

"Mary, Dr. Taylor does understand really doesn't he? But he has to pretend not to, hasn't he, to me?" Mary put me back to bed.

By the time Dr. Taylor came again I was all the time in bed, without talking. When I got stuck, bad all over, as if caught and being killed, I would bend over, my head on the floor. My words, if any, were always: "I don't want 'it' to go *in* on me." Whatever "it" was "it" was terrible.

One morning early I went to the kitchen. Jeff, one of the people who were in the house when I came, was by the sink, making tea. Bent on the floor, I rubbed myself against his legs. This eased me. He touched me. He gave me a drink. I crawled back to bed.

Another time, when I was caught with "it," Leon (Dr. Leon Redler, who was then working in Scotland) came for a weekend. Sitting on a kitchen chair, with me on the floor, he told me say "mm, mm" for "yes" and "ugh, ugh" for "no." I felt his concern, asking me questions to ease it. This helped me. Then taking bread, he broke a piece and put it to my mouth. At first, I ate. Then the thought came, eating will push

my feelings down. I refused more; Leon went. Mary put me
to bed. Then it was terrible. Whatever was wrong? Leon was
a therapist; Leon understands. If Leon gives me food, it's
right to have it. In refusing, I had "gone against," gone
against Leon, gone against therapy. This was terrible. Everything was wrong. I had failed. Not co-operated. What did
Dr. Esterson, Aaron, say about "going against"? "Have
patience with yourself, don't tear yourself to bits."

Maybe Leon would give me another chance. Crawling out
to the passage, I ate some crumbs of bread from the floor.
Back in bed, everything was still all wrong. Somehow I lay
with it. The next morning Leon sat in the Box with me.
Joan (Cunnold) whom I had sometimes seen about, gave up
her job as a psychiatric nurse to look after me.

One day she took me to the bathroom. She held me and
we went upstairs. Usually my eyes were shut. "Mary, you
can open your eyes. Or, you see, you stumble."

In the bath, the water was beautiful, so warm, with my
hair floating like weed. Someone calls, Joan goes. Everything
changes. I'm bad. Joan comes back. I'm all wrong. No
words. It's stuck. Somehow it seems right to hit Joan. She
lets me. Then, all sweating and sick feeling, it seems I'm
blacking out. Why am I so weak? Joan gets me to bed. I'm
hot and cold. Panting and breathless. My heart is pounding.
I feel I'm dying. Joan stays with me, soothing me and
wrapping me up. Then she fed me with a bottle and laid me
on my side with my neck stretched, one arm partly under
me. The pain seemed to get it into my body. Staying how
Joan left me, I went to sleep.

One day, Joan asked me: "Would you like to come up on
the roof? I'm having tea with Mary Garvey up there."

"Ugh, ugh," shaking my head. Joan leaves me. The
thought suddenly comes, "Oh God, I've gone against; gone
against Joan—against therapy." Hopeless, despairing: "Oh
God, what can I do, how can I get right." Pulling something
around my naked self, I crawl upstairs, dragging myself half-
way across the roof. Joan was talking to Mary. I lay,
listening. It was sunny. This was the roof. Exposed. Light.
My longing was for dark, for being inside. No further could
I go. Broken, in tears, somehow I dragged myself back, down
the stairs into bed. It was terrible. How to lie, to stay.

Would Joan *ever* come? Sobbing, sobbing in anger, despair, everything was wrong. Oh God, God bring Joan—please— *please*. My crying was that of a baby, that's how it sounded. Joan came. She'd hold me tight. Cuddled me. My breath came. Slowly in whispers. "Joan, Joan, *why?* Why? Everything was *wrong*. I wanted it right. Maybe I should have stayed in bed." Joan shouts, "Mary, bring me two clean sheets please." Joan rocks me. No more talking. They roll me. They lay me. They feed me. They "put me." They leave me.

On another occasion, when Joan invited me out of my room, I was in no doubt I wanted to go. She took me. "Mary, there are some visitors tonight. We are having dinner in the sitting-room, here just opposite to your room. Would you like me to bring you in?"

"Mm, Mm."

David, Dr. Cooper, has arrived. He is talking near my door. "Mm, Mm, Oh, Oh, Ah, Ah, Ah." The noises get nearer. He touches me. "Have some wine," holding the glass to my mouth. Mm, Mm—swallowing. Ah, Ah-ing, Oh, Oh; Aaron comes, visitors come, the chorus gets bigger. All big noises. All around me. Another glass is put to my lips. Mm, Mm, the noises are beautiful. Loud, loud, noises we make.

Joan comes, someone carries me in. I feel the company. Once I stole just half a tiny wee look. Safer to be, sit how I was put. Hum and sway. Taste the wine. Sid was there, Ronnie was there. Listening, listening, safe, secure, sleepy, I got sleepy.

"Mary would you like to come back to bed?"

"Mm, mm."

"David, the David who is our visitor, is going to carry you back to bed. I'm here. I'm coming."

"Mm, Mm."

In bed. Some of David's wine. *Sleep, sleep.* Bliss, beautiful. Soon after this I got a vaginal haemorrhage and had to be taken to the physical hospital. Joan came every day to see me, but it was terrible. I wanted to explode, to scream, to throw things, to bash myself to bits. Joan explained, it's not possible to be as you are at home.

"No, you can't have your Teddy. You must pretend, appear to be normal, like the other patients. Eat up your tea."

"Joan, I mustn't, it will push my feelings down."

"Well, drink your milk."

"All right."

Sid came: "Hallo Mary, how are you? I've brought you some sweets—a box of chocolates and liquorice allsorts. I thought you'd like them."

Everything went queer. "Sid, Sid, I mustn't, I can't. My feelings. I want to keep them up—to carry on, when I get home."

"Well, shall I put them in the locker? In case you might want one."

"No, no, Sid."

"All right love, I'll take them home. There's some children next door I can give them to."

All the time I lay, very still, keeping together. When a priest came I explained how I would be going down, going through madness, when I got home. He said he would pray for me. I went to confession and Communion. I knew whatever my mental state, had I ever been in danger of death at home, Ronnie would have got a priest. Although I was so bad—feeling, I did, as at home, sleep at night. The other patients had sleeping tablets. The night nurse asked how many you wanted. I said, "No thank you, not any." The sister knew I had nervous trouble and was resting.

The hospital doctor told me, after they had done a dilatation and curettage, that my haemorrhage was due to emotional trauma.

I was three weeks in hospital. On the day I was going home I wanted to scream and hit everyone, when waiting, waiting for them to come for me. At last, they came: Raymond, a member of the Philadelphia Association, in his car with Joan and Jill, who had come to live in the house. As soon as we got in the door I hit Jill, don't know why. Raymond pushed me up the stairs. Joan had made my room beautiful, with Teddy on the bed. Everything seemed right. Ronnie comes, I squeeze and squeeze him round the middle, laughing. Then I lay in bed. It didn't seem right. I sit on the kitchen floor, whining. It was terrible. Back in bed, I wet the bed. Joan put me back on the floor, she brought me a cup of tea. It seemed I mustn't have it. Something was wrong. Joan went. What to do about the tea? I might take it. That would be wrong. I fling it across the floor. It's still all wrong.

After three days, I was not eating or drinking, only lying on the floor, except once, when I slid my body along the floor and banged my feet against a partition where there was a meeting. Ronnie came:

"Let me help you up. Come with me. There's other people in the room. You can open your eyes. Let her sit there, on the floor."

I'm murmuring. Coming home, I didn't talk any more. Ronnie speaks: "Mary, different people are going to feed you. Will you eat and drink what they give? Do you agree?"

"Mm. Mm. Mm."

Very agreeable. Joan puts me on a rubber mattress on the floor. This seems more like the pads. I so love Joan and Ronnie and Aaron. Soon I would be right down, in the basement, in the Box. Several times a day they fed me with food, marmite, eggs, fruit, a bottle with warm milk. Gradually, as I got more down, the food got less and less. This was right. Everything would have been wrong otherwise. My shits didn't come any more. After about two weeks the District Nurse would come to give me an enema.

This was right. Everything had to be put in me and taken out. I had not myself to take in, nor give out. My water didn't come for some days. Once when the nurse had sat me on my pot, the enamel pot that Peter and I used as children, she started to plait my hair. It was agony. I screamed and screamed. Joan came. She explained I didn't like my hair touched. Then the nurse got the shits out. It was too stuck to come and hurting me a lot.

Sometimes Joan washed me. I liked this, and when Joan moved me in bed. Used to the feel of Joan, it was all right if she touched me or smoothed my hair. But if anyone else touched me, everything could get suddenly bad and be very terrible. Once it happened with Anna, quite out of the blue as she was feeding me. Aaron came. He said it was something in Anna. This time the badness was stopped. My eyes still shut—I kept on sucking as Aaron took the bottle. Then he played a bit with me with the bone ring he had got me to bite on. It had a bell so I knew when someone held it for me to bite. It helped me.

Once Ronnie came, with David. They spoke my name. I was very still and far away. Then downstairs Ronnie was playing the piano, a child's hymn, "There's a home for little children above the bright blue sky." Everything was right, at peace. I felt secure, safe, comforted.

Gradually I got more and more still. Obviously I was now no longer going out to the clinic. When Ronnie fed me I was quite still and completely together. Sometimes my limbs seemed heavy and stuck, it seemed I was a little animal, gone to sleep for the winter.

My body did often seem apart. A leg or an arm could be the other side of the room. Often it seemed I was floating and moving as if in fluid. Wanting to be always in the dark, it was wrong if the light was put on. My door, if it was shut, would make me feel bad. Usually it was left open, though noise could be very disturbing.

There was talk of Dr. Berke coming, he was the doctor who had been with me in Ronnie's office the day Ronnie said he was going to get a place. His name was Joseph Berke, Joe, Ronnie called him. It seemed he was coming to live in the house. The day drew near, I so wanted him to come. He was going to stay in the house. At last the day came. It got to night, late at night. Then I heard voices, an American voice. I kept very still, my eyes shut. Joan and Aaron came, and there he was, Joe. They left him.

"Something is in my eye."

"I'll have a look. Can't see anything."

"I still feel it."

"I'll get some warm water to bathe it."

I take a quick look. He drew back, very quick. He was the same. Dark suit, glasses, black hair, a beard. Joe bathed my eye. Nothing came out, but everything was right. Then Joan and Aaron said I was very hot. So Joe came again. It seemed he was going to examine me. Then he went. Everything was wrong. It was terrible. The night was so black. But the morning did come. Joe was still here. Joan and Joe came with some milk. Joe fed me. I knew he understood, I had not to take it all. I did steal a look. They didn't see. That was my secret—the little looks I stole. There was nothing else to steal.

Once, when Joe brought me a little water in a glass, I

started to drink. Then, knowing it was "wrong," I spat it out. Joe played with me. Everything was right. Joe understood. There was no "gone against" feeling. Then Joe brought me water. Joe understood. He fed me so most of it spilt. It seemed then I was in a garden with beautiful flowers, chrysanthemums of all different colours.

Joe was big and strong, he got me upstairs into the bath. My ears seemed so big, and my body all head. The water was glorious, it lapped in and out of my mouth. Holding my breath, my head stayed under. The water was all round me. Soon there would be a tube left in me and all the food running through the tube into my tummy would be just like a cord running straight from Joe's tummy into mine, me tied to Joe, floating in the warm water.

One night there was a lot of music, Ronnie came in to me.

"We are having a party, they are dancing, would you like to come?"

"Yes, if you think so."

He put a coat over me. We went out of my room, somewhere, my eyes were shut. Joe came. With Ronnie and Joe holding me, I danced and danced and danced. Faster, faster, into the music we went, then down, down, on the floor murmuring with joy. There I'lay till a strange boy coming near frightened me to a panic. Joe carried me back to bed.

Although I lay as if in a stupor for most of the time, I was very aware of what was going on. Touch seemed to mean everything. By it I drew away or inwardly moved nearer. Once, I was not dreaming, I saw a woman knocked down in the snow by a man in a fur skin. Then, it looked like the same woman, she was standing near an old-fashioned car in which there were children. In my room, sitting on the top of a small bookcase, was a boy, with longish hair and a big bow at his neck, as worn in the past. My eyes were shut. It all seemed real, yet not a dream, nor an imagining. When it seemed so real that there were spiders and insects on the floor, I put out my hand to prove to myself they were not really there, alive, crawling all around. On the walls too, were tiny, moving black insects.

The wall behind me seemed hollowed into a great space, into which I was going. Though, actually lying still, curled up in my bed, it sometimes seemed I was the other side of the room. Inwardly, I "saw" the room differently. It went round, to the left, as if bending into a narrower room or a corridor. Beyond was a great expanse. It was empty, endless, very beautiful with ridges of hills, and a cloud-blown sky.

By now I was very sleepy and still. Except when Joe rolled me. Then my water would just come from me. Joe made me laugh. He bit me. Instead of the bone ring, I bit Joe. My murmuring got very low. It seemed a tube was in me and soon I would be in the Box. Before, when I had cried, it sounded as if it was a baby crying, now there was no noise, nothing, yet—everything. In a sense I seemed complete.

Once a nurse came with Dr. Taylor. They took some water from me and blood out of my arm. One night Ronnie came.

"Mary I want you to eat now. To eat what Joe gives you."

Joe came. He held me.

"What would you like? Jelly?"

"Mm. Mm."

"I'll make you some nice jelly."

He went. Everything was nice, right. Then, something, don't know what, made a panic. I moved. I screamed. Joe came back. "What's the matter, the matter with me?" It's because I screamed. They didn't mean me to eat really, they were going to tube-feed me. Only now I had moved, had screamed, they couldn't tube-feed me. I had "gone against." It was all my fault. The Box, the Box, when was I going to the Box. Joe calmed me. "Nothing is wrong. It's not your fault. I would have tube-fed you, though I don't like putting tubes into people. But Ronnie, with all of us, decided it would have been a danger to your life physically." It seemed a bit better. They decided. Then I moved and screamed. No, I hadn't really changed them. That was right. I tried to catch the truth—though feeling, all the time, I was causing them.

Joe helped me to let it rest; he gave me a black spider on a string and lifted me out on a couch. They were moving me upstairs, to a room in the Flat.

Chapter Seven

The visit of my parents—up and about—living it out

They wrote to say when they were coming. Joe read me the letter. It was very worrying. The day they were expected Joan came to me: "Mary, I'm going to buy you some new clothes, what would you like?"

"Nothing black."

"They've got some nice pinafore frocks in Marks and Spencers."

In a whisper: "Could I have trousers? I've never had them."

"Do you like these, brown corduroy? Maybe I could get you something similar to mine?"

"Yes, yes, I like those."

Joan measured me: thirty-six inch hip. She went to the shop and came back loaded.

"Mary, open your eyes. Look what I've got."

"Oh, Joan, marvellous."

"Try on the trousers."

"They fit, and the shoes, green."

"Here's socks; brown, green and red. Hold up your head, see if the jumpers fit; green, red and mauve."

A girl who lived in the house, Anne, came in through the window, looking at everything, holding things against herself. I went all queer, turning away, unable to look. Anne went.

Joan fitted the brassière on me, blue.

"Stand up. Look pink knickers. What jumper would you like?"

"That one, mauve."

"Look, this is for cold weather. It's like a vest only shorter, I wear them."

Mm. I hadn't seen such a thing before, but Joan wore them, so it must be right. The jumpers had polo necks. I'd always chosen V-necks, but now I supposed polo necks must be best for me.

"Now I've got you a surprise."

"Oh, Joan, what a beautiful smell, lovely scent and talcum and soap."

"Do you like this shade lipstick?"

"Yes."

"This is 'Quiet Pink' nail varnish and here's cream and eye shadow."

Joan puts all this on me. We go downstairs. Joan sits me on a chair, in the sitting-room. Joe is there. I sit very still, keeping together. At dinner, there's ice cream. Then Joe puts me to bed. The next morning, I'm lying awake, my eyes shut. No one has come. The door is open. That's right. I hear Joe. He sits on the bed. He touches me. I have a quick look, when he doesn't see me, see him.

"Your parents are here."

"Ugh—er—"

"I was going out of the front door. They were there."

Joe holds me. My heart is pounding, I feel all weak. Breathless and cold, as if collapsing. It's a terrible shock.

"Do you want to see them? They are downstairs."

I'm fainting, falling to pieces. Knocked out. Joe holds me. The minutes pass. My breath comes, I'm whispering, "Joe, I can't." We rest longer.

"I'll go and tell them. You don't have to see them."

"Later, with you, I could see them? Not alone?"

"Lie still, I'm coming back."

I fear my parents, coming in on me. Joe returns.

"I explained you couldn't see them today. Your mother said, 'Oh, I do feel ill.' They've gone." My breath returns. It's safer. I'm still here.

Later in the day, Joe took me downstairs. Ronnie told me: "Your parents are coming to Wimpole Street tomorrow, to see me. You don't have to see them." I'm still numb and cold.

A few days later my Father came. Joe was out. I was in bed. Helen, a girl who lived in the house, told me: "Your

Father is here. He has called to collect his camera, which he forgot the other day. He would like to see you."

"Helen, Joe said I'm seeing my parents together with him."

"Shall I see if your Father wants to wait today until Joe comes in?"

"All right."

My eyes shut, I lay dead still in my bed. Joe came. He sat with me.

"Like to come with me to see your Father? We'll make a tape."

"Don't leave me."

"Here, put this on, hold my arm."

We got to the Games Room. My Father kissed me.

"Hello dear."

"Hello." I'm rather weak.

"Mr. Barnes, I've got a tape recorder, is it all right with you if we make a record?"

"Yes, yes."

My hand was on Joe's knee. The other side of me, sat my Father.

"Father, could you give some money to Kingsley Hall?"

"You know, Mary, private places are not really for us. We can't afford this sort of thing."

"This is not a nursing home. You could have ten thousand pounds and not be granted a place here. Or you could be here without any money at all."

"Dr. Berke, would you say Mary was manic depressive or schizophrenic?"

"Those terms relate to how a person behaves. In certain circumstances Mary might behave in a manner you could call schizophrenic. Here in Kingsley Hall, Mary is a member of a community. She is being helped simply to be herself."

"Mary, you have always been worse than Peter."

This frightened me, my hand was on Joe. "Yes, but I've been worse in order to get better. Here I go back to before I was born, and with Dr. Berke I re-grow. Peter can't do that in the mental hospital."

Father seemed puzzled. "Well dear, I think I'd better be getting off. We are staying at Welwyn, everyone sends their love. I'll be coming again to see you with Mother."

"Goodbye, Dad." We kiss.

"Yes, I know my way down. Goodbye Dr. Berke, pleased to have met you."

Father is gone.

I bash and bite Joe.

The next day with John Layard, a Jungian analyst who lived in Kingsley Hall, and Joe, I heard the tape recording. They pointed out to me the ways I had resisted my Father's attempts to control me.

The day my parents were expected to visit me, I was up and about with Joe. Someone let them in and announced they were in the Games Room. Joe brought me in, I kissed them, lightly. Joe went for the kettle. I had coffee, the same as Joe. My mother had tea. We all had a biscuit. My hand was on Joe. Mother sat across the table, opposite to Joe, next to Father.

"We didn't really know what to bring. We brought you some sweets and fruit."

"Thanks."

My Mother starts: "Well, how are you dear? Ruth and all the family send their love."

This is dangerous, all the love messages, I'm choking, afraid my Mother might come "all over me," that I might get bad if she touches me. This does not happen. I am with Joe. With my Father I am very cross when he tells me.

"We went to see Peter, he seemed well. He talked to us."

"Peter can't really *live* in that place—only like a turnip."

"Mary, Peter is happy in the hospital, they've got television."

I'm bursting. "Peter could get better here, really. He's always been stuck in it ever since he couldn't go to school that time."

"Peter was all right then, he was reading Freud and doing Yoga."

"*What*, Father, you say because he could do those things, he was 'all right.' You *know* how he was then, he never spoke, stayed in his room, never came to meals."

Mother intervenes. "We went also, Mary, the same day, to see Uncle Doug, in the Cheshire Home. He was well and sends his love."

"Oh, that was a long way Mother, all in one day."

"Yes dear, I *was* tired."

"Joe, do you think my parents could go to see Sid?"

"Yes, if you like."

"Can I give them Sid's address?"

"Yes, here it is."

Mother asks Joe: "Where did I go wrong?"

He replies: "There isn't time to go into all that now."

My Mother tells Joe: "Thank you, Dr. Berke for all you are doing for Mary."

We kiss. "Goodbye."

At the Games Room door Joe suggested to me, "You can go down the stairs."

On the stairs, my Father touched a radiator.

"My dear, are you warm in your room?"

"Yes, Joe stokes the boiler."

At the front door my Mother said: "It's cold, don't linger, get in, in the warm."

In the afternoon, Joe took me out, to get ice-cream.

From being in bed all the time, without speech, and without feeding myself, to being around the house and speaking was a big leap. There were many falls. Waking early, I would lie and listen, with my eyes shut. Cautiously, in secret, I might get out to use my pot. My body seeming still together, I would get back into bed. Listening, sleeping, moving a little, I was aware that Joe was out or around, the door left open, the curtains drawn, the light off; the day would pass "right." There would be sounds of Joe, growls drawing nearer. "Who's that? Who's there? Well if it isn't Mary Barnes." Joe rolls and rolls me in the bed, shakes my head about. It's all full of life. "Tap, tap, who's there?"

"Mary."

"Mary who?"

"Mary Barnes."

I was at home, inside my head, all here.

"Oh Joe."

Growl, a big bite. "Come on, here, put something round yourself, come to dinner."

In a whisper: "Yes."

Taking my hand, Joe helps me downstairs, my eyes opening a little. Joe sits me down. The light is dim, with candles. Joe puts food on to my plate. Serves himself. Feeding me,

Joe also eats. Sitting, listening, my eyes shut, I am aware of all the people. Sometimes Joe talks. Sometimes Joe touches me.

Maybe he is away, on the telephone. Everything is coming in on me. Joe returns, growling, biting.

"Want to go to bed?"

"Mm. Mm. Mm." Up we go. Wait for Joe. He pulls the clothes back.

"In you go—see you in the morning."

The light is off. The door is open. Keeping very still I collect myself, together, then taking a little peep, I go to sleep. My prayer on such a day as this, would be "Dear Jesus I love you, Goodnight." Sometimes Joe got me up during the day, sitting me still somewhere. In the same space as Joe I might open my eyes, taking a few quick looks.

Helen, a girl who lived in the house, was laying the table.

"Would you like to put these things on the table, Mary?" Everything was dangerous. She was "coming in on me." I kept together, quite silent and still. The danger passed. Talk, movement, anything extra to what I really felt I could do, brought disaster. In a flash things went from "right" to "wrong." Everything in the house seemed to do with me. I was like God, omnipotent, controlling. It was a great relief when in time, I emerged from this baby state.

One morning, quite early, Joe came, rolling me. "Come on, want to get up. Race you down the stairs."

Wait. Wait. Struggling into bra, knickers, jumper and trousers—there was never a moment to lose. Joe might go. "Joe, Joe, just a moment. Oh, oh, I'm ready."

Joe tears down the stairs. I'm panting behind. Joe takes me across the Games Room, into the kitchen. Joe sits me down. There are other people there. Getting used to the room, I'm exploring a little with tiny looks. Joe is moving about. He goes to the fridge.

"Like some nice soup?"

"Mm mm," nodding.

Joe heats it in a pan. Puts some in a bowl.

"Come here."

Joe puts me up to the table. The soup smells good. Joe is sitting, still, the other side of the table. It's safe. I feel all nice and beautiful, everything is so wonderful.

"Mary, I'm going out today."

A bomb has fallen. I'm shattered. Everything has gone. I'm away, stuck, can't move. Joe takes my hands, across the table, I've no words. It's silent. We sit. Joe looks very intense right at me. I'm looking, my eyes open, right into Joe's face.

"I'm going to Trafalgar Square to read some of my poems. I'll be back tonight."

No movement. Stone still, like a dead body in a chair, cut off from all life. The barrier was as a mist, of the density of steel.

"Eat your soup." Joe spoons some to my mouth. No movement. Dead. Nothing. Nothing. Nothing there. Nothing for it to go into. Nothing to hold it. Nothing to come out. The wall cannot open. Joe touches me. Still sits holding my hands. No words. I'm straining, straining to get through something. I can't. The wall. The blank. Nothing. Joe's face is all strained, puzzled, puckered. What is it, what is it? The soup is forgotten. Joe moves about. I remain. No movement. Joe comes near.

"Mary would you like to sit in the other room?"

"Mm mm," sad and far away. My head down, my eyes shut, Joe leads me next door. He puts me sitting up, on one of the sitting-room chairs.

So I sat all day, exactly as Joe left me, my eyes shut. In the evening Raymond came. I screamed and screamed and screamed. Raymond took me in to dinner.

Joe returned. He sat on the other end of the table. Raymond put me to bed. The next morning Joe brought me food, in bed. He plays with me. "Tickle, tickle." I laugh and laugh. He covers me: "Oh where's Mary Barnes? She's gone away—she's all *gone*." Holds me covered away. Peep —"Oh she's there, is that Mary Barnes? Oh, she's come back —bite her nose—crunch, crunch, growl, bite. She's gone away—she's come back." My head butts into Joe. "Bite off her ear." Big squeeze—"is that *all* you can squeeze, is *that* all?"

I'm laughing, breathless, my arms clasping harder and harder round Joe's middle. Joe releases himself. "I'm painting my room, want to come and watch?"

"Mm mm, all right."

Day by day I became more active.

"Mary, don't brush your hair in the kitchen."

"Oh, *Joan,* oh, where are my shoes?"

"Where you left them, across the sitting-room floor. Wait, I will tie your ribbon, but *wait* just one minute."

"Mary, can't you see Helen's doing something? Move yourself. There's no need to sit right there on the floor, where everyone has to walk round you."

"Oh, oh, I've got to be ready—er, er—"

"Now, don't start that noise. When Joe was out yesterday she was two hours sat outside his door, whine, whine, whine."

"Hold still, how's that? Have I tied it tight enough?"

"Mm, mm."

"Joe, turn round, you have something on your trousers."

"Oh er—thank you, Helen."

"Come on, race you to the front door."

Scrambling, panting out of the front door, across the road after Joe, round the corner. Joe stops, bends with growls and laughter. Breathless, I hold his hand and off we go. First the greengrocer man.

"Hullo duck."

"Hullo."

"Yes, sir."

Joe gives the order. *Marvellous.* Two packets of figs and big oranges. Everything is right. The money?

"Oh, put in two more pounds of black grapes," says Joe.

"Right, sir."

Next the Co-op Food Store.

"Do you want to push the basket?"

"Ugh, ugh," shaking my head.

"All right."

Joe pushes and shops; I'm looking and looking.

"Choose all your favourite biscuits," says Joe. Mm. Wonderful, lots and lots. Chocolate, fruit, honey—oh the warm loveliness. I'm so full of happiness. We get to the butcher, Joe is looking in the window.

"How much for fifteen people? How long do you cook it for?"

"Well, Sir, that's it then, and the duck for *tomorrow* night?"

The world falls. I'm shattered. All wrong. Joe is ready. I just stand.

"Come on, here, take my hand. What's the matter?"

No words. Joe is like a lamp post. I'm a stick. We cross the road, into the fish shop. Joe is ordering *fish,* fish, fish. I'm in a daze. It's *too* much. What *have* I done? It's not fair. I punch Joe, hard, and again and again. What *have* I done—that we are not having duck? Stuck. No words. Punch again hard. Joe is trying to order and hold me.

"Nice mackerel, Sir, you can bake them." Bash, bash.

"Or a piece of filleted cod." Groans of "it."

"Oh, I say."

The fish shop lady gets alarmed.

"It's all right, she's only angry with me. I'll take three pounds of that. Would you fillet it please?"

"Certainly, Sir." Punch. Punch.

At last, outside in the road, Joe gets hold of me.

"Now stand *still. What* is it?"

I have no idea that Joe is not fully aware of why he's being hit.

"You know, you know, you *changed* it, it's not fair, what have I done?"

"Changed what?"

"The duck, the duck. Why? Why?"

Joe smiles. "Now, *listen*, it's *nothing* to do with you. We never were going to have duck tonight. I always meant the order for duck for tomorrow night."

Slowly, disjointed: "We are having *duck* tomorrow night."

"You mean you didn't change anything?"

"No. That's right."

"Then, it *can't* be to do with me?"

Very slight sigh of relief.

"No."

Joe takes my hand. "Come on."

I'm rather numb, weak and shaken. Very quiet, not stuck, though holding together. We get to the cake shops. It's easier. Joe orders. "Want a cream bun?" "Mm." Real dairy cream. I pick the biggest. Out we go. Give Joe a lick. Fill my mouth—full. Mm. Home. Up the stairs. Joe gives me a push. Into the kitchen. Sit on a chair. Joe has gone. I'm lost. Joe comes back.

"Want an orange?"

Mm. Joe cuts me up an orange to suck. He makes himself some eggs. Marvellous. So safe. Warm. Home. Joe. Everything is right. Joe chews loud. I suck, big sucks. "I gotta go out now, to Sid's." The earth has parted, I am sunk. Dead. "I'll be back." I moan, Joe lets me follow him to the front door.

"I am not going out to punish you." "No, Mary you cannot come." Joe holds me. I'm so sad, faraway. Everything has gone. The door is shutting, I fall to the ground. Oblivion. Stuck. Will be back—back—a moment is a year. Someone touches me, it's Raymond.

"Mary, come upstairs, it's so cold on this stone floor." I groan and groan, start to move; it is too bad. Keep still. Raymond goes. Very gradually, I turn, open my eyes, move, lie back. Somehow, slowly, I got myself upstairs. Joe came back. Joe always did come back.

Terrible were the times when tied in a knot I would say: "Joe, you have to say that, I know, you don't *really* mean it."

"Mary, I *do* mean it. I know you weren't talking, and I didn't mean to step back on you, but I don't want you always to *follow* me about. I'm in the house. In a short while I'm coming to the sitting-room. Then you can sit in the same place as me." Lie on the floor. No Joe, whine and whine.

"Mary, if you don't stop that noise I'll have to put you to bed. You can't be down here with the other people like that." Whine extra loud, want to go to bed, Joe takes me up. We play biting, crocodiles and sharks.

"Who's got the biggest mouth?" Joe puts his hand in. Sharks! I scream and scream. Joe laughs. He takes my arms. Stretch, big stretch and again. He pulls the bedclothes over me. Out of the door. The light if off. It's nearly night. I'm half asleep.

After I had been up and about a month or two, Joe had to go away to Paris for four days. At least a week beforehand Joe told me he was going. He left at night, calling in my room to say goodbye. "Be a good girl. See you in four days."

"Mm," I murmured, half asleep, keeping my eyes shut,

in order not to see the actual going of Joe, and the shutting of the door. Four days was like four years, but I resolved to be good. The first day was very quietly spent lying about the sitting-room, sometimes on the divan, sometimes on the floor. Teddy was held, Teddy was put aside. "Joan, Joan are you going out?"

"In a minute."

"Please bring me something nice."

"What?"

"A toffee apple."

Joan returns. "Oh, marvellous, Joan, please tuck me up." Joan tucked me up with Teddy on the divan. It was just about tea-time. Soon everything was very quiet and lonely. Creeping up to my room, I lay very still, in the dark with Teddy. The next day, it got light. That seemed strange, that it was light and day. To me, inside it was dark and night. Time to keep still, to lie in bed. To get up, to move, was all wrong. Joan came. "Mary are you getting up today?"

"Ugh, ugh." Joan left.

The night came, there was Raymond.

"Mary, sit up. I have some dinner for you. Open your mouth, swallow."

"Ugh. Ugh." Everything is wrong.

"Raymond, I mustn't, Joe means me to go down again."

"Have a drink."

Raymond lays me down. It's best to keep very still. Certainly not to eat. That felt all wrong. So I stayed. Until.

"Growl, Growl, who's there? Well, if it isn't *Mary Barnes*. Come on down to dinner."

Somehow everything is different.

"Oh, Oh Joe, Joe." Punch and hit. Squeeze and butt with my head into Joe's tummy.

"Race you down the stairs." Breathless panting, living.

At this time, although up and moving around, I still had no shits. Joe told me: "Don't worry about it. No need to put your finger in to see if you can get some." After about two weeks of no shits, the District Nurse came. She gave me an enema. For the first time after an enema, I passed my own shits, into my pot, in the sitting-room. The nurse had not to put in her hand to get out my shits. It seemed everything had left me. I lay in great relief resting on the floor.

The nurse emptied my pot and covered it with newspaper. This seemed very strange. I never covered my pot then. The nurse left me. She seemed quite nice, but, as always, I had not spoken to her. It was too dangerous to speak to people who did not really understand.

Once when Joe was going to take me out it rained.

"Why can't we go Joe?"

"Because it's raining. I don't like going out in the rain."

"But Joe, you *said* we were going."

"Look, Mary, because *you* like going out in the rain, it doesn't mean that I like going out in the rain."

"But Joe, it seems all wrong, what's the matter with me?"

It was a long time before I was separate from Joe.

What helped me to get a feel of my own body was dancing. Sometimes when Ronnie played the piano, at other times alone in the Hall downstairs, I would fling myself about, dancing with my arms, kicking with my legs, whirling and twirling my body in the air. Often I danced with a ball, throwing and bouncing it. Sometimes Leon danced with me. Other times, I sang as I danced. Rock-a-bye baby, folk songs, hymns, bits of anything and everything. Dancing and singing alone in the Hall, or playing with a bat and ball, I felt movement, was aware of myself. People sometimes played ball with me. "Give me a catch." This was all right. But, "Mary why don't you speak to us? Come and sit in the kitchen with Helen and me." This was all wrong. Speechless, my body motionless, I would wait until such a person had gone.

It was ingrained in me that my badness must be punished. So great was the badness that Joe also must punish himself on account of it. To see Joe suffer so on my account, caused me to get stuck, to go dead.

"Joe, Joe?"

"What, what's the matter, Mary?"

"Joe, what, *what* have I done?"

"What do you mean, what have you done?"

"Joe, Joe, all that salt. All right, I know you have to do it. But, but?"

"Look, Mary, this is *my* dinner. I like a lot of salt."

"But, but?"

Everything is wrong. It won't come right. Joe chews loud.

Puts on more salt. Oh *God*, what have I done? Why does Joe so have to punish himself?

Looking at Joe's hands. He remarked, "Doctors shouldn't have dirty finger nails."

"Oh Joe, *Joe*."

"What's the matter?"

"Why, *why* am I so bad?"

"I haven't not cleaned my nails because of you."

"No, really, no?"

"*No*."

Joe bites me. "Where's the ball?"

"In Teddy."

Oh, play ball. Bash with Teddy. Roll on the floor. Shout loud. Scream and be wild. Hit with my hands, kick with my feet. Be a boy, all trousers and roughness. Never in those days did I wear a skirt. Within a few weeks of first getting up, all the jewelery and make-up was shed. My feet were always bare and my hair was long. There were a few rare quiet moments, as when I would carefully wrap Teddy in a yellow counterpane Joan had given me. Then I would sit, on the floor, rocking myself and Teddy. Sometimes Joe had visitors. "Wait here, I'll be back." Time passes. What is the matter? Where *am* I? Oh God, God where's Joe? What have I done? Oh why did I run downstairs, rushing up to Joe? Oh God, why do I "go against?" Groan and rock. Bang my head on the wall. Curl up. Lay down. I can't move. I'm stuck with "it." There's a noise. Is it? Can it be? Really? The noise gets nearer. God, God. "What's that there?" My legs stretch. "Well if it isn't Mary Barnes."

"Mm Ugh Mm."

Joe rolls me. We grunt. We are pigs. We are crocodiles. Crunching, biting, roaring into lions.

"Race you down the stairs." Panting, breathless.

"Come and get some chips." Run all the way. Two bags. Run home, into the kitchen, tomato sauce. Up on the roof. It's cold and windy. Mm. Mm. Beautiful chips. Stuff them in. Eat loud. Sit with Joe.

"I gotta make dinner, want to watch?"

"Mm. Mm."

"Sit there." The kitchen is warm, Joe is there. He gives me tastes. Everything is safe and right.

In November Leon came from Scotland for a weekend. I got myself up. "Hullo Leon." It seemed they were going out.

"Joe? You going shopping? Can I come? Put something else on it's cold."

Everything seemed different, strange. We went down the road. Leon was talking to Joe. Something is wrong, why am I all terrible? We go in the Co-op food store. Suddenly, I'm all exploding, falling apart. I'm all in pieces. Where am I? What's happening? I'm all splintered, showering away. I run to the door. Leon comes after me. He holds me together, tight. I'm standing between Leon and the traffic fence, squashed together, gasping and breathless. Can't we get home, *why* did I come out? Joe come. What's the matter, where am I? What am I?

We get home, Joe sits me down, still. I'm in the sitting-room. Everything *looks* the same. Joe's books, the divans, the table. It's the sitting-room. Here's me. There's Joe. Leon has gone upstairs. I'm coming back. Holding myself still, together. Must stay still, quiet, together. Usually, I went shopping alone, with Joe. I had been jealous. We go to the kitchen.

"Hullo Joan, is there some milk?"

"No it hasn't come yet, he's very late."

Everything is bad, black again. I am caught, the day seems lost. Oh God, what have I done? Why do I go against! Everything is miserable and dying. How could I have gone against Joe? It seems I must have "gone against." Like when the front door bell was broken. That was terrible. Then the boiler was off. It was cold. They said there was no coke. The man didn't deliver it. Why? What had I done? Oh why was I so bad. Oh God help me to keep with Joe, with the therapy. He didn't mean me to get up. He didn't really mean me to have that orange.

"Mary, it's not *stealing*, you can have it. Any food in the kitchen is yours."

"But Joe? It doesn't *seem* so."

Joan brought me food in bed.

"Joan, it seems wrong to eat it and wrong not to eat it."

"Mary, it's all right you *can* have some."

Joan leaves me. Secretly I take a tiny bit. In my mind to

"go against" Joe was to "go against" my treatment. One of the boys who lived in the house once complained:

"Joe does so much for Mary."

Joe told him:

"Those who can receive the most often have the most to give."

It didn't feel right to wash myself, so I didn't. Sometimes Joe put me in a bath. This was perfectly right as it was also when Joe brushed my hair. To have done it myself would have been "going against." In the bath we played. Spouting whales, and mermaids and sharks.

"Who's got the biggest mouth?"

"Eat you up."

Back again. Melting into the water. Joe pulls me out.

"Want to soak and I'll come back, or want to come out now?"

"Come out now."

Gradually it got a bit easier for me to move myself more.

One day I went out alone to the station to meet Joe. Squatting down at the top of the stairs, I watched all the people. Some children were going swimming. They returned. One, two hours. Joe was coming, that was certain. John, a friend of Joe's, came, on his way to see Joe.

"Hullo, Mary."

"Joe's not at home, I'm waiting for him."

"It's cold. Come back with me. Joe will come soon."

"Mm."

"Have some chocolate."

"Mm."

We start to walk. Joe is right behind us. He was on that train.

"Joe, I knew you were coming. I've been waiting and waiting. It's You!"

Joe growls: I hit and bite and laugh. I'm so excited, bursting with joy.

About this time Morty (Dr. Morty Schatzman), another friend of Joe's from America, came to stay. He wanted to borrow my bedside lamp which was not being used.

"No, Morty, no please. It cannot be moved."

"All right, that's all right."

Nothing must go from my room. Nor could I give, except a lick of a candy bar, to Joe.

"What do you want, an ice-cream or a candy bar?"

This was important, a choice I could make. Joe never hurried me, I knew all the different chocolate bars. Peanut rings I always loved and toffee apples were marvellous. Later, Joe gave me pocket money. Sometime before Christmas, as a present to the house, Joe bought a heater for a bathroom on the roof. This was wonderful: I must have been very good for Joe to do such a thing. Everything was good and right. Then it all changed, the heating went off and it wouldn't work.

"Mary, it's nothing to do with you. It's the electrical fitting."

"But Joe!"

"I'm not angry with *you*. I'm not punishing you."

All was black and gloomy. It seemed the fault lay with me. Somehow I must have gone against Joe; I seemed empty, all apart.

Joe took the heater, and me, to the shop. Joe was very cross.

"But can't it be altered?"

"No sir, I'm sorry, nothing can be done, we shall just have to take it back."

It was being returned, we couldn't have it at all. My mind went blank. Deadness came all over me. Joe took my hand. He walked me home.

Chapter Eight

The pest—IT, my anger

Joe sometimes told me: "Don't be a pest." I had a story about a pest. There was a snake who was choking a man. A pest tickled the snake, and the snake let the man go. One evening Joe came home with Leon who was by now living at Kingsley Hall. He had been out all day. I'd lots to tell him. My play, the things I'd cut out of cigarette-tin lids in the basement, how Mary had come down twice to see what I was doing, what Joan had given me to eat. All the day was bursting out of me.

"Joe look what I made, see this—"

"Mary, I can't stop now. I'm going to talk with Leon."

"Can I come?"

"No, stay here. We are going up to Leon's room."

"But Joe look—"

"Mary, I haven't time now."

Running after them across the Games Room.

"But, Joe it's ages since—"

"Look, Mary, Joe can't stop now."

"But Leon, it's not fair. Joe, wait."

"Look, *Mary*."

Whiney noises. "Er, er."

Joe turns round with his hand. Flaps it across my face and carries on, upstairs with Leon. He had been out, all day with Leon. Now when it's my turn, he's gone upstairs with *Leon*. My face hurts. *Joe is a pacifist*. I start to go after. On the stairs my nose starts to bleed. The blood pours down my white jumper, on to the floor. A big red splash.

"Look, Joan, *blood*. *Joe* did it!" Joan laughs. I'm quite proud.

Upstairs, outside Leon's room, it's cold and windy. I'm on the roof, weak and wobbly, very frightened. Shall I? Shan't I? Dare I? My nose is bleeding. Tap. No answer. Joe and Leon are talking. Look over the wall. Nose is dripping red. Go back to the door. Listen. Softly:

"Joe?" Loud from inside: "Mary, go away, I'm busy." Bit louder:

"Joe, Joe, my nose is *bleeding*. I'm opening the door." Leon looks. Joe takes me in. "Come here." He puts paper up my nose. In the wash place Joe cleans me up. Back in Leon's room, Joe tells me: "Sit still. Hold your head back." It stops. "Lot of blood on my blouse."

"Yes," says Leon.

"I rather like it. Shall I wear it to dinner?"

Joe tells me: "Mary, go and change your blouse."

"Joe, what's the matter with me, I seem to want to keep it on?"

Leon answers: "Mary, if you want to wear it to dinner —Joe, don't you think . . ."

"Leon I don't want your interpretations. Mary, go downstairs."

Back in the Games Room I sit quiet. Want to keep the blouse on. Go to my room. Joe comes. "It's dinner time." Go to dinner with Joe. Nothing seems really right. I'm wanting to make it right.

"What's that, Mary, on your blouse?"

"Blood, Joe hit me. He made my nose bleed."

Joe must be proud, glad for the people to see what he made. Leon looks pleased. Joe got up.

"Joe, what's the matter?" He was going upstairs. I ran after.

"Mary, I don't want you to follow me."

"But Joe, please tell me, why is everything all queer? This is my blood, you made it come."

"Oh, Mary, come on back to dinner." Aaron spoke. It was not nice to be so demanding of Joe. That is what Aaron showed me. The dinner finished. Joe put me to bed. For some time I kept the blouse, all bloody. Then, wanting to wear it, dyed it from white to blue.

"Joe, can I have two and sixpence for the dye?"

"Yes, here's half a crown."

It came out a beautiful shade of blue, much nicer than it was before.

Occasionally my anger burst out of me.

One day in the Games Room, with my dolls and balls, playing snap, and surrounded by orange peel, papers and nut shells, I was lying on the floor. Joan was around.

"Mary get some of this mess cleared up. Come on, get a brush, I'll help you."

I moved towards the brush. Then, without "knowing" what I was doing, I was bashing and bashing Joan. It was terrible. I was all apart, terrified. Joan was a therapist. Joan was as a Mother to me. What would happen? Where was I? All was lost. Joan sat with me, and laid me down.

Another time, one night, Joe did not come to take me to bed. Raymond saw me sitting, very still.

"Mary, it's very late. Joe will probably not be back to-night. I'll take you up."

We went, very slowly, up the stairs. Into bed. Groan with it. Don't move. Raymond has put me. Keep still. Sleep, water in the bed. In the morning, wait for Joe. Awake, lying, still the "clumpy" feeling comes. I'm numb and swollen up. It seems my hands, my head are like balloons, fuzzy, woolly, very big. Years ago, as a child, it happened like this, some-times at night when sleep walking. About this time my speech, when it came, which was not very often, was blurred, slurred and not always understandable.

"Mary, what is it? Speak slowly. Say the words separately."

"Where is Joe?"

"He's gone out. Let me brush your hair."

"Ugh. Ugh."

Joe was out. I would wait on the floor, by his door.

Oh God, bring Joe back. What have I done? Joe comes. "Mary, I have not been out to punish you. You are angry with me, but your anger doesn't kill me. It doesn't even hurt me, not one tiny bit."

Like a taut stretched wire, my whole being was played upon by all that happened, in the house and to Joe. Every tiny incident was fraught with hidden meaning. My door is open, Joe shuts it. Feeling bad, the question comes again: *"What* have I done?"

It took a long, long time before what Joe said got through from my head to my heart. Before what I accepted in my mind caused a change in my feeling.

When I was bad time seemed endless. To be able to think that in two, four, six hours, the feeling would lift, was not possible. *It* was so awful at the time, that there didn't seem any before or after. The only possibility was to live one moment at a time. When really bad, I never spoke, knowing the only safe thing was to be still, going into a sort of half-sleep, stupor state. When I was very bad at night, Joe would lay me down in bed, with very few clothes. The cold helped. Joe never spoke. Other people might try to talk with me, I knew better than to attempt to reply. Though I might moan or groan. It just had to lift before I could move, without stirring it worse.

It, my anger, always did lift. But when caught in its grips I was stone still, immobile, dead. To me, at this time, IT coming out was very dangerous, it might kill anyone. When I was rather wild about the house, people used to say of me: "she is very strong."

In December '65 I had a dream that I think must have been about IT. Walking along a road near a town I saw a man in a dark suit and beret. He reminded me they would soon be testing the bomb. Behind a wire fence were men in grey uniforms moving about. Entering the town I went, with a crowd of people, into a building like a pub. We went down, deep inside, to be safe from the bomb, an atom bomb, being tested.

From being in a passage deep underground, I then found myself again on the surface. I was very worried and frightened. Little bits of black dust, as paper, from a fire, presumably from the bomb, were outside on things, on people; on me yet not harming anything. It was from the bomb, but nothing was hurt.

In the dream, to me, the passage underground was my deep inside and the bomb was IT, my anger. The bomb burst, as anger coming out of me, yet nothing was harmed.

During the day IT, my anger, seemed to split and tear at me, cold and frightened and fragile. At times the IT seemed stronger than my very strong body and will. Instead of using my strength, I became as a slave bound in chains of my own making, stiff, set, unable to bend. Joe had then to specially help me, such as by leaving me alone on the roof to scream till he was ready to fetch me. My trust of Joe was enormous, I thought how clever he must be, so young in years to have got so far. To have known so surely that he wanted to be an analyst, and to have worked so hard with himself.

To suffer myself, to stem my own rebellion, was the fight that at times became so intense within me that I hardly knew how to live with myself.

Joe understood: "Do you wish you'd never been born?"

Somehow, not of myself, most certainly of the guidance of Joe, and by the power of the prayers of others for me, I got through. One of the worst times was when, very angry, hard and stiff like a cold hard poker, I couldn't bend. Joe was with me, we were near the front door. I was in my nightdress. Suddenly beside myself, I ran out of the door, screaming.

"I'll go to a mental hospital."

Joe dragged me in, slashed me across the face, crying in anguish:

"Oh why do you make me *do* this?"

My nose poured blood, as it always did. I broke, I cried and cried, as a dam bursting, in great flood. The relief! My tears, the blood, my crumpled body. Joe held me and hugged me. My whole being poured and flowed, was loosened, supple, warm. Joe put me to bed. People were sympathetic to me, Joe was rather a brute.

I never loved Joe so much. My hardness he melted and the relief of physical pain he had given me. Never had I needed it so much—and been so unable to break myself. Quite hard, horrible and hating, Joe brought me back. The big bear, with a flop of his paw, had saved me.

Chapter Nine

The start of the painting—Wallpaper Stories—the
Art School—painting at home

Towards the end of November '65, one Saturday, when he was going out, Joe gave me a round toffee tin of grease crayons which he had found in the house. He sat me at a table with these and a lot of scrap paper. He showed me.

"Here, just scribble."

So I did, all colours all sorts of scribble, on and on, all day.

Joe came home.

"Look what's come, it's for you, in red. A woman kneeling with a baby at her breast."

"That's very nice, do some more."

Out of the scribble, pictures came. Suddenly, I would see what I was doing. Red was marvellous. All the papers had to be kept, every tiny bit of scribble.

One morning I was moaning about the place looking for more material. Joe came along: "Here, here, look, there's plenty of paper, sheafs of it." Joe collected a bundle of oddments for me. Soon I was settled at the dining-room table, very busy with my crayons. Suddenly, there was a violent eruption. A girl who lived in the house exclaimed, "Hey, look what she's drawing on!" Other people came to look. Someone said "Map sheets!" and snatched a pile of my papers. I tore them back, screaming, "That's mine, that's *mine.*"

"You can't have them," they said.

"Yes, I can, I *can,* Joe said, they came from Joe, that's my drawing." I stomped about in a fruious rage, grabbing

hold of all the papers. Some of the scribble was on the back
of stencilled diagrams of how to get to Kingsley Hall, as if that
mattered. They were *my* papers.

I quickly ran off to my room and put them all on the
floor under my bedding and lay on them. That was safer.
Eventually, the storm died down.

The next thing was the walls of my room. By this time I
was living in a room on the roof. It felt like being on the
edge of a mountain. There was paint and brushes about the
place, left over from decorating. These I took to my room.
All over the walls I painted moving figures, running, dancing,
swimming. A mother kneeling with a baby at her breast, a
baby as a bud, like a flower, and over my bed in red an
outline of Christ crucified.

At night, by candle light, the figures moved me to sleep.
In many colours on my door were twining stems with leaves.
The table became bright orange with a bird. Much as I now
loved my room, the roof still did not seem safe. Looking over
the wall I felt the pull of the height, it could make me
giddy. Leon once said, "Come out and sit on the roof."

"No."

"Why? Because you feel you might throw yourself over?"

"Yes."

"Well you won't, see, because I'm here and I won't let
you."

That time I did sit with Leon on the roof. When in this
roof-room I got tonsillitis. Unable at first to say in bed,
feeling I would slip off the roof, I spent the day, first on the
floor of Joe's room, and then on his bed, which I wet. Joe
was out; when he came back he did not punish me, he only
held me. I felt weak and loving with the pain of my throat.

"You go up now and I'll sit with you till you go to sleep."

"Joe, it seems I might slip off the roof, can I be inside?"

"All right."

I went in the Games Room and slept between two
chairs.

The next day, Doctor Taylor came. In bed in my room
he ordered antibiotic tablets for my throat. I stayed on the
roof another few weeks, during which time I got very bad
and one night, when Joe was out, bashed up my room. In

the end, Joan, whom I had chased down the stairs, helped me and I went to sleep in all the mess. The paintings were not damaged.

Downstairs, the sitting-room was being turned into a double bedroom, Joe allowed me to move, on condition I would share this room. These walls later got covered with layers of painted papers.

Meanwhile, I continued to paint moving figures, first on odd pieces of wallpaper, and then on wallpaper backing paper that I bought from Mr. Allen in the paintshop across the road. Sometimes, Mr. Allen gave me tins of undercoat paint. My brushes were such as were about the house in old paint tins. The wallpaper I spread out across the Hall or the Games Room floor. From children romping or playing ball or dancing, I went on to stories. The first was the Mermaid story.

"Joe, come, walk with me and I'll tell the story."

"That's a very nice story."

Saturday morning some children came in the Hall. "What's all that, Modern Art?"

"Yes, sort of. Want to hear a story? The words are in me."

"OK."

"Start here."

We walked the length of the paper to the story of "The Tramp and the Children." Tuesday afternoon the old men at their meeting in the Hall were looking at the story of The Ship. I told them this story. Some of the rolls were full of people going into animals, coming out and going in again, dying and being re-born, being eaten and themselves eating.

One afternoon, Joe, Leon and I went round to Taylor's, the local stationery shop. They were going to help me buy painting things. I was thrilled, real painting. Joe thought I had talent. Joe started.

"What's the largest book you have? Any bigger paper?"

"Yes, Sir, this one."

"I'll have that, and Joe, some of these colours?"

"Yes, all of them, and Mary, what about these?"

"Mm, coloured pens."

"Yes, Leon, those two crayons."

"What, Joe?"

"Watercolours, yes, I have all those."

With the biggest book and a great variety of colour we start home. Suddenly, everything was wrong. This wasn't real, it was just "a thing." I couldn't move.

"Oh, come on, what's the matter?"

"Joe, I'm not right." The book and colours were dropping. "The world is ending tomorrow."

I groan. Leon adds, "No, it's ending today."

"Oh, Joe!" bending and groaning.

"Just *look* at you, you've got a new sketch book. Crayons, paints—and look how you are!"

We got home. All sadness and gloom, I looked at all the new things. Something had happened. It didn't seem right. Later, Joe explained I didn't trust myself or know what I wanted, still less how to get it. Going against Joe was really going against myself. My fear of love was even greater than my fear of anger. All twisted up and matted together in my mess state, I didn't know much what was happening.

Joe assured me it was all right to paint. "Mary, those things are yours, it's *right* to paint."

Paint I did. Gradually, it seemed to *me*, perfectly right again, to paint. Painting, when I wasn't too "bad" to do it, got me together, my body and soul. All my insides came out, through my hands and my eyes and all the colour. It was free and moving, loving and creative. The early picture stories became known as "The Wallpaper Stories." Here are some of them.

The Mermaid Story

A bird dropped a seed into the ground, and a mermaid came from the seed, and she wandered through the world; over mountains and into valleys. She longed and mourned for the sea.

A man met her and she trusted him and he threw her into water.

In great sadness she discovered it was not the sea but a lake. Such were the tears of her weeping that the land was washed away, and she swam freely into the sea.

There, on the bottom of the sea, by a rock, with a merman, she rests in peace.

The Wind and the Flowers

Some flowers were growing in a field, their heads held tall and high. One day the wind blew so hard that she battered them to the ground. The flowers were very sad and a big cloud came and rained and rained until the flowers were growing as lilies in a pool of water.

Then came the wind again and he blew them up and carried them high above a mountain and dropped them in a deep gorge between the rocks in the deep of a mountain pool.

The flowers were afraid for the rocks were overhanging them.

But, one day, the sun found them and he shone brightly down through a slit in the rocks.

The flowers warmed, and dropped their seeds, and slept, and the stream of the mountain carried the seeds right through the depths of the mountain to the open air, and there in the cool, by the water, the stream left the seeds.

Sheltered by the mountain, secure from the wind, yet open to the sun, the seeds grew in peace and quiet and as plants, they held high their heads and flowered; and dropped their seeds, and they died, in the richness of the grass and the damp of the water.

The Egg on the Sea

A bird drops an egg on the side of a cliff. It falls into the sea and floats on the waves in the warmth of the sun.

In the egg a beautiful lady is growing, and one day the egg cracks open by the break of a big wave and the beautiful lady feels herself in a flood of great water.

She is in fear and is carried by the waves. She feels herself floating but is sad for there in the sea there is none like her. She realizes she has no tail, as a fish, and she breathes air, and wonders about her legs.

Then, one day, as she is weary and tired, the sea washes her on to the shore, and she lies warm in the sun on the sand.

Then she moves, and raises herself, and stands. She feels she can walk, and she sees before her, another upright figure. She walks towards him, he welcomes her and she feels free, as she moves, like him.

Death of a Family

One day, a little boy went to see his Mother, who was sick in bed, and because her heart was weak, she fainted when he hugged her hard.

He thought she was dead and that he had killed her and he was so frightened that he ran away and lived in a hollow tree in the wood, with a squirrel.

Above them in a nest lived their friend, the bird. One day the bird saw the little boy's Mother through the window of her house. She had been in hospital, in a bed with a temperature chart, but now she had returned.

He told the little boy, she is still alive. The little boy returned back to the house.

His Mother was in a storm of anger, at his going away, and she hit the little boy so hard that he died.

When the Father came home, he was terrified and he ran out in a panic to telephone the doctor.

On the way, he fell into a hole in the road and was killed.

It seems they were all killed by fear. The little boy feeling his love had killed his Mother, was very frightened and ran away. Going later, in trust to his Mother, he is killed by her fear and grief and love, turned to anger.

The Father was beside himself and ran into his death.

On Christmas Eve, 1965, Joe and Leon and I went to Midnight Mass in Westminster Cathedral. Afterwards Joe gave me a book of paintings by Grunewald and Leon gave me a book of Australian aboriginal paintings.

Then Joe took me to the Tate Gallery. We looked long at the feeling painting by Edvard Munch of *The Sick Child*.

The holidays over, in January '66, Joe took me to Art School. Before we started, I had at home a bout of "not knowing" whether Joe really meant me to go or not. This feeling made any real obedience very difficult, practically impossible, at times.

"Come on, I'll give you five minutes to make up your mind. Then I'm going out."

"Oh, Joe, Joe! Do you mean it *really?*"

I had an idea perhaps Joe meant me really to go to bed, to go down again. The minutes ticked by; I sat in a lump. Suddenly I knew, for sure.

"Joe, Joe, hurry up or we shall be late, let's go."

"Mary, don't drag, wait a moment."

We got there, to Cass College. Up the stairs, we passed people with portfolios and women in slacks, all looking very earnest and business-like. I kept hold of Joe's hand.

"Look, Mary, there's the library."

"Mm."

"Here's the office." Joe went in first. I was enrolled. We bought pencils and the largest sketch book they had.

"Where's the Life Drawing?"

"Upstairs, Sir."

We got to the room. Not a sound, everyone was drawing, one or the other of two naked women. Joe found me a seat, a sort of stool and easel thing. He asked a master to sharpen my pencils.

"Here, your pencil. I gotta go now. Just *draw.*"

"Ugh ugh."

Everything was so strange. I messed about with the pencil and paper. Then I just did it. A master came. He started to draw over my drawing. I got all terrible, wanting to hit him and tear my book away. He was sitting on my stool. Then everything was dead, I wanted to run away. The school went on all day. Michael, a coloured boy, with pink trousers, took me out to lunch. That was better. His friend gave me a sweet.

Back in school, I sat in the other group with a different master. He left me alone. That was Mr. Pitchforth. I drew and drew. Just how it came. Lots of drawings, more than the other people made.

I dashed home, running up the stairs. "Joe, Joe!"

"What have you got?"

"That's good, very good. Show Jutta." She was an artist who lived in the house.

"Then, Jutta, what do you think? He drew *over* my drawing. It, my inside, was so bad. Suppose I had hit, I might have got taken away, to the mental hospital."

"Mary, he should not touch your work. That's *right,* how *you* do it."

"It doesn't matter about 'official ways?' "

"No, always do it as it comes to you. You see, what *you* have done is alive, it's powerful. Anyone can do what that master has done. Do you see the difference?"

"Oh, yes, Jutta, I can really do it?"

"Yes, *yes.*"

"Joe, Jutta says it's right. That's marvellous."

My doubts ended.

At school, Mr. Pitchforth encouraged me.

"I've been at it too long to be free, like you. Keep on, as you are doing. Do you understand why I do not attempt to teach you anything? Why I leave you alone?"

"Oh yes, *yes.*"

Mr. Pitchforth saw some of my story scrolls, from home.

At painting in oils, there was a similar difficulty. A master came:

"That's very strong. Perhaps background . . ."

He took my brush. He stood back, dismayed when he saw what he was doing. He gave me back the brush. I was *furious.* How to keep my hands off him? Somehow I got home, with the painting, a life group. People at home were sympathetic. Ruth, with whom I shared a room, said she would have been cross had it been her painting.

Half a day a week I went to Sculpture class where we modelled the head of Molly in clay. I liked this, except when the teacher talked about proportions and did measurements. I just got on with mine.

"Mary, that's strong, it's really got something of Molly. Do you all see, sculpture is not photography?"

This put new heart into me. The teacher had doubted my ways but decided to leave me alone. She helped me cast the head in plaster.

About this time, Dr. Maxwell Jones stayed a few days with us. He asked me:

"Mary, how do you manage at school? Do you get there in time? Can you communicate with people?"

"Oh, yes, Max, I get there in *good* time. Of course I be with the other people. It's not home, but you know, well, I just be, how I am." Actually, I didn't speak in words much. The people at school accepted me as I was. Except when I was working and needed to be left alone, it suited me very nicely that they thought I was very young, which I was, in all my ways. Alone, without Joe, especially away from home, I did want to be "looked after," bought a cake, taken to the library, sat with at break-time.

Before my birthday on February 9th, I was full of beautiful ideas. Joan would make me a cake. We would have jelly, and ice-cream. Friends would come, people I used to know, they would see my paintings. How to go about it? Of course, make out invitations. Fancy pieces of paper with pretty pictures. When I was sitting in the middle of all my efforts, Joe came to my room.

"Do you think we could have a party? I'd love a birthday cake."

"Yes, sure. Put them away now, and come to dinner."

Somehow, it didn't seem right. Joe didn't *really* mean me to have a party. Everytime I thought of it, the whole matter seemed wrong. The only thing to do was to tear up the invitations, nothing made it right.

When the day of my birthday came, IT, my anger, was terrible, first sending me up in groans outside Joan's door, then getting me stuck in a chair in the Games Room. Someone was saying, it was the National Assistance lady, "Well, except for cases like *her*—that no one can do anything for." It was so bad I wouldn't move or look out. Then Ronnie came.

"Ronnie, it's all this birthday business."

He touched me. It was eased. Gradually I got back to my room. The children who were really four or five years old were playing on the park swings under my window. In the evening Joe came home. Everything was easier.

"Look what I've brought you, for your birthday."

"Oh Joe, what is it?"

"Open it."

There was mauve ribbon, in bows, and the most beautiful mermaid paper.

"Oh, oh, Joe. It's marvellous—a mug with a fish symbol of Christ."

Joe sat with me. Life was full of joy. The colouring of

the mug was green and blue. There was some ribbon for my hair. The big bow I pinned up and all the beautiful wrapping paper I stuck on the wall.

When I telephoned Mother Michael about going to see her, as Joe had suggested, she asked, "Mary, how old are you?"

"Forty-three, Mother."

"What, you are *only* forty-three, is that *all?*"

"Yes, that's all."

I was so happy.

I'd got very excited at the idea of going to a Ball at the Art School. It was from midnight to six in the morning. In my mind, one of the teenage boys would take me. I'd got a new dress, gold slippers and a gold evening bag. Although older in years, I was then in all other ways much younger than a teenager. Fortunately, with the help of Joe, I chose that weekend to visit Mother Michael. Joe saw me off on the train to Llandovery. "Leave this outside, it won't go on the rack."

"No, no, Joe I want it here, where I can hold it." This was a very big case of paintings and all my party things.

"All right. Give my love to Mother Michael."

I was off, for two nights. My first time away from home.

As soon as I got to the convent, in the guestroom, I showed Mother Michael my spider.

"This is what Joe gave me. He sends his love, and this is what I did. 'God and the Flowers,' a wallpaper story. It hasn't got written words but I know it. Shall I tell it?"

"Yes, do."

"Mary, that's a lovely story. Look, here is Sister Mary with your tea. I'll come back later. Do eat plenty. There's lots of milk."

In the evening I put on my new green dress and the gold slippers; the gold bag and all my paintings I showed to Mother Michael. Together we enjoyed it all.

In my past life I had taken courses of things and passed examinations. Art was different, but still there was the idea of a "set course." Joe suggested I apply to St. Martin's School of Art. After the application, when some of my work was in, I saw Ronnie one day on the tube.

"Ronnie, it's the Feast of Our Lady of Lourdes, I'm going

to Warwick Street Church of the Mother of God to say thank you, that I've come so far. About St. Martin's, it's better, more important, you know, to get 'right' than to go to Art School or to have paintings or anything?"

"Yes, I know."

When the letter came saying there was no place for me at St. Martin's, I knew at once it was all right. Ronnie had seen to it; that first things would be kept first. It was right, to stay more at home in order to get straight. Even so, I was furious that St. Martin's had no place for me. Wanting to bash them up and tear them to bits made me angry with Joe, who reminded me:

"You were very cross at being refused a place by St. Martin's."

Later Joe went to the school to see an artist there about my work. He said the work was "of great promise." The work we had sent in was some sketch book scribbling and a scene from one of the wallpaper stories that I had framed.

One Wednesday afternoon after school, I was telling Joe about painting, Life painting, and ordinary painting, still life, or a group of people. Joe said, "It sounds dull."

"It was."

"You don't *have* to go to school."

"You mean, just paint at home."

"Yes."

"All right."

Being registered for the term, I was still able to use clay from school and library books, but I didn't attend classes any more.

During March Joe took me with some of my paintings to the studio of Felix Topolski. The paintings we took were St. Joseph, the Red Christ, the Black Crucifixion of St. Peter, the first Crucifixion I did, when Joe had suggested, "Paint the Crucifixion," and a very large one of the Crucifixion in which there were several figures. These works were in oil on wallpaper backing paper.

Felix Topolski liked my pictures. "They should be putting paper up all over the walls of Kingsley Hall for you to paint."

He showed me hardboard he was painting on. Also some

of his recent work; the visit of Pope Paul to the Holy Land, Pope John and Edith Sitwell.

"Look well at that painting, you cannot always see it, at once, the face."

Back home, I started using hardboard. When people looked at my paintings, and didn't always see what I saw, this no longer surprised me. My work seemed to well up from within me. To grow almost of itself. It wanted to come as it liked. Then it seemed to give back to me. "The Feeding of the Five Thousand" was the first one I did on canvas. Stretched on the wall above my bed, a mattress on the floor, it was about seven feet across and six feet high. The longest time I then worked was about seven hours, doing "An Angel on the Verge of Hell" on several strips of wallpaper backing paper.

When not painting I often sat about the floor, as when the men came to tune the piano.

"Hullo, love?"

I was bad and couldn't answer. Teddy was with me, my red and black balls in his back that opened.

"What's up?"

Silence.

"Young girl like you, got your life before you. Got a boy-friend? Go dancing?"

Holding Teddy, I peep out, touch my hair.

"Sometimes I dance." Pause. "Ronnie plays the piano."

"Oh, so you dance, then?"

"Yes."

"Well, they shouldn't let the piano go so long, it needs tuning."

"Mm." I watch.

"That's it. It's all right now. Goodbye love. Take care of yourself."

"Mm."

They go.

Ronnie once asked me, "How much of your life do you think you have lived?"

"Perhaps nearly half, maybe I'll die at about ninety."

When very young in years, about seventeen, I looked much older and would be taken for the wife of my Father and the Mother of my much younger sisters.

In the Spring of '66 my bearing and behaviour could be very deceptive to strangers. As I felt, so I appeared. Sulky, excitable, shouting, screaming. My speech always muddled, unclear, when hurried, went from a sheer jumble of running words, into mere sounds. My pronunciation was queer. I was going back to my real girl self through my pretence layers of girl on boy.

My anger was enormous. Sometimes it just got stuck. As on one afternoon, Joe was out, when I had some lumps of dry clay. It marked like chalk. Not in a mood for painting yet wanting to do something, I chalked up the Games Room. First the floor, scribble, scribble in white, all over, then the locker tops, the armchairs, the billiard table. Grunting and moving and scribbling. Then lying in a heap in all the mess.

"Look what she's done." Everyone saw it. I wanted to hide. Joe was in. "Come to dinner." I was still bad and didn't move, nor speak. Jesse, a friend of Ronnie's, had called, "Come with me, Mary." He took me in to dinner. All the people were very cross with me. I'd relieved myself while making a mess but it seemed I was now in big trouble. Really frightened I sat very still next to Jesse.

"It shouldn't be allowed."

"Why doesn't she clear it up?"

"What did you do it for?"

"Mary, tell us why you did?"

"Why doesn't she talk?"

Ronnie spoke, "Mary, before you go to bed, tonight, all that mess must be cleared up."

My head was bowed, there was silence. I make a move. Jesse moved.

"Come on love, I'll help you."

We got into the Games Room, I was very sad and sorrowful, Jesse held me.

"I'll get the water." He went out, past all the people, still sitting at table.

"Here's a bucket, swill it over—mop it up—we'll soon get that lot clear. Don't worry. Stop *worrying.*"

Apart from this big mess, there were still about the building some black breasts I had painted on walls. The desire to paint walls was very strong within me. With the help of Joe I asked:

"Could I paint on the walls up the back stairs?"

A lot of people said "No."

Ronnie said, it was at dinner, "It is not mad to draw on walls. Artists all through the ages have wanted to cover walls."

Sometimes when too bad for work, I would seem to be full of a seething rage that burst out of me. Not knowing what brought it on, or how in any reasonable terms to get rid of it, I would seem as a leaf battered about in my own storm. At times, wanting to destroy myself, yet knowing not to, I never regretted whatever else I did, or got, at the time, to ease me over the moment. A lot of IT was bashed out on Joe. The whole boiling sea of it would come surging out, exploding me to bits. Terrified, in a panic of violence. I would want to tear anything to bits, fling over chairs, smash glass, or tear my flesh apart.

If I ever said anything to myself, it was "suicide is a form of pride, suicide is a form of pride, oh, God, oh, God." The panic was intensified because I couldn't "feel" people, warmth, affection, love. They could feel and feel towards me, but it couldn't touch me, which was desperate.

"Where was Joe, why couldn't I feel him? I'm dead, I *can't* feel."

"You're here. In your body."

I touch my body.

"It's together. Your body has not fallen apart."

"I can't *feel*."

"I have to go now."

"What have I *done*?"

Why do they go? I can't, I can't be alone. Not talking, I bury my head. A dead sleep comes. No dreams. It's solid. I can't move. Awake, it comes again. For no reason, it's on me. What to do. Nothing, Nothing, Nothing. Lie with IT. At this early time I rarely could. When insight, understanding in words with change of feeling, came through talk, it was easier. Also it was getting looser. I was freer. Here in the Spring of '66 I was full of IT, a mass of tight anger. When it flared I was as a devil caught in a trap and the more I struggled to get free, the tighter the trap fastened. Slowly, slowly I learnt to be still in the trap. With help I would gradually be released. The spring would uncoil.

Joe has a painting of mine of this time, St. Ignatius of Loyola, when he has gone away to struggle with himself. It doesn't look like a human being. Joe says, "That's *exactly* you."

I came to realize there were two things, the shattering of the anger and the shame of the destructions. I felt my anger, not only killing me, but everyone and everything around me. Then I punished myself.

Anger, torn to bits, deadness, not fit to live. My cry towards Joe was, "I'm nothing, *nothing,* you are *everything* to me. I'm nothing to you."

Joe told me, "Paint the Crucifixion."

I did, again and again. From crucifixion to resurrection. Going down and in, coming up and out. Being re-created, being re-formed. Joe did it: he was able to because I trusted him. Now in the spring of 1966, IT, my anger, seemed to threaten to submerge and drown me. No human activity, nothing seemed able to take, to consume, IT. Slowly, for brief spells, I was coming towards the possibility of lying with IT, to a state of "being," without "doing."

I had an awful dream. Two women were in bed in a house. They had had operations on their breasts and their testes had been removed. I didn't want to be there. A man was bossing me about. I didn't want to do what he wanted. I wanted to be liked but I was hated. In the end one of these women wanted to see my paintings. I got some out and felt better. At this time, my sexual feelings were emphasized in my painting. Joe told me, working at home, "Study different artists. Start with Matisse." I did. At the Courtauld Institute, seeing the life drawings of Matisse, I felt a strong resemblance to some of my work. Oskar Kokoschka also attracted me. I looked specially at eyes. At home on canvas, the Hanging Crucifixion came, with the whites of the eyes showing. Rouault I was drawn to. I went to many exhibitions, seeming to drink in something.

A few times, feeling like swimming, I went to the local baths. I just had to jump off the very highest board, something I had never done before. The water would be coming up to me, and smash, my body sank in it splashing up, all arms and legs.

When Easter came I went away, to Aylesford, intending to stay four days at the Priory. Joe was going away for Easter. This had caused me to feel "not right." Then on the morning of my going Joe was talking to a girl in the kitchen.

"Joe, hurry, it's time for the train."

"Wait, it's not all that late. I'm talking."

Why was Joe talking to *that* girl, not me? Why did I have to wait? Joe came. I was all bad and crying. "How can I go away like this. Can't go."

"Yes, you can. You're jealous and angry with me."

"Oh. Oh, all right, I'll go."

Somehow everything was wrong. It didn't get right. At church in the evening my tears came. In my room I couldn't get undressed. In bed with my clothes on the thought came, suppose I get worse bad, wake up with IT. People don't know me. Wish I was home. I'm going home. It was very late. I knocked on the next door. A man opened the door.

"Do you belong here?"

"No, I'm a guest."

"I'm going back to London, will you tell them? They can let me know if there is anything to pay."

"Yes, I'll do that."

Quickly I rammed my things, papers, crayons, doll, back into my case. It was dark, I bolted. Running all the way to the station, I just got a train. In London, the tubes had stopped. I got a taxi.

Home at last, what a blessing. Ring Joe.

"I'm back, Joe, I was bad. Do you think I'll sleep? It's still bad."

"Mary, go into the kitchen, get a raw onion, cut it. Go into the lavatory, eat it and spit it out. That's badness coming out. Go back into the kitchen. Make some nice warm milk. Put honey in it. Stir it gently. Drink it very slowly. That's goodness going in. Something nice and good in your tummy."

"Joe, I'll do it."

"Goodnight. I'll ring you Mary, on Sunday."

From the beautiful mug Joe gave me I took in sips, the goodness in. Bears liked honey. I was a baby bear. Now I could undress, in my own bed with all the paintings, glowing in the candlelight. On my pot I did shits, licked the chocolate fish Joe had given me for Easter, then curled up, with my Rosary and Spider. I went to sleep.

On Easter Monday, in the Dining-Room, I painted a big canvas of the Mother of God. Her breasts were revealed, the succour of men. She was before the world, bordered by gold, and above her were the sun and the moon. In my room a few days later on hardboard, I painted "The Hand of Thomas," showing the five wounds of Christ going in from the surface of the painting. David, Dr. Cooper, specially liked this. Then came "disintegration" a large oil on hardboard. The Devil is clawing at parts of people he has broken but he does not engulf them, for St. Michael the Archangel is spearing the heart of the Devil.

My painting had emerged from black lines and breasts on the walls and paintings in shit, to moving figures and scribble on paper: from undercoat paint and wall brushes, to pencils, crayons, charcoal, poster paint, water colour, and oils.

The Temptations of Christ was a canvas nailed to a wall in the Dining-Room. I started it; the Devil came on, horrible, the Devil, the Devil. God, make him come bad. How is it? I waver. No. Let him come, how he wants. Now the temple, gold. The mountain all colours. The desert. Use the stick end of the brush. Quick, quick. Christ is silver, cool. More orange and yellow. I'm mad with the force of orange and the sheer light of yellow. The devil is clawing and clutching, Christ is smiling. He is still. It's a painting. It's finished.

The Devil fades, Christ is at peace.

The picture seems to look at me. Did I do it?

Yes, it was a movement of me, from me.

Strange. Power, Awe, of God, of myself.

Colour, colour. It seems to blend, to meet, to fade. It's warm, it's cold. Anger, fear, hate, love, it's all there, in the colour. A pouring out of power. A shedding of the essence of the world, through the eyes of the soul. The yellow roundness of the moon. The green, blue sea, still and quiet, that was the "Moon on the Sea." Black of his lice, brown of his bent body, brown of the walls he is bent into. Blue of the sky, he is crouched beneath. That was "St. Joseph Benedict Labre." The paintings were speeding, around the house.

Some American students of Theology and Psychology came to see us.

"Those paintings, those paintings!" a student exclaimed.

The professor said, "You have tremendous talent. Are you selling any paintings?"

"Well, not just now. You see, I have to keep everything till Ronnie and Joe see what's to be done for the best."

One day in the middle of painting, I had a fight with Peter, a boy who lived in the house. There were two particular chairs from which I painted. Peter, who did tapestry, was winding his wool between them.

"Peter, please could you change chairs?"

"Yes, all right. Wait, no, not unless you give me reasons why you want these chairs."

"Peter, I just have affection for those two special chairs. The paint things go on them. What do *reasons* matter?"

"Mary, you have to give me *reasons.*"

"It's not fair, you said yes."

I hit Peter.

"Don't touch my wool. You tangle that and I'll mess your painting."

"I don't touch other people's work. Hitting them is not touching their *work.*"

Peter was stronger than me. I couldn't win. He just got hold of me so I couldn't move. It was not possible to paint. Everything went dead and bad. Leon came.

"What's the matter?"

It's difficult to move. Somehow I manage to talk.

"Peter hit me, it's not fair. I always paint from those chairs."

"Come over here. Talk with me, to Peter about it."

Leon listened to all. Then he suggested I might ask Peter again, very nicely for the chairs. Peter was nice. He agreed I could have them. Painting continued.

About this time I wrote a prayer which I kept by my bed.

Dear God,
Through my submission sanctify me.
Through my weakness sanctify me.

Through my anger sanctify me.
Through my jealousy sanctify me.
Through my love sanctify me.
Through my sexual feelings sanctify me.
Through Joe sanctify me.
God live through me.
Breathe through me.
Work through me.
God, how I love you,
In all things.
Through all things.
Beyond all things. Love, Mary XXX

Chapter Ten

*My friendship with Stanley—the Love Muddle—
more about my paintings*

Stanley was very quiet. He never talked. We became great friends, able to romp and fight each other.

"Joe, Ronnie, look. Stanley is here, in my room. He's cutting his whiskers with my scissors." Stanley smiled. He seemed happy.

Stanley would come to my room, the big double room that I shared with Ruth, and carefully inspect everything, just as I have looked in people's rooms. As we got to know each other better, Stanley would run off with my brushes and paint, keep my scissors and little knife always on him, in his trouser pocket. It seemed Stanley never properly went to bed, undressed, under the clothes. Sometimes, when he was out, I looked in his room. Everything looked untouched. In his lower drawers were all the empty tins of baked beans he had eaten. Stanley loved baked beans.

"Give me a spoon of baked beans. I'll give you a bite of this cheese on toast."

Stanley looked cross. He didn't want to share. Like me, Stanley didn't want anything of his to go away.

"Stanley, can I come in? That top drawer, it's open. Give me back my things."

"Stanley, go away from the drawer, please let me take my book, what Joe gave me."

"Come on, Stanley, I give you another tin of undercoat paint—what Mr Allen gives me."

"Stanley, look, it's not fair. Those things are *mine*. You broke two brushes. How can I paint?"

153

"Come on, give. All right, I take *your* waste paper basket."

In a flash, Stanley was on me. He got me down, my head bumping the stone floor. Sitting up, he grabbed my head to bash it down. There was no doubt, Stanley was really seeing red. This was no romp. A boy, he was much stronger than me. Very softly, I whispered, "Please, Stanley, get off me. I will go out of your room."

He released me. Later, I went back when he was out and helped myself to my things. This often happened, Stanley took. He went out. I got back. He took again. Leon suggested, "Mary, do you think you could do a painting for Stanley?"

"I don't want to get bad. I'll see. Maybe."

"Stanley, on this piece of wood, I did this painting for you, to keep. It's yours.

"Stanley took it. But he didn't look very happy about it. Really he wanted my company. We sat together in the kitchen. We were not popular.

"Mary don't get paint on the chairs."

"Stanley, you have burnt another saucepan."

People discussed "what should be done about Stanley," "how Mary could be coped with."

My anger was coming out. Joe used to help me about, the other people in the house.

"Mary, you hate yourself, then you feel other people hate you. They don't."

"Joe, they laugh at me."

"So what? People sometimes laugh at me."

People coming near me, especially if I was painting in the Games Room, would cause me to go dead still and rigid. This was "in case they might come in on me." Unable to explain anything, in words, this seemed the safest thing. They would pass by, not touching me, or attempting to talk with me. Apart from people who "understood", Joe, Leon, Ronnie, Joan, David, Sid, and Aaron, Stanley was the only person it was "safe" to be with. Sitting watching me paint (rather as I might watch Joe), he might pounce on a brush as I put it down, and romping, he might get a bit rough. But these were things that seemed natural to me. I don't want my body damaged, but mental things threatened me more.

Unable to cope in ways that "grown-up" people used, I seemed at sea. Ronnie once said at dinner to the other people: "Mary has no ego boundaries." Just in going my own ways, being as I was seemed at times to make other people angry. Then I was surprised: "Why, Joe, I'm just getting on with myself." Stanley was also in a sense "just getting on with himself."

Sometimes, he really seemed to want a fight with me. One evening after dinner, there was a painting of my Teddy near the Games Room door. Stanley was going in and out of the door.

"Just you watch it—how you go by that painting."

Stanley jolts the door back, bolts into the Games Room.

"Cowardy custard, belly full of mustard." I'm running after him. Ronnie came in and put the light off. Stanley stops running. He touches me. We start romping on the floor. Suddenly I feel Stanley really "see red." His hands are on my neck beginning to squeeze. Gasping, very quietly, I say, "All right, Stanley." He lets go. That was the end of the fight. Stanley once gave Ronnie a good kick in the ribs: I should like to have seen it.

Another morning, Stanley had taken my brushes and run out of the house.

"Leon, Stanley has gone off out with my brushes."

"Are you going after him?"

"I'm not sure which way he's gone."

"Well, you go one way round the block and I'll go the other."

We both got back before Stanley, who soon appeared.

"I've been after you with Leon, give me those brushes." Leon was near.

"Bastard," shouts Stanley. Leon is on the floor. Kick, punch, Stanley was really bashing.

Sometimes at night, after dinner, we danced to records. In a circle Stanley danced between me and Leon. He could tap the rhythm of the music with his hands and feet when watching the dancing. I loved it if Stanley danced with me. Realizing he was too angry to really play with me, I accepted he could only show he liked me by fighting and stealing. Younger than me, Stanley was at times like my

brother with whom, as a child, I used to fight a lot. And
people who were "more like me" it seemed easier for me to
accept, be natural with.

On one occasion, I went out all day, it was Spring, a beautiful day, and I came home, happy, with an arm full of
bluebells. My room was in chaos. Worried, frightened, furious, mystified, whatever had happened? Why? Why? My
shrine was torn to pieces. The clay crucifix scattered on the
floor. Joe's head and hands painted on a board, torn to
pieces. Some things were missing. *Stanley*.

First his room; not there. In the Games Room, "Stanley."
He bolted up the stairs with me behind him. In the flat
Stanley got into Ronnie's chair. As I got hold of him, he
clutched me in terrible fear. I felt his terror and my anger
went. Ronnie appeared.

"Stanley, really I *have* to tell."

"Ronnie, he's messed up my shrine. Torn Joe's head and
hands to bits."

"Stanley, *why* did you do it? Why?"

He was cold with fright.

Later it occurred to me. I was out all day—very rare for
me—and these were what to Stanley "took me away from
him:" God, that was my shrine, and Joe, that was the painting. Understanding helped me to forgive Stanley. He must have
felt so bad—extra bad to how he usually was.

When I had a letter from France my passport disappeared.
I guessed Stanley must have been worried that I might be
going away. He let Jutta, who lived in the house, get it back
for me with a lot of other things.

"Stanley, believe me, I am *not* going to France, though if I
were I could still go even if you took my passport."

One evening I was cross. Joe was out. Stanley came into
my room. It had been suggested that Ruth and I lock our
door, but at this time I couldn't bear the thought of being
shut in. I always left the door open. Stanley picked up a tool.
Thinking it was mine, I shouted "Stanley, put that down."
He ran out of the room, I followed, screaming: "Stanley give
me that." Raymond touched me: "Hush, quiet, Mary, you'll
frighten him." Stanley bashed a door with a hammer. Then
he dragged me along the floor in a rough romp. Later, when

I was angry and much in fear of my violence, I came to know how liable one is to panic and bash if shouted at.

Soon after this, in the flat, when I was feeling bad, Raymond was helping me. Stanley pulled up a chair to sit and listen. (Some years later I remembered this when my brother Peter pulled up a chair to listen in exactly the same way.) At this time Raymond's room was opposite to mine. He had a record player which Stanley was allowed to use. One night, when Raymond was away, Stanley played a Beatles song, over and over again. It was about a holiday sweetheart. Eventually, shutting my door, I went to sleep. In the morning, I woke to the same music.

One afternoon Stanley was looking at the cover picture of a magazine. It was of a bull-fight: the bull was goring the fighter.

"Leon, isn't that a beautiful book that Stanley has got?"

We all look: Stanley is smiling.

"Sometime, do you think, Stanley, that I might borrow your book, I'd love to see inside."

Mildly, in a casual way, Stanley replied:

"Yeah," giving me the book.

In the late Spring of 1966 I told Joe: "Remember how I was on the 1st November last year?"

"How were you?"

"In the Games Room it suddenly pierced through me, about the convent. I was bent up in myself. It seemed so strong, so completely without doubt. Then I realized it was the time of prayer, in Carmelite convents, and that I was kneeling as the nuns do. It was All Saints' Day. That also came vividly to my mind. Then I rather dismissed it all, because I was mad. Well, it could be true. I want, in time, to go back to the convent to be a contemplative nun."

"Yes, well, that is quite possible. If that's what you really want, when the time comes I'll help you get there."

"Joe, really, how can I manage, about my sexual feelings?"

"Everything you need for your wholeness is within you."

"Mm. I want to be a Saint."

"The saints. Oh yes, Mary, but you can't *force* yourself there. You have, in time, to suffer towards it."

In time, Joe helped me to a deep understanding of sacrifice and love.

Meanwhile, my idea of suffering was rather, as Joe expressed it, to "excommunicate" my sexual feelings, than to encounter them. My fantasy of marrying Joe and getting a baby became very strong. Why shouldn't I have a baby? For me, having babies was all mixed up with shits and water. Having big shits and lots of water was for me having babies. If there was a real baby in the house I would keep right away. When I had told Ronnie: "Even if I put my shit all over you, you would still love me." My shit to me meaning babies, this was saying to Ronnie: "You would still love me even if we had a baby." My Mother's view was that making love was a crime for which she was torn with guilt at having a baby. My brother and sisters and I caused her such shame and punishment that she hated us. Everytime she saw us reminded her of how bad she was to have had love and babies. It was "wrong" for my Mother to have what she wanted. She had wanted a baby.

To me, likewise, any love was a crime. It was to me a very frightening thing, my shit. To dare to "have my shits" was daring to have babies. It had been possible in Kingsley Hall to have my shits on me without shame and punishment. So maybe I could have shits on a man, have a baby without punishment. I trusted Ronnie, so much so, that I could envisage putting my shit on him. To water on Joe's bed was to give him "a baby." Joe in not punishing me was saying, "It's not wrong to have babies." When very bad and frightened, I had no shits or water, not being "fit to."

Much later, I bathed another girl, Catherine, of her shits and showed her, "I'm not afraid of, don't hate, your shits." A shitty blanket I put round myself. With my dolls, I played babies, kissing Teddy.

"Mummy's little precious one. Your ribbon is choking you. Let's make it loose and smooth. That's better. Mummy tuck you up, nice and warm. Big kiss."

To me at times, Joe was very strongly "my Father." In the fantasy of my family I "marry my Father." To me, my young sisters were my babies from my Father. Deeply embedded in this, I never, in real life, moved away from it. How was I going to marry Joe? How to get a baby from

Joe? Maybe Joe would give me a baby. Then I'll go to confession, bring the baby up a Catholic, and keep my own Faith.

"Mary, I'm never going to marry anyone."

God doesn't give a man an idea of not marrying without purpose. "God, please give Joe the Faith and a vocation to the priesthood, *and* please get me back to a Carmelite convent."

When Joe did marry, my ideas of the convent temporarily subsided. Still not quite free, separate, Joe being married meant in a sense that I was married.

As my Mother was, so was I. Afraid, unable, to give and receive love, my idea of this warmth of heart was distorted. My Mother, physically, always had "heart trouble." To me she said, "Mummy loves you." What this came to mean to me was something very dangerous. To be loved was to be possessed. To give myself up. Then came the absolute despair.

To me it had seemed the only possibility of love was to "imagine" I was loved when my Mother cuddled Peter. So strongly was this implanted in me that, only recently, seeing someone much concerned for Peter had made me very angry. Trying to take, steal, to myself the love of this person for Peter, I was starting to desert myself, to imagine I was Peter. No longer at the mercy of the past, seeing what was happening released me.

The situation I had put myself in was that love could only come to me, if I left myself and became someone else. The price of love was the loss of myself.

I had an innate love of myself. It was impossible to "lose" myself, to totally "put myself into other people." God is love. I must by the nature of my being, "have myself," have love, have God. So always when trying to do these wrong, false things, I felt bad, was all wrong, not right. My plea was, I must "get right."

On the other hand, any attempt to get, to give love, of and for myself was thwarted, barred, frustrated, impossible. The attempt would make me feel very bad, guilty, ashamed. Why? Because due to the past the condition imposed upon me with regard to the giving and receiving of love was the loss of the self. There was I, stuck.

To feel love from the heart is life. Unable to love, I wanted to die. It was not possible to lose myself. Not possible to live without love. How could I possibly "have myself" *and* love? My Mother felt if she let herself be loved she would be controlled, possessed, stolen. She must, therefore, control my Father, in order that he, from making love with her, did not go on to control her. The penis of my Father, his love, meant to my Mother, "I am coming in on you, I shall possess, steal you, you will be no more." I was not free from my Mother. She was "inside me."

Joe putting his finger in my mouth was to me saying, "Look I can come into you but I'm not controlling you, possessing, stealing you."

My fear of people coming in on me, was my fear of love. They were as a penis coming in on me. They were out to take me over, steal me, possess me. Keep still, rigid, maybe they will go, was how I dealt physically with people coming near me. My Mother wanted to be rigid, frigid, her vagina shut to the penis of my Father. In myself, I was tight, tense, in the grip of this love knot. Had I been married, I would have been as my Mother, in a state of terrible guilt every time my husband made love to me. Any baby from me would have been twisted as I was, in the womb and after. Any man making love, having sex with me, would have been stealing me. Any mention of sex was very frightening to me, a suggestion of stealing, of my very self. To speak to Joe of sexual feeling was very risky. The whole matter was fraught with danger. My body showed forth my shame, my strain, my worry. Not able to move easy, as a child to dance, to use my hands, my body needed the oil of love. My parents jarring on each other seemed embodied in me, disjointed, ill at ease. In a sense I was in a real state of disease. When angry, wanting to steal things, I was "paying back," doing with things what my Mother did with me.

My Mother wanted to "be a baby," to go back. Being physically ill many times she got looked after. Joe told me: "Some people like you spend their lives physically ill and having operations, in order to get themselves looked after." Joe explained to me: "If you feel loved you feel guilt. If you enjoy yourself you feel guilt."

The shame of having a warm heart, of enjoying herself was very strong in my Mother. It was difficult for my Mother to be softhearted. One of my biggest troubles has been a hard heart. Physically I would get a pain, "Joe my heart has gone hard." It was like a solid lump of stone in me. I was so very angry, so full of IT, my anger. Caught in my despair, a seething hatred of myself and everything that lived seemed at times to possess me.

It was only "safe" to be dead. Death was secure. Love, life was an intolerable risk.

Feeling affection could also make me want to leave people, not only out of fear of supple hearts, but because my Mother, in my past ways, had always pulled me back, run after me, gone to great lengths to keep her grip on me. Therefore, other people loving me would likewise pursue me.

Joe waited for me. Freely I had to come, to Joe.

Always, with my Mother in me, was the lurking, abiding hope, that perhaps, "after all my Mother does know how to love." This was part of the horrible mesh of the web, that at times violently did I fight free of. The grip of the past that Joe was breaking me from. The spider in the web was my Mother. Joe gave me a toy spider. My brother was always terrified of cobwebs and spiders. Sometimes I chased him with a spider. When in bed, I saw, hallucinated, spiders. The clutch of the past was coming out of me. Gradually, my Mother became a separate, individual person. Slowly I worked free from the past, from the web.

When first at Kingsley Hall I wanted externally in the flesh, my family with me. To, with me, so I thought, "get right" and help Ronnie, get me right. How easily might I then have slipped back into the lure of the web: "Surely I *can* trust my Mother, surely, she does know how to love."

Sometime afterwards with Catherine I seemed to see the grip of the web. Seeming to come out, then back in, she was dazed and choking with the mesh. At times she looked suffocated. Remembering how frail I'd been, how compelling, how enticing is the web, I realized the danger when starting to struggle free of being actively involved with one's own family.

Not to be possessed and controlled can be very very frightening. The hospital* with its drugs and physical treat-

---

*I use the word hospital in the usual accepted way. To me the word denotes a place of healing, of therapy. Kingsley Hall is, in this sense, a real, true hospital.

ments and compulsory admission is controlling and possessing. There is a terrible gripping fascination about the web. A whole lifetime could be spent making outside of oneself, webs to match how one is inside. To go into madness, to start to come out, to leave the web, is to fight to get free, to live, to move, to breathe. To spew out the spider. To see my Mother outside of me, as she was, a separate person, was the desire of my tormented being. Emptied of myself, torn to shreds, then matted together all wrong, in a thick lump, was the state I seemed to be in. I was starving for myself.

Joe, to me, was the means to my true attainment of love, of myself. I wanted Joe. So much, for so long, all the time. Any "intrusion" of anyone else towards Joe was murder. I wanted to kill them. Joe was my life. Unwinding through Joe, Joe, to me, was the same as me. If anything happens to Joe, meant if anything happens to me. If Joe dies, I die. If Joe is with someone else I am left. I am lost.

Until I started to "get separate," to be able emotionally to gradually dare to "live alone," to "be free," this was the hell I was in.

I wasn't torn from my Mother's breast, I never even had it. Sitting with Joe, my head to his breast: "You want to suck?" "Mm."

When Catherine lay me down, put her head to my breast, I knew what she wanted, felt her fear of her own demands. When I lay very still, she would come and go, as a little bird.

When I got an idea of the breast, a safe breast, Joe's breast, somewhere I could suck, yet not be stolen from myself, there was no holding me. I was out to suck Joe. To suck him dry. My greed was enormous. Also it was terrifying. Joe conveyed two things to me. My most terrific greed would not really eat him up. He would still be there. Love was safe. You can love me. I love you. You still have yourself. You are not destroyed. You are not possessed.

How could I let myself experience love?

Only by discarding the lessons of the past, and by re-learning in the present, for the future, for all the rest of my life, and beyond it, in so far as the freer I become the most responsible I am and the higher I can reach.

Through the mistakes of the past had I been cramped.

My body was not "free." When still a child, I was clumsy, hopeless at handwork. The creativity in my soul had been forever contained, as in a tight bud. I was cut off, divided from myself. Walking the tightness of my own wire, my own life, I had to fall, to break to pieces.

Through the true desire of my being, the mad state, I came to know the truth. That I wanted to go back, to come up again. Through the skill of Ronnie and all who worked with him I was able to follow through, the desires of my being.

People did not understand, yet tried to boss or control me. When this happened I was terrified.

I wanted to be around, yet was afraid to be seen. I wanted my things around, yet was afraid they might disappear. Thereby life became very dangerous and difficult.

When I was first about the house, after being some nine months in bed, I felt "at home" and used the dining-room as a living-room, leaving my things about. Some people got very worried:

"Mary, other people don't leave their things about, you must keep yours in your own room."

Very frightened, twisting my body about, in a baby voice: "Don't boss me, I don't tell other people what to do."

"Speak properly, slower."

Screaming, running away: "I do what *Joe* says."

Soon realizing I couldn't cope in any other way, I stopped speaking. I tried to dodge people "who did not understand" and generally ignored what they said. Had I tried to change to suit them my anger would have "gone in on me."

The whole house seemed like a mine field that might explode, any minute. Standing, exposed, painting, I might be struck down dead any moment. The strain was intense. But I wanted to paint, so I did. It seemed the paintings were me, exposed, raw on the walls all around the house. Joe loved my paintings. He encouraged me to paint big.

One day Ruth Abel came, from *The Guardian*.

Ronnie told me: "Mary, there's a lady I want you to meet, to show her your paintings, and your room."

"Yes, all right."

She was very interested.

"This is a painting of Christ and His Mother. He is about to be taken from the Cross, into the arms of His Mother. Being God, he can smile—from a dead body. His Mother, she's still alive, on her way of the Cross, is in great grief and agony. Christ is seeing in a flash, all that was, is, and will be, as he conceived it, before the beginning of time. The painting is of a peak point in time, between the Crucifixion and the Resurrection, a pause in the breath of God."

The lady listened, really interested. My speech got slower.

"This is another painting that means a lot to me, 'Christ Raising the Girl from Death.' She is somewhat 'holding back' as if a little reluctant to come, not yet fully wanting to return."

"For how long do you paint?"

"Perhaps for five or six hours, then, the same day, I may do another painting. Stanley often sits watching me, all day."

"Does it seem long?"

"Oh no, time goes from me. It's just like a few minutes, doing a painting."

"Do you know what you are going to do?"

"Not exactly, it just comes from me. You don't, in a sense, know what you're doing, not when you're doing it."

"Does it tire you?"

"Yes, but in a refreshing way. When it's finished, I lie on the floor. Then I fall into bed and go to sleep, all covered in paint. Paint all over my trousers, on my face, in my hair."

Leon told me: "Mary, mind my jacket."

"Why, whatever's the matter?"

I loved paint. Surely Leon would like some on him. It was then almost impossible for me to realize how other people were not me.

One evening a South African artist came to dinner. Harry Trevor.

"Mary, would you show me your paintings?"

"Joe, may I, now?"

"Yes, go on."

"Harry, that's the 'Head of a Girl', there's 'The Mother of God'."

"Mary, you have what Beethoven has in music, it's a perfect pitch or blend in *colour*. Even among artists it's a very rare gift."

Harry really made me realize that I had been given a gift of God. This moved me, inside. Later, thinking of Harry and Table Mountain, I painted "Mist, Mountain, and Sea."

My paintings seemed to come, through the colour, to move, to change, to become complete.

About this time, May '66, I dreamed of being in a room, looking at a long table, at which were sitting separate groups of women, having coffee. I looked at them. One in each group was "a famous woman." One who had spent her life in good works. I did not somehow think much of them. Then I was in a Hall. Women were at tables doing sewing, one was in bed. Some of my paintings were up. "Now I am going to take the paintings down. Have you all seen them?" To the woman in bed I took a painting, on a tray. She put something on the tray. It was a new rosary. I was very pleased.

Later, I realized this was a future or prophetic dream. Leaving the painting, I went to the source of its spring, to the root of my being, wherein was my Faith.

Every Wednesday evening, after dinner, we had a meeting. Joe would be there, but, even so, it was a terrifying ordeal. This particular evening people were discussing my paintings.

"Mary, there's far too much of your work about the place."

"She put up another one today."

"You won't discuss things."

"Why doesn't she talk?"

Joe mentioned, "Mary does say things through her painting."

Terrified, I wanted to disappear right into Joe. The conversation changed. After the meeting Joe spoke with me.

"Mary, try to get some of the paintings down. Roll them up."

"Joe, can you? Is it really all right to roll paintings?"

"Yes, artists do roll their canvasses."

The next day was very vivid. Exhausted, I had gone to bed late and got up late, going straight out to the eleven forty-five Mass at the Church of the Guardian Angels.

In the hardware store, Mr. Sargent noticed me.

"Hullo Mary, you look nice. Got a new dress?"

"Mm." I felt good.

On the waste land I found a board to stick a painting on. It was still rather worrying, the thought of rolling them up. Apart from the ordeal of having to "take myself down."

Coming up the front stairs across the Games Room, I suddenly realized my paintings weren't there. I was so used to seeing them, they were to me, part of the place. A visitor had remarked:

"To me, Kingsley Hall wouldn't *be* Kingsley Hall without Mary's paintings."

At first, I couldn't seem to believe my eyes. It stunned me. Then I was angry, had they *really* thrown me *out*? Why? Why? Who, who, would have done it? Helen had spoken against the paintings.

"Helen, Helen." Where was she? In a panic:

"Mary did you do it?"

"No."

"Peter, you didn't do it?"

"No, Mary I didn't."

"There's Helen, you did it? You did it?"

She didn't answer. "You *did,* I can see. I'll *kill* you."

My hands were on her. Peter Tollimarsh pulled me off. I ran to the phone. Couldn't get Joe, couldn't get Leon. I got Ronnie.

"Mary, try to hold it, until tonight, then we will see about it."

I went up to Joe's room, away from the others. I lay on his bed.

Later, everything seemed quiet. I went down and put all the paintings up again. It had never occurred to me that anyone would take them down, especially without telling me.

Someone said, "There's a note inside your door." It was stuck on a painting on the door. I hadn't seen it. The note was from Helen saying she had taken the paintings down.

That evening, after dinner, everyone was very angry with me. They demanded that my paintings come down. I knew that David and Ronnie and Joe and Leon liked my paintings and were not disturbed by their being up. But the anger of all the other people was so much I didn't know how not to run away.

Joe helped me take the paintings down. Worn out, in a

temper, I tore down "The Head of a Girl." Joe caught hold of me:

"Go and get some Sellotape and mend it."

I did.

This painting was of a full blooded girl I had met on the tube, with some boys. She had said, "Show us your paintings."

"This is 'The Mother of God.'"

An hour or so before, standing on a seat in the hospital chapel I had unrolled her before my brother, Peter.

"Do you do portraits?"

"Not usually, not in a usual way."

"Our stop—cheerio."

Back home, that day came "The Head of a Girl."

By the time we got down to the Hall, taking down paintings, David and Leon were helping. I did not seem to be anywhere. Everything went from me. I was lost, dazed. Joe held me together. Upstairs, there was music and dancing. The other people had been to the pub, celebrating the coming down of my paintings.

We hadn't yet had time to roll up the paintings. They were scattered in the Games Room. Someone was reading a newspaper spread across "The Mother of God" canvas. My anger was terrible, a girl's foot was against the bottom of the canvas. Someone was shouting:

"Mary Barnes must go, she must be got rid of, out of this place."

My temper was up. Why *should* they? What right had they?

My body bashed. Someone fell. Joe got me out of it.

The next day was hell. They were going to have another meeting, as to why I had put the paintings up and whether I was to be allowed to paint outside my own room any more. I spent the day in Joe's room. In a bad state, unable to contact anyone, afraid I might bash, my own room, next to the kitchen where people congregated and talked about me, was very dangerous. I stayed the whole day on Joe's bed, on which I watered. Very bad, I knew better than to move. The roof edge was perilously near. I was afraid I might kill myself. Although not eating or drinking, I was very awake, my temper smouldering.

Suddenly I threw all Joe's books on the floor. Lay again, with IT. Then picked up all the books. In the late afternoon, I beseeched Joe's mother "Pray for me, pray for me. Oh God, take her straight to heaven." She was in New York, dying of cancer. She had in fact died about this time.

In the evening, Joe brought me down for the meeting. Sid was there, which helped a lot.

"Come on Mary, eat some dinner."

Sid didn't hate me. Joe and Ronnie helped me. I ended up in tears. Joe put me to bed.

The next morning, Joe told me a Baby Bear story. There was a little baby bear who was always black or white. Then, later in the story, she got brown, like all the other bears.

Then Joe went to America, to his Mother who had died. From there he sent me a beautiful card of the Mother of God, holding a thorn—the thorn of the flesh.

Later I asked Joe, "Why do people get so agitated about my paintings? There's never all this terrible trouble about crockery smashed or windows broken?"

"Mary, your paintings are very powerful. They go deep down into people."

In my mind the whole matter of my paintings coming down was worked out in this way. Joe must have decided it was for the best, if my paintings came down. With Ronnie and Leon, a means was found to get the paintings down, without forcing me to "go against" Joe. Because I wanted the paintings up, Joe couldn't take them down. So what must have happened was that Joe had to put it into the mind of Helen to take them down.

At first, Joe was as the Devil, later, in this way, as God. I must have been getting very proud and vain about the paintings. It was not helpful to me to be so admired by visitors. For my ultimate good, Joe had therefore got my paintings down. I must trust Joe. He did everything for the best, that I may become whole, sanctified.

I mentioned it to Joe:

"You did put it into Helen to take the paintings down, didn't you, Joe?"

"No Mary, I didn't."

"All right, I believe you."

But in all my feeling such belief was not possible, not

then. About a year later, when looking through some paintings the truth suddenly pierced through me. No one but Helen had known that Helen was going to take my paintings down. Soon after the paintings had come down, I had a period of intense loneliness.

"Joe, the house has been dead, all day. There was no one about, I wanted someone to come and pick flowers with me, by the canal."

I wandered about cuddling Teddy. Looking over the wall, I saw people in their back gardens. I sobbed, "I'm so *lonely.*"

I had been allowed one wall in the Games Room on which I might put a paper or canvas to paint.

Somehow the painting seemed to dwindle off. I did the "Garden of Gethsemane—my Father, if it be possible, let this chalice pass from me, neverthless, not as I will, but as thou wilt."

Peter told me, "Mary, this is one of the best paintings you have ever done."

Then came "Abandonment and Love" in which Christ abandons Himself in Love, to be crucified.

There was a brief revival of the paintings about the house. With the help of Jutta, I put some up very early one morning in the Games Room. Ronnie had arranged something.

"Mary, some men from *Paris Match* are coming to talk with me, and you, and to take photographs. *They* think your paintings are *marvellous.*"

Later Joe gave me some beautiful big photos the men had taken of me in the Games Room with paintings, me on the floor, on my bed in my room, and me doing a painting.

Now I seemed very babyish, wanting people to do things a lot for me.

Inside my room I painted "The Schizophrenic Christ." Sideways, the Head is split against the Cross.

My baby ways increased. I would be sitting on the floor, pushing along on my bottom, and Joe would turn round:

"Mary mind, I'll tread on you. Don't keep following me everywhere."

One evening when Joe was out with David, I put shits from my pot all over myself and in my hair. When Joe came I was frightened to touch him because of my shits.

He went up on the roof. I followed him. Joe was not afraid. He bathed me. I dreamt of being in a big sink with all my shits. It was being cleaned off me. Snakes were rising up.

One day, I borrowed a picture book of Ronnie's.

"Oh yes, I'll take great care of it."

There was a beautiful picture of a little bear. I put a bit of my shit on him. It was my favourite picture. Later that day, up in the flat, I watered on Ronnie's chair. Teddy was with me. Someone found me there all wet.

"Come downstairs, where's that book?"

"Look, Peter, she's put shit on *Ronnie's* book."

Everything was bad and terrible.

Ronnie came in: "Mary, we are going out to eat."

"I know, I'm bad."

"It's not because of you. There's no food in the house. Look, the fridge is empty. Do you want to stay up, or do you want to come to bed?"

"Bed."

Ronnie put me to bed. He touched me. I slept safe and easy. There were shits in the bed. In the day I kept my nightdress on.

At the weekend Joe helped me to get cleaned up. IT was very bad and "going in on me."

Ronnie was sitting out on the roof. I lay near him, stuck with IT, in a dead heap.

"Mary, you shouldn't be out on the roof in a nightdress."

I ran down to Joe. Ronnie was after me—"And just you do your hair nicely. Wear a *pretty* dress, to sit on the roof."

I'm bursting, bashing and bashing Joe, growling in rage.

"Do my *hair*," punch, bite, scream.

"I can't. I can't." Bash, bash.

"Is that all you can hit?"

"Pretty *dress—dress, dress*," tearing at Joe. I just can't hit hard enough. IT was bursting out of me. Full of anger, like a pipe bursting. IT was gushing, all over Joe. Bite, punch, Punch, in the end, when I was exhausted with screaming and growling and hitting, Joe took me in the kitchen. He gave me a drink of milk, then put me to bed.

Chapter Eleven

*The start of my second period in bed—the time of
Joe's holiday and the return of Joe*

May 1966. I wanted to stay in my room, alone, in complete
bareness. The walls were covered with paintings, layers thick.
The curtain, dividing my end of the room from Ruth's was
covered in paintings. There were lumps of wood about,
charred. In the winter I had collected wood from the wasteland to burn in the fire, and to make charcoal for drawing.
In the grate were ashes and in front of the ashes were
paintings. The hardboard "Christ raising the Girl from Death"
stood there, in front of the ashes.

There was my shrine, patched up from the time of
Stanley's massacre. On the table, on the floor, were great
pots of flowers, masses of white syringa, from the wasteland, where there had once been a garden. Wild flowers
from the canal, sculpture, clothes, balloons, the tiny Chinese
cup and saucer that Joe had given me from his family
things, when his Mother died.

The flowers were dying, withering into dryness. I got dry,
going down, down into my depths. Joe came with me and
Leon helped and Ronnie was there. In the beginning I wanted
to be alone, because I feared my badness would kill people.

"Joe, suppose I had spoken or moved. Mary G. might
have stayed then. I might have killed her."

"Mary, has your anger ever even hurt me?"

"No, but suppose I hit someone—not strong like you—I
might kill them."

Joe would growl, very loud and bite.

"How's the *monster* of Kingsley Hall today?"

I just laughed. It was so funny and nice to be with Joe as "The Monster of Kingsley Hall."

I tried to spin out as long as possible, a chocolate crocodile Joe had given me, he was beautiful. I loved crocodiles and sharks.

At first the other people came who "did not understand." They brought food. I just had to lie perfectly still, without looking or speaking, then they went away.

Stanley never came. Not once. I was in bed, my door shut, and Stanley never intruded. I so loved and respected him for this. I was going down, into myself, and only people who really understood were safe, to be near me.

Sometimes, when very bad, it was difficult to move to Joe.

"Come and sit on my lap."

Joe doesn't *really* mean it. He really means me to lie still. I mustn't get out of bed. He's "testing me." Mustn't do a "too much thing."

"All right, that's all right." Thank God, Joe understood. It was "right" to lie still in bed.

One day, when full of IT, I moved, pulled down a canvas off the wall, bashed a plate. The Chinese cup and saucer which I loved was accidentally broken. Then I lay, still, dead still.

Joe came. "Come here."

Terrified, I sat on Joe's knee.

"Mary was bitten by the angry bee, the getting out of bed bee, *and* the bashing bee."

Joe was nice and laughing, not cross. He "took the sting out." Back in bed, everything was nice and safe again.

Joe gave me a Rule: "Keep the bed dry. Use your pot. Every morning early empty your pot in the lavatory."

"All right, Joe."

Very early, as it got light, I would lie listening. Not a sound, everything quiet. Cautiously, coming out of my door, I would scurry back at the slightest sound. Like a little mole coming out of a hole, the hint of a footstep, I was back inside. The coast clear I would scamper like lightning with my pot to the lavatory and run back again. The early morning was my best time for moving. Then I would lie very still and perhaps sleep again. Movement, when I was bad, could start IT up. If I thought of something, where can I put these big scissors, farther away, wait until tomorrow, when I'm emptying my pot, then throw them behind all those boards.

My fear of killing myself was never far from me.

Once, I was angry with Joe and my aunty had just died in the house where I was sent when Peter was born. I thought, I'll go down to that house, then I'll go and drown myself in the sea.

"Joe, I got bad, it's gone now, I'm not really doing it, but I had a dreadful idea of going under water, in the sea, and not coming up."

"Mary, do you want to go and see that house?"

"Joe, no. I'm in bed now, going into myself, I don't want to go out."

"Come upstairs."

We sat on the roof. Leon was there. Joe started to brush my hair. "Stand up." Weak and wobbly; everything started to go "queer."

"Oh, Joe."

"Sit down, put your head between your legs."

That was better, but everything was wrong, stuck. Oh dear, I'd gone against Joe. Why did I speak? Joe meant me to fall, to faint.

Joe went to take Helen to work. Oh, why was I so bad? Why did Joe go?

"Brought you an ice lolly."

"Mmm."

Starting to suck, everything went worse.

"Ugh ugh."

"What's the matter?"

"Joe, I can't, mustn't."

"All right, you don't have to have it. Give it to me."

"Mmm."

"Want to go back to bed?"

"Mmm."

One evening Ronnie came. He sat on the chair.

"Ronnie, it's right that I'm in bed, staying in bed? Of course, I have not to 'go against.' If you say I must get out of bed, then, well, I have to."

"Mary, would you get dressed and come and have dinner with us?"

"It's too much, dressing."

"Later on I'll send Jutta in to dress you."

"All right."

Jutta came and dressed me.

"Do you want to sit outside, or wait here until I come for you?"

"Wait here."

By the time we were sitting at table, I was quite bad. Ronnie was carving and serving:

"Mary, would you like some chicken?"

"Ugh ugh."

"A tiny piece; it's good for you." He put a minute bit on my plate. Everything was too much.

"Ronnie, Stanley is not here. Why do I have to come? It's not *fair*."

"Do you want to go back to bed?"

"Mmm."

"Come on."

Ronnie put me to bed. That was better. I lay very still, holding myself together, everything seemed very worrying. I heard the door open, I slightly peeped. It was Ronnie, smiling. "Goodnight."

He gently went. Oh, the relief! Everything was right then. How I loved Ronnie. Goodnight, Jesus. Go to sleep.

Soon after I came to bed, Liz, Leon's wife, who was a psychiatric nurse, called to see me.

"I've brought you a flower."

"Mm."

"Here, in this egg cup."

I peeped out.

"I'll put it here, by your bed."

"Mm."

It was nice. Then it seemed all wrong to have it. Liz had gone, I quickly hid it on the window sill.

Joe came.

"Mary, tomorrow, when Liz comes, she will give you a bath."

I liked Liz and baths, but—"Joe, does she understand, really?"

"Liz is a psychiatric nurse."

"Yes, but there's lots of psychiatric nurses. Only Joan really understands about Ronnie's work. Suppose I'm bad? Please, Joe, not."

"All right, all right."

Liz was a very slight person. Probably I was aware that physically I might have overpowered her.

Once when Joe came, he opened my window. At once, grabbing his legs, I pulled him down.

"What's the matter?"

"Ugh ugh?"

"Don't you want the window open?"

Groaning with IT. How not to "go against" Joe.

"It's just open a tiny bit, I've almost shut it." That seemed a bit easier.

Caught, unable to "go against" Joe, yet becoming equally unable to consent to what I didn't want.

With regard to the dreadful despairing thought that I might have drowned myself, Joe told me:

"I don't want you to have any unnecessary pain, but some pain is necessary in order to get better and that pain I want you to have."

Lying in bed, after the strain of the previous months, was a relief, but it was also a deepening of my misery as I went down into my despair. Lying, biting the bedclothes, groaning with IT, waiting for IT to pass. Was IT, my anger, resolving?

At the time, I didn't know, in words, what was happening. The point was, it was beginning to happen, the resolution of my anger. Joe was helping me to let it happen, to lie still, to let myself be, with IT.

Sometimes Joe would ask me "Want a bath?"

"Mm Mm."

"I'll go and get it ready? Back again. "Mary, you can't have a bath, there's no hot water."

This was agony. *Why? What* had I done? Did Joe really mean the water was cold? Better not say anything, try to let it pass.

In time "There's no hot water" came simply to mean, the water was cold, not hot, that was all. Mary Barnes: water. Two separate things. I wanted a bath, I couldn't have a bath but I was not being punished. Sad, but not dead with shame, or broken to bits with anger.

One evening when Joe took me to the bath, I started to feel queer. The water was really hot, it had been beautiful lying soaking.

"Mary, stand up, let me dry your leg." Everything seemed more queer. Better not to speak. Must do just as Joe says. Hold up my leg. Gasping and weak, I seemed to slide. Myself couldn't hold up any more.

The next thing, I was lying on the ground.

"Hold under her arms." Then I was in bed. Joe and Leon were just going.

"Goodnight."

"Mm Mm."

Lots of shits just ran out of me into the bed. Such a relief. I was in bliss. How wonderful, going *with* Joe, not against, I had fainted. Such a peaceful experience, I'd never before fainted. Of course Joe had meant me to faint. Of that I was in no doubt. Going to sleep that night I really felt in heaven.

One evening we had been playing.

"Where's Mary Barnes?" On my head: "Tap, Tap, who is there?"

"Mary Barnes."

"Oh, is *that* Mary Barnes?"

"*Yes!*"

Peep out, look at Joe, shut my eyes, quick again. Joe growls, bites. *Sharks.* I'm screaming: "Who's got the biggest mouth?" Mine stretches wide. "Eat you up. Mm. Mm," nuzzling into Joe.

"Mary, I want to introduce you to Noel and Paul."

This was alarming.

"What Joe?"

"You know, Mary, in a few weeks I'm going on holiday. Noel and Paul will bring you food. I want you to meet them."

"Oh no, no. *Please* not, Joe."

"Mary, I'd like you to get to know Noel and Paul."

In terror: "But Joe do they *really* understand?"

"Noel has worked with sick children, he's a psychologist."

"They are therapists?"

"They are people who can help you."

"But Joe, what about Leon, and Ronnie and Sid and David. Are they all going on holiday when you do?"

"Yes."

"Oh." This was terrible, whatever was to happen? If I was bad, people coming in on me could make me spill all out, disappear. For some time Joe said nothing more of Noel and Paul.

Dodo, a photographer, who lived in the house, wanted to take some photos of me in bed in my room. It was one evening, when Joe was with me.

"Will you have Dodo take the photos?"

"All right, but, but—no, Joe, really not, please. *Please* don't let her come in."

"All right, that's all right." Ronnie was outside with Dodo.

"Mary, what about if Dodo comes in while I'm giving you a bath and just photographs the room?"

Clutching Joe: "No, please not, Joe." Everything was going bad. Joe went out. Ronnie looked in. I screamed "Get out." He went. My agitation was terrible. Ronnie came back, what a relief. If I had killed Ronnie! That's how it felt. The punishment was never, ever seeing him again. Complete desertion. The relief of seeing him again—and he was smiling, as nice as before.

Joe came back. "Mary, it's quite all right, I'm not angry with you, you don't have to have Dodo in to take photos." Things seemed easier.

A few days later: "Joe, you know Paul's voice; he was in the kitchen saying to someone 'You are mad.' Does he *really* understand? Therapists never say that. They say "They are like you' or 'You like them.' You have to see yourself that you are mad."

Early one morning Ronnie came in: "Mary, I've come to say goodbye, I'm just away on holiday." It was difficult to move.

"Mm." Peep. He had his coat on.

"Noel and Paul—"

"Oh Ronnie—*please*, you know how dangerous it is to trust people who do not really understand."

"Here would you like some milk?"

"Mm."

Ronnie fed me from a glass, spilling most of it. This was right, Ronnie knew I mostly mustn't have it. He touched me, I was easier. He went.

Joe's holiday was getting near. The worry was enormous. Somehow it seemed Joe didn't really mean Noel and Paul to come to me. They were here like me, like all the other people, they really wanted to go into themselves.

"Joe, suppose I got bad when you were away. What would happen? Noel or Paul might put me into a mental hospital? If there's no *proper* therapist, Sid, Ronnie, Leon, everyone away? Whatever will happen?"

Then one morning, when I was so full of weariness and worry, Aaron, Dr. Esterson, opened my door.

"Oh Aaron, I'm so worried. Joe is going away. I can't look after myself."

"You know Noel and Paul, don't you?"

"Mm." Noel and Paul looked in the door.

"You'll have Noel and Paul bring you some food, won't you?"

"Mm, yes."

Then Aaron came in with Mary.

"What would you like, some fruit juice?" said Mary.

"Er. Mm. Mm. Er. Bottle—some milk." They went out to see about it.

Listening, awake, I waited. Would they really come, someone, who, Noel or Paul?

Noel came with a bottle and orange. I stole a look. Sucked quick.

"I dreamt I was in the room opposite. You came to me." This was worrying, Noel was coming to me, not me to him.

"You are a therapist? Joe says you have looked after very baby children and helped them grow."

"Yes, that's right."

I liked Noel. He seemed safe.

Paul was in the room. My eyes shut, I took a quick glance when I thought he wasn't looking. Noel went. Then he came back. Paul fed me with an ice lolly. He was nice. It seemed they understood.

In the evening, Sid came. "Hello, Mary, would you like some grapefruit?"

"Mm."

Tinned grapefruit: Sid fed me. "Listen love, would you like to come out and sit with me, at the table?"

"Mm."

"They're getting another room ready for you."

This was right. To be going somewhere away from all my things, somewhere bare without paintings. Only what the therapist gave would I have.

Soon it was time to go upstairs. Leon and Sid took me to the room in the Flat, where I went before, from downstairs. Joe came also, with my Teddy. It was beautiful, going to sleep there, all safe and sound.

The next day when Joe came, he took me into the Flat sitting-room. It seemed too much. Moving and talking, sitting in a chair, out of bed.

"I'm going now, want to go back to bed?"

"Oh *yes.*"

Joe went. I got so bad, groaning with IT and wetting the bed. Where were Noel and Paul? Crying, I crawled downstairs and lay on the Games Room floor. Noel was touching me.

"Come back to bed."

"Mm."

Paul brought a clean dry sheet.

"Don't worry that the bed was wet, I'll sit with you." Noel held me. That was better, IT got easier. Eventually, I went to sleep.

In the morning when Joe came.

"Joe, I got bad and was wet and cried with Noel."

"That's all right, Noel is not angry with you. It's not naughty to cry."

Joe brought up my pot. His holiday was getting near. Paul brought me warm milk in a glass.

Joe was going on three weeks holiday. Four days was the longest he had ever before been away. I could hardly bear to think of it, still less to speak of the matter. A few days before Joe went Noel came.

"Joe will soon be away."

"Yes, now I want him to go because the sooner he goes, the sooner he will come back."

Every day Joe came. That last time, the beginning of August was on a Saturday afternoon.

"Mary, I have some friends in the building. They have a little baby. Would you like to see the baby?"

"No no—please Joe, don't bring the baby."

"That's all right, you don't have to see the baby."

I was Joe's baby still wanting to be held. Too much, the idea of seeing Joe with another baby.

"I'm not going yet, I got a present for you, I'll be back."

That was nice. A big surprise coming. Joe came back. I knew, for the last time.

"There, do you like him? See he has hair."

Joe was pushing him against my face, a pink dog doll with great big eyes and woolly hair that brushes up all rough.

"Mm, mm, he's beautiful."

I held him. Joe held me. Tears were coming to my eyes. I couldn't look, and didn't when Joe went. The door shut. Hidden down in the bed, I kept very still, cuddling the doll. Donk came to be his name. Had I let Joe show me the baby, he wouldn't have given me Donk, so I felt.

The next day Noel and Paul took me into the sitting-room of the Flat. My eyes were shut; Paul suggested: "Open your eyes, look around the room." They were eating. "Would you like some food?"

"Mm!" Paul fed me

"I see you like cauliflower. Have some more potato? You don't have to have it, if you don't want it."

"Ugh, ugh."

"That's all right."

"Want to go back to bed?"

"Mm, mm."

To be out of bed seemed to make me very bad. At first with Noel and Paul, I did not know how to tell them, or even to know, it was a "too much" thing.

In the morning Noel came.

"Mary, we are sitting on the roof having breakfast; would you like to be with us?"

"Mm."

Noel took me out. They gave me kippers. That was nice but the roof was terrible.

In a whisper: "Noel, please can you put me back to bed?"

"Yes, you want to go back to bed?"

"Mm, mm."

It was such a relief to get back in my bed, in my room. Paul brought me food. Fed me. There seemed lots. We went on, it was finished, Paul went. Then I got so bad I was groaning with IT, holding on to the bed, biting the sheet.

In time the truth dawned. I ate too much, more than I wanted, because to have refused, to have left it, would have been "wrong," naughty. I would get very angry if I refused food, but afterwards wanted it. However, a really bad feeling would come over me if I ate food not wanted because I didn't know how to say no. In my mind, not to take what Noel and Paul gave could be "going against" Noel and Paul. That is to say, going against "therapy," my treatment. Gradually some idea filtered through that "going against" was really "going against" myself, what I wanted. At times not to "go against," to eat food, could make me very bad. Therefore, the only "right" way in the matter became what I wanted. Therapy treatment then, was coming to know what I wanted. Through the food, with Noel and Paul, I seemed to realize this. The "right" thing had always been what someone else wanted of me. Or to get what I wanted: "Joe doesn't *really* mean me to eat." Not simply—"I don't want it." Not separate, my desire had to go through some-one else. As if I was a tiny baby, I could only be satisfied through "Mother" gauging my needs. In the womb, the food of blood from her, to me. The trouble with me had been my real Mother *hadn't* really wanted me to have it, food. She had never had any milk in her breasts. She couldn't, she hated me. Yet told me she loved me, and wanted me to eat.

Underneath in us both was the truth. I had to starve to death to satisfy my Mother. Yet at the same time, innate in me was the desire to live. Food was necessary for life. "Joe doesn't mean me to eat." Seeing Joe as my Mother was, "My Mother never meant me to eat." Mother had felt bad about giving. I had felt bad about taking. Quite unaware of the truth, we padded ourselves against it.

Mother strove to fully feed me. I made big exhausting efforts to take it all in. We were so unhappy. At times the battle was intense. When I just *couldn't* eat and my Mother simply *must* feed.

Through all the food I had from Joe, and Noel and Paul, the past was broken. They were not my Mother. New ideas set in. They loved me. I could eat according to the needs of my own body.

Joe would say, "Mary, if you feel hungry, eat, if not, don't." This simple advice took some time to follow. It was always very dangerous to ask for anything.

One afternoon, when I was on the roof with Noel and Paul, Joan passed by.

"Hullo Joan, look what Joe gave me, Donk."

"What's he bringing you back?"

"Don't know."

"Noel, would you help me move a case?"

"Oh, yes, Joan." They went.

Everything was so light, so outside, so bright. How to get in.

These color illustrations by Mary Barnes appear on the following four pages:

Peter Before Christ—the first finger painting Mary did. Oil on hardboard, 4ft. x 3ft., May, 1967

Triptych showing Mary and Elizabeth—the friendship of the New Testament (left). The Nativity, and Ruth and Naomi—the friendship of the Old Testament (right). Finger painting, oil on wood, 7ft. x 6ft., February, 1969

Gathering Manna. Finger painting, oil on canvas, 6ft. x 5ft., December, 1968

The Blinding of Paul. Finger painting, oil on hardboard, 4ft. x 3ft., June, 1970

Spring, the Resurrection II. Finger painting, oil on canvas, 7ft. x 5ft., December, 1968

Mary Barnes, Summer 1971

Dr. Joseph Berke

Three studies of Christ in Agony

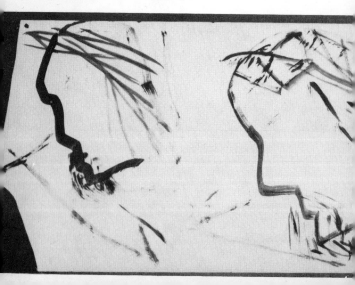

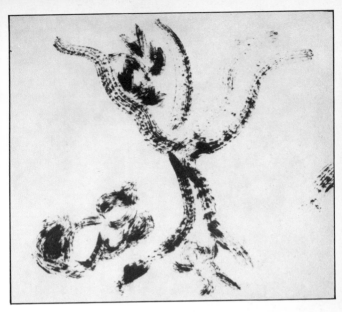

One of Mary's first drawings

Mary painting the Triptych (*Photograph by Karen Hagen*)

Mary in front of
her painted door
(Photograph by John Haynes)

Mary in front of her mural
*Christ Triumphant—Three
Stages of the Sacrifice of the
Lamb* (Photograph by John
Haynes)

Me, bad, taking in good-
ness, warm milk and honey
from the mug Joe gave me

My mother and me
with a sore throat
and how I feel all
over. To tell my
mother.

Me, a crocodile eat-
ing Joe — crunching,
gobbling, biting

Mary showing Joe some sections of her thirty-three-foot
painting *The Way of the Cross* in her new studio, 1971

"Paul, do you think I could have a bath?"

"Maybe, if the water is hot."

Noel returned. Paul told him, "Mary wants a bath; I'll see if the water is hot."

I'm sitting very still, holding together. Noel comes back: "It's all right, are you coming?"

"Mm."

Paul helped me up: we all go to the bathroom. Something seems a bit queer.

"Want your hair washed?"

"Mm."

Everything was like Joe did it. Lying soaking my hair in the water. But somehow it was all "wrong."

"Want to go back to bed?"

"Mm."

Noel and Paul went. Then I was so bad, groaning with IT.

Ever after, as with Joe, I waited until they "gave" baths. It was all "wrong" to ask.

One evening Noel and Paul took me to the kitchen to have dinner with them. Sitting with Teddy, my eyes shut, I felt very exposed.

Mary G. came in and Noel talked with her. Paul served me, "Mary, you like chicken?"

"Mm."

"Have some wine and an orange."

I ate, stealing quick looks.

We went back upstairs.

Another night Noel came. "Would you like to come and eat with us? A friend of mine, a Norwegian psychologist has come to dinner."

"All right."

On the way we came to Stanley. I brushed against him. Noel took his arm, "Come on, Stanley." This was nice, Stanley was coming to eat with us.

I had two helpings. It was special; Norwegian soup, made by Noel's friend, Berit Wahl. She told me, "Mary, you have nice hair, shall I comb it?"

"Mm."

Usually my hair was just left wild. She put it up, with hair grips.

"Do you like that?"

"Mm." But something was queer.

We had music and danced. I lay on the floor. Noel took me to bed; my hair was still up. It was some days before the last of the grips fell out, on the floor. I tried not to notice them, fearful that Noel or Paul might put them back in my hair. They didn't.

We had picture postcards from Joe and Leon. Mine, from Joe, was of the sea. I kept it in bed. Noel and Paul had the Church of the Holy Family at Night, in Barcelona.

"Noel, that's such a beautiful card."

"Would you like to have it on your wall?"

"All right."

Noel pinned it up. Something was wrong.

"What's the matter?"

"Noel, please not."

He gave me the card. That was right. The walls must be bare, nothing on them. My curtains were often drawn and this was "right." If they were pulled back I would feel very bad, but be quite unable to explain why, having to wait for Noel or Paul to draw them again. That was very often the trouble, just not knowing how, or why I got "bad."

Noel and Paul were clearing up downstairs and one day Noel took me down through the Games Room. Everything looked as if I had suddenly died, left life in the middle. Brushes and paints and paintings. It looked desolate, dead.

"Noel, those brushes should be in turps."

"What's that painting?"

"Disintegration."

"I like your paintings."

"Do you?"

"Yes."

I was terrified, talking in whispers. We went back upstairs. It was a relief to get back into bed. This time in bed I did sometimes have shits. Paul relaxed me, so I could pass it, myself. It hurt a lot, not wanting to come out. But Paul knew how to help me, just let myself be. It almost seemed like magic, from all the strain and pain, to the joy of shits just coming, easy and free.

First, Ronnie came back from holidays. I was feeling bad, he touched me. I got easier.

By this time I was often lying with IT and when bad

could not do anything more than that, talking was too much. Instinctively I knew in order to "hold it" I must keep still and silent.

Then Leon returned. "Joe is on the way back. Like some food?"

"Mm." I looked at Leon.

Two evenings later there were big Joe noises all up the stairs, getting nearer and nearer. The door opened and there was Joe, all growling and biting and laughing. I'm all squeaky and squealing and banging my head into Joe. Everything is so marvellous, so wonderful. Joe is back. Joe is coming again. I sleep well.

The next time Joe came, he took me down to dinner. We sit down, Joe moves his chair in to the table. I move mine. Joe got up, went over to the sideboard, came back. "Mary, I'm going to call Leon."

Joe leaves me. Something seems wrong. Shouldn't have moved my chair. Keep still. I'm bursting. It seems I want to explode and can't. Everything has gone from me. Oh, why did I "go against," why did I move my chair? Someone brings the dinner in. Joe is still away. Will he never come? What *have* I done? I can't move. I can't speak. Dodo, a girl who lived in the house, wanted to serve some food on to my plate.

"Mary, have some potato?"

My body swerves round. It's stuck and stiff. Ronnie was there.

"Would you like some cauliflower?"

Turning a bit, I nodded. He served me. Joe is back, Leon has come, Joe sits down again, next to me. I can't eat, I'm bad. Ronnie puts the lights out. The candles are on. That's easier, Joe is there. He is talking with the people. Usually, like Joe I eat loud with big chews. Now I can hardly touch my food. All the people are talking. Joe is there. I want Joe. Everything is tight; tense; I'm holding together.

"Joe, I feel bad. Please take me back to bed." We go upstairs.

"I'll come back and say goodnight."

Lying very still in the dark, I get some relief. My body "lets go" a bit.

Later Joe told me: "You were jealous because I left you to call Leon; you could have asked to come with me."

"Joe, it never occurred to me. I just couldn't seem to move."

With Noel and Paul I could be angry. "You won't hurt us, we won't let you." I was glad to hear that.

When I had been around in the house, the girls used to say of me, "She's very strong." I was very frightened of this big bomb in me, all my anger. It was sapping my life away. Everything seemed to go into this terrible thing inside me. I couldn't spew it out. Gradually, as I lay with this lump, this unexploded bomb in me, it seemed to soften, to dissolve. But it was often very difficult to wait for this to happen. There was the urge to throw it out, to explode it, outside myself. As if trying to tear it out would get rid of it.

I've seen other people have this state. Sometimes they explode as I sometimes started to do, when around with Joe. It's a terrible experience, the shattering of the bomb, and the more you try to throw it out, by violence, the more it seems to cling, to stick inside you. When I was near danger, Joe would be with me without talking. Then leave me, cold in the bed. This seemed to freeze it, the bomb inside me. Then, in easier circumstances, it could start to melt. When it really softened a lot, I wanted to love. Then I found it difficult at times to contain my love, when other people felt too bad, too explosive, to be loved.

Not long after Joe was back from his holiday, he came in one morning.

"Want a bath?"

"Mm."

It was so beautiful that Joe was back. In the bath Joe told me, "We are having a change of rooms, I'm going to see Noel about fixing up the room downstairs for you, where Stanley used to be."

Soaking in the bath, I thought how Stanley, until very recently, had sometimes sat outside my door singing. I was glad to be going to his old room. Paul told me Stanley had started to talk. Joe came back:

"Want to come out now? I gotta go. Or want to come out later, with Noel?"

"Want to come out now, with you."

What a blessing, to know something, definite. With so many questions, it was so difficult, often impossible, to decide myself. Whether to have the door open, the light on or off, whether to eat or not, to go to the sitting-room with Paul, or not.

Usually, I didn't have to decide things about the room. Noel and Paul saw to that. Then, because it would have made "everything all wrong" to have altered it, I always left things like the door or the light, exactly as Noel or Paul left them.

Joe brought me downstairs, to the middle floor, inside the house again. It was a wonderful room, all clean and white. The walls, the ceiling, everything was newly painted white, by Noel and Paul. Joe brought down the yellow curtains, from the upstairs room, and my pot covered with the cushion.

"Goodbye Mary, see you Monday." The door was shutting, Joe had gone. I took a peep. There were rush mats on the floor. The bedspread was patchwork, pretty.

I lay, looking out.

Chapter Twelve

Autumn 1966—coming insight—how I used my
paintings to seduce people—bonfire night

"Hullo, Mary." Joe has come. I'm all hidden in the bed.
Can I, can't I look at Joe? He's sitting near. Joe touches me.

Something dreadful has happened, my beautiful mug with
the fishes on it, that Joe gave me, is all broken on the floor.
I threw it. My sheet had been nearly getting torn, but then
there had been Joe noises all up the stairs.

"Oh, oh, Joe, Joe. It only just happened."

"You were very angry with me. I was late."

"Waiting and waiting, it seemed years. I nearly tore the
sheet."

"You haven't hurt me by breaking the mug."

"No? My arms get tighter round Joe. My head goes into
his soft woolly pullover. It zips up the front and it's greyish
blue with big white patterns. So safe and beautiful—like
Joe. We sit a long time, the bad is going.

Joe got a dustpan and brush.

"Here, I gotta clean sheet. Get out. I'll make your bed."

"Mm."

"Sweep up the pieces." Joe took them away, the dreadful
day was nearly over.

Some days later I was very excited, for Joe had told me,
"Next time I come, I'm bringing you a present, a big surprise."

Joe came. I didn't mention it. We sat awhile. Seeing Joe
was the main thing.

"Mary, I gotta present, remember, I said today I was
bringing you a big surprise?"

"Mm mm."

Joe brought in a big parcel and something smaller. They looked like sticks of chocolate.

"Oh Joe, it's, oh—it's crayons!"

"Conte crayon."

"Oh, Joe, that's marvellous, a sketch book."

"That's the biggest I could get and here, oil pastels."

"Oh, oh." I'm smoothing the pages of the book, holding the pastels and clutching Joe. Everything is heavenly. Joe has to go. I start to pastel. Rocks, all colours, one on top of the other. Suddenly, everything got bad. I wanted to burst, it was all inside me. Bang, like a big balloon it went.

"Noel, Noel." Where was Noel, what was happening? Screaming at the door, "Noel." Yelling in the dining-room. "Noel." Smashing a glass. In a terror of panic, screeching, "Noel, *Noel*. Joe, Joe."

"What's the matter, what's the matter?" He held me tight, together. "Oh. Oh." Joe took me back to bed. Groaning and holding Joe.

"I don't know, I don't know. I'm bad. I'm bad."

"What happened?"

"I was pastelling, then everything went bad, *very* bad."

"You got angry that I went."

"Oh dear, oh dear, oh dear." I was going dead, unable to feel Joe.

"Would you like some milk?"

"Yes, er no. No." If I wanted milk, Joe would go, Joe mustn't go. Joe put the book and the pastels away.

Oh God, what would happen? How could I stay? Joe was going. God, God.

"Here, cuddle the Teddy?"

Held Teddy tight. Don't look, the door is shutting. Lying still. Everything is quiet.

No Joe. No milk, maybe? I creep into the kitchen, and start to nibble a biscuit. There's a sound. I scamper back.

Noel came. "Oh, Noel, I was bad—I was so bad. And Noel—I started to take a biscuit."

"Mary, I've been out, I'm just going to get you some food."

"Mm." What a relief, Noel was not angry. He came and ate with me.

For some time I did not know whether to pastel or not.

"Paul, it doesn't seem *right*."

"Shall I put the book over here?"

"Mm, no *no, please* Paul."

"Where do you want it?"

"Please can it go *outside* the room, and the pastels."

"All right."

Noel brought a desk in. It had been Joe's. I wanted it. Two days later I was in agony.

"What's the matter?"

"Oh, Noel, Noel, the desk."

"Don't you want it? Shall I take it away?"

"Oh yes, please, *please*." It seemed wrong to have anything.

Noel was clearing my old room. "Would you like any of your paintings in here?"

"No. No."

"All right."

Sometimes the pastel book came back and it was "right."

One evening Joe took me upstairs to the flat. Ronnie was there, drinking beer.

"Want some?"

"Mm."

Suddenly Joe was going, "Mary, do you want me to put you to bed, or do you want to stay here?"

Everything was going from me, I couldn't think.

"Er—er—want to stay here." Ronnie was still there.

"Do you want to come downstairs to see me off?"

"Ugh, ugh."

My body was turning away. Everything was getting black. The door shut. There was silence. I heard the noise of Joe's car. It was going away. There seemed nothing left. Nothing to live for, I went dead, sad, desolate. Tears came, silently, I was long alone, desolate. Then, in a tiny whisper, it seemed a struggle, to know it, to say it.

"Ronnie, please will you put me to bed?"

"You see, it's quite simple." Ronnie was standing, we went downstairs to my room. "Do you want the door open or shut?"

This was terrible, how to *know* which was "right." Ronnie helped me opening and shutting the door. "Shut." It seemed I "hadn't gone against." The door was shut because I had wanted it shut. It was neither a reward nor a punishment. I was bad, sad, forlorn, because Joe had gone. But there was no "Oh God, what *have* I done to cause the door to be shut." Something was separate, me, the door, Ronnie. He was not cross with me. In the tinest way there seemed an inkling of the truth, a glimmer of light. Things seemed strange, and weak. But I was there, in bed. Lying still I went to sleep.

One day when Noel had taken me to the kitchen for food, we were making animal noises. Helen asked me, "How does a donkey go?"

"Oh the donkey I know, Henry, at the convent, goes 'Arh, Arh.' He's hoarse, he's got asthma."

Noel suggested, "Maybe you will write a story about a donkey."

"Mm."

In my sketch book with the pastels I made:

The King and the Donkey

Once, in the country, amidst the oranges and the wild flowers, was born a baby donkey named Saleh. His master, Hussein, was a kind and rich man and Saleh grew strong and happy.

Then, one night, in a terrible storm, the house of Hussein was struck by lightning, and so killing was the fire that everyone in the house was burnt to death.

Saleh, in his stable, felt strange to feel so warm in the dark. He went out and felt stranger still to see such light and, as he heard the crackle of the flames, now reaching his stable, he felt very frightened.

It was wet, he had no dry place, no soft hay. He grew cold and hungry. He wandered about. His coat was soaked with rain, his ears were full of water, and his eyes were wet with tears, he felt no one loved him and he was lost and sad.

Such was the beginning of the life of Saleh, as a stray, hidden, stealing, donkey. Men tried to catch him so he had to hide, and no one fed him so he had to steal.

He stumbled, through days and nights, and over rocks and into ruts, and he grew thin, and his coat got sores, and he felt sick, and he got kicked.

He never knew quite what to eat, and he got so weary of

trying that he could hardly breathe. One wet, cold night, he slipped in the mud, and such was his tiredness that he hardly felt the rain, or all his emptiness and pain.

He was dying; in fact the man who fell over him thought, at first, that he was dead. But Saleh sighed, and the man stroked his head. He loved donkeys, and just now he needed one, his own had been stolen only the night before.

He got Saleh to his feet and patted him and somehow he got Saleh home. His whole home was a stable, so Saleh lived in with the family and he was now called Abraham for this was a Jewish house.

He soon grew strong and well and Joseph, being a poor man, was tempted to sell him. Abraham sensed danger and big tears fell into his hay and every day he ate less and less. Joseph loved him and was worried that he was so poor, that his wife was trying to do with less milk and his donkey with less hay.

Then, one day, three men came to visit them and they brought gifts for the baby. One of these gifts was some gold, and, at once, Joseph went out and bought a goat for milk, for Mary, and lots of hay for Abraham.

Then, he started to look for a bigger house, but, in the night, an Angel told him, "You must go into another country." Thank goodness, thought Joseph, that I did not sell Abraham, such were his tears that I thought not first of money.

So now, quickly, they set out. Abraham, who had before spent so long in lost wandering, now strode surely along, as if he had always known the way. Every night, Angels came, with hay for Abraham, and with milk and honey for Mary, and with meat and wine for Joseph.

So it was, that with the milk of his Mother, and with the feet of the donkey, the King of the Jews reached Egypt.

Abraham was the first donkey that this king ever rode.

Joe read it: "Mary, what a beautiful story."

Eventually, I gave this original copy to Noel.

One morning I woke up with pains in my knees, perhaps rheumatism. My throat was sore, there were spots in front of my eyes, my head ached.

"Ronnie, what's the matter with me?"

"You are getting all your Mother's illnesses." Joe also told me this: "Do you remember how sick your Mother was?"

"Oh yes, terrible throats, migraines, very bad. Dreadful rheumatism, awful headaches."

"You didn't cause your Mother to be ill."

"No, I didn't, did I?"

"No, you didn't."

It seemed my Mother was "coming out of me."

With pastels in my book I did, "Two Devils in a Web," me and my Mother. This I gave to Joe.

On October 7th I was having food in the kitchen with Noel and Paul. Jutta was arranging flowers: "It's Ronnie's birthday." Back in bed I made a present for Ronnie. A birthday card, the birth of day, and a story, "The Hollow Tree." Paul came.

"Look, words and pictures for Ronnie."

"That's nice, would you like to give it to Ronnie yourself at dinner?"

"All right."

Noel came. "This I have for Ronnie. Paul says to give it at dinner time."

"Ronnie is going to be late."

"Oh dear. How can I give it?"

"I could write Ronnie a note, telling him if it's not too late to come to see you, as you have something for him. Or, give it to me and I will leave it upstairs where he will see it, when he comes in. Or you could give it to Ronnie tomorrow. He won't mind having something the day after his birthday."

"But, Noel, I *mind*. I want to give it *myself* to Ronnie, today, his birthday."

"I'll write a note for Ronnie to come down for his present, however late it is."

"Yes."

That was settled, Ronnie came. He sat on the floor. This is what I read.

The Hollow Tree

There was once a tree in the forest who felt very sad and lonely for her trunk was hollow and her head was lost in mist. Sometimes, the mist seemed so thick that her head felt divided from her trunk.

To the other trees, she appeared quite strong, but rather aloof, for no wind ever bent her branches to them. She felt if she bent, she would break, yet she grew so tired of standing straight.

So it was with relief that, in a mighty storm, she was thrown to the ground. The tree was split, her branches scattered, her roots torn up and her bark was charred and blackened. She felt stunned, and though her head was clear of the mist, she felt her sap dry as she felt her deadness revealed, when the hollow of her trunk was open to the sky.

The other trees looked down and gasped and didn't quite know whether to turn their branches politely away or whether to try to cover her emptiness and blackness with their green and brown.

The tree moaned for her own life and feared to be suffocated by theirs. She felt she wanted to lay bare and open to the wind and rain and the sun, and that, in time, she would grow up again, full and brown from the ground.

So it was, that, with the wetness of the rain, she put down new roots and by the warmth of the sun, she stretched forth new wood.

In the wind her branches bent to other trees and as their leaves rustled and whispered, in the dark and in the light, the tree felt loved and laughed with life.

It came to me why talking had been impossible, especially when I was feeling very bad. I had been "going away" in my speech, in my paintings, in my shits.

Sometimes I went two weeks without shits.

As a child, my Mother used to give me food, then sit me on my pot, saying, "Do a big job for Mummy. Try hard." Time is passing, "Mary, hurry up, you're not just there to sit, you're there for a purpose, you forget that." Straining myself, "I wish you'd start talking." Mother is getting strained. "All that waste stuff inside you, you'll be getting poisoned. You just sit there till you do do it. Think what you're doing." Nothing happens. "Oh dear, I don't know what to do with you, you'll have to have a dose of syrup of figs, and that's bad for you, you'll get into a habit of having medicine. Then you won't be able to do it yourself. Now I must change Peter. That's a good boy, see Peter's done a big job. It's time for his bottle. Mary, take that thumb out of your mouth. Now stop whining. Look at Peter, how good he is. It's no good looking up there at the sweet tin, you had one after dinner. Sweets are bad for your teeth. What are you shaking your head about for? Come and see Peter. He's taking all his feed. Careful, don't poke his eye."

At about the age of six years I did poke Peter's eye with a bit of old iron.

"There you go again, to think I never gave you one of those dirty dummies and here you are, sucking that thumb again. I won't have it. Get away and play now. Mary, be a good girl, don't tug at my dress, I've got Peter, ssh, he's going to sleep."

"Ugh. Ugh. Ugh."

"Now don't be a baby, it's time you started talking. You're over tired, its time you were in bed. Careful now, I've kissed you goodnight once. Mary, be gentle, you're pulling my neck. Now go to sleep and stay asleep, all night. I've got Peter to feed in the night.

"Eat nicely, show me how you can use a spoon, no not your fingers, keep your pinafore clean, be quiet, look at Peter."

Sad, longing, angry; every suck, every cuddle he had I stole.

It was the only way, imagining myself to be Peter. If only I could have got back, inside Mother. Before he came, he was there, in my place, filling out Mummy's tummy.

How it all began, that too I knew in ways more imprinted than anything I would later be told. It was all terrible, *that* happened. Your Mother was terrified, she might die, there was a baby on the way. Birth was dreaded, Mother was worried.

"No, don't touch, leave me alone."

"We have a girl, I wonder will it be a boy."

The feelings, the thought of my Mother, was mine.

How her parents had longed for a boy. After three girls they had a boy. He died at six weeks, of whooping cough. Then my Mother was born, the last child, another girl.

Becoming separate was crawling free from all this, emerging from a maze. Sometimes it was like being in a tight tunnel, and when I exploded the tunnel burst. Then I was lost, smattered, like a cough in the air.

"What's that there, a ghost?" Joe was solid, here, I was not anywhere.

I remember, some months before getting to Ronnie, being with Monique, a blind teacher, and very sensitive. She could tell she was passing a building just by pressure of the air. Monique told me, "Mary, you are so elusive. With other people I get a sense of, feel their presence. Why not you?" We held hands, she wanted to know me beyond my flesh.

Of a carving she could say, "This is exciting, the shape, it's stone. " A sculpture, not alive, yet complete in itself, fully satisfying. Physically, I moved, I was not stone, yet what I was was a mystery, unknown, still unknowable, for this was two years before the time of Kingsley Hall. Monique, with her acute sensitivity, had tried to touch me where it was not yet possible to touch. Most people accepted a surface, Monique knew there was more, and tried to touch.

Like an anemone in the sea, I fled away, just wasn't there.

Always elusive, when I exploded into the air of Kingsley Hall, there seemed nothing left.

This lost "going away" feeling, I knew all too well as a child.

Then, struggling free, like a fish getting back into the sea from a net, I swam, gradually, as if I had never been caught.

The sea was so vast. Alone, would I drown. Nets were enticing, how to get into someone, how to swallow someone into me. How to suck every breast that appeared.

The sight of the past was falling away. The sea was free. My inside made my outside.

The happenings of the day brought the truth. Joe told me: "Mary, a friend of mine is coming to dinner. He lives in a big house, in the country."

I was in bed, Leon came. "Joe's friend, Steve is here, want to come out to the dining-room to dinner?"

"Mm."

"This dress?"

"All right."

Joe came late to dinner. Noel was there.

"Mary, meet Steve."

"Hullo."

"I believe you do some painting?"

"Oh yes, lots and just now, I'm mostly in bed, I'm doing some oil pastels."

Noel helps: "Perhaps in a minute we could show Steve some of your paintings."

"Marvellous." A visiting psychiatrist also wants to see my paintings. I am itching to go, Steve looks nice. Joe comes in, he makes a few growls. Everyone is talking, will they never finish? This is passing.

"Noel, Noel—you want to—er, Steve, I wonder—"

"Oh yes, I want to see Mary's paintings."

I'm up. "Are you coming?" The visiting psychiatrist tags on, I'm ahead with Steve. -

At this time the paintings were in the basement. With Noel I pulled out and held up as many as possible.

Canvas after canvas. "And that's the crowd pushing at the back, a few at the front, as crowds always are." They laugh. "What is it?" "The Feeding of the Five Thousand— that's what it is."

"Mary—"

"What, Noel, just two more."

The visiting psychiatrist asks, "Are you going to sell any of these paintings? May I come and photograph some of them?"

"Oh that's all to do with Ronnie and Joe. Just now they are all being kept here together. You'd have to ask Ronnie and Joe about taking photos."

"But they're your paintings."

"Yes, but it's all to do with Ronnie and Joe."

"Steve, look this is one of Pentecost, tongues of fire. Noel, do you think Steve would like to see my oil pastels?"

"Ask him."

"Would you, Steve?"

"Yes, very much."

"Come up to my room."

In my room the visiting psychiatrist starts to ask me questions.

"Before, where was I? Oh, here, where this story in my

pastel book is—in the Holy Land. Steve, shall I read it—
the King and the Donkey story?"

"Oh, yes."

Then I showed Steve all my pastels, Noel helped.

"Mary, it's getting late; do you want to go to bed?"

"Mm Mm." Showing so much was quite exhausting.

The next day, I'm dreaming of Steve. Joe comes. He
brings me an ice lolly, a strawberry Mivvy. Somehow it's
different. I don't show Joe any paintings, I'm sucking the ice
lolly. Joe likes me, there's no need to show. I speak with Joe.

"What was it?"

"You were seducing him with your paintings."

"Mm, Steve."

"And he had a big house, in the country, and lots of
money."

"Oh, *Joe!*"

Everything was quite clear. It all seems far away. He was
a big house and money and the country; I was paintings. I
told Noel.

"Mary, he was nice, I liked him."

"Oh yes, but Noel. . . ."

I was where I was. The bubble had burst.

Usually, at this time, I stayed in my room. Food called
breakfast or tea was often eatable, whereas "dinner" was
not. My Mother had never agreed with eating much near
bedtime. "You won't sleep, it's not good, a heavy meal at
night." However, sometimes at night, I liked to go out to
dinner. Paul came: "Mary, have on your pink dress?"

"Mm."

Holding Paul's hand, I get to the table. Ronnie is there,
and a visitor.

He stands, we hold hands across the table. "Glad to meet
you, I'm Erling Eng from the States."

I feel very alive, it's dim, there is candle light.

The visitor is talking to Ronnie. He speaks of himself, from
the heart. It's warm and rich, we become quiet and still.
The sizzle of candles deepens the silence of love. Ronnie
is speaking: "We must become poor in spirit, be as nothing,
empty ourselves. We are all within the body of Christ. Let
us enjoy the divine presence, now and for ever."

Joe had brought me some fruit, in a reindeer bag from Selfridges. Great big oranges and grapefruit. My mouth was *in* an orange, sucking, hard.

"Mary, want to come up on the roof? It's Guy Fawkes' night. I bought some fireworks. We are just going to let them off."

"Er, yes, yes."

"Here, put your trousers on. Jumper, lift up your head, it's cold."

"Here, hold this milk bottle, it's to set a firework off from."

Joe holds my hand, we're on our way, out of my room. First we sit in the flat. Everyone is there. I sit on the floor, near Joe, holding the bottle. Because Joe had given it to me to hold, I clutch it tight, couldn't put it down. Joe got up. "Come on, let's go." We all get out on the roof.

The sky is beautiful, red with fires and gay with soaring rockets. I stand near Sid, by the bathroom door. That's a bit sheltered. Joe has some big bangers.

"Oh Mary, Golden Rain."

"Oh, Sid."

Joe is ready for the milk bottle. "Mary put it here. That's right. Now a rocket. You want to light it?"

"Here's the taper, light it first, here." I jumped back, quick, it went right up, beautiful.

We had a Catherine Wheel and coloured fire and sparklers. It was glorious, I loved the smell.

Back in bed, I guzzled more fruit. Joe brought huge oranges.

"Look at *this*, this is an *orange*."

It was enormous. "Mm, Joe."

"Next time I come, I'll bring you the biggest orange you have ever seen."

Sometimes I drank milk but, mostly, now I only ate fruit. Leon brought me a coconut. I could hear the milk. Gradually I got a hole in the eye, drank the milk, then bashed the nut on my floor. Paul came: "Mary, have you eaten all that, all that nut?"

"Mm, it's all gone." Joe brought me another.

One night Joe came in with a red plate. "Mary, shall I get you some dinner?"

"Yes, all right."

Paul came in with dinner on a different plate. "Here, Mary, here's some dinner." Paul goes.

I start to eat, something is wrong, very wrong, I'm getting bad. I went out, after Joe. Everyone was sitting at table, I'm groaning with IT. Caught in the vice, tearing my hair, ripping my nightdress. I'm on the floor, sitting rocking my body, shaking my head, lumps of hair in my hand. What was the matter, what did I want, how to get relief? Tormented, trapped, I screamed.

Joe got up, took me back to bed. "You wanted your dinner off my red plate."

It was so terrible how bad I was. Then I went dead. I believed what Joe told me, but, as yet, the thought didn't change the feeling, especially when it was as powerful as this.

Joe went. Somehow I stayed with it, eventually going to sleep.

Gradually, eating less, going out of my room less, I was becoming more able to lie with IT.

One big trouble of this period was that it wasn't "right" to accept things.

Noel told me, "Mary here is a letter." I turn away.

"Shall I read it to you? It's from your Mother, something about a duck, it's quite funny."

"Ugh ugh."

Joe came. "Mary, someone has sent you a present. Do you want to see what it is?"

"Ugh ugh—no, *no, please* not, Joe."

"That's all right, I'll put it in the drawer outside. You don't have to have it."

Oh, what a relief. Joe understood. I mustn't have things.

One evening I was caught between not being sure whether to have or not to have. Joe brought me an orange stuck with cloves. It smelt good.

"Look, Mary, Roberta made it for you." Roberta is Joe's wife.

I took it, smelt it. "An orange. But Joe, should I *have* it?" Maybe I'll eat the orange. No, no, I can't. "Joe, please take it away. It doesn't seem right."

"All right, you don't have to have it." Joe went, with the orange. I got bad, very bad. Leon came in. He held me.

"Mary, we are all going outside, to a Chinese restaurant to dinner. Joe will come to see you when we get back."

The idea was with me "This is not me, my badness hasn't sent them out." Even so, I was bursting and groaning with IT. Terrible imaginings came of tying a stocking round my neck. It was like a nightmare of suffocation. I was bad, Joe had gone out. I was angry with Joe.

I make up my mind, I'll keep still, suppose Joe doesn't call in to say goodnight, well that would be for the best. Joe understands, I must trust Joe. If Joe doesn't come, I'll just keep on, keeping still.

Joe came in: "We've been out to eat. Goodnight, Mary." The door shut, my feeling eased.

Eating less and less, getting thinner, feeling in myself that Joe "meant me to go down," I was becoming very aware of my anger. Except for going on the pot, I didn't move out of bed. My shits were very rare, perhaps once in about two weeks, except when Joe gave me some brown pills. Joe used to tell me, "If you don't drink, your kidneys will pack up. Here, drink this." Joe gave me a pint of water.

"Joe, have you got some salt?" I ate teaspoonfuls of salt from a glass.

"Mary, I'm going to ask Noel to buy you a dressing-gown. Think what sort you would like."

"All right, Joe." This seemed right. Going to the bath, Joe put a blanket round me, but a warm dressing-gown would be nice.

Noel came. "What colour dressing-gown and slippers?"

"Red. With a sash, a dressing-gown like Liz has."

"I'll see what I can do. Heike is coming to help me choose." Heike was a girl who lived in the house.

It was a long afternoon. At last they came.

It was beautiful; warm, red wool.

"Oh, oh, Noel, I never in all my life had a dressing-gown like that."

"You like it?"

"Mm mm."

"Try it on, see, here's the sash."

"Mm." Everything was so wonderful.

"Look, try the slippers." Thick wool inside, leather, real leather, it said, strong warm slippers.

"Just right."

Joe came. "Show me your new dressing-gown and slippers too."

Jumping about with it on. "Look, Joe, sash—and buttons."

Joe reads the label, "Made in France."

At this time, Joe used to remind me, "Mary, I don't know all you are thinking and feeling." Getting separate, I came to really accept this fact. My feeling seemed to be coming up to my thought. My thought was going down into my feeling. At last my head was coming down into my heart. It was becoming more possible to lie long with IT.

Noel would light a candle, sit in my room with me.

Relaxing, I "let go." It was not talking. But something was happening. IT was looser, resolving, not gripping so tight.

I could tell Joe about the pretence girl I had been on top of the pretence boy. The real girl me, was becoming more bare, uncovered. I lay exposed and feared.

Joe told me, "The more you suffer, the more free you get." The old swelling up, clumpy feeling that I knew as a child, especially if sleep walking, seemed to leave me. It was a feeling of walking in space, exactly as a man in a space suit seems when about in space. I've seen this in a film.

I was getting clear. My mind seemed sharp, vivid, though my body was weak.

The moment mattered, but so did the century.

Changing, growing, through a moment, I yet seemed like a yew tree, staying deep green, and quiet.

Chapter Thirteen

Christmas 1966—further experiences with Noel and Paul

Leon brought me a big, enormous red balloon. We tossed it a bit, I was too weak to play much. It was good to look at.

I hadn't wanted any Christmas cards.

Joe had gone, it was Christmas Eve. The house was very quiet. I didn't expect to see anyone, not until after Christmas. Feeling, by now, separate, distinct, I could lie quiet, myself and God, alone, for two or three days.

Waking early, I got out on my pot.

Where was the Mass, the Mass at dawn, it was getting light. I stretched my hand for my missal, it seemed so heavy. The drawer was shut tight.

The words rather blurred. I looked at the sky, cold, red. Then I shut my eyes and went to Mass inside myself. "Dear Jesus come into me."

Lying in bed, I thought of baby Jesus. How Mary, his Mother, just in being and receiving, had given so much.

Suddenly, in the afternoon, there were noises of Joe. The door was opening. "Hullo Mary. Big surprise, Christmas day. Father Christmas has been." Joe was full of parcels, all growling and warm.

"Oh Joe," I'm all excited, hitting the bed and Joe, wanting to see all the things.

"Here, undo it."

"It's yellow, the biggest cracker I've ever had." It was full of things and always stayed a cracker because it didn't bang and tear. I still have it.

Then there was Squeaky, a beautiful mouse, all blue and

green with orange ears. I took her in bed with me. Also, there was a new book, all about the crocodile who stole the sun.

We played crocodiles and bears. The big bear, and Teddy bear, and baby bear. I sat on Joe's lap. Everything was beautiful and full of joy.

When Joe had gone, I lay with all my Christmas things on the bed.

In the evening Liz came. She looked very beautiful, fragile and holy.

"Mary, I am now Leon's wife."

"Liz, I am very happy for you."

We embraced, she left.

Paul came, with a glass of red wine. "Would you like to eat, some almond paste dessert?"

"No, no, Paul."

"All right."

I sipped the wine.

Leon came. "Peace."

"Mm."

"If you are with God, set towards God, everything that ever happens can only bring you nearer to God." We touched. He drank from my glass. I drank from his. It was whisky, Ronnie's drink. I was drowsy. Leon had gone. There was a knock on the door, the door was opening.

"Can I come in?"

"Oh, Ronnie." He stood against the wall.

My room was dark, just the light of the fire.

"I'm thinking of the passivity of the giving of Mary. Of Christ as the Victim, giving from the Cross."

I seemed part of the Crucifixion. Ronnie told me, "Then there was the Resurrection, the Resurrection, the Resurrection."

Ronnie was saying it softly, over and over, "The Resurrection, the Resurrection."

I was swaying, half asleep. He slipped out. The Resurrection, the Resurrection, it was going over and over in me. I slept.

In the night, I woke, feeling sick. Out on my pot, I was near the sink. It didn't seem right to drink water. I didn't. Christ could have got off the Cross. He did not. Back in bed, without being sick I slept again.

The next day, in the afternoon, I coughed and some blood came up. "Noel, Noel."

"What's the matter?"

"Look."

"Lie down, Joe is coming soon."

Joe came. "Just lie still. I'm going to make you some nice jelly."

"Is it my throat? Will I choke?"

"Mary, I think it's just a bit from your chest, and it's stopped. I'll take you to have your chest X-rayed, later. Keep your throat moist."

"Mm."

During the night, I took sips of water from a spoon. Something in me seemed to have broken. Now it was quite "right" to take the water.

One day, a little while later, I knew Joe was coming to take me to be examined by Dr. Taylor and to have my chest X-rayed.

Paul came: "Mary, I've come to help you get ready to go with Joe. What clothes?"

"Paul, *clothes?*"

"Yes, you are going in Joe's car."

Something was wrong, stuck.

"Paul, did Joe say I was to put *clothes* on?"

"Yes, Joe said to be dressed. He is coming in fifteen minutes."

"Really, Paul?"

"Yes, here's your trousers." Everything is easier, I put my arms round Paul. It seems it's really "right." Suddenly, I'm bad again. Stuck, wrong. "Oh Paul, Paul, dressing is such a *strain*. Paul, why not a dressing gown?"

"Because Joe said clothes. Socks, jumper."

"Oh dear, oh dear." The badness won't go.

It was many months since I had been out of my room and longer still, nearly a year, since I had been out of the house. It was very strange and frightening, "going out." I was wholly concerned, in every way on "going in" and staying "inside." Going "out" was a foreign, alien idea.

Joe came, "It's very cold, you need your clothes."

"Joe it seems you really meant me to go in my dressing gown. Why am I so bad?"

"You're angry because *you* don't want to go in your clothes. We'll take your dressing gown to wear for the examination."

Joe takes my hand and the dressing gown. We go out of my room, down the stairs. I'm holding together, very quiet and still.

I'd been afraid with clothes on I might get left alone, or expected to do something in the hospital.

Joe stayed close with me, all the time. Dr. Taylor told me, "Those spots you get in front of your eyes are not serious. They will go. You're a bit thin."

"Dr. Taylor, sometimes, when I was a nurse, I got thin."

"Joe, she'd better have a blood test, too, at the hospital." Dr. Taylor wrote it all down. We carried on, in Joe's car, to St. Andrew's hospital. Everything was very quick. We hadn't to wait. In the X-Ray place, I breathed deep. They took two pictures. Joe was there. We walked back, it was a long corridor, to the laboratory, where there was a man who took blood from arms. He took mine. On the way back, Joe told me, "You were good at the hospital, want an ice-cream?"

"Oh, yes."

In the corner shop Joe tells me, "Choose what you want."

"Orange Ice Lolly."

Joe took a choc ice. "Choose one for Paul."

"Choc ice."

Soon after Christmas, early in 1967, Noel came one evening.

"Mary, Joe is on the phone, he wants to speak to you."

"Noel, is it right?"

"Right to telephone? Joe said he wants to speak to you."

"I go. Noel, it's right to go?"

"Yes."

I'm excited and nervous.

"Joe, Joe?"

"Mary, I just want to tell you I can't come to see you tomorrow. I've got a meeting. I am coming the next day to see you."

"Oh, yes, yes, Joe."

"Goodnight Mary." Joe has gone. I feel good, absolutely believing Joe.

Noel carries me, I'm still very light and thin, back to bed.

Suddenly Noel was in anguish: "Where is *God?* God, where is God? Mary, why do you have to suffer so?" Noel was crying, "Don't die, we want you to help us."

Without words, not able to explain, I was just quiet with Noel. He was quite separate from me. I realized that as never before. My feeling was so distinct from his. He took me by surprise. The difference between how he was at that moment, and how I was, was so striking that I felt more separate than ever before.

At this time, although wanting to live, I was also accepting in my heart to die. I felt I could only ever help Noel and Paul, from heaven, where I wanted to go.

Separate as I was from Noel, I was not at all so from things.

Anything moved in my room spelled agony. Behind the movement of an object there was a sinister reason. What had I done to cause Noel to move that plate? Any movement, a change, was a mystery. Disturbed for the day, I would lie puzzling over the matter. My peace and smoothness were shattered by the slightest external deviations.

Once Noel wanted to borrow some tweezers.

"Mary, someone has a thorn in his hand, may I borrow your tweezers?"

"Oh, Noel." Not able to say more, I just groaned with IT. Noel didn't take the tweezers. I still felt bad at night. He had asked me in the morning.

Many of my things, paintings, clothes, books, were still in my old room. Noel had put the paintings in the basement. Unused as I was to going outside my room, I one day brought most of the paintings up from the basement. Two days later the boiler burst and the basement was flooded.

One day, I went alone to my old room, and in a drawer found my watch.

Noel brought me my rosary and *The Imitation of Christ,* things I really wanted very much, yet, at first, I questioned. "Is it right to have them?" I was still very much "in" my things. It is the cause of terrible anxiety to lose anything, to have to put things, especially paintings, away.

One evening Joe came.

"I got good news for you. Your chest X-Ray was clear. Your Haemoglobin was 96 per cent."

I was safe from hospital, although not wanting to go to hospital, I had within myself realized the possibility. I had thought, if in hospital, when the priest comes, I shall go to Communion and I shall eat food. Somehow I imagined, away from home, it would be "right" to do these things. At home there was still the perpetual question, "Does Joe really mean me to have it?"

Having spoken to Joe about going to confession and Communion, I was then caught in the tangle, "is it right" or is it going against Joe? Does Joe really *mean* me to go to the sacraments?

Joe had arranged for the priest to come. My feeling, when caught like this, was so violent that to force myself against it was physically suicidal. To feel I was "going against" Joe caused me such agony that Joe, understanding the state I was in, asked the Father not to come.

A week or so later, the feeling eased, it seemed "right," not "going against" Joe, to go to the sacraments. Joe took me in his car to evening Mass. It was Saturday, for Joe, as it was for Christ, the Sabbath.

I had my missal, there were some changes in the words of the Mass.

It was very quiet, just a few people. We sat at the front. I was very aware of the presence of Joe. Something was going on that I was inside of. Joe was looking on, from the outside.

Confession, Communion, hearing Mass, the core of my life. The Mass seemed a dance moving to the music of souls, carrying them forward to the life of Christ.

The priest was facing us, just as St. Peter faced the first Christians, across a table, the altar of the Mass.

To me, there seemed no distance in time, between now and the Catacombs. Nothing separated me, a part of that movement, from its roots. The newest greenest shoot is a part of the tree. The sap runs through the centuries of years. Joe had opened me more to the blood of Christ. "He that eateth my flesh and drinketh my blood abideth in me; and I in him." so aware was I that night of myself in Communion with the vigour of the life of Christ.

The catacomb of the depth of my own soul was a part of the catacomb of the life of Christ, forever going down, forever surging upward and out, watering the land.

Paul asked me, "How was it?"

"Beautiful, quiet."

"Mary, once when I was alone, cycling on the continent, I went into a church to shelter from the rain. It was dim, just candles glowing—and people praying. There was I, a little schoolboy, drenched with the wind and the rain, coming into all this."

Noel had been sharing with me a book Ronnie had lent him, *The Catacombs* by Aldred Heidenreich. I wrote some notes, later made into a pamphlet, *Links with the Catacombs.* When Noel and Paul invited Alfred Heidenreich to the house and he came in to see me, I wanted to tell him how his book had caused me to really realize how today I was individually, and communally, aware, alive spiritually, just as people were in the time of the catacombs. But somehow, this did not seem possible.

Alfred Heidenreich asked me about myself: "Who looks after you?"

"Noel and Paul. Joe comes, to help me."

Because of his book I wanted somehow to meet him, inside, to convey to him "it's all here inside you, around you, life is not lost, it's still growing." As it was I felt such a gap that, although not myself doubting the truth, I could not transmit to him what his book showed that he, himself, was missing.

When I was speaking to Joe about the convent, he reminded me, "You go there, not to be 'looked after' but to suffer and grow."

Chapter Fourteen

Spring 1967—painting again—four times going

down

Noel and Paul were still bringing me food. Sometimes now they left food in my room for me to eat when I wanted. This was now possible. Previously, I had begged them, *"Please,* take it away. Please, *please,* don't leave it." Mother had never allowed us food in our bedroom.

"You are not ill, you must come to the table for it. You'll get into bad habits now, you'll never grow out of them."

Usually I still ate only fruit and milk with additions of soup and jelly. Paul made jelly with fruit in it. Noel and Paul gave soup in beautiful bowls that Frances had made. She was an art teacher who lived in the house, and Paul's girl-friend.

One night, when Paul brought soup, I was wanting to scream, being all twisted inside, disjointed and jarred, lying in a knot. Nothing would untie, and the string wouldn't break. It couldn't slip undone. Paul handed me the soup, standing like a poker, "I've got a bad back." Too much. I threw my bowl of soup at him, screaming.

"Bloody mental nurse."

Then I was all crumpled and crying. It was terrible, the shock of what had happened. Nothing was damaged, there was soup on the fire, on Paul, on the floor.

Paul helped the badness to ease and gave me more soup which I ate.

On February 9th, my birthday, I feasted so much, I was sick. Too many salted peanuts and raisins, I went on to chocolate, a big tin of fruit, ice-cream, chocolate biscuits, wine, whisky, a coconut, a big mixed bag of dried fruit, cream eclairs, oranges and peanut toffee—I just kept eating. At night I felt queer. Paul came, he wasn't cross, we both knew why I was so sick.

One night I put an apple in the front of the electric fire. Eating baked apple in the middle of the night was very nice. But then I got so bad about it, I told Noel. He was not angry and Paul brought me a saucepan to heat some soup in. My fire was a tiny one, an electric fire.

This was the start of the cooking. Saving the skins of my fruit, grapefruit, lemons, oranges, I made candied peel and marmalade.

Turning my fire up, on the stone floor, I made oatcakes. From this I got on to frying and stewing and steamed pudding.

When no one was about, I would scuttle into the kitchen and collect up all sorts of bits, for cooking. Seizing food from the fridge, I would pounce on the fruit, stuffing my dressing gown pockets, then scan the shelves and dart back into my room. Then thinking, maybe there won't be any of this or that tomorrow, I'd run back for some more, just to ensure my lamp "would have oil."

I got quite greedy, though I gave Noel and Paul some tastes. Wrapped up in all this cooking and eating there was Mary, becoming just a great big tummy.

One evening, when Noel took me to the kitchen, I saw Paul eating peanut butter on top of jam. Everything seemed bad, I was dead, in a cloud.

"Oh dear, whatever had I done, that Paul had to do that."

Later, when eating spoonfuls of jam with cold cauliflower, I suddenly thought, maybe Paul likes jam and peanut butter. That was nothing to do with me, what he was eating.

Feeling very raw, and exposed, I was much afraid of other people. Only Noel or Paul were "safe" to come into my room, except when a friend of Noel's came to stay, Dag, it was all right to see him. Also, Morty, a friend of Joe's, Dr. Morty Schatzman, came to see me, and I read him the story of The King and the Donkey.

Then Joe went away for a week to a conference, and I went "down" again. It seemed I shouldn't eat or drink, so I didn't. Dag, not Noel or Paul, came in to see me.

"No, Dag, I don't want to eat."

"Milk, water?"

"No."

During this week, although feeling weak, I was compelled to keep getting out of bed to scribble some notes in a pad I had in a drawer, with a pencil. Afterwards, when making books, I put some of these writings with my paintings, to make "Writings and Paintings for Ronnie and Paul, Mother Michael and Joe." I was writing of my soul. Of love, of heaven, of suffering and sanctity, of death and of God. Here are two of the writings.

The Presence of God

The truth can be revealed to me though all things. God is Truth and God abides in all His creation. God lives within all men. There is no place where God is not. He is manifest through every breath of air, through the dark of night and the light of day; in the depths of the sea He slumbers, and in the clouds of the sky is He revealed.

The world is clothed in the glory of God, and the earth shouts with gladness and is vibrant with His joy, and in awe, in the whispered hush of dawn, the world kneels, and adores, Him who *is* its breath and being.

Aflame with His Love, wrung with His sorrow, magnificent in His glory, the World abides, in Him, now and forever.

Death

The floodgates of my soul are open, and the water of my life, flows out, into the endless sea of light.

But as Joe says, just now I am not quite holy enough, too greedy with food, to quote more of these writings.

Early one morning, I slipped out to the Park, Victoria Park. (Except to go to the hospital with Joe, I had not been out for a year.) The may was out, some hung over a wall, I smelt it.

Hurrying on into the Park, I ran across the grass. It was wet with dew, and green with such a vividness, brilliant beyond all grass I had ever seen before. The sky was such an intense blue, and the brown of the bark of the trees and the white of the clouds was so strong, I felt never before had I seen colour.

The horse chestnuts were out.

The penetration of colour, of silver birches, of water, of red may, burst into my soul. Leaves, trees, green, green, water, sky, clouds, earth, brown earth, how good it smelt, the grass, the wet green grass.

I kept touching the grass, ran barefoot, touched the bark and the leaves. The growth was amazing, the life was so green.

Running home, I scurried up the stairs, shoes in hand.

Breathless in my room, I listened, not a sound. No one was up. Back into bed. My feet were blistered. My soul sang with the spring. During the spring I had this dream.

Two men were sitting on chairs at the other side, the opposite end, of a heavy bare wooden table, from me.

One was big and fat in a dark suit. The other was small and slight in a brown religious habit with a white knotted cord round his waist, which in speaking he rather lightly flicked in a carefree manner. He had dark hair, his head was bare. He said:

"God is within you."

I said, "Yes, I know, I came to know 'through' Joe."

Then I talked anxiously and excitedly of my experiences here and with relief was saying, "I know it's all right, well, now *you* have come, of course it will be all right."

They had come to stay here.

In the dream, I was definitely here, in Kingsley Hall, although the place did not appear as one of the rooms here. All was bare, the room in the dream, except for the heavy wooden table we sat at, I at one end, and they looking at me from the other end.

I thought the man in the religious habit a priest of an order, probably a Franciscan.

On waking, I felt quite certain it was St. John of the Cross, having been dwelling on his words, "All good things have come unto me, since I no longer sought them for myself," and, thinking of his writings, on the Dark Night, the time more of meditation when the soul is, itself, struggling towards God, and of the Ascent, the time more of contemplation, when God works in the soul, the soul giving itself over entirely to God.

At one time, it occurred to me that there was likeness between the writings of Ronnie and of St. John of the Cross.

I had a picture of St. John of God which I had thought of as St. John of the Cross. The dream caused me to look at the picture and read correctly underneath, St. John of God. It was his face, except that he had no moustache as in the picture, that I had seen in the dream, St. John of God, in the habit of a Franciscan.

Very early one morning, I ventured out into the Games Room.

It seemed strange, a foreign land. I crept about touching and looking, a deer in the forest, ready to flee at the slightest sound.

There were people in the house I had never seen, odd things about that I didn't know. The Games Room looked deserted, not used any more. It seemed a desolate land.

There was a piece of hardboard by a window—heavy—awkward to carry. But I got it to my room, and stood, listening, inside the door.

Everything was quiet, the board went under a mat, under the bed.

What was I doing? I wasn't painting, not now—"down" in bed.

The day passed. Dusk fell. I was going to paint, Peter before Christ, that's what I wanted to paint.

It didn't seem "wrong" to put on the light. There were tubes of paint. The board stood by my bed. Squeezing hard, I got the paint on my fingers, made the eyes of Peter, blue eyes. Then black hair, lots of black, and red of the love of Christ and yellow for the Light of God.

"Whom do you say that I am?"

"Thou art Christ, the Son of the Living God."

Christ above, illusive, looking down. In the response of Peter the future seemed sealed.

Blessed art thou Simon Bar Jona—Thou art Peter—Upon this rock.

Brown of the rock of Peter and green beyond for the growth to come.

The smell of the paint was in me. Excited, absorbed, two hours had been as two minutes. The feel of the paint on my fingers, touching the surface, my hand in the flow of the paint. The feel of a curve, of a line. I danced within as my fingers turned, in the paint, instinctively moving, up and down, in green and blue, red and brown.

The painting grew, it changed, it moved. It became complete.

I lay and looked, then secretly quiet, got back into bed.

The next day Joe saw it: "Dag, come and look, Mary's done a painting."

Noel and Paul came. They liked the painting, and they still liked me. I was more important than the painting.

This was the start of the finger painting "Peter Before Christ."

Getting out my picture scrolls of the Wallpaper Stories, I started to write the stories in words.

Joe gave me a book, *Where the Wild Things Are* by Maurice Sendak. It was glorious; animals with big teeth and trees and vines growing through walls.

I wanted to make my stories into books. Joe told me, "Do lots of pictures and just a few words on each page."

First I made, "Three Stories for Two Christophers," then "Ten Myths and Three Stories of Division," for Noel and his daughter, Natasha.

All day, every day, I finger painted and wrote on large sheets of paper. Sometimes I scooted out for more paint. Going on the tube and up an escalator seemed like being in fairyland, wonderful, and new.

Although I painted in bed and only dressed to go out for paint, I was, by now, in the house, going myself to the kitchen for food. This could be quite a dangerous venture. It was "safe" to go out at night, like a mouse, but at night there were "only the crumbs." Somehow, I had to make the trip when there was food, during the day.

If I moved quickly, when Noel or Paul told me, then there was some protection. Otherwise, I had to face the kitchen alone, in the light of day. To get "caught" in the kitchen seemed so perilous that I would peep out of my room, and bob back many times, perhaps waiting several hours, to catch a "safe" moment. Even so, sometimes when just about to flee back to my room, with food, I would get "caught." Someone would come in the door and I would have to pass them, to get out. Terrified, in a panic inside, I would try to look as if I wasn't there, and somehow slide out, back to the safety of my room.

It was so difficult to get my body near another person. There was no question of talking, except to Noel and Paul. Other people seemed so big and powerful.

In my room, Paul helped me, in the evenings, to pin up all my manuscript pages to dry. The King and the Donkey, God and the Flowers, The Hollow Tree, The Cross of Christ, and all the others were up on the walls. From floor to ceiling became covered in stories.

I learnt the names of new people living in the house, Francos Gillet, and Paul Gillet, who were brothers, Ian Spurling and David Bell. People I had known before helped me to feel I still "belonged" to the place. Bill Mason, an artist friend of Leon's encouraged me with my painting. It was good to see Sid at table. He is an anchor in any storm. Raymond came around. Connections with the past, that seemed to me years ago, and of a different world.

Sid had been to America with Ronnie. He brought me back a fan.

"Mary, when I was in Chinatown, I saw this, and I thought of you, so bought it—for you." It was very pretty, with a pink tassle.

This time as I was getting up, going out, I was different, changed, no longer completely the child. It seemed being more totally myself, although in fear of being with others, I was more secure, "at home" in myself. At least, outside in the road, I walked and paused, rather than run everywhere with tremendous physical energy.

In the hardware store, Mr. Sargent looked bewildered.

"Mary? You *are* Mary, aren't you?"

"Yes, Mr. Sargent, it's *me*, Mary." We laughed.

Previously Mr. Sargent had run across the road with sweets for me. He had felt my difference, the change of my growth. The way I bought a candy bar caused the sweet-shop man to look twice at me. I realized he must be thinking back to the days with Joe of long looking and choosing, usually to end up with a peanut ring.

Mr. Allen in the paint shop, the greengrocer man, the fish shop lady, the Co-op man, they were all the same. I had changed.

In June, Joe gave me another book, a sweet smelling Sandalwood Scroll book of Chinese painting.

From this, to me, came "The Sun Book." It is a long canvas made in two parts and stitched together in the middle. For very little children, it most specially is for Catherine, a Mongol child. Round, sun covers in sweet smelling wood, round pages, each one a sun, is how I see the sun book.

The words are very few. Over twelve pages they go like this:

THE SUN BOOK

1. For Catherine from Mary Barnes.
2. Today the sun is feeling shy and hides behind a cloud.
3. Now the cloud has moved away and the sun has come to stay.
4. *Let's Play, Let's Play*.
5. Now the sun is beating down and the flowers weep and wilt.
6. The Sun, He glares, the Sun, He stares.
7. Now he's in a haze of heat.
8. To shine so hot is very hard, the Sun feels quite apart, and goes inside to rest his heart.
9. Now he's really sleepy and the birds are going to bed.
10. Look the sun has spread his coverlet right across the sky.
11. I wonder why?
12. Goodbye.

In June Joe suggested I paint "Fire."

This painting I did naked in my room. Smearing the paint on the board, I then wiped my hands across my body, as if using a rag.

The painting was exhibited at the International Congress, "Dialectics of Liberation."

The fire I painted was the pillar of fire, God, going before the children of Israel. There was Moses with the bones of Joseph.

God is the fire that dwells within. If the wind is right the fire draws well.

In the fire are many colours, the different lights of God, springing from the well of birth, flowing into the sea of heaven.

The first time "going down" seemed mainly body.

IT, the anger, was coming into my body. My body got stuck with IT.

From bending myself up I was bent by others with my head drawn back. This got pain into my body. All my expression was through my body.

Back, down, to the baby, to the foetus in a womb. My head felt big. My body got weak, immobile, nothing coming in or out, I was down near my beginnings, as a seed in the earth before split into life.

Then there was the time of violent growth. Up and about spreading over the house, stretching myself, in new ways. When Joe understood, when others didn't. When I was what I was, I could be no other.

An impact from the past could throw my sight back. Hilary, my cousin, came to see me. I felt my growth, ahead of the past. When Anne came, a close friend of the past whom I had nursed, I felt again my surge forward, despite the vomiting up of the food she brought.

This time over Christmas '65 through the spring of '66 was a time of being up and out, of doing, of exploding, of running and screaming. The house was a minefield, every happening a bomb. Life was frantic, loud and aggressive.

June '66 down, in bed, going inside myself for the second time. A time of terror, of destruction.

"I am a killer!!" Too dangerous for anyone to be near.

How to keep still, to save myself from my own destruction.

The monster of Kingsley Hall. A very frightened Mary Barnes, in bed with her eyes shut.

Up a bit, as if to breathe. Writing and pastelling in the autumn of '66.

Then down again, the third time, less body now, more mind, understanding coming. Moving away out of the web, getting separate.

A more tender, fragile time.

How to hold it, my anger, in peace, to resolve.

Blowing up balloons with Joe, not floods of tears in a panic.

Lying alone, feeling my fear, feeling my love.

Finding myself, finding God.

My body and soul together. The meaning from within of much that I seemed often to have before only accepted from without.

Joe, lead me deep into myself.

At one point I imagined going down from my middle floor room to the ground floor, to be put, to lie still in what was then the meditation room. When first going down in '65 I had wanted to be put in the Box in the basement. Being "down" inside the house seemed the same as being down inside myself.

Freedom and submission of the will, the "loneness" of life, the use of penance and fasting in the attainment of wholeness.

In bed, not in a convent living the life of a nun, I yet came to understand it as never before.

Masturbation had left me. It gradually went. Aaron, Dr. Esterson, had always told me, have patience with yourself. Brother Simon of Blackfriars, Oxford, reminded me of a monk who, after going out and committing fornication, confessed not that, but despair. Joe had said, "All girls masturbate and what about the Desert Fathers? They masturbated, of course."

Joe also cautioned me, "You mustn't make excuses for yourself." In my mind, the Desert Fathers didn't masturbate, they were "spiritual men." What was I, then, a snail, the slime of the earth?

As Mother Michael had told me, Saint John of the Cross suffered greatly on account of sexual feelings. I had often appealed to him to help me. It seemed he, like Mother Michael, must have been of the opinion that if you risk nothing you gain nothing. I wanted to go the full stretch of the Cross. The masturbation business seemed a bit like smearing shits, some of the mud to be got through.

Geoffrey Moorhouse in his book *Against All Reason* mentioned that in a certain community the monks are advised to leave and get married if by the end of the novitiate they haven't stopped masturbating.

I feel it's just possible, so great was my state of self deception, so clever was I at deceiving others, that if God had not rescued me through mental breakdown I might have worn a habit, been a "nun" outwardly, without ever really encountering all my anger, jealousy, sexual feelings and guilt. All my sexuality would have been forever dammed up by the block of emotional drift, caught up in a whirlpool of frustration, bitter and strained.

Now free to reach forth, if not through the physical expression of love by pentration of the penis of a man, then through the giving and receiving of love that is yet, without its full physical element, warm and living and growing. Such love, in my previous state of division, within or without marriage, was not possible for me. Like my Mother, all love for me was ridden with guilt. To me now, all guilt feelings, the deadness that brings me to a standstill, is a terrible binding evil.

At the end of the Lord's Prayer, "deliver us from evil" means to me, "deliver us from the grip of guilt, from the deadness that stops all giving and receiving of love, the wall that divides from God, who is Love." What every priest and nun must encounter and suffer in the giving, the sacrifice, I feel I am really only just beginning to know. Joe reminds me, "everything for your wholeness is within you."

Coming up through this down time of purification, I continued more outwardly to meet myself, to contend with my own demons and to grow. I was rather like a silk worm, gobbling up leaves until I subsided again into my own cocoon.

This last, fourth time of going down was in the spring of '67. It was short and drastic, six days without food or water. I seemed all spirit. For a very intense week working by discipline as well as feeling, I wrote of my own depth, of my soul and its needs.

Coming more out and up, I yet seemed to remain, to contain, within, this time of going down. The spirit was willing but the flesh was still weak. Sickness with too much food, then beautiful writings. Then still a hard heart. My heart would physically feel like a bubble that has set hard and was wanting to be pricked. If I cried it didn't melt.

My life took on a certain structure. Painting, writing, reading the Mass of the day. My growth seemed more secure. I looked to the future as a time wherein I would grow strong enough to physically, outwardly do more, yet retaining the inner state of being I had come to know.

Joe reminded me, Ronnie says, "Life is therapy and therapy is life."

Moving free, I came to know the healing that is within all that happens.

In a particular way, Joe recreated, reformed me. I was able to let him, because I trusted him. This trust has been rewarded. Since the spring of '67, I have grown up. To an increasing extent I have become much more involved with people both at Kingsley Hall and in the outside world. Also I have had two successful exhibitions of my paintings.

Sometimes I have felt like going down again, but never so strongly as before.

"Shall I put the book over here?"

"No, no _no_, _please_ Paul."

"Where do you want it?"

"Please can it go _outside_ the room, with the people."

Part 4

With Mary at Kingsley Hall by Joseph Berke

Chapter Fifteen

Baby Mary

Kingsley Hall is a three-storey brown-brick building in the East End of London within sound of the bells of Bow Church. Before Mary Barnes and other members of the "anti-psychiatric" community moved there during 1965, Kingsley Hall had a long and honourable history as a centre for social experiment and radical political activity. Many of the social services which British people now take for granted were pioneered at the Hall. Many leading Socialists met their electorate there. At times of crisis, out of work East Enders could always get a meal at Kingsley Hall and often a place to bunk out as well.

In 1931 Gandhi chose Kingsley Hall as his official residence during a six month visit to London for the purpose of negotiating the independence of India with the British government. This gesture had the same impact on the working-class of London as Fidel Castro's staying at the Hotel Theresa in Harlem had on the coloured population of New York in 1967. Local residents still remember Gandhi, dressed in the traditional cotton garb of the Indian poor, walking about the neighbourhood.

Gandhi lived on a straw pallet in a small room, more like a cell, which had been grafted on to the roof of Kingsley Hall. His meals were provided by the milk of a goat. The goat shared the room with him. Top level members of the British government and diplomatic corps used to travel to meet Gandhi in this cell in the heart of working-class London at the break of dawn. He liked to rise early. Presumably it was easier for Gandhi to negotiate the fate of India at five or six o'clock in the morning than for the government ministers for whom dawn was a deathly hour and the East

End of London a foreign land. Unfortunately the great Indian leader did not get his way, but a round blue "Gandhi stayed here" plaque was placed high outside Kingsley Hall to commemorate the historic visit.

The building had been erected by two spinster sisters, Muriel and Doris Lester, about the turn of the century. I was told the Lesters used to pass through Bow in an open carriage while travelling to and from the city-centre of London. On these occasions they could hardly miss the extreme poverty of the working-class inhabitants of the area and they were appalled by it. Unlike most others who were equally appalled by the terrible condition of the poor people but did nothing to help them, Muriel and Doris decided to devote their considerable wealth and personal energies to serving the needs of this community. According to local legend, this decision was taken during one of their horse-drawn journeys through the East End.

For many years the Lesters lived at Kingsley Hall. They inaugurated and personally supervised a wide range of activities, from child care to adult education.

During World War Two practically the entire neighbourhood was destroyed by German bombs and rockets. Amid the devastation, Kingsley Hall stood fast, some bent window frames but a minor concession to the blitz. However, the Hall never did regain its pre-eminence as a settlement house. The neighbourhood had been radically affected by the war. Many people had died or moved away. Then too the Lesters were getting on in years and could no longer take an active hand in running the place. Most importantly the government itself had begun to implement many of the reforms which the Lesters had advocated and inaugurated.

When Dr. Laing and his friends first visited Kingsley Hall in mid-1964, it was being used as a student hostel and community activities centre, but was not flourishing. The Lesters (by then in their 80s and still active and alert) were looking for someone or some group to put the hall to a more vigorous and socially redeeming use. Ronnie did not exactly fall madly in love with the place, but the absence of other prospects and the possibility of being allowed to live at Kingsley Hall rent free for several years tipped the balance in its favour. So an agreement was made with the trustees and by mid-1965 people began to move in.

For an elderly East End building, Kingsley Hall was quite spacious. And it even possessed a few amenities such as central heating (which sometimes worked), a roof garden and bird bath. The ground floor was divided into a small entrance-way leading into a vast meeting room which in in days gone by doubled as a church hall (the Lesters were very Christian ladies). A cross and painting of a religious nature adorned the walls. One of the windows was stained glass. Gandhi was represented by a portrait. This room could comfortably hold a hundred people. In turn it led to a much smaller room which had seen service as a library, but which metamorphosed into a meditation room once the community got going.

However, if when entering Kingsley Hall you didn't pass into the main hall, you would find on your left a door which opened into a tiny chapel, or on your right, a door leading to the main stairwell. Half-way up this stairwell there was a complex of cloakroom, toilets and washroom. Eventually these chambers were utilized as a bedroom by several residents.

On the first floor there was a large recreation room chock full of such goodies as a billiard table, ping-pong table, piano (out of tune), comfy overstuffed chairs (never enough), a rug and a TV set. When the central heating didn't work this room was exceptionally cold because of its extensive windows. The windows overlooked a small balcony and across the street, a housing estate. Kids from the housing estate took great pleasure in breaking these windows, so the room often remained even colder than necessary.

Straight on from this recreation room was the dining-room, with its long table around which the community gathered for the evening meal, when the evening meal was made. An extension of the dining-room was used as a bedroom. From this dining area, there came a mini-hallway, flanked on either side by single bedrooms, and on the left by a double bedroom made pleasant by a working fireplace and unpleasant by the noise from the kitchen next to it.

This kitchen was the heart of the community, as well as the centre of sociability. A quick glance or sniff into the room would immediately put one in touch with the emotional pulse of the community. If the room was clean, or freshly painted, the milk bottles taken down, the garbage removed, and food stacked high in the larder, then things were going well. If empty milk bottles flowed like spilled milk in a corner, or the dustbin was overflowing, or the walls looked like a Jackson Pollock abstraction, but with egg yolk substituted for paint, and if the larder was bare, then matters weren't too good.

On the other side of the hallway, past a water closet, was the back passage of the building. Upstairs it opened out on to the roof and then on to three cell-like rooms. A plaque indicated which Gandhi had occupied.

Two of the three bathrooms in Kingsley Hall were also located on the roof. This Victorian remainder didn't make it too easy to have a bath in the winter. However, in summer, it was nice to take a bath, and dry off in the roof garden a few paces away. On a clear day (none too often) one could see (and smell) the gas works and miles and miles of housing estates.

Past the garden there was another cell and the entrance to a small four-roomed self-contained flat, as well as the main stairwell. The flat included the third and only indoor bathroom, a mini-kitchen, a meeting room, two single and one double bedroom.

During the five years Mary Barnes lived at Kingsley Hall she managed personally to occupy two of the rooms in the flat, one or two of the cells, three of the four first floor bedrooms, the meditation room, the chapel and also the basement which one could get to by going down the back passage. Other rooms tended to be occupied by her paintings. Mind you, it was unusual for her to actually live in more than one place at a time.

When I moved into Kingsley Hall in September 1965, Mary was ensconced in the bedroom opposite the kitchen. She lay naked, covered by a blanket in a twilight state (awake, asleep, in a dream, all at once) on a mattress. I was horrified to see how thin she was, almost like one of those half-alive cadavers the army liberated from Auschwitz after the war. I said hello, she opened her eyes, immediately recognized me, and whispered a greeting. That surprised me. I didn't think a person in her condition could be so lucid.

Later I learned that she had been eating very little since coming to Kingsley Hall, and for several weeks had refused almost all the food offered her, even the baby's bottle with warm milk which the Kingsley Hall residents had tried at her request. Mary wanted to go far down into herself, return to a period before she was born, when she was a foetus. And she wanted everyone at the hall to help her do so. She had the idea of being fed by stomach tube, with additional tubes in her bladder and rectum to remove liquid and solid excrement.

This situation had precipitated a monumental crisis of which Mary was generally unaware. Some residents insisted that she be sent to mental hospital as soon as possible. Others, including Ronnie and myself, thought that what she wanted to do was not unreasonable, that it would be interesting to see if someone could regress so far, and that it might be possible to tube-feed her.

For some days this matter was battered about while everyone tried to coax Mary to drink some milk, or at least some water. We were all afraid that she might die. Mary wasn't.

After one particularly long and heated discussion it was definitely decided that we couldn't do what Mary wanted. Although many of us were doctors, we had not come to Kingsley Hall to practise medicine. And in any case, we didn't have the facilities at Kingsley Hall to engage in the complicated and potentially dangerous procedure Mary desired. Furthermore we had to impress on Mary the need to take adequate nourishment, both for her sake and to alleviate our anxiety about her physical condition.

Ronnie took upon himself the task of conveying the situation to Mary in as direct and unconfusing manner as possible. He did not simply say: "Mary, we have decided that for your sake it would be best if you were not tube fed." Rather he told her that it was not within his capacity or mine or that of the others to tube feed her. However, this did not mean that the procedure might not be profitable for her. If she insisted upon it, we would try to find some hospital where she might be fed in such a way. But offhand, none of us knew any. In the meanwhile we did not want her to die from malnutrition. So, if she wished to remain at Kingsley Hall, she would have to start eating.

Faced with this ultimatum, Mary cried and argued against it with all the considerable skills still at her command. Why was she being punished, what had she done, why was Ronnie going against himself and so on. At the same time she considered what had been put to her. After she was convinced that we were not just trying to stop her from "going down," and that she was not being punished, she relented. That night I gave her a whole bottle of warm milk.

After my arrival at Kingsley Hall, I had begun to take an increasingly important part in caring for Mary. With the resolution of the "tube" crisis, I became the primary person responsible for maintaining Mary's life support system. However, I could not have done so without the aid and encouragement of other members of the community.* At one time or another everyone had a hand in keeping Mary fed and warm and clean. And on the frequent occasions when Mary seemed too impossible to cope with, the sympathetic words of those at the Hall kept me from chucking it all in.

I did find it rather disconcerting to feed, with a baby's bottle, someone who looked like a forty-year-old woman. Fortunately the bottle bit didn't last too long, for after Mary decided to eat again, she would drink her milk from a glass and save the bottle to suck on, much as a baby sucks on a rubber nipple. More to the point, Mary could make anyone who spent time with her believe that she had become a baby again, by the way she talked, moved, and acted. After a while you simply stopped thinking of her as Mary the adult, and started to see her as Mary the baby, or as a three-year-old,

---

*These included members of the Philadelphia Association, the Mental Health Charity of which Dr Laing is the director. In 1965 it included three psychiatrists; Aaron Esterson, David Cooper and Ronald Laing; a psychiatric nurse, Joan Cunnold, who had taken on the primary task of looking after Mary; a psychiatric social worker, Sidney Briskin; a businessman, Raymond Wilkenson, and the writer, Clancy Segal. Originally, all the members of the PA had intended to move into Kingsley Hall and start a community together, with assorted friends and colleagues. I had come to England to work as a Research Fellow in Psychotherapy and the Social Sciences with the Philadelphia Association.

or as a six-year-old, or teenager according to her wont. Yet throughout all, she never lost her intellectual faculties. She could suddenly switch from a baby or a little girl to a mature nursing sister who would argue quite rationally and convincingly about some issue affecting her stay or that of another at Kingsley Hall.

Some medical men might consider this behaviour to be a form of "hysteria." But this label is usually applied to a person who dissimulates roles or personalities, many of which arise from identification with external individuals. Mary was not like that. Whoever she was, she was herself, and she was very much "in" whoever she was. Moreover, Mary manifested an unusual temporal differentiation of self, which can be seen as an ability to exist temporarily on several different levels of the self at or about the same time. In other words, she was capable of simultaneous multiple regression. (Regression is a return to an earlier version of oneself.) However, there was always a primary level of self to which Mary had returned and from which she could move "up" or "down." Once I had formed a relationship with Mary, her primary self, say "baby" Mary, was easy to discern. And general movements up or down, that is, towards adulthood or towards babyhood, were also pretty clear. But it was hard to follow sudden shifts of position based on an internal incident, like a memory or dream, or an external event of which I might not be aware. Mary often responded to my confusion by bashing me one. At least then I knew where we were at.

On such occasions and many other times as well I have confronted myself with the question: "Why the hell did you ever get involved with a woman like Mary?"

The answers vary with my mood and retrospective awareness of events at Kingsley Hall. When I was living there, I might have replied to such a query: "Because I'm a damn masochist." Nowadays, I would say that it had a lot to do with Mary's embodiment of the thesis that psychosis is potentially enriching experience if it is allowed to proceed full cycle, through disintegration and reintegration, or death and rebirth, as Ronnie was fond of calling it. Mary had elected herself to the position of head guinea pig, although the nature of the experiment had been determined *by her*. That Mary had her "trip" all worked out years before she had ever heard of Laing or Berke or the rest of us tends to mitigate the criticism that she was simply acting out our fantasies for us. Anyway, Mary is too strong-willed (pigheaded) to do what anyone else would want her to do for their sake, and not her own.

For myself, Mary was the right person at the right place at the right time. As soon as I got to Kingsley Hall, I realized that the best way to learn about psychosis would be for me to help Mary "do her things." And so I did. Secondary benefits were that I got to meet an unusually charming woman, that I was catapulted straight into the middle of Kingsley Hall politics without having to spend time on the sidelines, and that by identifying with Mary and vicariously participating in her experience, I allowed myself to approach and come to grips with my own tumultuous emotional life, which is in some ways similar, and in other ways quite different from that of Mary.

Getting to know Mary was simple. I imagined where she was at and then met her on that level.

Our first encounter consisted of my growling at her and she growling back at me. Mary loved this and would shake with fright and laughter. She thought I was a bear who was going to eat her up. Sometimes before giving her some milk, I would growl menacingly and then bite her on the arm or shoulder. She would scream, bite me back, then scream again. As she got stronger she would race around the room after me on all fours and I after her. Other times we would pretend we were fish and reptiles hunting for prey. Sharks and alligators were great favourites and we would snap and bite at each other just like the real thing.

Another game was for her to grab ahold of me and squeeze me around the middle as hard as possible. I would say, "Is that all?" and she would squeeze harder and harder and I would say "Is that all?" and she would drop back to bed exhausted. Fortunately Mary is much smaller than me so that her squeeze didn't hurt too much, although sometimes she would catch me off guard and knock the breath out of me.

The biting and squeezing played an important part in the early stages of the relationship between Mary and me. Because she found that I was not engulfed, incorporated, digested, poisoned, mangled or otherwise injured, no matter how hard she bit or squeezed me, she allowed herself to relax with me, and worry a bit less about the deadly effects of her greediness. Similarly, when Mary realized that my greediness, and/or her own greediness which she attributed to me (projected) would not destroy her, she began to trust me. Since the destructive effects of her greed (real or imagined) terrified her, it was not a matter that could be worked out calmly over tea. It had to be demonstrated in the flesh.

But I never had to stop and think, "Well, I'm going to visit Mary now. What shall I do today? Maybe some growling. Let me see." I never knew what would happen. I just let it happen. It was something that came naturally once I allowed myself to meet Mary on her terms. The resultant transactions often took place at a psychotic level, and if that was the way of the day, fine.

The reason why most psychiatrists are unable to communicate with people who have entered the deeper levels of regression is that they do not utilize their own enormous reservoirs of primitive emotion to make contact with such individuals. They try to force the other to speak in rational modalities long after he or she has decided to declaim in an "irrational" tongue. And by "irrational" I do not mean "unintelligible." I am referring to the language of the infant, the melodies of primary feeling, which are, in themselves, quite comprehensible.

By the same token, it is unnecessary, if not positively confusing, to employ primitive mannerisms in a relationship with someone who is willing and able to speak as an adult. Whenever Mary chose to talk in a calm and straightforward way about what she was feeling, or any other matter, I was glad to respond accordingly. In fact I encouraged her to try to formulate in words whatever it was she was trying to communicate by other means. The problem was that Mary was often too frightened or guilty to let herself become aware of her most fundamental feelings and desires. She hid these experiences from herself, and did likewise with me or the others at Kingsley Hall.

Mary took the first step in allowing me to help her, by helping me to figure out what was going on beneath her tumultuous exterior. It was less terrifying for Mary to work through me because she did not have to take immediate responsibility for the net increase in understanding. Secondly, she dimly perceived that I was not imprisoned by the same fears and guilts as herself. So, I could permit myself to see what she could not. By identification with me Mary started herself on the rebirth road.

Only later did Mary dare to open up a direct link between her emotions and her perceptions of them. The initial process of her coming together was akin to my trying to put together a jigsaw puzzle without having all the pieces. Of those pieces which were about, many had had their tabs cut off and their slots barricaded. So it was nigh on impossible to tell what went where.

This puzzle, of course, was Mary's emotional life. The pieces were her thoughts, her actions, her associations, her dreams, etc.

Every once in a while Mary would begrudgingly bestow on me an undamaged piece of the puzzle. And then, as if beset by a paroxysm of fear or guilt, she might try to take it back by denying what she had said or done, or by putting me off the track with other beguiling, but irrelevant, thoughts or actions.

The first round of this titanic struggle between the forces of light and dark was fought over the issue of food.

At Kingsley Hall Mary's eating habits expressed a curiously ambivalent attitude towards food. Some days she would stuff herself with all the sweets she could get hold of. On other days she would refuse to eat at all. In her "down" periods milk was the only nourishment she allowed herself, yet she was quite capable of rejecting milk as well, and her refusal to drink milk always precipitated community crises of monster proportions.

Superficially there was no problem. Didn't Mary go about painting breasts all over the walls? Wasn't the message clear? She wanted a breast, she wanted many breasts, she wanted to be fed. Then why didn't she take the food that was offered her?

Ah yes, but the breasts she scrawled, dabbed, smeared, and splattered through Kingsley Hall were not ordinary breasts. They were black and were made of shit, so smelly that people gasped upon entering a room. Later, when such productions were forbidden, the breasts were made with black paint. These breasts so omnipresently hung about her home were not good and nourishing, they were bad and poisonous. They rode the walls like storm-tossed waves across a demonic sea. They proclaimed the orgy of hate and destruction which lay lightly concealed beneath the pale skin of baby Mary.

However, it took some time before I realized that baby Mary was not only concerned about getting the good, but was also preoccupied with evacuating the bad. During the early stages of our relationship I was tempted to exclaim, "Mary, you want the breast, you want my breast, you want me to take care of you just like a baby at the breast, you want me to love you, let me take care of you, let me feed you, let me give you nice warm loving milk." But it became obvious that it wasn't words that mattered so much as deeds, and even when deeds and words coincided and were seemingly accepted by her, the ensuing state of relaxation could revert to one of agony for the barest of reasons. All I had to do was turn my head, or look inattentive, or blink an eye while feeding her, and Mary began to pinch her skin, twist her hair, contort her face, and moan and groan. Worse shrieks followed if I had to leave the room and get involved in another matter at about the time she was due for a feed. Suffice to say that if my acts and/or interpretations had been sufficient, such agonies would have been averted.

So I said to myself, "Berke, you had better stop trying to tell Mary what you think she is wanting, and pay more attention to that with which she is struggling." What came through was Mary's despair and anger.

One day, after Mary had vehemently refused lunch, I spoke with her about these feelings. She acknowledged the despair, especially when she felt bad and all twisted up inside herself. She completely denied any anger.

"No, Joe. I'm not angry. Why do you try to confuse me?"

I stood my ground. "Mary, the way you scream and carry on sure seems like anger to me. If you aren't angry, why do you hit me and refuse to eat the food I bring you if I am a minute late, or get called out for a phone call?"

"No, Joe. I would never go against you." And so on.

It then occurred to me that the act of eating was of less immediate importance to Mary than the occasion of anger. She certainly rejected all offers of food when she got in a rage. Yet, Mary seemed unable to make the link between the most overt expressions of anger and her experience of it. And since Mary didn't feel angry when she was angry, it was almost impossible for her to understand the reasons behind this anger.

Of course, Mary had refused to admit she wanted my breast or anything else. She felt so deprived that her frustration had sparked off volcanic attacks on the world. But since she wouldn't recognize Mary Barnes, the volcano, she couldn't see that her overwhelming sense of deprivation had anything to do with the shit she spewed forth on me and others at Kingsley Hall. Hence my attempts to convey to her what I felt she wanted fell on deaf ears. One piece of the puzzle had come into place.

Breasts aside, I suspected that other sources of real or imagined deprivation were stoking Mary's fury. And my suspicions were later to be proved correct. But it was very difficult to get at them without having Mary relate her thoughts or expectations at the moment she felt angry. Therefore, a priority in the first months of our relationship was for me to help Mary to become aware of her anger.

My Mary strategy revolved around the twofold process of attending to her physical needs while pointing out her anger to her as soon as it manifested itself. This was a taxing task. Mary avoided awareness of anger as a vampire does a crucifix. Even when she broke some crockery, or bashed a doll, or overturned furniture or spoke of suicide and murder, she never connected these actions or words with the feelings that occupied the innermost recesses of her soul.

Another difficulty was that Mary continually attributed to me anger which was clearly hers, yet she lived in mortal fear of my getting irritated or angry with her. Concurrently she was an expert in the art of provoking me and other members of the community with a host of controlling, domineering and bitchy mannerisms. As a result, a lot of my time with her was spent in differentiating my anger from hers and vice versa.

Tremendous guilt, anxiety and panic took hold as Mary

began to appreciate the nature of her explosive emotions, and then the intentions that lay behind them. This was a gradual process. First she recognized rage when it was directed towards strangers, secondly towards people at Kingsley Hall with whom she was not closely involved, and lastly towards Ronnie, me and her parents. Several years passed before Mary could look straight into my eyes and exclaim, "Joe, I'm angry with you." Many of the ensuing events which both Mary and I describe relate how this came about.

Chapter Sixteen

Naughty Mary

After Mary moved into Kingsley Hall, she had the idea that it would be good for her and her family if her mother and father and brother and sisters all joined her there. To Mary, this was an obvious step in the evolution of her "treatment." To others, Mary's scheme was seen as another attempt to overwhelm the community with remnants of herself. Since Mr. and Mrs. Barnes lived in South Africa, and no one had broached the matter with them, the question was academic. From what Mary told me about her parents, Kingsley Hall was the last place they would have wanted to live. But the issue was an interesting one. Many of us were engaged in the study of family structure, and we were in contact with psychiatrists such as the American, Ross Speck, who emphasize the importance of getting together all the members of a family, no matter how distant or how many, in order to work out problems which seem to surface in just one of two individuals. So I was quite pleased when I read the letter from Mr. and Mrs. Barnes informing Mary that they were coming to England on a holiday and looked forward to visiting her.

At first Mary was also pleased, but as the time came near she became increasingly apprehensive about seeing them again. It was a difficult time for her; she was just beginning to "come up" after a prolonged period in bed. Fortunately, the impending reunion stimulated her to get up and about. Everyone tried to help her as best they could. Joan brought her some marvellous clothes. What a grand occasion it was when Mary, all dressed and perfumed and manicured, walked into the games room. We were thrilled, especially because we had been worried that her parents would come, see her in the emaciated, weak condition of the previous months, and then get all upset. Mary was still weak, but she was beginning to look like a *mensch* again.

On the appointed day Mr. and Mrs. Barnes arrived spot on time. After greeting them, I went and told Mary they had arrived. Mary paled, turned cold and started to shake. She refused to see them. She was too frightened. What she didn't realize was that her fear was not so much of her parents, as of her anger towards them, of her wish to destroy them.

Mary remembers, "I'm fainting, falling to pieces." This refers to how she experienced her anger. It was so intense, yet so repressed, held in, that it threatened to explode and blow her apart. We see this metaphor of her body—exploding—repeated time after time.

Similarly her anger threatened to explode on to other people, in this case her parents. She says, "I fear my parents coming in on me." The anger is transformed. Instead of exploding from within outward, it is put on to her parents and perceived as coming from without inwards.

In the circumstances of the reunion her Mother gave an interesting retort. She didn't say, "Mary, I'm angry with you because I have travelled thousands of miles to see you and you won't see me." No mention of annoyance crossed her lips. Instead she said, "Oh I do feel ill." This reply immediately induced intense guilt in Mary, ostensibly for not being hospitable, but actually for showing hostility towards her parents. It is a manoeuvre which is typically seen in families of "schizophrenics."

Later in the week Mary was sufficiently composed to meet her father with me. A tape recorder provided an auxiliary memory.

For the most part the conversation was quite civil. Mr. Barnes was politely inquisitive about Mary's health. Mary was politely inquisitive about the state of the family, which was dispersed about South Africa, Australia, and England. Matters heated up a bit when Mary took on the issue of Kingsley Hall, and her father the issue of Mary's "illness." Mr. Barnes seemed quite unable to understand Mary's point of view. He replied to Mary's comments about herself and her brother by changing the subject of the conversation, sometimes slightly, sometimes completely. Mary got very

angry when the issue of her brother Peter was raised. Con
sequently, after Mr. Barnes had left, I got bitten and bashed
another indirect expression of the feelings fermenting in
side Mary.

After listening to the tape, Mary was proud that she "had
resisted my Father's attempts to control me." Her resistance
consisted of refusing to accept her father's definition of her
condition, of the circumstances of her life, and of that of
Peter as well. To be sure, Mr. Barnes did likewise.

Fortified with the knowledge that she could survive meeting her father, Mary began to look forward to seeing both
her parents. This meeting had much the same façade as the
previous one with Mr. Barnes alone. People talked at each
other rather than to each other. Mary tried to convince her
parents that she was much better off in Kingsley Hall than
in a hospital, and her folks went on about the marvellous
facilities, like TV, at the hospital where Peter was staying.
At moments like these, Mary would dig her fingers into my
leg in lieu of bashing Mr. or Mrs. Barnes. I tried to sit non-
chalantly while wincing with pain from Mary's digs. Within
the limits of their capacity to appreciate a radically different
viewpoint and life style, the Barneses were warm and sympathetic to what we were doing at Kingsley Hall, rather
more than Mary gave them credit for, and rather less than
would have permitted mutually satisfying communication between them and their daughter. A glossy veneer of good
intentions covered the inter-generational power struggle
which had then lasted close to four and a half decades.

In the ensuing weeks Mary was a joy to behold. Every
day brought new problems but also new progress as she
started to spend more time out of her room and about the
house. She would dart from room to room like a scared
rabbit, frightened that the others would "come in on her."
The issue was anger, always anger, and most always experienced as coming from without, rather than from within.
Coupled with the fact that Mary thought she controlled
everything that happened in Kingsley Hall, especially everything that I did, difficult moments presented themselves and,
in turn, were slowly resolved.

What I found hardest to take was Mary's insistence on
being with me every moment of the day. By necessity I be-

came an expert in Mary-dodging as I did my chores about Kingsley Hall, cooking or cleaning when I was on the roster for such, or shopping, or dealing with the million and one unusual, often amusing, events which pulsated through the life of the community. Towards me, Mary behaved like a little puppy dog, always wanting to play; and when I wasn't immediately about she was sad and lost, sitting in front of the door to my room, whining and crying the world down.

I remember the day I told Mary I was going out for the afternoon to participate in a poetry reading at Trafalgar Square in protest against the war in Vietnam. Mary mutated from a warm cuddly puppy dog to a cold hard stone very quickly. She felt, "A bomb had fallen. I'm shattered. Everything has gone." Here we have a bird's eye view of the transformation of Mary's anger. First she heard that I was going out for the day. This news hit her like a bombshell. The immediate response was rage, experienced as a bursting bomb inside herself, and projected into the external world, into my words, so that the rage was seen as coming from without. In consequence Mary felt torn apart, shattered by a tremendous "external" force. But not only her—me also, because she identified very closely with me, in fact, did not feel separate from me. So the disaster was compounded; not only Mary, but Joe too, was threatened with destruction.

Who's away? Mary's away. Joe's away. Everyone is dead.

Turning into stone was a last desperate measure to deal with the imminent collapse of Mary's world. She tried to prevent the bomb from bursting by making the shell casing so strong that it could never explode. This casing was her body. Hard bodies, stones, lie immobile, can't hurt anyone.

Mary confused the cause of her anger, my going out, with the result of her anger or rage. Mary confused the agency of the rage, herself, with the object of it, me. No wonder she felt tied up in knots.

That it was anger we are discussing is further confirmed by the fact that in the evening, when Raymond came to take her to dinner (instead of me as was usual), Mary screamed and hit him.

In the morning we played "peek a boo" and "hungry bear" and "dangerous shark." Mary squeezed me as hard as

she could (which was quite hard, I assure you) and I, i
turn, squeezed her. This put her shattered body all bacl
together again, and, from her point of view, mine as well
Similar incidents occurred over and over while Mary grad
ually learned that when I went out, I did not leave her for
ever, and that before I came back, her rage had not blow
me apart.

This rage was so earth shattering, so people-destroyin
that Mary could not refer to it by name. "Anger" was a
quasi-magical word for her. To pronounce this word wa
tantamount to conjuring up a cataclysm. Eventually Mary
did allow herself to take heed of her explosive inner feel
ings, which she nervously referred to as "it", then "It,"
and lastly, after she was pretty confident that I would no
be harmed by the word, "IT."

"IT" was an atomic bomb. "IT" threatened to burst ou
of her. "IT" turned her to stone. "IT" was the shit she
found so hard to get rid of in times of stress.

"IT" came in on/over on Mary whenever she felt she
was being punished. This was quite often. On these fre
quent occasions Mary experienced an all-pervasive badness
This badness was so awful, so terrible, so twisted up in he
guts, that Mary would easily have killed herself, or others
in order to alleviate it.

The sense of being bad was intimately related to an
omnipresent, almost overwhelming guilt, that she carried
within herself at all times. In other words, Mary was always
full of guilt, but sometimes she felt more guilty than others
Consequently she was never sure that whatever she did was
not bad, and she was always avoiding doing anything which
might possibly be considered bad, such as taking an orange
from the larder. Mary had a super superego.

Worse yet, she continually attributed events which hap
pened around her to her 'badness," because she equated in
ner and outer, and me with her. The latter was a deliberate
attempt to cope with her "badness" by incorporating a big
hunk of "goodness", i.e. me. With "Joe" inside her, she felt
she had a better chance to win the struggle between good
and bad.

Sometimes this strategy backfired. For example, when Mary
started to take her evening meal with the rest of the com-

munity, she noticed that I liked to put a lot of salt on my food. This horrified her. She immediately stopped eating, or even moving except for a slight whimper. Since she didn't like salt, she thought I didn't either, and was only using it to punish myself. Since, in her mind, Joe being punished was equivalent to Mary being punished, she must have done something very bad. Why else would she/Joe be punished? Therefore Mary felt very guilty and upset.

Furthermore, Mary noticed that when I ate, I ate noisily, with gusto. According to the way Mary had been brought up, such a practice was strictly forbidden. Since, to her, we were inseparable, she felt guilty and liable to punishment because of the way I ate. This guilt was compounded by the "fact" of my suffering (eating salt) on her account.

In this situation, the various guilts and punishments which accrued to Mary were cumulative. Her conscience wouldn't let her off the hook by figuring, "Ah well, noisy eating is a crime, but eating salt is a punishment, so I'll let one cancel out the other." The problem was even more dicey because Mary often felt guilty about telling me why she was feeling guilty, so she couldn't comment on why she was upset.

Mary's "inner"—"outer" confusions led to a slew of self-recrimination when things went wrong around Kingsley Hall (my buying a heater for the bathroom which then didn't work) or didn't match up to Mary's expectations (fish for dinner instead of duck). It took some mighty hard talking on my part to convince Mary that someone's change in plans or a blown fuse were not calamities which she had personally instigated. (In many cases, I think she would have, if she could have.)

The experience of punishment was always accompanied by anger, which generated great guilt (for the real/imagined destruction wrought by the anger on whomever or whatever Mary saw to be the agency of the punishment) and, in turn, the experience of more severe punishment (for "going against" the original punishment). This vicious spiral of punishment-anger-guilt-punishment took months to figure out, and years before Mary could break out of it. In the meanwhile Mary kept complaining that her "badness" kept causing her "to get stuck," and most terrible, "to go dead." Getting stuck meant that she could get caught at any spoke of the spiral. She didn't have to start off at the level of punishment. Just to respond in any angry manner to someone or something would immediately involve her with guilt, then punishment, then further anger, etc. This spiral served as an emotional amplifier of all the feelings with which Mary found it most hard to cope. No wonder she spent so much effort denying that she ever felt angry or guilty. To do so was her way of trying to "unstick herself," to avoid climbing on to this ever escalating spiral of "badness." In extremis this meant that she had "to go dead."

Mind you, there were many occasions when Mary really did misbehave. Mary, the pest, would rear her ugly head and intrude upon my relations with friends or visitors at Kingsley Hall, or prevent me from going out, especially to the Langham Clinic in the centre of town, where I worked as a psychotherapist several days a week. Then Mary was not just naughty or "bad," but very very bad.

Usually I kept my cool. Infrequently I would respond to Mary's provocations by screaming at her to go away. This kept the pest at bay.

Twice I completely lost my temper and bashed her. I remember one of these incidents very well. That was when Mary tried to prevent me from going out to the Clinic. The other remains a hazy blur. That is when Mary tried to prevent me from going to talk with Leon Redler, an American psychiatrist and old friend of mine who had recently moved into Kingsley Hall. My memory seems to have combined these two incidents into one; I am sure this is because I still feel guilty about hitting Mary, and reluctant to publicly reveal this example of my own violence.

After reading Mary's account of my blow-ups, I thought she had made a mistake and divided one drama into two. But I checked with Leon and he confirms the essential features of Mary's version. Nevertheless, I shall report what happened as I remember it. Readers can make their own comparisons.

Even when she was lying in bed all day, even when I had seen her for hours, Mary had the uncanny ability to figure out, almost to the exact moment, when I planned to go out or meet someone at the Hall, and then make a huge fuss about it. Looking back, I suspect that I used to let her know about my plans in advance via subtle changes in my tone of voice or body movement, of which I was not aware, but to which she responded.

In the days after Mary began to realize that my going out did not represent a total abandonment of her, but before she perceived the existence of her intense jealousies, I often found myself in the position of having to sneak out of Kingsley Hall the back way in order to avoid her. Later on, it generally sufficed to tell Mary a few hours ahead of time that I would be meeting someone and didn't want to be disturbed, or that I would be away for a while, for me to be able to be alone or leave the place without too much bother. Still Mary could and did revert back to her obnoxious and most trying ways without warning. Such was the case on the afternoon I exploded at her.

It had been a difficult day. The coke hadn't come for the boiler. The shopping had taken longer than expected. And I had to hurry Mary's lunch in order to get out in time for a clinic appointment.

Everything had seemed OK when I said "goodbye" to Mary. She didn't seem upset, but a few minutes later, just as I was starting to walk down the front stairs, I heard her tearing after me in nothing but her nightdress, pleading with me not to go out, crying and tugging on my coat.

In no uncertain words I told her to go back to bed and that I would see her when I got back. Still she screamed and screamed. I continued to walk downstairs, Mary holding on with all her might. Half-way down, I stopped and tried to reason with her. This seemed to help matters a bit and I thought she would go back to bed. Then I realized that it was getting very late and I made the mistake of proceeding down the stairs without taking the time to stick her in bed.

Mary tore after me, leapt in front of me just as we got to the door, and in what almost seemed a cold calculated manner, screamed that if I didn't remain with her, she would take off all her clothes, go into the middle of the street, and yell that she wanted to be taken to a mental hospital.

That did it. Without a moment's hesitation, I stood back, made a fist, and hauled off at Mary as hard as I could. The connection felt great, as all my anger, not only from her screaming on the stairs, but all the anger accumulated and held in over dozens of similar incidents, was released, all at once. Then I noticed that blood was pouring out of Mary' nose and all over her face and gown. I was horrified, and thought, "What way is this for a doctor to treat his patient?"

This first reaction on my part is an extremely interesting one, because I tried hard to avoid the role of doctor at Kingsley Hall. I, like the others, endeavoured to embody the proposition that once we entered the doors of the place we functioned simply as equal members of a community True, in other circumstances or at other times, any one of us might have been or might still be patient or doctor, but at Kingsley Hall we were just people.

Fair enough. And as far as the formal social relationships of the place were concerned, there were no doctors, so there could not be any patients. Doctor-patient describes a strictly defined social situation which did not characterize what took place at the Hall. None of those who outside Kingsley Hall were practising psychiatrists ever "treated" any other member of the community at Kingsley Hall. Those few individuals who were in psychotherapy with Laing or one of the other therapists had their sessions elsewhere.

However, those who had been trained as doctors found it difficult not to relate to others as doctors. Similarly those who had been trained as patients found it difficult not to relate to others as patients. In this regard, Mary was the chief offender. She interpreted everything that was done for her (or for anyone else for that matter) as therapy. If someone brought her a glass of water when she was thirsty, this was therapy. If the coal was not delivered when ordered, that was therapy. And so on, to the most absurd conclusions.

To be sure, I had many conflicts on the issue of doctor-patient delineation too, but I didn't like to admit them to myself. I remember how surprised and annoyed I was when, not long after I had arrived at Kingsley Hall, one of the residents, a young girl also named Mary, acidly complained that I "came on to her" like a doctor. Years of medical training, not just on how to write a prescription, but on how to behave in the presence of whomever one was writing the prescription for, had had their prescribed effect. At least five months passed before I was able to engage in the usual social transactions at Kingsley Hall without automatically paring off so and so into "that nut" or "that social worker," etc. It took even longer before the others confirmed my impression that I had shed my doctor mask and no longer behaved like one.

Clinging to medical mannerisms was an expression of intense anxiety about being perceived as a "nut" or "schizophrenic" by other members of the community or visitors. All the other psychiatrist/residents of the community had the same problem. As for Mary, her clinging to the idea of patient expressed the anxiety that people might not otherwise take care of her.

I think that anxiety about being confused with "the mentally ill" is why the staff at most mental hospitals rigidly conform to a strict standard of dress and demeanour, and resist attempts to de-institutionalize their relationships with patients. It was terribly amusing when such personnel used to visit Kingsley Hall.

As soon as they noticed that most of the residents dressed and talked alike, one could smell their anxiety reaching record heights as they struggled to divide us up into staff and patients. Nine times out of ten their observations about who was who were dead wrong. I can't count how many times Mary was seen as the chief nursing sister, or one of the "psychiatrists" was seen as a "schizophrenic" and spoken to as such. Great waves of embarrassment always broke across the face of a visitor after he learned that the "poor crazy" he had chatted up was Dr. Laing or Dr. Berke or Dr. Redler.

No doubt these same visitors would have been as surprised to see me take a swipe at Mary as I was when I realized what I had done. My mental doubletake about being a doctor was an expression both of anxiety at seeing her bleed, and of guilt about transgressing a role which I had not consciously been playing, but with which, unconsciously, I was obviously still involved.

Within seconds after being hit, Mary bounded upstairs, blood pouring all over, yelling, "Look what Joe's done, look what Joe's done!" Full of shame I bounded after her trying to get her to shut up, then stop the bleeding, then change her clothes. It must have been a funny scene to watch for

I also was trying to wipe the blood off the stairs and bannister at the same time as I was running after her.

Mary, God bless her devilish soul, managed to elude me and ran up on to the roof, still exclaiming, "Look what Joe's done!"

Here is the point where my memory starts to fade and I possibly combine two incidents into one. I recall her passing by Leon's door, Leon coming out, Mary hurling herself into his arms, Leon taking her into his room, I following, and then getting very angry with Leon when he didn't agree that Mary should immediately change her clothes (the bleeding had stopped). I stormed out of the room in disgust and fury, not least because Mary had succeeded in preventing me from keeping my appointment.

By dinner time everyone in Kingsley Hall had heard about, if not seen, my gory handiwork. I anticipated terrible criticism. None came. People had long since cottoned on to what Mary was like close up.

As for Mary, she was very proud of her bloodstained blouse and kept it on display, much to my continuing annoyance. The next day she told me how grateful she was that I had hit her, that the tear tinged blood had brought great relief to her, and that she loved me more than ever.

That was good to know.

Chapter Seventeen

Mary paints and shits

Mary smeared shit with the skill of a Zen calligrapher. She liberated more energies in one of her many natural, spontaneous and unself-conscious strokes than most artists express in a lifetime of work. I marvelled at the elegance and eloquence of her imagery, while others saw only her smells.

Was painting the royal road to Mary's unconscious? Could it provide a means for her to reveal the mysteries of her inner world? I was determined to find out. While waiting till Mary was sufficiently together before suggesting she try crayons and white paper, besides her body products and the living-room walls, I remembered the words of John Thompson, "Be aware of the ways by which men will reveal themselves!" John had illustrated this advice with an account of how he had managed to communicate with a young man, who had spent many years of his life as a "catatonic schizophrenic" in the back ward of a New York State medical hospital.

Dr. Thompson had been asked to see this person by his parents after all other treatments had failed. In preparation for his consultation two nurses had carried the patient from his bed and plunked him on the floor of a vacant room. There he remained, head buried in his chest, arms and legs rigidly fixed in space, when John entered the room. The man did not move or talk, and had not done so for several months. John sat next to him, silently, for an hour, and then left.

The next meeting and the one after were conducted in exactly the same way. On the fourth go round John became aware that the man was aware of him. He said so. The man immediately made some violent jerking motions with his body, picked up his right arm, as if to strike John, and rhythmically waved the arm over his head as he exclaimed, "Don't give me that shit, don't give me that shit." Then he fell back into a catatonic stupor.

John said that he came away from that meeting convinced that the person was trying to communicate with him but didn't know how. The movements of his arm had been vigorous and outgoing, but also shy and restrictive.

At the next meeting the same drama was repeated, but on this occasion it occurred to John that the movements of the man's arm were akin to that of a painter. So he took his pen and put it in the man's right hand, and took some paper and placed it on the floor between them, and waited to see what would happen.

John didn't have to wait long. The man grasped hold of the pen tightly and, in a few minutes, fashioned a technically proficient, Giacometti-like, drawing of a thin, tortured individual.

John placed another sheet of paper on the floor. Quick as a wink, another drawing appeared, to be repeated several dozen times in the course of the afternoon; yet nary a word passed between them.

During the next few years, John met with this person regularly. Each time the man would draw or paint (he progressed from pen and ink, to charcoals, to coloured charcoals, to oil colours), and John would comment on the theme or style of the communication. The man had found his mode of expression. Later he became a well known painter.

Before I left New York John showed me the large collection of drawings and paintings which this individual had given him and which recorded the progress of a man from catatonic to communicant to artist. I thought of this person's first drawing on the bright November day when I gave Mary white paper and an old tin can full of crayons and suggested that she might like to use them. She did. The result was an outpouring of scribbles, then drawings, and then, with the help of some old paint she found in a closet, wall paintings.

Mary's first efforts were like primitive cave paintings—light, mobile outlines of archetypal figures—Madonna and

Child, Jesus and Mary, and babies inside babies inside babies inside mother. They adorned the walls of her rooftop cell and then white strips of wallpaper hung from ceiling to floor. Always curves and circles and whirls and bold splashes intermingling freely and joyfully. Dozens, hundreds of paintings overflowed her room and were hung wherever a wall allowed, throughout the Hall. People were startled, then suffused with the joy which Mary radiated whenever she was working. Every day she discovered new ways to present the same figures in ever more sophisticated and intricate poses, always retaining the delightful innocence of her first splashes of paint. Then came the colour, all sorts of colours, reds and greens and blues and violets, an outburst of brilliant hues which made the paintings glow so intensely they seemed to leap out at you and draw you right into the centre of them.

Within a short time after Mary had released a cascade of lithe coloured figures and flowers, she began a series of delightful stories which, in her own words, were about, "the persistence of life, of death and renewal, of sleep and creation. Also of *change;* the flowers in water becoming lilies, and back in the soil, reborn as flowers of the field. A story of movement in growth in accordance with environment, Man, plants, animals suiting themselves to live, to grow, where they are, where they are born."

The stories give the story of Mary. They are parables about elemental characters like seeds and birds and fish and children who search for, insist upon, and are rewarded with the proper environment in which to flourish. For Mary the seed, Kingsley Hall was the soil, I was the sun, and her paintings were the flowers.

Over the ensuing months Mary coupled her natural talent with a bit of hard learning. I thought it would be good for her to familiarize herself with the work of other artists, as well as learn some tricks of the trade (technical proficiency) by attending classes at a nearby art school. For Christmas I bought her a book on the paintings of Grünewald (appropriate to the season). Leon presented her with a book on aboriginal paintings (appropriate to her early works). Mary herself went to the local library and took out books on the impressionists, cubists and expressionists. It was a turn-on for me to take her to the Tate Gallery and share her unfettered enthusiasm for paintings which she had only previously seen in reproductions, if at all.

Mary also profited from my introducing her to a number of artists who were my friends, including Harry Trevor, Felix Topolski, David Annesley and Jesse Watkins. They all liked her work very much and encouraged Mary with their comments as well as by showing her their work, and, at times, even painting along with her.

Going to art school was a difficult decision for Mary because she doubted whether the school would provide a nurturing environment. More importantly, she was not yet a social animal, and she was afraid of blowing up at the people with whom she would have to come into contact. Sure enough, no sooner had she returned from her first afternoon at the school, when she rushed over and hit me and told me how bad she had felt. Why? Oh, because one of the instructors had dared to draw over one of her drawings. For Mary this was tantamount to picking up a knife and cutting her body apart. She did not differentiate herself from her drawings or paintings. They were experienced as one and the same. She felt she had been mutilated. Seeing how upset Mary felt, I assured her that she could draw as she liked and didn't have to work in an academic mode if she didn't want to. Others in the house concurred.

To understand why Mary got so upset, one must realize that she did not just view the instructor as an authority against whom she had to rebel, but as an omnipotent authority who, because he was an authority, must always be considered right. To draw or paint in any way but this meant that she was going against him and had to be punished. This generated a spiral of anger and guilt which threatened to tear her apart. When this happened, Mary could not paint.

The next day she attended a different group. Fortunately the new drawing master was wise enough to leave Mary alone, except when she asked for help, and then he was most tactful with his suggestions. He too agreed that the power and vitality of her drawings more than compensated for her lack of technical expertise.

Another class which Mary enjoyed was sculpture. Having

had a lot of experience playing with her shits, she took to moulding clay as a duck takes to water. Her models are expressionistic, they capture the essential features of an object without getting bogged down in detail. Sometimes grotesque, other times tender, they convey a sense of how Mary had been using her hands long before she entered Kingsley Hall. Both as a child and as a professional, whenever Mary felt tense and anxious, she used to go to the toilet, take hold of her shits and mould them into little figures. This was her way of making babies, and it yields an important clue to what her anxiety and sense of "badness" were all about. Of course, we have no record of these creations, because they were always anxiously flushed away. At Kingsley Hall Mary did likewise. She had a chamber pot in her room and used the raw material it contained to best advantage when she felt bad. Not a bad way to learn sculpture!

Cass College lasted about four- months. Mary's attendance began to peter out once she picked up a few basic techniques and sucked up all the encouragement the staff had to offer. Furthermore she decided that any work which could be done at Cass College could be accomplished just as easily at Kingsley Hall. Little did she realize how soon this breezy expectation would be shattered.

Many problems arose throughout the period when Mary was learning to draw and paint and sculpt. In the first place, she did not always enjoy her new found freedom of expression. Soon after she took up a crayon and brush Mary began to worry about falling off the roof of Kingsley Hall. She even had thoughts of throwing herself over the roof. These frightened her. Then she got sick and had to stay in bed a while. Next she started to get caught up in IT and moaned and groaned whenever anyone went near her. It seemed that she was punishing herself for taking up painting. (She experienced this situation as if she were being punished by an outside force.) But why? One reason, which Mary did not disclose till after her first exhibition, was that she was afraid of competing with her mother. Mary felt terribly guilty that her mother, whose hobby is painting, mostly flower scenes in a realistic style, would be upset if she found out that Mary had become a better painter. At the same time Mary felt a tremendous desire to paint and surpass her mother's accomplishments, hence the conflict.

Another reason had to do with her *fear* of making the other residents at Kingsley Hall envious of her new found skill, and in particular, of all the attention and admiration that accrued to her because of it. Of course, her accurate assessment of what might arise at Kingsley Hall commingled with a *desire* to make everyone around her envious and jealous of her in order to feel important.

An over-enthusiastic evaluation of her paintings on my part added to her troubles. It led me to suggest that she apply for a diploma course at St. Martin's School of Art. I thought Mary could profit by advanced training in painting and sculpture. My attitude was quite ridiculous. It cut across my own dictum that a person should swim in his or her own waters. Mary was not at all prepared to engage in the social contacts such a course would have necessitated. In retrospect, I think this advice was precipitated by my intense anxiety that a storm was brewing at Kingsley Hall which would adversely affect Mary's drawing and painting. By getting her into a good art school, I was hoping to protect her and her art from this storm. Instead I made matters worse. Mary got terribly depressed after St. Martin's turned her down.

When Mary felt depressed, her paintings became dark and sombre and foreboding. The images turned in on themselves and melted one into the other. These scenes really spooked people at Kingsley Hall, especially when she placed the paintings all over the house. This happened when she felt insecure. She would try to deal with her fears that Kingsley Hall would explode or be destroyed or that she would be got rid of by enveloping everyone within the rubric of her imagery.

In the spring of 1966 a gathering social crisis at the Hall led Mary to feel very insecure indeed. The community had become polarized into two increasingly antagonistic camps. Each had a general idea about how Kingsley Hall should be run, and each disagreed with many ideas of the other.

Aaron was the informal spokesman for one of these groups and Ronnie spoke for the other. Roughly the former felt that the social structure of the hall was too loose, that there should be clear-cut rules which everyone had to obey or be dismissed from the community, and that this could best be maintained by a qualified, mutually agreed-upon chief executive who would be known as the Medical Director of Kingsley Hall.

The others (including myself) believed that Kingsley Hall had been working pretty well both as a community and as a place where individual members of the community could work out their "madness." We didn't disagree that it would be a good idea if regular meetings were initiated where people could talk to each other about their problems, but only if these meetings were non-coercive and arose out of a genuine need, rather than from a theoretical model of "therapeutics." We were against formalizing roles like Medical Director, because a) this would inhibit the freedom of the residents to develop spontaneous and mutually helpful relationships with each other, and b) the attendant social operations might be defined by the local medical authorities as constituting a nursing home or half-way house. The community could then find itself bound by a set of extremely restricting and (from the standpoint of the organic development of the community) alien rules and regulations as to how people should behave and by what means they should live. It was the whole point of Kingsley Hall that this was something we had to discover for ourselves. It could not be imposed from without. Being defined as this or that by the local medical authorities was always one of the gravest threats that Kingsley Hall had to face and defend itself against, not just at this time, but on several other occasions as well. c) Authority should not be imposed from without. The role of Medical Director would be an imposition on the community. Authority could only be established by what Ronnie referred to as "presence." "Presence" has to do with all that which leads other people to respect you. If a person has "presence" then others will know it without having to be told. If one doesn't have it, then in order to establish authority, one has to resort to force. The resultant authority is based on fear, not respect.

While Ronnie lived at Kingsley Hall, he was the leader (guru) of the community. A combination of erudition, experience and charisma led many residents to particularly respect him. Therefore, to change the rules by which people were respectful presented a direct challenge to Laing's leadership as well as to the integrity of the community.

On the other hand, Aaron's criticisms of the way we operated were both timely and useful. Things happened so quickly at Kingsley Hall that the community didn't often take the trouble to think about what was going on and how it was changing. The community needed someone, with a strong character, like Aaron, to take the bull by the horns, yell, "Whoa," or, "Slow down," and then, by his own personal example start us all thinking about what we had been doing, instead of just doing what we had been thinking about.

As the storm clouds began to appear and the chill winds began to blow, life at Kingsley Hall became less pleasant. It became impossible to ask friends or acquaintances around, because a prior agreement for the visit had to be arranged from both camps. This was almost impossible. Then the usual high-level, all evening dinner discussions were replaced by glares, stares and recriminations.

This drama did have its amusing sidelights. For a long while Aaron used to walk about Kingsley Hall carrying a biography of Stalin. About the same time Ronnie began to interspice his lofty metaphysical comments on the state of mankind with quotes from Lenin.

Mary and her paintings provided a sensitive barometer of the extent of the tension which everyone experienced during this period, but few expressed so directly. Mary was terrified of divisions in the community because whoever she sided with, she would be "going against" the other and would therefore be liable to severe punishment. Moreover, she did not distinguish between her inner and outer worlds. Since various parts of herself were ordinarily at war, and since she identified Aaron and Ronnie with these opposing internal factions, she thought she had personally caused the conflict at Kingsley Hall. Concomitantly, she had to deal with a marked increase in her usual level of inner disturbance, "IT," which was then seen as happening all about her. (It was!!) The situation is common in children who see their mother and father fighting, but don't know with whom to side because they love both parents.

Consequently, Mary felt under enormous pressure to stop the conflict and bring both sides together. One of her first acts was to take a piece of chalk and scribble white lines about the Games Room, over the chairs and tables and walls, all over. She connected every object to another and to the room itself by a chalky line. I think that if the other residents had not stopped her, she would have extended these lines all over the house, over and into everything.

When the community gathered for dinner, people were furious. How could Mary do a thing like that? Had she taken leave of her senses? Surely she should be expelled from Kingsley Hall! Etc., etc. Perhaps they thought that Mary had tried to envelop them in a gigantic spider web. I don't think anyone appreciated the importance of her chalking as an act of social reconciliation. (Everyone is connected to everyone else and to everything else.) And even if people did, the community was not in a reconcilable condition. So, they turned on Mary. Fortunately Ronnie was able to cool the most overheated tempers by insisting that Mary clean up the chalked lines before she went to bed. She was helped in this by Jesse Watkins, an old friend of Ronnie's who was visiting that evening. Once a naval commander, and now a well known sculptor, he himself had passed through a ten-day experience of emotional death and rebirth some years back and still retains a vivid memory of what may be termed psychotic states of mind. So, Jesse could well understand what Mary was up to. (His "trip" is detailed in Chapter seven, "Ten Day Voyage," in Ronnie's *The Politics of Experience*.)*

Mary had tried to unite the community with her. She succeeded in uniting it against her. Whereas the residents did not settle their disagreements, they did agree to hold Mary responsible for them. "The problem isn't with ourselves, the problem lies in Mary. Get rid of her and everything will be OK." The price of peace was their allowing Mary to turn herself into a scapegoat for the ills of the community. How strange that a group of people devoted to demystifying the social transactions of disturbed families should revert to behaving like one!

*The Politics of Experience by R. D. Laing. Published in the United Kingdom by Penguin Books and in America by Pantheon Books.

Mary had taken into herself and expressed the disturbance which no one, including Mary could cope with. Throughout this spring and summer she remembers a seething rage which threatened to tear her apart and anyone or anything with which IT came into contact. She didn't want the rage. She tried to expel it in any way possible. What she didn't realize was that she was acting for the whole of Kingsley Hall.

The community didn't want its rage either. So several residents tried to have Mary expelled from the community. What people didn't realize is that the rage they were trying to expel had little to do with Mary Barnes.

When most full of fury, and most confused about the origins of IT, Mary would lie in her bed, twist her body into a knot, tear at her clothes and hair, and moan. It was a pitiful state, and not immediately amenable to consoling words from me. Mary referred to IT as a trap from which she couldn't escape because the more she struggled, the more IT closed in on her. This was only partly true. Through her continued painting Mary had begun to extricate herself from that part of the trap which was of her own making.

Mary had previously endeavoured to rise above her emotional pitfalls by converting to Catholicism. Symbols of her profound, almost mystic faith abounded in her paintings. But she had never painted the crucifixion. I wondered if she saw, as I did, the many similarities between her torments and the suffering of Jesus on the cross, especially in the spring of 1966 when she seemed nailed to the conjuncture of her disturbance with that of Kingsley Hall. So, I suggested she paint the crucifixion.

What followed was an astonishing transformation of her life's agonies into dozens of huge brilliantly coloured canvases all depicting the death and resurrection of Jesus. In the image of Christ with his head turned painfully aside, his mouth shrieking in desperation, Mary had finally and convincingly captured her own history on fields of red and gold and orange and yellow.

Later Mary expanded her themes to include Saints, Devils, biblical stories and landscapes. Watching her work was a great thrill. I recall one occasion, early one afternoon, when

I walked into the Games Room just as she was about to begin a painting. She had nailed large sheets of white paper, maybe eight feet high by twelve feet long, on the wall facing the dining-room. Without so much as making a preliminary drawing, Mary took up a brush, dipped it in one of several quart buckets, and sloshed away at the wall. Within minutes, vigorous, yet delicate dashes of colour covered an area several times the size of Mary. Then she picked up a smaller brush and started to fill in the characters. Never once did she stop or look up, although as she worked, she would often laugh, or talk with or even scream at this or that figure (or vice versa—she played all parts), as the figure began to make his presence known in the painting. From time to time a beatific smile would break across her face. It was as if, at that moment, she had transcended all her troubles and entered an ecstatic reverie.

Leon came in, then others. Mary did not notice. She was totally engrossed in her work, in herself. No one spoke, only an infrequent gasp or cough interrupted the drama that was unfolding across our wall. From time to time Leon would point to this or that figure and I, or someone else would nod, or smile, or perhaps just look on, too enchanted to reply.

One hour passed, two hours, then Mary stepped back from the burst of colour lying resplendent in front of us and sank to the ground, exhausted. She had brought to life the Transfiguration of Christ. A majestic Jesus, his hand glowing in gold and silver, could be seen soaring through a bevy of old testament prophets on his way to meet Elijah, illumined in oranges and reds and as brilliant as a mideastern sunrise. Beneath Jesus there lay lall the apostles in violets and golds and greens and blues looking up in wonderment.

How long had Mary been thinking of creating the transfiguration? "Oh Joe, I hadn't thought of it at all. I never think about what I paint in advance. It just comes."

It sure did, and also the Temptations of Christ, a monstrous confrontation between Christ and the Devil, the Crucifixion of St. Peter, and many more. All of these got hung up and about Kingsley Hall.

The paintings generated as much hatred as love. "Mary is

trying to engulf us, to dominate us, to control us, her damn paintings are all over," exclaimed one group of residents.

"No, you're wrong, she's embarked on a great spiritual journey," insisted still others.

Neither side had a monopoly on the truth. Mary's paintings were beautiful and they did give a welcome respite from the difficulties of day to day life at the Hall, yet one could feel the tension rising in the air as more and more of her work got plastered about.

Could Mary have tempered the hostilities by restraining her flow of paintings? Temporarily, perhaps, but since she was not the cause of the conflict (although she thought she was), it would have inevitably flared up again, paintings or no paintings. What Mary did not realize was that the very way she had chosen to deal with her anxiety about other people's anger, that is, by exerting control and domination over the angry others in order to cool them down, was, in the circumstances of Kingsley Hall, bound to produce the opposite effect.

Previously she had some success in squashing overheated emotions in herself and individuals external to herself by taking up the career of nurse or nursing tutor, or schizophrenic, where the exercise of intra- and interpersonal control and domination is of paramount importance. Therefore, from Mary's point of view it was not unreasonable to try to control and dominate the atmosphere at Kingsley Hall through the intensity and omnipresence of her paintings.

The effects of her efforts were exaggerated because of a voluminous amount of publicity which came Mary's way as soon as visitors to Kingsley Hall heralded her paintings to the outside world. Although she did have a way of "playing up to the gallery," it would be wrong to blame Mary for enjoying the first fruits of fame (including an article on her work in *The Guardian* by Ruth Abel). It would also be wrong to blame Mary for the envious anger this article begat in some residents. ("Damn Mary's all over the place, both inside and outside Kingsley Hall!")

Mary was terrified by any expression of envy or jealousy. ("The whole house seemed like a mine field that might explode, any minute.") A request to the community that she be allowed to use the walls of the entire back stairwell was her way of trying to cope with this fear. Completing such a project was equivalent to her saying, "I am the painting. The painting is me. I can't stand your hating me. I want you to love me. Love me by looking at me and letting me touch you."

Yet the very idea was also equivalent to her waving a red flag in front of a wounded bull. The answer was an emphatic, *"No!"* from most of the residents. I thought, *"Yes,"* but remained silent. It would have been politically inexpedient to have done otherwise.

Years later Mary was allowed to paint the whole of the dining-room wall. This magnificent iconography was shown in colour on BBC TV in the spring of 1970. She also wanted to paint the entire ceiling of the large downstairs hall. Unfortunately she never got permission to do so from the trustees of Kingsley Hall. The result could have been Mary's "Sistine Ceiling."

At that moment, Mary did not take "no" for an answer. She whined and cried and asked again and whined and cried. That was definitely counterproductive. People not only reiterated the "no," but screamed at her to take down her other work as well. All sorts of meetings were called "to deal with the Mary problem." For days all anyone talked about was how to deal with Mary, how to teach her how to live in a community, how to get rid of her, or, in the case of Leon and myself, how to cool the situation.

The painting continued, but with darkened colours and chaotic brushwork. Her images grew sinister and ominous. Hideous monsters appeared who tore at and devoured other hideous monsters. People paled when they saw them. Mary couldn't tolerate the disturbance they saw (a strong reflection of their own!) and stopped using the Games Room and other places where the pictures hung. From this period, one work was beatific, a full length portrait of a black madonna, on a field of black.

Mary's dark, violent images particularly tormented Helen, a thin, semi-quiet American girl, whom a friend once described as, "never quite there, always everywhere." One day she tore them off the walls. Mary had been out shopping. When she returned and found her paintings missing, she blew her top. Poor Helen would have been strangled to death if Peter Tollimarsh, another resident, hadn't pulled her away from Mary, who, after gaining a second wind, went and posted them all up again. What Mary refused to realize was that Helen had expressed the will of the community.

Coming back to Kingsley Hall that evening, I no sooner walked in the front door, before chill winds blew my way. People no longer saw me as Mary's helper, but as her accomplice. I felt hard pressed to deflect the tidal anger that was moving in my direction, as well as Mary's.

Dinner was a sombre affair. The "anti-Mary" faction had tasted blood, and now moved in for the kill. The issue was no longer whether Mary's painting should remain up, but whether Mary should remain at Kingsley Hall. I decided to go along with the majority decision in favour of the removal of the paintings in the hope that a vote against Mary's continued residence in the community would be deferred. It was. Leon and I helped Mary put away her work. The others made merry with song and dance, a celebration which extended to the local pub and then back again, courtesy of Her Majesty's licensing laws.

The next few weeks were taken up with some heavy politicking on Mary's behalf. This was made exceedingly difficult by the fact that one sector of the community felt that Mary was a perfect example of what was wrong with Kingsley Hall.

"Don't be wet," went their retort. "She has to be curbed. She needs us to set limits for her."

Ronnie agreed with limiting Mary's painting to her room, but remained curiously ambivalent as to whether Mary should be eliminated from the community. I was furious when he seemed to treat Mary simply as a pawn in a power struggle. I couldn't see how he could ruthlessly dismiss Mary's contributions to Kingsley Hall, aside from his own intense relationship with her. I thought, "This whole business is crazy. Mary is a red herring. Compared to what else goes down here, her shit is but a drop in the bucket."

In the midst of all this turmoil, I received the sad news that my mother, who had been sick, but not gravely ill, had suddenly taken a turn for the worse and died. I hurried back to the States. Mary prayed for her and for me.

Upon my return a couple of weeks later, I was relieved to find that Mary had not been chucked out. She even had been doing a bit of painting. The Mary issue had cooled down. But so had Mary. A marked change had come over her. She no longer wanted to do things for herself. She didn't want to go out of her room, except to follow me around. She didn't want to eat much. The latter message sufficed to tell me that she had plunged into another period of regression, her second "down" while at Kingsley Hall.

The change in Mary's behaviour and state of mind was topped off by a greatly renewed interest in her shits. Normally she liked to muck about with the contents of her pot, smear, make little figures or just look at (admire?) her faecal products before cleaning up and getting on with her business. But now she seemed positively fascinated by the stuff. She would play with it for hours at an end, especially when she felt unloved ("Joe is away") or "bad" (full of IT).

One day Mary presented me with the ultimate test of my love for her. She covered herself in shit and waited to see what my reaction would be. Her account of this incident amuses me because of her blind confidence that her shit could not put me off. I can assure you the reverse was true.

When I, unsuspecting, walked into the Games Room and was accosted by foul smelling Mary Barnes looking far worse than the creature from the black lagoon, I was terrified and nauseated. My first reaction was to escape and I stalked away as fast as I could. Fortunately she didn't try to follow me. I would have belted her.

I remember my first thoughts very well: "This is too much, too bloody much. She can damn well take care of herself from now on. I want nothing more to do with her."

Half way down the front stairs and nearly out of the house I felt a slight change of heart. "Stop a minute. What are you getting so worked up about? It's just shit. What's wrong with shit? It ain't any different from the stuff she used in her early wall paintings. Touching her shit won't kill you. Yes it will. No it won't. Stop mixing up her shit with your shit.

Her shit is just shit. Ain't going to hurt you none to go back and help her get cleaned up, and if you don't you will never have anything to do with her again. Is that what you want?"

The last point was the clincher. I liked Mary and did not want to give up my relationship with her. I knew that if I didn't turn around and face that poor, sorry, shit covered creature, I would never be able to face her or anybody like her again.

It wasn't easy. I practically had to push myself back up the stairs. Mary was still in the Games Room, her head bowed, sobbing. I muttered something like, "Now, now, it's all right. Let's go upstairs and get you a nice warm bath."

It took at least an hour to get Mary cleaned up. She was a right mess. Shit was everywhere, in her hair, under her arms, in between her toes. I had visions of the principal character in an oldie terror movie, *The Mummy's Ghost*, of the Mummy as he (she?) rose up out of a swamp.

You have to hand it to Mary. She is extraordinarily capable of conjuring up everyone's favourite nightmare and embodying it for them. Until that day, however, she hadn't succeeded with me. When she did, she came over with a bang.

During the bath I jokingly told her all the monsters she reminded me of. With some hesitation, and then with hearty laughter she joined in my gruesome reminiscences. While this was going on, the "rational" part of my mind switched on. "Mary was just trying to exercise/exorcise her disturbance. The shit is her anger, her badness. But it is also herself, an important part of herself. How can she love herself, if she can't love her shit. If she can't love her shit, can 'Joe?' Who is 'Joe?' 'Joe' is her own goodness which she projected back into herself. 'Joe' is the last judgement. She must have been very frightened that 'Joe' would be frightened by her shits. If 'Joe' had been frightened, she would have felt totally unlovable. That I have stayed with her means that 'Joe' was not frightened, and that she can still love herself, no matter how much 'badness' is inside her."

That night Mary went to bed clean, well fed (warm milk with honey) and reasonably content that there was some goodness still left in the world. I went to bed exhausted.

Chapter Eighteen

Mary "goes down" and "comes up" again

On the road towards self-renewal Mary passed through several "downs." The most profound occurred in 1965. It lasted the longest and presented the gravest threat to Mary's life. Subsequent "downs" took Mary less deep into herself, made fewer demands on her life-support-system and lasted for shorter periods.

Her upward movement followed a helical trajectory, seemingly covering familiar territory, but always at a more advanced level of psychic integration. For example, from the summer of 1965 to the summer of 1966 Mary emerged from her bed to play with her shits, cover walls with her shits, cover walls with paint, cover herself with shits, play with her shits, before returning to bed. Although she did go into herself again, she had begun to become aware of "IT" and to tolerate "IT" without feeling torn to bits, and she did retain the ability to communicate her feelings through her painting and sculpture. Equally important, once Mary had gained experience in the art of regression ("regression in the service of the ego") she became quite adept at it and "going down" held less terror for her.

Could Mary have avoided a "down" in the spring of 1966 if the social climate of Kingsley Hall had been less disturbed?

Possibly. I think Mary's down was a response to being scapegoated by the residents. It also represented another attempt to bring people together by creating a crisis about herself. If she couldn't bring people together by what she did (her paintings), she intended to bring them together by what she was (a deeply regressed individual).

I have now used the term "intention" or "intend" in reference to Mary on several occasions. Do I mean that she behaved like a Pentagon games strategist, thinking out moves in advance, anticipating her opponents' reactions, and responding in kind?

Obviously not. Mary's moves and countermoves had not been thought out in advance at all. Most of the time she was completely unaware of the social effects of her actions. Nevertheless, these actions and her "presence" did generate many of the important transactions that occurred in Kingsley Hall. We need to differentiate between "rational intentionality" and "psychotic intentionality."

"Rational intentionality" refers to *consciously* considered moves and countermoves. "Psychotic intentionality" refers to *unconsciously* considered moves and countermoves. Each is purposeful. Each may include multiple simultaneous levels of perception, "thought" (conscious or unconscious), and decision. Each may produce effects which are parallel, tangential or opposite to each other, and which are consistent or inconsistent with any one of several levels of intent. Inconsistency most commonly characterizes "psychotic intentionality" as does the engendering of effects opposite from what is seemingly wanted.

In real life the two intentionalities are not mutually exclusive because the would-be rationalist is not able to predict all the variables that influence his decisions. "Rational intentionality" often masks the psychotic variety. (Consider Dr. Strangelove in Stanley Kubrick's film of the same name.)

Mary's behaviour at Kingsley Hall characteristically demonstrates "psychotic intentionality." She was not aware of what she wanted, but what she wanted was expressed by how she was, what she became and in the interpersonal situations that sprang up around her. What she wanted was also revealed in her dreams, and years later, in her memories of what took place when she "went down" and in her associations to these memories. Significantly, Mary engendered situations which were opposite to what she did want. Her plethora of paintings provide a good example. Instead of resulting in people loving her, they resulted in people hating her.

Observe that the way Mary expressed or masked her intentions ("psychotic intentionality") is a common occurrence and is not limited to people who have entered a psychotic state.

With Mary, *guilt* was the key to why she did not allow herself to want what she wanted, and also to why her actions brought about results which were detrimental to her intentions, rather than consistent with them.

Mary has not mentioned that in mid-January 1966, Roberta, my wife-to-be, joined me from the States. We then took an apartment away from Kingsley Hall. Although I still maintained a room there, having a separate place meant that my life was not centred at Kingsley Hall.

For a few months I continued to spend about half the week with the community (Roberta often with me), more during moments of crisis. But from Mary's standpoint, any break in the relationship between us was a disaster, especially if another woman was involved. Mary responded by resurrecting the "pest." This embodiment of obnoxious intrusiveness had lain dormant for a while. Roberta's presence was all it needed to come to life again.

Mary wouldn't leave us alone. If we were sitting together she would come between us. If we were asleep in our room, she would walk in and lie down between us. If we locked the door she would stand outside and howl. If we forgot to lock the door and went out, she would steal into our room and pee on the bed. Several times we had to drag her screaming out of the room. She wouldn't leave of her own accord.

Considering that she had never previously dealt with anyone like Mary (or with a place like Kingsley Hall), Roberta put up with "the pest" with heroic patience, far above and beyond the call of duty. Meanwhile, I felt hard pressed to cope with Mary without divorcing myself from her trip. First, I politely but firmly told her to cease and desist. Second, I told her that I realized she felt lost and abandoned, but that her actions were driving her away from me, rather than bringing her closer to me. Third, I set aside a specific period to be with Mary. She knew that this was her time, and that no matter what else was holding my attention, I would be with her at "her time." Fourth, I screamed at her. Of these realistic measures, the latter two were the most effective.

Occasionally we had "think sessions." The purpose of these sessions was to consider what was going on in her, in me, between us, and at Kingsley Hall. Topics ranged from the polarization of the community (totally denied: "Joe, you're wrong. I know people love each other and only want to help me get better"), to her sexual desires and jealousies (partially denied: "Joe, I want to go back to the convent to be a contemplative nun." Me: "Say ten 'Hail Marys' and we'll talk about it in the morning"), to feelings of anger and rage ("Joe, I feel so bad today." Me: "That's because you want to kill me and Roberta.")

Communal mayhem and sex were indigestible. Rage and violence were not. This was the highlight of the spring for both of us. Mary had finally begun to accept her own experience of rage. We spent hours going over how, when and where she felt angry. This was fundamental stuff. IT was the regurgitated remnant of undigested penises and vaginas. Mary had to appreciate her vomit in order to get to the meat of the matter and be nourished by it.

I encouraged Mary to yell and scream and kick and bite. I used my superior size and weight to absorb her squeezes and bites and blows. Deft footwork kept me from being kicked in more vital places. These primitive exchanges had many beneficial effects. Mary grew more able to "stay with IT" as her fear of her anger diminished. She began to see that her own experience of being tortured and murdered by other people had something to do with her own desires to torture and murder the very people whom she thought were going to "come in on her." She gained the ability to recognize the multifold ways of her anger. When she recognized IT, she could ask herself the all-important question, *"Why?"* It dawned on Mary that she was a very jealous lady.

Roberta's staying at Kingsley Hall proved a help rather than a hindrance in my relationship with Mary. It forced Mary to confront her anger and rage sooner than she would otherwise have done. It enabled me to focus Mary's attention on the issue of jealousy. Whatever happens to me and/ or whomever I am with is fair game for the fantasies, dreams, memories (and as Ronnie puts it, the memories of fantasies, dreams of memories, memories of dreams of fantasies, etc.) which pass between us.

Mary Barnes was a hotbed of sexual desire and frustration. This imprisoned sexuality touched every aspect of Mary's life and everyone with whom she came into contact. It lay behind Mary's ubiquitous *guilt*. Mary didn't know this. She didn't even know there was something about her sexual desires that she didn't know, but she encased herself in legions of fear and punishment to make sure she never found out. However, once Mary had confronted her rage and paid attention to her jealousy, she was able to pass through her veil of fear and guilt and make the major discovery that this rage and her sexual frustrations were related.

Unfortunately, Mary's emotional infrastructure was overwhelmed by the combination of sexual jealousy and social chaos. This aroused more anxiety, fear and guilt than Mary's newfound consciousness could cope with. In consequence, the spring of '66 saw Mary enter a "down" from which she did not return for almost a year.

I disagree with Mary's assessment of her condition during this period. She says she "went down" in the spring and then came up for a brief while before plunging down again in the fall. I think she confused an "up" with a slowing down of her rate of descent. From my observations, I would say that her "down" began in February, accelerated in March, held steady in April, and plunged forward in May. By June she had taken to bed and was refusing to eat. Her body had begun to look like a bunch of bones loosely covered with skin.

The "Mary problem," which had been temporarily overshadowed by communal infighting, came to the fore with a vengeance. Meeting after meeting was called to discuss the state of her appetite. People eagerly awaited the latest news, even a whispered rumour of Mary having eaten something. "You say she took milk from Joe today? That's good!" "You say Joe wasn't about and she didn't take anything? That's bad."

"Mary" had succeeded in uniting a group of people who otherwise wouldn't have come together. Wasn't this her intention?

Mary embodied the spirit of Kingsley Hall, hence the tremendous anxiety on the part of the community that her body and spirit remain intact. This was a pressing problem. I had made plans to go away on holiday in August, so had Ronnie and Leon.

Who was willing to feed Mary in August? Two newcomers to the community, Noel Cobb and Paul Zeal, raised their hands. Noel is an American psychologist who had practised in Norway for several years. He had written to Ronnie asking to meet him and seeking to participate in his work. Paul Zeal, a degree in philosophy at the University of Bristol fresh under his belt, had written Ronnie about the same time for the same reasons.

By June both Noel and Paul had been coming round Kingsley Hall fairly regularly and had asked to join the community. In the true manner of Kingsley Hall no formal vote was ever taken on their request. I doubt whether anyone ever said, "Yes, do come in." They just came at a time when there was room and when they were needed. No one overtly objected in words or in deed. Assent was silence, an offer of a pint of bitter at the local and an invitation to help out with the housework.

The issue of feeding Mary was intimately connected with the struggle for control of Kingsley Hall. Therefore, Noel's and Paul's arrival on the scene, and especially their caring for Mary, had an important bearing on the future of the community.

But Mary threw a spanner in the works. She rejected all attempts to introduce Noel and Paul to her. She didn't believe that they were therapists. "Mary, of course they're therapists, they've come to care for you while I and the others are away."

"But Joe, how do I know they are proper therapists? Do you know how dangerous it is to trust people who do not understand? What if I go bad?"

No assurances, entreaties or exhortations from Ronnie or myself could get Mary to change her mind about Noel and Paul. She refused to accept them as therapists, she would only allow therapists to feed her. I could have wrung her neck.

Although it made life very difficult for me, Mary's cageyness did have some basis in fact. Paul had not had prior training in psychology (a point in his favour!). Neither Noel nor Paul had had experience in dealing with people like

Mary before. My insisting that they were "therapists" was rooted in the social realities of the moment. It was also based on an intuitive feeling that both would do a good job. (They did, once Mary accepted them.)

Of course, no one, not even me, fits in with Mary's version of a "therapist," a cross between Jesus Christ and an earth goddess. And even if someone had come to Kingsley Hall as a trained therapist, this was no guarantee that they would have or could have taken care of Mary. Many a person came to Kingsley Hall with the idea of helping others in the community and wound up having to be looked after by the community.

In the meanwhile the fate of Kingsley Hall hung in the balance. Ronnie worried about Mary and encouraged her to eat. He redoubled his efforts to find appropriate people to keep the community going in his absence. Otherwise he began to wonder out loud whether his best move would simply be to move out of Kingsley Hall and start another community elsewhere.

At the "Mary meetings" Ronnie suggested that we look for a pattern in Mary's "downs." If such a pattern existed, and could be linked with some important event in Mary's history, we might be able to understand why Mary was as she was.

We noticed that Mary usually entered a "down" in the summer and nosedived in the fall. This pattern corresponded with the seasons in which her mother had become visibly pregnant with, and given birth to, her brother Peter: summer and fall. Could it be that Mary's "going down" in the summer and fall was a reliving of the anxiety and fear and anger associated with the birth of her brother? We discussed this with Mary. She thought we were on to something, but still she wouldn't eat.

It took Aaron to resolve the feeding crisis. He simply went into Mary's room, looked her straight in the eye and, speaking with a tone of voice that meant no funny business, told her that she had to eat, and that she had to accept food from Noel and Paul. Mary acquiesced. Never again has she ever refused to eat.

I admired Aaron's straightforward, no-nonsense approach. It avoided the ambivalence about her taking food from Noel and Paul which I must have conveyed to Mary in the way (tone of voice and kinesics) I insisted that she allow herself to be fed by them.

Unfortunately Aaron did not continue to be associated with Kingsley Hall. He moved out before the end of the summer. All things considered, I think that the community came out much the worse by the loss of Aaron's continued presence. And by "community," I do not just mean the Kingsley Hall crowd, rather the larger network of people who included friends and alumni of Kingsley Hall and members of two other loosely associated communities. A more inventive and fruitful move on the part of all of us would have been to help Aaron get a house and start a new, but associated community. There is no "right way" to run a community. Individual personalities and their creative interplay properly determine the structure and character of "a place." Whatever Aaron's place would have been like, it could have contributed to the development of the network.

The story of Mary's stay at Kingsley Hall provides an essential but incomplete picture of life in the community. Before proceeding with her saga, I would like to introduce you to some of the colourful characters and extraordinary activities which made Kingsley Hall more than "a place where people could freak out." Keep in mind, however, that *no single person or incident is typical of Kingsley Hall.* Frequent and radical change was the community's consistent feature. As Mary would say, it had many "ups" and "downs." Furthermore, so much took place at the Hall that even the keenest observer could only relate a part of the action. The following is a composite snapshot of one day in the life of Kingsley Hall.

The "day" began in the early afternoon. The clatter of milk bottles or the sound of a record player would announce that someone somewhere was stirring about. Folks might then drift into the kitchen for coffee or tea. The energetic types would make sausages and eggs for themselves.

Who was going to do what about the place had usually been decided the night before. There were always dishes to be washed, floors to be swept and groceries to be fetched from the Co-op. Later, the long dining-room table had to be set and dinner started. Even when these tasks had not been

formally allocated, they were completed by residents who
sensed what had to be done and did it. This procedure
seemed to work very well, but was replaced by a job roster
after complaints about anarchy in the kitchen. The roster
helped to bring the slackers to public attention. It mobilized
efficiency and cleanliness. But it was hard to get someone
to draw it up every week. That was considered a "low level"
job. So after a while, we sank back into happy or unhappy
anarchy, depending on whether things got done, or not.

Not everyone who stayed at Kingsley Hall was asked to
pitch in with the housework. There was always a minority
who had chosen to "go into themselves" and who had to
have things done for them. Mary is an extreme example
of such a person. At any one time there might be two or three
regressed individuals in the community. There was a great
deal of prestige associated with this "down state." I remember one girl complaining that she hadn't been able to "go
down" and asking people to help her do so.

Dinner was the main meal of the day. It was the principal
occasion for the community to gather together. During the
early history of Kingsley Hall, a collective euphoria dictated
that we have not just a meal, but a banquet. Even in
harder times great efforts were expended to make the table
look nice and to prepare one tasty course and dessert.

While I was a resident, dinner was served between 9:30
and 11:30 in the evening. Twenty people sat around a table
garlanded with flowers and illumined by four white candles
atop a tree trunk candelabra. If visitors were present another
table extended the seating capacity to twenty-six. Loaves of
bread and bottles of red wine crowded platters of vegetables
and meat and fruit. Light ale was also a favourite drink, as
was Scotch when Ronnie or a guest felt in a generous
mood.

Ronnie sat at the head of the table in front of a handsome
arched window also illumined by candles. No other light
broke the darkness. Among those who sat around this table
at one time or another were Leon Redler and his wife Liz,
Morty Schatzman and his wife Vivien, Jerome Liss, Grace
Conner and Roberta and I. Leon, Morty, Jerome, Grace
and myself had known each other since medical school days.
Grace was then a physicist working in the department of

radiology. She had turned her two-room apartment over Oscar's fish restaurant on New York's upper east side, into a haven for freaks, dropouts, and assorted other people in states of personal distress. During our years of training, Leon, Morty, Jerome and myself served Grace in the capacity of ex-officio "consultant psychiatrists." The practical experience we gained at Grace's pad came in handy at Kingsley Hall.

Of the five of us, I was the first to join the community, then Leon, and finally Morty and Jerome. Grace spent the summer of 1968 at Kingsley Hall. She had just struggled through her second year of medical school and found life at the Hall a welcome relief.

With a mane of golden hair flowing in all directions, Leon proved a prime mover in the community. He was a great help to Mary and especially to Stanley, a young man with whom Leon developed a close relationship. Stanley didn't talk very much, but liked to communicate in deeds. He used to get people to think about him by pinching their morning mail and salting it away in a chest of drawers piled high with empty soup cans and odd tins of Mary's paint. Mary has provided us with a vivid account of her relationship with Stanley. I expect Leon will do likewise in an anthology on Kingsley Hall which he is bringing together and to which he will be contributing. Kingsley Hall was such a complex animal that the more written about it the better.

Jerome stayed at Kingsley Hall for a couple of months in 1967. However, his primary interest was gestalt therapy and encounter groups. He is principally responsible for introducing encounter groups to England.

Morty was the "senior presence" at Kingsley Hall during 1968. With the help of Vivien he got the community back on its feet after it had gone through a period of collective depression and chaos. During his stay the community developed a strong inner cohesiveness. Consequently it was better able to function as a retreat for people in emotional crises.

Around the table one might also find a number of distinguished psychiatrists and psychologists to whom we had extended an evening's hospitality. They included Lyman Wynne and Loren Mosher of the United States National nstitute of Mental Health; Murray Korngold and Fritz Perls rom California; Ross Speck, whose talent at ferreting out uppressed rules and regulations once provoked a brawl; and Maxwell Jones.

During and after dinner Ronnie would expound on philosophy, psychology (paranoia/metanoia), religion, mysticism, and many other subjects as well. It was a delight to listen to him organize and synthesize a variety of complex deas with the ease of a concert pianist demonstrating variations on a theme by Bach or Mozart. It seemed that he could step inside a work of art, whether by Freud, Heidegger, Sartre, Beethoven, Bartok or whoever, and convey the key notes more simply, directly and eloquently than the master himself. At the same time he would point out connections between "A" and "X," "Y" and "Z" in seemingly unrelated fields of science, act, politics, etc. Ronnie is closer to the Master Game Player (see Hermann Hesse's, *The Bead Game*) than any other person I have ever met.

Sometimes Ronnie the raconteur would come to the fore. Then we would be treated to tales from the Gorbals, medical school, a Glasgow bughouse or the army. Any incident that could amuse, shock, dismay, edify or provoke the assemblage was fair game. My favourite was "the great appendectomy race." Aaron and I were also experts at the medical horror story and we used to spend hours trading Ronnie tale for tale.

However, the majority of the community, and visitors, were not medical or paramedical men and women. Many were artists, writers, actors or dancers. And these individuals did not necessarily come to "go down" or see how we dealt with others who "had gone down." They came because friends lived there, or because they liked community life, or had heard that Kingsley Hall was a "groovy scene," or to demonstrate their wares at the poetry readings, film shows, music and dance recitals, and art exhibitions which took place in the big hall downstairs. Their presence added an extra dimension to life at Kingsley Hall. They emphasized touch and smell as well as sight and sound. They showed how easy (or hard) it is to pass beyond the limits of verbal expression in order to reveal experiences which are remarkably like those which occur in dreams or psychotic reverie. At the least Kingsley Hall was never in any danger of suffering from medical claustrophobia.

John Keys, an American poet, and Calvin Hernton, an American poet, writer and sociologist, joined the community at the same time as I. We had all come over from the States together, an eleven day voyage on an Italian ship called, "The Happy Castle." The journey was so amazing that Calvin has written a novel about it, *The Scarecrow People*. The two poets came for the night and stayed for awhile.

Calvin and Ronnie made some fine after-dinner scenes together, as they tried to "sus out" each other. For these ocassions Calvin never forgot to shade his eyes with two pieces of black glass. Ronnie would put on a deep guttural Glasgow accent. A candle, two glasses and a bottle of Scotch were all that lay between them. The following are excepts from a poem entitled, *In Gandhi's Room,** in which Calvin has documented these confrontations:

> .... This is the *PLACE* the *HALL*
>   the *BODY* of *GANDHI*
>   the *ROOM*
>   1931 September December Come In
>   *THE GURU IS WAITING*
>   Fish and wine, bread and milk
>   And twenty-five indisputable existential
>   Queens of terrible mercy ......
> ....   *"What can I possibly say to you so*
>   *that you will hate me for the rest*
>   *of my life!"*
>   cried the Guru, sitting
>   Yoga fashioned on the long table
>   among the ruins of wine bottles and fishbones
>   and bread ends
>   Ticking my genitals with his toe ......
> ....   *"What can you and I do together?"*
>   said the Guru.
>   *"Get naked,"* I replied.
>   And the dance began. ....

*"In Gandhi's Room" by Calvin C. Hernton. Originally published in *Riba*, Number 1, London, Spring 1968. Reprinted in *Fire*, Number 10, London, Fall 1970. Available from *Fire*, 1 Sherwood Street, London W.1.

Sean Connery was another guest who "danced" at Kingsley Hall. He came during the height of his James Bond fame. The community had been informed of his visit in advance. We expected (were hoping?) that he would drive up in an Aston Martin and knock on the floor with a sten gun, his other hand wound around a blonde or two. Instead he brought a side of smoked salmon and remained quiet and reserved the whole evening. So much for cinematic fantasies!

Dinner was not rushed. It usually took several hours before the last drop of wine was downed and second cups of coffee had begun to grow cold. When this point had been reached, a restless soul would announce, "Enough of this talk. Let's dance." Alternatively someone would turn on the record player full blast. Then a half dozen residents would push, pull and heave the long table over to the side of the wall, dishes and all, and a space would be cleared midway between the door to the Games Room and the door leading to the kitchen. Impromptu, unrestrained, free form dancing ensued to a background of the Beatles, the Rolling Stones, Flamenco, or whatever was favoured by those who possessed the records. For a while we got a rather stiff dose of whirling dervish music courtesy of a "Folkways" aficionado.

One evening, just as the dancers were starting to build up a sweat, we heard a great flapping sound in the next room accompanied by meows and scritches and more flaps. Ian, who owned a white dove which he allowed to fly about the house, rushed into the room along with Helen who owned a black cat. The black cat had ripped off the white bird, from stem to stern! Great peals of anguish were forthcoming. What could be done? Could the bird be saved? Should the cat, a bevy of white feathers and blood running down its mouth, be killed?

Amid the turmoil, a half dozen doctors initiated a reasoned discussion about what could or could not be done for the bird. Half thought it should be put out of its misery. Half wanted to pick up needle and thread. Finally it was decided to zip the bird off to the emergency room of a local hospital. Perhaps the casualty officer could save it. In the meanwhile the community split into those who believed the

bird would survive and those who didn't. Bets were take
60-40 against the bird making it through the night.

Dawn broke. The dove came back completely swathed
bandages. A few dozen stitches, a stiff dose of penicillin a
the steady hand of a surgeon had done the trick. I lost £

Sometimes the dancing spilled over into the Games Roor
This was dangerous. Our working class neighbours used
get up and go to work before most of Kingsley Hall we:
to bed. They didn't appreciate any noise coming from o
direction. About 3 a.m. one particularly noisy morning, t
good burghers of Bow emphasized their desire for a sol
night's sleep by forming what looked like a lynch mob,
couple of dozen strong, and banging on the downstai
doors vociferously demanding that we shut up. Fortunate'
the police came and saved us from the full brunt of their ir

The noise problem was never solved. Special plastic foar
sheets over the windows reduced the decibel count, but di
not eliminate it. Here was a good example of a basic cor
flict in life styles between us and our neighbours which mac
life at Kingsley Hall less pleasant than it might have been i
more isolated or sympathetic environs.

4 a.m.—5 a.m. Sheer fatigue works wonders in quietin
the place down. The record player is shut off. The dancin
stops. Ronnie, sitting in the lotus position in the middle c
the dining-room floor, resumes a dialogue with the few re
maining residents or visitors still awake. He is fresh an
alert. The conversation continues until everyone has droppe
off to sleep on the floor around Ronnie. He then gets u
and goes to bed. For a while there seemed to be an un
written rule that Ronnie never went to sleep before the las
person packed it in. "Night" had arrived.

My '67 summer holiday was the first step in weanin;
Mary from her "need" to be with me every moment o
the day. This separation set Mary further along the road t
"separation."

When I returned to Kingsley Hall I was immensely re
lieved to find that Mary had got on with Noel and Pau
and that her scarecrow frame had begun to fill out. Bab
bottles were a thing of the past. Milk and juice, cooke

vegetables and raw fruit were the order of the day. Ice cream, candy and cake were in too.

Although Mary kept to her room during the day, she tiptoed out at the crack of dawn to empty her chamber pot. This simple act was of enormous benefit to Mary and to whoever was caring for her. It meant that she kept clean, the laundryman kept calm, and the Kingsley Hall compost heap kept to its proper place on the roof garden and not under Mary's sheets.

Before I had left, I told Mary that eating and emptying the pot were part of her "treatment" (according to her vocabulary). She accepted my advice because she saw it was necessary to establish a balance between encorporation and evacuation. My contribution lay in anticipating what she wanted and conveying her own wishes to her in a way and at a time when she would accept them.

By mid-summer it had begun to dawn on Mary that it was she who decided her "treatment," not "Joe" or anyone else. Therefore to go against the "treatment" was to go against herself. This was a major breakthrough. Once Mary allowed herself to want what she wanted, she didn't have to use me or anyone else as an intermediary in order to avoid the excruciating guilt associated with "being in the wrong." What an overblown conscience Mary had had. How exhilarated and frightened she must have felt when she finally understood that her whole right and wrong "business" had been a delusion.

Mary's newfound freedom "to want" gave her the opportunity to sort out her desires and needs from those of the people with whom she had confused herself. This is an inner/outer differentiation, that is, between her internal experience and someone else's experience which, by definition, is external to her. Throughout the fall Mary practised and sharpened her ability to separate her inner world from outer realities. She no longer got terribly upset if I had to change or cancel a meeting with her. My reasonable explanation remained a reasonable explanation and not an excuse for a hellish punishment. This was great for me. I never failed to feel a tinge of guilt at such times even though I knew my guilt was "irrational" and was playing into her manipulative hands. Another example. Ronnie found that he could put Mary to

bed, shut her door and leave. A year earlier his leaving
would have precipitated a flood of tears. On this occasion
Mary did not think that she was losing part of herself. She
saw that "she," the door and Ronnie were separate, unique
entities.

Distinctions between Mary's inner experience and outer
inanimate events also became clearer. The apocalypse was
not at hand if the bath water turned cold, the Co-op ran out
of oranges, or the electricity failed. Whereas these situations
affected her, Mary realized that she did not cause them.
Eventually Mary's consciousness could weave through and
around all manner of 1) inner/outer; 2) inner/inner (two
parts of her own personality); and 3) outer/outer (two
separate external events) animate and inanimate events. And
her consciousness could do this without getting confused by
or entangled in chance similarities and contiguous relationships between one level of experience and another.

So far, I have demonstrated inner/outer distinctions which
had a spatial dimension but not a temporal one. They extended from one point in space, Mary, to another, Joe, but
within a time zone that was relatively the same for both of
us—our present. Yet, Mary was caught in a multidimensional
trap. She had to separate herself from relationships which
had taken place in the past, apart from people or events
in her present. The distinctions she had to make were not
just between the here and there, but also between the then
and now. If she could manage this, she would probably find
the "real Mary." This person had been buried under more
than forty years of conflicting identifications with her mother, father, brother, sisters, uncles, aunts, extended family
members, school teachers, and anyone else whom she had
incorporated with or without projected fragments of herself.

Mary's "present" was her "past." Her situation was equivalent to that of a woman who had forgotten she had put over
her head a magic set of goggles which transformed present
to past. As a result whomever she met, whatever she did,
was seen in terms of the mother she had known when she
was two years old, or the Sunday dinner she had eaten
when she was three and a half, etc., etc. This explains so
many of Mary's sudden, ostensibly inexplicable actions, atti-
tudes or moods while at Kingsley Hall. Recall the incident

in the Games Room when Mary suddenly attacked Joan after Joan had asked Mary to clean up her mess. Since Mary was wearing the magic goggles, the mise-en-scène immediately reminded her of a similar incident way back in her past. Something inside her went "click," and lo and behold her reality was no longer Joan and the Games Room, but somewhere in her childhood home being asked by her mother to clean up "that awful mess you have just made." Mary had attacked her mother. Joan was an innocent bystander who had had the bad luck to be cast into a Mary Barnes scenario without being asked if she wanted to play the part. Mary's own description of this event confirms my interpretation. She says, "Then, without 'knowing' what I was doing I was bashing and bashing Joan. It was terrible. I was all apart, terrified. Joan was a therapist. *Joan was as a Mother to me.*" (my italics). Quite true. Joan did serve Mary as a surrogate mother, both in the role as "helper" in the community, and as a character out of Mary's past.

Joe Berke was continually mobilized by Mary's memories, dreams and fantasies in a similar way, hence the curious sense of unreality I occasionally experienced in her presence. These situations never became real for me till I figured out who I was supposed to be for Mary and in what scenario. During the first months of our relationship I was not entirely successful at this enterprise so I sometimes walked away from Mary wondering whether I had been with her or not, and if not I, who? By 1966, however, I had a pretty good idea of what and who I was for her when we were together. "Mother" took the lead when she was Mary the baby. "Father" and "brother Peter" vied for second place. In order to protect my own sense of reality, and to help Mary break through her web of illusion, I always took the trouble to point out when I thought Mary was using me as someone else. As Mary came to trust me more and more she accepted my comments, even after I had picked the wrong character. Without getting too upset, she would say, "Oh no Joe, you're 'X,' not so and so." My big solid physique was a great help at these times. It was difficult for Mary to confuse me with her mother, a short arthritic woman, when she saw me towering above her.

Mary saw her past as a spider web in which she was

enveloped and from which she was struggling to break free. The spider was her controlling, dominating, all-possessive Mother. I think that the spider was Mary as well.

Escaping from the web was not a simple matter of cutting the meshwork and stepping outside. Mary had to face the existence of and her attachment to the sticky, adhesive, enveloping interrelated strands which penetrated in and through every aspect of her life. Each was a fantasied umbilical cord bringing pseudo support and satisfaction to a life which had not been able to use the outside world to gain nourishment and pleasure. Why give up, even become aware of the web, without some promise of a viable alternative. Fortunately, Mary's stay at Kingsley Hall and her relationship with me and Ronnie and the others provided the necessary alternatives. She then began the long process of letting loose her strangelehold on the past (she experienced this as the past letting loose its grips on her).

How did Mary accomplish this? Perhaps the first thing she did was to hallucinate spiders. She considered these hallucinations to be her way of exorcising her mother. I see no reason to doubt her. Later I gave her a large fearsome black rubber spider to play with. She kept this toy in her possession wherever she went. Mary thought that as long as the spider was outside her, it couldn't be inside her. Same reasoning held for the monster spiders which were some of the first figures she ever painted. The symbolic importance of these spiders once prompted me to suggest that this book might have been titled, *The Rosary and the Spider.*

Another technique was for Mary to come down with an assortment of aches and pains. This brought her mother out of her bowels and into the open. We knew it was her mother we were dealing with because every time I pointed out to Mary that her symptom assortment made her resemble her mother, they disappeared.

Mary also struggled to break her entanglement with her father. She felt that the only way she could be loved by her mother was to imagine that she was her father, or her brother Peter, too. Conversely, she believed that the only men who could love her were replicas of her father or brother. This false belief lay at the root of much of the guilt Mary experienced whenever her sexual feelings came to the fore. It meant that Mary saw every man through an incestuous eye.

Taking off the goggles which turned the present into the past was a precondition for Mary allowing herself to want what she wanted, especially as so many of her wants were of a sexual nature. Similarly, getting directly in touch with needs and desires made it possible for Mary to be sustained by an outside world which was not nearly as hostile as she imagined.

Although it took a long while before Mary realized that living in the present and expressing her own wants went hand in hand, she allowed each to take place during the course of her growing up and finding herself. By Christmas 1966 she observed, "The sight of the past was falling away. The sea was free. My inside made my outside."

Truly, Mary's inside did make her outside. When she felt bad, twisted up, entangled, injured or dead inside, her outside world was seen in the same manner. At such times, she would become pre-occupied with inside events and would not be able to take interest in anything that went on outside her. Good signs that internal problems were being resolved and that Mary had begun to effect a separation between inner and outer worlds was a renewed interest in, and involvement with, the mechanics of her life-support system as well as painting, meeting visitors, walking about the neighbourhood and participating in Kingsley Hall activities. To the extent that these good signs increased in number, intensity and complexity, Mary could be said to have entered an "up."

Mary's lighting brilliant red, blue and green sky rockets and bangers and sparklers on Guy Fawkes night heralded the onset of a slow sustained period of growth and development which culminated in the spring of '67 with a flurry of cooking, painting and trips to Victoria Park, a mile or so away from Kingsley Hall.

It was wonderful to watch Mary satisfy her essentially eclectic appetite by the sweat of her brow. Great efforts were expended to make sure that the food, the fire, the finished products all came out just right. Mary transformed a twelve-inch single-bar electric heater into a combination grill, stove and oven. The latter was what her room felt and smelled like when she concocted new candies and other delicacies. To say Mary has a sweet tooth is an understatement. Her tooth is the sweetest.

Eventually the electric cooker took on a sculptured quality as layer after layer of variously coloured soups and fruits dripped on to the metal holder and were baked into it. Moreover, Mary's creative ingenuity spilled over into her room. It came to resemble what modern artists call "an environment," and what Mary saw as a "tummy." Canned goods, bananas, oranges, grapefruit and biscuit boxes piled high atop each other vied for space amid food encrusted pots and pans, old clothes and assorted crucifixions.

Significantly, Noel and Paul no longer had to stock Mary's tummy, Mary supplied herself with whatever she wanted from the larder. She did this like a house mouse. She would wait till the kitchen was clear of people, then scurry inside, grab some fruit or cans and dash back to her room. Months passed before Mary felt free enough to simply stroll into the kitchen and take what she wanted whether others were there or not.

That Mary could cook for herself, and supply herself with needed food items, either from the larder or from the local grocer when she went out, indicated that she had taken into herself the capacity to nourish herself. Previously she thought that this nourishment could only be provided by some outside figure, originally her mother. Once Mary had separated herself from her mother, she did not have to repeat to herself the relationship which her mother had had with her. Mary did not have to feel guilty when she wanted to eat aside from times when her mother wanted her to eat, she didn't have to feel guilty about eating in her room, or taking food from the larder, or even being greedy. She could stuff herself with all the food she wanted and no internalized mother would punish her for doing so. Furthermore, she no longer felt that "mother" would only love her if she did not eat. She could eat and still feel love. This love was the love which I or others at Kingsley Hall felt towards her when we took care of her. When she ate her previous visions of a threatening punitive mother were superseded by a smiling encouraging happy "mother."

From Mary's standpoint, she had replaced a "bad" internalized relationship (her identification with her original mother) with a "good" one (her identification with "Joe"). This new relational structure gave her room to operate, both internally and externally. Most important, it laid the basis for her uncovering her "real self" by allowing her to discover who she was not and showing her how to continue the process of sorting out who she was from who she was not.

Mary learned about the existence of projections (bits and pieces of herself put on to others) and introjections (bits and pieces of others taken into herself), how to distinguish the one from the other, and how to separate herself from either. But the ultimate lesson was that the source of herself is herself, not "Joe" or anyone else. By 1967 this message had begun to sink in.

pass her mother's acceptance, hence the conflict.

Another incident to do with her fear of making the other residents of Kingsley Hall resentful of her new found skill, and in particular of all the attention and admiration

Part 5

The "up" years by Mary Barnes

Chapter Nineteen

I meet my parents again

Though I was still very afraid of my parents, there was in me a desire to meet them, and in January 1968 I saw them again. The gap was very wide. How to cope? Their anger at my change, at my freedom, in the inner escape I had made from them, was enormous. They felt my change as an attempt to harm them, to hit them, almost as if in expectation of punishment.

I saw them, and all that had happened, as a means of my salvation. My family, the circumstances of my birth, are a part of the providence of God, of the Divine wisdom.

I wanted so much to show my mother and father my love, my respect. It was very difficult, for they felt I was accusing them of conscious wrongdoing in the revelation of unconscious motives.

We did meet, at times, on a superficial level. With my mother, especially as she seemed to understand something of my painting, it was much easier. Also, she had never, like my father, tried to make a substitute partner of me. Above all, she was much nearer to herself, more aware of the truth than my father.

Alone together, my mother and I spoke of the death of my mother's eldest sister, an aunt of whom I had been very fond. Mother stroked my hair, I felt her love. We touched each other. Mother's hands were all knobbly with arthritis, her body was twisted in pain.

I felt very much "her little girl"—it was warm and safe to be near her. Then my father appeared, instinctively we moved apart.

Neither Mother nor Father understood the meaning of psychotherapy. We didn't talk about it. Not once was I asked anything at all about the past two years of my life, or about where I lived or with whom I lived. They seemed to want to forget, or not be associated with anything concerning "mental illness."

To them, Peter was being "looked after," dismissed, in the, to them only possible place for him, the chronic ward of a mental hospital.

My mother, in reference to my long hair, spoke about "wild women of the west," as if there was something "wrong," not nice about having long hair. Secretly, in church, I felt somewhat consoled remembering, Mary, the Mother of God, probably had long hair. An aunt of mine once told me, "Mary, now you are so much better you should *do* something about your hair." It seemed long hair was to *her* a sign of sickness.

My mother had always worn her own hair short, in a fringe, because that was how she liked it. Although I didn't like this hair style, it never occurred to me that my Mother was "bad" or "sick" because she wore *her* hair in that way. There never could be anything "right" or "wrong" about a hair style.

Very often I felt hurt, wounded by sheer apathy. Would they never say anything to me?

I ventured to read them some stories, "The Hollow Tree." Nothing, what was wrong? Squashed, dismissed, alone in bed in my room, the naughty child who had dared to "show off."

Later my Mother did display some of my paintings of her friends. This, my Mother's appreciation of my painting was a great joy to me. Later, when my Mother was angry, she again "didn't understand" my painting.

All the time I saw the way my parents hurt each other. To themselves, as they saw themselves, they were "happily married," they "loved" each other. My sister Ruth remarked, "I couldn't live like that. I would have got divorced or separated."

There was no way to tell my parents. Once I tried. "Why do you so hurt each other?" They looked amazed. "Mary, whatever is the matter with you?" I was to them completely mad, and I felt it. To suggest "why are you so cruel to each other" was to get oneself slaughtered. The deception was complete. If only something would break—if they hit each other physically.

I hated them hating each other, and longed to love them together. They seemed intent on total destruction and anything that penetrated their deceptive barriers to this aim was doomed to death.

The "normal, satisfactory, happy family." It was uncanny, sinister, how despite the factual data forever before them, they kept up the façade of apparent "happiness." Didn't they want to know, didn't they want to understand, now whilst still in this life? The answer was no, a most definite no. Sadly I held my peace, what was the use, a storm in which I got battered and they merely swelled in superior pride at my "illusions," my "madness."

My Mother thanked me for coming to see her. "I can't come to the station, I'd only be in the way." How often had we wanted Mother "in the way." She had never felt fit to be seen.

Chapter Twenty

Spring and Summer 1968—my time with

Catherine

They were painting the house and with some of the paint
I painted the door of my room, a tree with bare branches,
and roots, stretching up to God and rooted in God.

Muriel Lester, the person who founded Kingsley Hall, had
died and the house was being prepared for her memorial
service.

When the day came I was very angry, screaming at Ronnie
that it was a lot of whitewash and that I wanted clean
sheets on my bed. Noel and Paul had put clean sheets on
my bed when I was good, so I felt, now everything was
bad, and if I got clean sheets that would mean I wasn't
absolutely bad, hated, thrown away.

Noel got money from Pamela for me to get myself clean
sheets. I got striped ones, with a pillowcase to match, and
when they were on my bed life felt good again.

At this time I started going once a week to Joe's instead
of Joe coming to see me three times a week. This new arrangement was difficult for me because Joe rarely came to
Kingsley Hall.

On the way to Joe's, after leaving the Chalk Farm underground, there was a wasteland. It had once been a garden.
I picked masses of flowers from it through spring and summer—bluebells, roses, syringa and buddleia.

Joe would ask, "Did you leave any?" Then he said, "Mary,
there's only one person greedier than you. Do you know
who that is?"

"No."

"Me, Joe Berke."

Joe's sink would overflow, petals falling, water dripping. An hour later, with a huge wet bundle of flowers in paper, would I emerge, off for another week. My room, the dining-room, the Games Room, everywhere on Wednesday—fresh flowers—I had been to Joe's.

Morty Schatzman and his wife-to-be, Vivien, were living with us, at home. They helped me quite a bit, especially with regard to meeting other people who lived in the house. I was completely raw, like flesh without skin.

Visitors were a problem. Although I often felt like getting to know other people I never knew how. Once, when feeling bad and crying on the roof, I said to one of the other people, David—David Page Thomas,

"What am I? *Nothing, nothing!"*

He replied, "Is it not enough for you to be a suffering member of humanity?"

I realized it was, though I could not *then* know the fullness, the deep happiness of resignation, that resignation Christ must have experienced in carrying the Cross.

It did now seem safer to paint outside my room, and this time my paintings were tolerated in the Games Room. Through the help of Morty I was given the dining-room wall to paint and on it with my fingers I did "Christ Triumphant." Ten feet by twelve, it took eight hours and a step ladder to do it. The upper part was the three stages of sacrifice, the lamb in fire of the Old Testament, the Lamb of God, Christ Crucified, and then the Host, the sacrifice of the Mass. Below was the foot of the Cross, St. John, the Mother of God, Mary Magdalen, and Mary of Cleophus.

Then when I had finished it there was a storm. Terrified, my heart sank, but the painting survived. David, who had been upset by the painting, accepted a small work on hardboard, "Impressionist Cherry Blossom" which was what he wanted me to paint.

Joe gave me lots of old Dialectics of Liberation posters to cover the floor and benches in the Games Room so I could paint without spoiling the room, which had then been newly decorated.

Grace Conner, a medical student and friend of Joe's, came from America to stay for the summer. This was a great joy to me for I seemed to be able to "meet" Grace. Twice we went out together, to the cinema and to the Matisse exhibition. I painted "He Shall Come as the Sun" and a huge sun on hardboard for the Hamsptead Open Air exhibition. Then Roberta showed me some big sunflowers she was growing and I painted "Sunflowers." Everything seemed very much connected with the sun. This was the first summer I had "been around," met other people, in the house.

Geoffrey was my special friend. Fanning himself in my room, he told me, "You're my friend, you are." His feet in the kitchen sink, Geoffrey turned, trembling, frightened, "How long have you been here?" On the roof Geoffrey lay, very bad. He lit fires in the yard, then on the roof, and some people got frightened and wanted Geoffrey to leave. I couldn't understand this. I was afraid of the other people but not of Geoffrey. This was always my difficulty, how to cope with my terror in the house, of being with "other people" who were not therapists and who were not mad.

I did a lot of abstract paintings of my anger, one of which Claus, a visiting Swedish psychologist, particularly liked. In clay I made a "Head of Janet," a girl who lived in the house.

It seemed to me at this time that I wanted to meditate. The little chapel downstairs became my room for this. In went a little crib, a clay sculpture of the Mother of God, finger paintings of Isaiah and St. Joseph and the Sacred Heart. Also an incised clay of the Crucifixion.

As soon as I settled in there with my prayers, Morty promptly decided he wanted to use the room. He reminded me I was well behind with my rent for the one room I already had.

I took a dim view of this, though I realized that Morty must have acted the way he did in order to avert the anger of the house from my head. The chapel had previously stood empty for months and I had given the promise that when I sold paintings I would pay rent.

Christine Doyle came from the *Observer* and for the first time my own name was used in the press. I remained in rent trouble for the rest of the summer, being given notice several times, though I had a short break being away at the Buddhist monastery in Scotland and at the convents in Wales for two weeks. After this, with the help of Peter Barham, a visiting psychologist from Cambridge, some relief from the rent was gained, on condition that I paid something every week.

Before leaving for Scotland I had a lot of terribly angry dreams. Joe said one of these was a healing dream. This dream was about Joe being sick. His forehead was burning. He had swollen angry spots, like blunt boils. It seemed I was not supposed to visit him and that he had osteo-arthritis in his knee. I went to see him. His life was feared for, he was so ill. Roberta was there, his wife. Joe was not cross, but glad to see me. I seemed to wake, melting with relief.

Outwardly I was, though not always realizing it, in a great heat of anger. Anything seeemed to make me feel bad, very bad, out of all proportion to the event.

Bill Mason, a friend of Joe's, came to advise me about sticking some paintings on to hardboard. He was some time in coming, but I told myself "this was therapy." The only "right" thing therefore was to wait, not to ring him again. In waiting, my anger rose.

Then there was a letter from the Presteigne convent asking me to change my plans as they had some nuns coming to stay. Agitated, aware that I was bad, very bad, I went for help to Joe's. He was out and my anger frightened Roberta, who was expecting a baby.* On the phone Joe gave me some relief. "You're angry, very angry with the nuns, but you won't let yourself feel angry, what did Mother Anne say?"

If only I wasn't so vulnerable to such terrible feelings, to such "badness" at the slightest touch, it seemed.

Mother Anne was written to and I carried on, seemingly all right, by coach to Scotland.

At the Buddhist monastery I met Kesang and Akong, whom I had already met when he had visited Kingsley Hall earlier in the year. On arrival at the monastery I joined the other people in a meal on the lawn, then being tired, was shown to my room by Kesang. About three hours later on waking from solid sleep I was very very bad. My first thought was to get home, at once. However on coming down the stairs I met Kesang, who got Akong.

*Later she lost the baby but Joe assured me my anger had not killed the baby. It seemed I was "in punishment" for months about this anger.

Walking about the garden I kept telling Akong all the badness inside me was coming out. I really seemed to, for I got all eased and sleepy and had warm milk and honey. The next morning after a lighter, troubled sleep the same thing happened but not nearly so violently. The day before I could have killed myself with badness. Now, with Kesang, I walked by the river and we talked and I got quiet and relieved. For the rest of my time at the monastery I was not bad and loved Kesang and Akong. Something inside me seemed to have melted and instead of being screwed up and hating was easy and loving.

When I got to Wales, the anger somehow took a different turn. At Presteigne I got a very bad cold and really felt ill and at Llandovery I was torn to bits with itching.

Mother Michael wondered whatever the rash was and sent me to the local doctor. He said it was gnat bites. In Scotland there had been swarms of midges and people were smearing themselves with skin cream. My skin was then perfectly all right. I had dreams of having babies, feeling the legs inside me. Then two babies, girls in big bubbles of fluid were born of me, with loud, ticking hearts.

One evening Leon and his wife Liz brought a young girl to the house. I shall call her Catherine. When on holiday in Morocco she had gone down into her madness. Liz was a friend of hers and had gone to Morocco to bring her back home.

When she first arrived at Kingsley Hall Catherine looked dazed and wandered about the house. Because there was then no room vacant in the house, her bedroom was the sitting-room of the Flat.

We first met in the chapel. It was my custom to call in there on my way out. Catherine was there, bent up, as if very bad with "IT," anger. I'm kneeling on the floor, she puts her head on my lap. "I want to get down in the dark. Put ashes on myself."

"Yes, I understand. I've felt like that."

I was remembering how when going mad I just had to get down *inside* the building.

She touches me, my hand.

"Yes," slowly dazed, "that's *you.*"

Touching herself—yes, that's me. Bewildered, frightened. "I'm not here."

Very quietly, "Catherine," touching her hand, "that is you. This is me," touching my hand. "Your body is here. You are your body. I *know* how you feel. You *cannot* completely lose yourself."

Silence.

"Mary,"—agitated—distressed—half-standing—"everything in the house is to do with me." Holding her, quiet.

"I know how you feel." We sit. She is sort of gasping.

Very scared, in a whisper, "They are throwing me out—they are throwing me out."

"No, Catherine. We want you. We love you"—holding her, gently kissing her head. She is very cold. We are near the crib.

"I want to steal. I thought in Morocco I gave birth to baby Jesus, really I'm barren, had no periods, don't want to marry and just have children."

"Would you like me to get your blanket, the one you brought from Morocco."

"Mm."

We rubbed noses. On the stairs, Vivien was going down for the milk.

"Catherine is in the chapel. She feels lost. I'm going up for her blanket."

"Mary, I'll go down to her."

Somehow, things don't seem quite right, but I left her to Vivien.

Some days later, on the stairs, Catherine took my hand and led me to a room downstairs.

"Lie down with me."

She put her head on my breast, as if to suck. Maybe she wants a bath, she's very cold.

"Catherine, shall we go up to the bath?"

She lets me take her hand and walk her to the bathroom. As I'm bathing her I'm wondering whether she would like to go to her bed in the Flat.

No, she seems dazed.

"Well, would you like to come and sit in my room?"

"Oh, yes, I would like *that*." She looks round the room.

"You have got a lot of things." We play with my dolls.

For some days, although aware of Catherine being around, I didn't really seem to "meet" her. (Joe told me, just tell her you have been like that, you understand how she feels.)

Then Ronnie came to dinner with Kris Kringel, a visiting American psychiatrist, and Morty Schatzman. They were talking with various guests up in the Flat. Catherine sat herself beside me. Ronnie was lying on the floor. We moved downstairs, Morty, Ronnie, Catherine with me.

We had some wine, Ronnie was talking to Catherine, I was lying behind her. Then it was time to eat—"and Mary wants some too." Ronnie was walking off and Morty with him.

Somehow it seems Catherine and I should stay where we were.

"Mary, I want some dinner."

"Let's wait awhile—lie down."

"No, no."

"Catherine, please—wait—keep still—I'll ask." Ronnie was right behind the dining-room door.

"Er, Ronnie—"

The door shuts, I'm in no doubt. There was a divan bed and Catherine should be lying in it.

"Ronnie means you to go to bed."

"But Mary, but—" She is angry, frightened, running across the Games Room. I chase after.

I'm kneeling on the floor lifting up my dress as I can't hold my water. The carpet is soaked. How to hold Catherine. She is sitting by the window—darts up the stairs, me after her. We are on the roof, Catherine is crouching down.

"Stand up, it's important—listen to me—Ronnie understands how you are—it's better you don't have dinner and come to bed." She runs into the Flat. We sit on the floor. Vivien comes in. They are coming up here for coffee. Oh God—coffee.

"Catherine, please," I'm whispering in her ear, "let's go down." She edges out.

We get downstairs, she lets me help her to bed. Ronnie is talking in the dining-room. We hear him for a long time. I'm kneeling over Catherine. Eventually she goes to sleep. It was Friday night. We stayed quiet until Sunday afternoon, though Catherine had one bad spell.

The children were playing below in the road.

"What's that, I must go out to them, they are to do with me." She darted to the window.

"Come back, they are outside, you are here, in bed."

I pulled her back to bed. Somehow she settled, putting her head near my breast.

Catherine could change very quickly, from a baby, cuddling my Teddy, to a university person wanting her lecture notes. This was her structure, students, lectures, meetings, the rope she tried to grab when her fear of letting go, of dropping down into her real self, to the baby she wanted to be, was too great.

"Men are so demanding, I don't really want to be with Nigel. Can we have an orange?"

"Yes, when Kris brings some more." Kris was regulating our food intake. Half a bottle of milk, half an apple, how to make it last. Instinctively I was vigilant. It was much more difficult for Catherine for she was full of anger, feeling very bad, broken, apart and trying to submit her will, something only possible with trust and love. Could she trust and love us enough? How could I hold her to herself? Joe had told me, "You have a very strong will."

When going into myself I would at times lie like a log, immune to interruption. This is what people sometimes called my obstinacy. Joe said I was obstinate in a good way.

How to convey to Catherine, persist inwards, refuse to be pulled out, let me add my will to yours; lay bare, grow, work through your madness, suffer yourself.

If there was pain in her body, was there more in mine? She must be free to be angry with me. I must keep quiet, very "in," apart, yet warm, loving.

I knew from my own past the disaster that can come from eating when feeling very bad. It was better to eat sparingly and to get dry. To be "wet" full of fluid was not good. It was silly, made one rather a "jelly fish" slipping about all over the place. Instead of being contained, enduring, like a camel in the desert. It was a long trek, the inner journey, too much water drowned the soul. A dinner at night was too much, like fuelling the boiler when you really wanted the water cold. Sometimes, as Joe had told me, I took more fluid, if my water got very little and dark.

Catherine was drinking enough, more than enough. "Mary, may I have a drink of water?"

"Yes—where's Teddy? You know Joe is a big bear. Ronnie gave me Teddy. You are the Baby Bear," smoothing her hair.

"Say some prayers."

"All right. Dear Jesus, please may we go to sleep? God bless everyone."

"When you went to Mass this morning you did go to Communion?"

"Yes."

Catherine sighs, satisfied.

"Have you got the spare Rosary?"

"Mm, here," unzipping Teddy's back. Takes it, subsides, with my hand upon her.

Catherine was very sensitive to my hand on her back. Gradually as she slept I would raise my hand. If not quite asleep she would always stir, as a baby may wake when the rocking stops. Often I laid her with one arm under her body and her head well back as I had been put.

How to keep the body still, when full of anger and worry and fear? When first going down into my own madness I had battled with distractions, strong tea, coffee, cigarettes, talk. Just to listen to people speaking, on and on, could make one yawn, be relaxing, like a boring droning lecture on a summer afternoon.

How to convince Catherine that some things, good in themselves, and ideal in usual circumstances, could now be adverse influences, hindrances to the immediate necessity of getting to herself.

It was a case of submitting the lesser good for the greater gain. One cigarette instead of tea, milk rather than tea, and being without books.

Unable to reason, Catherine was out of her reason, there could seem no sense at times in not following a sudden urge to read a book. This was her fear, her resistance to "being."

"Mary, what will happen? Shall I be lost in you? When you went out of the room it seemed I had gone away."

"Catherine you are not inside me. This is me, touching my body, and this is you," holding her hand. "We are not alone. Morty and Kris who really understand, are in the house. The other night when Ronnie was here with us both, he indicated to me that it was good for us to be together. It's because I've had similar experiences that I know how you feel, so I can understand.

"I used to feel a part of Joe as if inside him. It doesn't matter. You come through that to being really alone, separate from your real Mother and Father as you have never yet been."

"Can we do clay?"

Oh dear, I was talking too much—shut up—then she would.

"Let's have a bath."

"All right."

The water was warm. Her hair was like weed. We got quiet. She lay in bed. I boiled an egg, lightly. With her eyes shut she took it, slowly as I fed her. Then there was peace. When the milkman came there was milk, warm from a glass or cold, sucked through a straw. My breast was her bottle. I would kneel over her, and she would put her mouth to my nipple. This was satisfying to me. We both enjoyed it.

She felt bad, like "shit." "I used to put my shits all over me. Has Teddy had shits today?"

Catherine laughed. She plastered herself, in her hair, over her breasts. I put a shitty blanket round myself. "I'm not frightened of your shit"—and off we went, to the bath.

Catherine played a bit more, messing it in her hands, then we washed it all away. Very relieved and loving, Catherine let herself be cuddled and wrapped in my red dressing gown. It suited her flaxen hair. We had laughed and splashed water, and squirted it from our mouths, as whales in the waves.

From the Games Room Catherine moved to my room, to the Hall, to the Chapel, upstairs, downstairs, in and out of my room, unable to settle, unable to stay in, inside herself.

"How can we get back to how we were that weekend in the Games Room?"

"Be patient, stay quiet, it will come again."

It never really did except perhaps, for one day, in my room. Kris came that night and we ate oranges and Catherine slept until the noise of coke being shovelled suddenly woke her.

"What is that? I must go out, down to the dustbins, it's to do with me."

"Stay here, it's outside, you are here, inside." She is furious, punching a cushion, twisting her body and screaming. "Every minute I'm killing someone. Hate everyone. Hate myself. Am worthless." Catherine is opening her mouth and throwing her arms about. Eventually as she subsides, I put off all light and kneel over her until she falls asleep.

During the day she played with her shits, watered on my pot. Sometimes I bathed her, washing her hair. We played Fish and Mermaid and sometimes sharks, biting and splashing the water.

Once when I was having a bath Catherine silently came in behind me. In a daze she had taken off her clothes, stepped into the water, inviting me to bath her, which I did. She confided, "I want to go in, be how it was before."

Sometimes she slept in bed, fully dressed, afraid to uncover. Perhaps I could undress her, it was not always safe to do so for fear of shaking her away from herself, usually I left her as she chose to be, but once when she was rather in a panic and we had chased round the roof I continued the play into undressing, rolling in bed, covering up and going to sleep.

That was the night Maud Manoni, a famous French psychiatrist was visiting us. She was in the Hall giving a lecture. I was around the house after Catherine, who had, early in the evening got the idea of dressing up and going down into what she felt was a party. Always fearful for her, realizing the state she was in, I was trying with the help of Leon and David (Dr. Redler and Dr. Cooper who had come to hear the lecture) to help her to rest, to return to bed, to stay upstairs.

The "opposition" (other people who, not understanding the state Catherine was in, did not realize how much was at stake) seemed particularly strong that night. A visitor was trying to make a date with her, anyone might escort her downstairs. Somehow we stayed upstairs, eventually settling in my room. Then Janet, who was feeling bad, came in to see me, and we all ended up helping ourselves to wine from the buffet prepared for the guests.

Leon appeared and did likewise, and from there, Janet went to her room to bed and Catherine ran on to the roof.

I held her on my hip, we danced and growled and hit and screamed and then ran down to bed, in the Games Room. No sooner had I undressed Catherine, than the guests surged into the next room for their food and wine.

Naked, from under a heap of blankets on the floor I darted up to switch off all our lights. No one intruded. I kneeled over Catherine until she went to sleep. We had survived the evening.

My clothes were soaked. I'd done a big pee. In our times of stress and strain it was me that watered. Catherine would use the pot, saying "I want to do a tinkle." At times when movement could be very disturbing to her, I would suggest, it's all right, just let it come, wet the bed, knowing from my own experience what a relief it could be to lie in the damp warmth.

What did seem very important to Catherine was to be able to put her head against my breasts and sometimes she would suck with her mouth on my breast. This happened all through my time with her.

Silently she would steal into my room like a little bird, pull back the bedclothes, and putting her head down suck on my breast, then cover me over and creep away. She came, and went. Sometimes standing at the door, opening and shutting it, coming and going. It was like waiting for a little bird. One day you keep quite still, hand held out with food. You look at the sky, no sign. You go indoors. Next day, quite suddenly, the bird is there, perching on your shoulder. How still you have to be, caring, yet not caring, like God grows a tree, to let be.

Mistaken efforts to help Catherine often annoyed me. People would want to take her out, or to interest her in other things and trivial talk. Once Pamela, a girl who lived in the house, took her to the library and Nigel, a boy who was then living at Kingsley Hall, often sought her company. Weak, in a daze and very frightened, Catherine found great difficulty in resisting the pull "out."

I tried gently talking to Nigel, helping him to see what was at stake for Catherine. She would be quiet, going in, lying without talking in bed. Nigel would come, and they would talk, once about chess. From talking, Catherine would want more activity, to answer the phone, to see people.

Distractions, movement away from herself. At times I seemed bursting with frustration, unable to explain to her, unable to convince other people of what seemed to me her urgent need to be left, to "get in" and to stay in, inside herself. Conversely, my relief and sheer state of "being" with her when she did suffer the difficult pain of herself was immense.

I could see the change in her when she was "still." No longer wanting to read, write, talk or do anything she would let herself go and become clear and beautiful in spirit. For odd moments she seemed complete, then all would be shattered, lost, bewildered, fallen apart.

"Mary, I must phone, why can't I talk to Nigel? It's the beginning of term. I've some writing to do."

She couldn't seem to rest with me, nor yet alone, without me. How to help her get in?

"Mary can I do some clay, a painting?"

"Better lie still."

"But why? Let's have a bath."

"All right." How to *tell* her? If only I had all the skill of Joe and Ronnie. It was her life—she was losing it. Paul who had helped me so much when I was down, advised me, "Don't make rules for yourself."

"Please, Vivien, Karen, Catherine isn't well enough to answer the phone."

"But Mary—I can answer it." Again and again she would contact the disturbance and be drawn out into it. Maybe I was jealous if Nigel came, but no, I told myself, it's her *life* I fear for. If she doesn't go in, stay clear of the distractions of others, what can happen? Nothing but an evasion of the trouble, electric shocks, hospital, apparent "cure," another breakdown—recovery—the cover-over all again, then another breakdown. This was what I feared for her. The impulse to reach down, to touch the truth within herself was very strong.

Sometimes I got angry, with myself, with her, with the other people.

"Nigel, please leave us alone. Catherine, lie still, no don't go, not now."

"But Mary."

"Oh, all right." How to curb my wrath, my frustration, to let her go and yet to hold her.

Grave as the danger was from distractions within the house, what really tipped the balance was the intrusion of her parents upon her when she was in a very frightened and fragile vulnerable state. She was terrified, unable to communicate in words, and the impact was too much for her. Her parents had come on her birthday.

Catherine went to greet them. It seemed she wanted to show them all she had got and was looking to them to approve, to understand. Uncovered, as a little child, she couldn't really quite believe they "didn't know." They really didn't. We were unable to tell them. It was very difficult for Catherine to know which way to go. The grip of the past was upon her. Exposed, fragile as the tiny child, how could she not be swayed by the power of the parents? They were wanting to take her away.

I lay in my room, aware she was in difficulty. Then the door opened, Catherine was coming in and out. She came in, over to me, dazed and speechless. She seemed numb, put her arms round my neck. "Catherine, can you say what you want, tell them?"

"I want to stay." She was cold, frightened, lost and apart.

Her parents were in my doorway. Her father's hand was upon her, "Come on, sunshine." She seemed stuck, unable to move. Dead, she followed her parents out. It seemed she had gone, everything got very quiet outside. A car drove off.

Her friend, Liz, the wife of Leon, came to my room. She was sobbing. I put my arm round her. She had brought Catherine to us, she had so wanted her to stay, to get better. Leon came for Liz, people gradually dispersed. Somehow I felt that Catherine would be back and told Kris so.

There was a phone call from the police station. Cindy, a girl who lived in the house, took it. Catherine was ringing to ask for help, she wanted someone from the house to come and bring her home.

Cindy went with some other people. They found her with her parents. The police had explained to her parents that Catherine was free to make her own choice. Alone, with her parents and the police she had decided to return to Kingsley Hall.

Everyone was very happy and full of joy that she was back. Eventually, quite late at night, Catherine came to my room. She was dazed and quiet. Stroking her hair, I laid her down to sleep. It was the end of her birthday.

Soon after this, Catherine got sick with diarrhoea and vomiting. It came on rather late one evening and Morty arranged for me to take her to the London Hospital. The doctor who saw us told me, "It's probably gastro-enteritis. Take her home to bed and give her these tablets, two for the tummy, and one for sleep."

I spent the night with Catherine as she was very restless. She sicked up the tablets, then went to sleep. I lay on the floor by the side of her bed. In the morning Vivien came to her room, bringing us milk and more tablets. I wondered whether, now with this tummy upset, Catherine might rest more in bed in her room.

Morty assured me all was well, "Go away, as you intended this weekend, we will look after her." When I got back Catherine was around again.

On the Wednesday morning I was going out to Joe's. "Catherine, I'm just going out to Joe's." It was always my habit to let her know where I was.

On my return she had gone. Her sister, a trained nurse, had come and taken her to hospital. Various people in the house told me they had seen Catherine being walked off between her sister and another woman after her sister had failed to persuade Dr. Samuel Brill, the local general practitioner of Catherine, to commit her to a mental hospital.

To me, it seemed her sister coming was the end of a long battle her parents, in their ignorance and fear, had waged. Between the time of Catherine returning to us from the police, until the time of her final going there had been continued pressure put upon her to leave, her parents begging her, by way of phone and letter to return to them.

It seemed her parents had been unable to consider there could be treatment other than drugs and electric shocks. If only they could have trusted Ronnie or Leon—or just me, to tell them how it was possible to get through a madness, to be healed, to get sound, just by being with people who understood.

It was so sad, to realize how they must have thought they wanted to help her, yet were using all their strength to drag her away from herself, really simply because their entire trust was in drugs and physical treatments.

I wondered if her mother at all connected her present state with the circumstances of her birth. Catherine had told me, "I was born prematurely at home, taken at once from my mother to hospital, and put in an incubator."

Her sister was a trained nurse. That made me think of the time my brother was first taken to a mental hospital. It had happened through my intervention. As the "nurse" of the family I had rather told my parents, with the help of a doctor that my brother was "ill." I imagined Catherine's sister was much as I had been, recently trained, authoritative, deciding, the best of intentions with the most complete lack of true knowledge.

Catherine seemed the victim not only of her own lack of communication but also of our inability to reach through to her parents to help them to trust us.

Chapter Twenty-one

On to Christmas 1968—adventures with John—

weekend in Paris

After the time of Catherine, when the weather was no longer warm, I had a strange physical experience.

During the night I became so hot that sleep was impossible. It seemed my whole body was on fire, burning to a cinder. Never before had I known such heat.

I put cold towels soaking wet under my armpits, sponged down my body with cold water. The fire continued, it seemed inside me. Desperately, I went up to the bathroom on the roof. It was cold, the middle of the night, I lay in a bath of cold water, came down to bed dripping wet and slowly cooling off, went to sleep.

Later, trying to think of some explanation, I wondered with Joe whether it was to do with the cycle of my periods, the time being about that of ovulation. Never before had such a happening occurred. I thought too of the spiritual expression of the saints, "on fire with the love of God."

Morty was leaving. He did not expect to be with us for Christmas. Through Morty I had had the experience of three professional seminars, something I had not participated in for some time.

The first was a large gathering with Leon and Sid present —and I mainly just listened, only afterwards speaking, individually, to a few people. The second group was smaller and Mr. Gargon was there, the warden from the hostel in Wimbledon where my brother then lived. Morty had arranged for me to show some of my paintings and give a short talk. First Morty spoke, then Peter Barham, the psychologist from Cambridge who had helped me through my rent troubles, then I said my bit, reading two of my stories.

Then we came upstairs to the Games Room where people dispersed and everything felt easier: Irving Sarnoff, an American analyst at the Tavistock clinic, told me his wife was an artist. Could he bring her to see my paintings, would I come to supper and meet Sarah, his thirteen-year-old daughter? Mr. Gargon came to see my room, the Tavistock students were full of questions. It really was fun, and I felt quite ready for the next such visitors, a group of student nurses with their tutor. Peter Barham had arranged this seminar.

With regard to my own past nursing experience, I used sometimes to remember how angry I had been. Joe helped me to see how my anger was due to the fact that I had become a nurse in order to appease my guilt, the guilt of having "caused" all my Mother's illness. Glad as I was to see the students, I felt no inclination towards their work. In time with Joe I would come to help people more for the sake of the other person and not as a means to the appeasement of guilt.

One of the students asked me, "Do you go out?"

"Yes, sometimes."

"Can you communicate with people outside?" Morty afterwards told me the simple "right" answer. "Am I not now communicating with you?" At the time I rather struggled to convey the fact of my gap—how inside experiences cannot be transferred from without.

The tutor particularly liked my finger-painting on wood of tulips.

In November, when Peter Goodliffe came from Oxford to photograph some of my work I finger-painted "Peter the Fisherman." Father Gerald Pietersen, a young priest in South Africa, had asked my Mother what she would call a new church in a fishing village. She had told him, "Peter the Fisherman," and he consequently asked me to do such a painting.

Peter Goodliffe had a cine-camera and with the help of his assistant made a film of me doing the painting.

"Mary, what does the colour mean? Did you know you were going to do it like that?"

"No, I let it come, how it wants, that's yellow for the light of God, here, Peter is orange and red, lots of red, aflame with the love of Christ."

Eventually when the painting was dry, and well-varnished against the mists and salt of sea air, I saw it off to the docks, on its way to Cape Town, bound for the church of Gansbaai. Six foot by four foot, it was going in the porch of the church. The painting shows the saint as the Peter of his ministry, the first Pope. Strong in faith, he now "walks on the water."

About this time a Swedish journalist from the paper *Dagens Nyheter* came to see us. Karen took many photos of us all and of my paintings for this paper. When I saw the faces of Ronnie and David clearly shown and mine blacked out I was furious. Joe helped me to write at once asking the Editor to apologize to his readers and to print the photo again with my face properly showing.

One Sunday afternoon Morty asked me to meet two friends, Kieran and Charlie. They had come to get to know us all and wanted to make a film about life in the community. We walked around the house. I was speaking of my experiences. Kieran asked,

"Could I come to stay for a week?"

"Maybe, it depends on what the other people feel about it."

There was not all that enthusiasm on the part of the community for a film, but it was agreed that Kieran came to stay for a few days. People didn't feel like "being observed." I told Kieran.

"Tomorrow I'm going to finger-paint my big canvas, if you would like to come and watch."

"Oh, yes, I'd love to see that."

We became good friends and Charlie brought some of his technical team in. They brought lots of special foods and wine. We feasted for a week. Then, there was a big meeting, us and them. This was to decide were we going to have the film. I was all excited about it, thinking of photos of paintings, and what I might wear.

People started shouting. It seemed they felt a film could be very dangerous. Morty listened carefully, was very sympathetic. The film people were very keen, the cameras were downstairs. Bottles and glasses got smashed. Ian had an explosion. He shattered, fell to pieces. Vivien helped him down to his room. Kieran was frightened, crying. I put my arms round her.

"Mary, I wanted the film but what's the matter, what's the matter? It's all my fault. What's happened with Ian?"

"It's all right, he just got angry and it made him feel he was all splintered, going away, losing himself. I've been like that. You can't really lose yourself but you get terrified that you will. It's the shattering effect of your own anger, causing you to feel it's killing you and all around you."

"He'll be all right?"

"Yes, of course. His anger hasn't really hurt him, or any of us."

Kieran was comforted. Morty spoke with the men and they decided to pack up and leave. Ian's point was that if they wanted to make a film about Kingsley Hall, they would find it more useful, more helpful, to make a film about themselves, the results of which would be quite interesting and possibly terrifying. About the last we heard of it was from Ronnie.

"It never happened to me before; but as I was going to shake Charlie's hand, we missed; our hands didn't meet."

This time of year, autumn going into winter, gave me feelings of death, of going home to God. Especially as it got dark would I sense the comfort of dying, the very aloneness, the weary sadness of the fading day. Holding Donk, my dog doll, I read the pictures on my books, gifts of Joe: Animals of "Where the Wild Things Are"; the Crocodile Who Stole the Sun, the Jungle, and the Sea. It gets darker. I'm lying still; sleep is near. There's all the tunes from across the road. It's the Saturday night social; "Knees up Mother Brown," "Happy Birthday to You"—it's always someone's birthday, "Auld Lang Syne"—for the sake of Auld Lang Syne.

Laughter, noise in the road. They're going home. It's quiet. Into the sleep of night. They have all gone.

I'm away, in the dark, with angels and dreams.

As Christmas approached I made many cards, all of the sun, breast of the earth. A different sun for everyone in the house and a specially big one for Joe and Roberta.

For Sid and for Leon and Liz I made angels. Ronnie

got a fish, symbol of Christ, and when it got lost in the post I felt bad, very bad. That seemed all "to do" with Joe. What had I done so that Ronnie's card had got lost?

Joe said, "Make another and send it recorded delivery."

This I did, but still hardly able to really believe Ronnie's card had got lost It had been a specially nice fish with gold in the waves. Even now, with floods of imagination, I see it messed up, thrown away in the post, and my anger surges up.

Then I got on to angels in cardboard, a big one, and lots of little ones in gold, and blue stars, for the Christmas tree and underneath in clay a baby Jesus with sheep and Mary and Joseph.

Baby Jesus was still wet and someone messed him up. My anger started choking me and life seemed absolute hell, like when someone had splattered blood on my paintings. I knew my work wasn't me and how terrible it was to feel bad and that people mattered more than any "thing." Even so, it seemed a hard thing, making me want to run away somewhere where it would be "safe" to love and be creative, without stirring up destruction. That's heaven, perfect harmony, a place to be waited and worked for.

In the church there was a beautiful big crib with life size figures in the straw. I went to midnight mass. Candlelight, all the people, Communion, me and baby Jesus. Back home in my room was Joe's present all wrapped in wonderful paper. It was a marvellous book, "The Bald Twit Lion," and on the cover the sun, shining in the jungle.

Christmas had come. Dear Jesus I love you, goodnight.

On St. Stephen's Day I painted the stoning of Stephen and for the second time, "Spring the Resurrection" in which Christ still enshrouded is rising from the wild earth through bare flowering trees to the serene glory of the sun. Since painting "Time of the Tomb" I had been impelled to paint the Resurrection.

"Time of the Tomb" was a work done in November showing Christ crucified within a tree. It was the barrenness of winter with the glory of autumn fallen to the ground. Christ was going down into the tomb, to the sleep of winter, to die to live. Then on hardboard I had shown very early spring, Christ being as a bud, rising up through hazel catkins to pale rays of sun. Later, well after Christmas, on wood, came the third painting, "Spring the Resurrection." Here the spring is well advanced, with flowers on the ground; and the arms of Christ flung open wide.

When Morty left, James Greene, a psychologist, came to live at Kingsley Hall. He reminded me what a compliment it was to the nuns that I first went down into my madness, into a truer state away from my false self, at the convent.

At this time John Woods, who had come to Kingsley Hall from the Anti-University some months before, was going down into his madness and was much troubled by delusions. "I got to be looked after, I'm ill, I got delusions." John used to sit over the fire in the flat. He held a big crucifix to his stomach, as I used to hold my Rosary over my tummy when in bed. John's cross hung by a long string over his bare hairy chest.

"I moved into the big bedroom up here."

"But John, that's someone else's room. Your room is downstairs. Shall I come down with you?"

"No, no, I'm staying up here."

"Would you like me to get James?"

"Yes, get James."

John was shivering.

In the middle of the night my door burst open, John flung himself into the room, "They're after me, can I stay with you?"

"What, John?"

The black magic, Nigel's got a whip. James is in it, and Cindy." John was trembling, agitated, in a panic.

"Look, you've had like a bad dream, and just now it all seems real."

"You don't believe me?"

"Yes, but it's a sort of nightmare you're in."

"It's all right then?"

"Yes, nothing is going to harm you. Let's go down to your room."

We walk downstairs, John is very nervous. He bolts his door. I undo it.

"Let's sit down, I'll put your fire on."

John is very cold, though fully dressed. He always kept his clothes on, being far too frightened to undress. We sit on his bed. John seems to settle.

"I'll be all right now, you can go."

"Well, just stay still, but come up again if you feel bad."

"Maybe I'll go for a walk."

"It's better to stay in."

"I mean a walk in the Hall." John often paced up and down, round and round, the Hall. "Don't disturb me, I'm deep in thought," he would say.

John in a panic, tearing into my room, was as a two-year-old child. That is how I felt him, the baby in a bad dream, running to a "mother." I was not frightened because of how he was. His terror was quite real. He was afraid to be alone.

James suggested, ask him if he would like to go to church with you. "John, if you want to come to Mass with me?"

"Yes, call me in the morning." We got out in the street, John was disturbed.

"Hear, can you see, all those cars, going round the block. She's in one, they're driving her around."

"John, it's all inside you."

"No, listen to me, they've got her, in the black magic. Naomi—you know—Naomi—she was crucified last night. I killed her. Murder's been committed. I got to find out. I got to save her—go after her."

I knew of course that Naomi was John's ex-girlfriend. She had recently left him for another boy. John in his despair and anger maintained that she was caught in a "black magic" spell and that he must therefore go after her in order to save her. This was the basis of all his black magic delusions, into which at times he put various people of Kingsley Hall.

John began to walk rapidly.

"Just now, John, we are going to Mass."

"All right, you lead the way. Look I'm going to Mass for *her* not for myself."

"All right."

What had John got in mind? Was he aiming to start a search for the girl? Was he quite beyond reason, out of contact with external reality? From my own past experience I knew what it was to be caught "in a cloud," away from the world, other people and what was happening in the outside, in the here and now. Also did I realize how one can be half in and half out, in a state of misty awareness. John seemed pretty much inside his own cloud.

We got to the church. Johns pulls his trousers up and his pullover down. Blessing ourselves with holy water we silently enter the church. Here I was with a big burly Irishman, breathing deep and bending to the Lord. His whole being seemed to move, in the relief of home country. Still he is obviously very conscious of where he is. I'm wondering about Communion.

"You know, John—"

"Yes, I'm going to confession." He seemed quite lucid. A few minutes ago he had "seen" cars racing round the block and informed me he had crucified a girl.

"John try to make a very short simple confession." John nods, apparently devoutly attempting to remember his sins.

Father Brown was in the confessional. "Dear God, if John says he has killed a girl, please may it be obvious to Father Brown that he's got delusions." It didn't seem right that I should intervene. If John could come out of his web from the grip of the mesh of his own tangled past for a few moments—and wanted to go to Communion, well, who was I to stop him? Leave it all to Father Brown. John returns to kneel beside me. He whispers, "I can't go to Communion." He is obviously accepting the fact.

Mass commences, John is most devout. I realized that John was coming in and out of his own inner dream state. He seemed to be keeping a hold, at the moment, to the outside, to what was going on around him.

Together we stood, sat down, or knelt, in accordance with the words of the Mass. Outside the church we started to walk home. John didn't seem so satisfied about his efforts of communication with Father Brown.

He announced, "I want to *talk*. Is there a Dominican Friary around here?"

"No, John."

"A convent?"

"No."

"Well, a Catholic centre?"

"No."

John was getting determined. "Well, then a Church o England place?"

"No, John you can talk when we get home, to me o James."

John snorted and scuffled along, lagging a bit behind me Suddenly he sighed, "Oh well, what to do?"

"What do you mean, John, what to do?"

"Well, I mean, I suppose go mad! Dance about naked!" John is expansive, flinging his arms about.

"Yes, that's all right, you can be how you like." We ge home.

Almost at once, when inside the house, John seemed back in the clutch of his delusions. Especially James and Cindy he plagued with accusations of being involved in black magic He wanted to be called again for Mass. All went well But hardly had Father Brown finished saying, "Go forth i peace," than John seized my hand, "Come, quick, some thing's got to be done."

Urgently he strode out of church, taking a good grip o me. "John, what—careful—wait—the traffic!" We were half way across the main road.

"People's lives are at stake."

"Well, I don't want to be killed." A brief pause. The car streamed by. Then we ran. John raced down the road dragging me with him. Like a runaway horse, there was nc holding him.

In to the house, up the stairs he bolted. "Quick, hurry, nc time to lose, Cindy."

"John let's go first to James."

Bursting into Jame's room John goes as if to fling himself on James, in bed asleep. James rises up, as if to defend him self.

John has his hand on James's forehead.

"Say, in the name of the Father and of the Son and of the Holy Ghost . . ." John is insistent, grabbing James, holding something to his head. It falls to the floor.

"Mary, Mary—look down there—it's fallen, he's knocked it down."

"What, John?"

"The crucifix, my crucifix—I'm exorcising him."

"Can't you see it—move the bed, look on the floor—it's got to be found." We all look on the floor.

James shakes his bedclothes. John is fuming and stamping, the room is small. Cindy is at the door. I whisper, "Go into your room and lock the door."

"Look, look John is shouting." James and I are doing our best. It can't be found.

"Have you got another? I must have a crucifix."

"Yes, I'll get you one." John races after me down to my room.

"Here will this do?"

"Yes, snatching it from me, now quick, Cindy."

Back on the roof, it's now raining. John bangs on the door of Cindy's room. "Look John do it on the door, hold the crucifix there—that's effective."

John shouts, "Say, in the name of the Father—" "She's asleep. It's all right, John, that's exorcised." We are getting wet. John comes downstairs, still pretty hot. "Get me Simon Tug—on the phone."

I knew he meant Brother Simon Tugwell, a Dominican whom John considered an authority on exorcising.

"John it's too early—he'll be at Mass."

"No, now. Get him, I got to talk to him, it's urgent."

I try. Brother Simon is away, at the Buddhist monastery. Oh God, will John ever believe me?

"Now listen John, what I'm telling you is the truth"— my hand is on John—"I want you to believe this. Brother Simon is not there. He is away. You cannot speak to him."

"All right. I got to think."

John sits himself on the stool in my room. He subsides. He had been quite vicious—like the Church in the Inquisition.

The next day John was not around, and he wasn't in his room the following morning. I was wondering, had he gone chasing after Naomi, was he in a panic, too frightened to stay in the house?

Early for Mass, the church was dim, I almost fell on John, leaning over the front pew.

"Hullo."

"Hullo John." We sit next to each other. John is quiet. A long pause.

"How's James?"

"All right."

"How's Cindy?"

"All right."

John yawns.

"Anyone miss me?"

"No, I knew you'd be back."

"Will you come with me, to my room when we go in?"

"Yes."

Mass commences. We are in the road, walking home.

John is very slow, wearily sighing.

"Oh, my feet." He is shuffling and stumbling.

"Tired, John?"

"Yeah." Silence. "Oh my feet."

Nearer home. "Last night I went to the pictures."

"Did you, John? Any good?"

"No—cowboys and Indians. Saw Morty yesterday."

"Oh—how's Morty?"

"He's all right." We get in the front door. John is making clucking noises. We get to John's room.

"Put your feet up." He lies on his bed, pulls some blankets up. "Got anything to eat, some tea?"

"I'll go and see."

"Bread and cheese."

I go up to James. "John is back. Seems like he was walking around all night."

James gives me some whisky for him. It seemed John might settle. I left him nearly asleep, with some whisky beside him. That was the last I saw of John for some time.

Terrified of himself, of his madness, of being free, he went out to a very busy shopping street, Oxford Street, and showed his crucifix to some old women.

Apparently he wanted to exorcise them and they did not understand and called a policeman with whom John got into a fight. It took four policemen to capture him.

In time John made his way back to Kingsley Hall. He told me, "In the hospital in a padded cell I was naked with all my shits and water."

"John, you can have all that here and be helped through it so you understand and really grow from the experience."

In the hospital he had been given drugs and electric shocks.

David, David Page Thomas who lived in the house, and with whom John had spent a lot of time, told me, "Mary, he was afraid he might have hit you."

Not long after this happened I went to Paris to spend a weekend with Maria Boons, a French psychiatrist whom Joe had introduced me to. She had sent me a ticket.

We met at the airport. "Come, have some lemonade. How is Joe? What do you paint?" It was thrilling to see her again. "How was the trip?"

"Raining in London, then sky above the clouds, white light sweeping over the sky—and now, all this sun, and wind —and you."

We laughed. "What do you think? This morning we go to the Eiffel Tower—so you see all Paris—then this afternoon we go to see paintings, and tonight we see the ballet—lots of colour and dancing, not too much talking."

"Wonderful, marvellous, let's go."

I gasped. So much. All those happenings, in one day. We got to the car. Maria told me, "Tomorrow, my husband Jean Paul can take you to the Museum of Modern Art, then we go together to buy your dress. Sunday we go to Chartres. Monday what you like!"

It was still Friday. We got up the Eiffel Tower. I asked Maria to show me the Sacré-Coeur. "There, so far—but you can see—it's so clear." A photographer took a picture. Maria told me, "You are like a Slav and I a Swedish person."

It was very breezy and light with the sun. We came down, the trees were just flecked with green. Maria lived by the Seine near the Bridge of Mary. "My father felt this was the place for me, near Pont Marie."

Her house was beautiful, a huge mirror in the bathroom, a thick blue rug in the sitting-room, a tiny cane chair, wonderful old figures of Christ and the Mother of God. At night we sat by the window watching the water splashing white in the light. Everything was so new and exciting. Maria loved my present, a blue hyacinth in a box I had finger-painted. "We shall keep the box here, on the chest. The flower smells."

"Come, we eat, afterwards rest, then go to see the paintings." The food of Maria was delicious, soup, cold meats, salads, cheeses, wine.

"This is your bed. I take the covers off." High white walls, long yellow curtains. Donk, my Rosary, sleep.

"Mary, it's time, we have a drink, get ready, go—the paintings." I yawned. Where was I? Donk fell on the floor. Where was my Rosary? Must find that. Hold Donk in the cupboard. Joe gave me him. Rosary in my pocket—Donk in the cupboard.

"Mary, Mary are you awake?"

"Yes, coming."

I loved Maria. We were going to see paintings. There was an elderly lady with Maria.

"Mary, a friend of my husband's mother, from Tangiers. She has a bookshop."

"Oh hello, will you sell my book? I'm writing a book."

"Yes of course."

Maria intervened.

"Mary, I go for the car, then together we all to go see the pictures."

Maria drove in and out through the side streets. "That's the University where I teach the students—tell Joe you saw it—we do lots of activities."

"Maria—look."

"Yes—lots of markets, and churches."

We got to the gallery, a small house with a garden, off the road. It was where the artist Jean Dubuffet had a collection of work done by various people during mad states. Maria, who was a friend of Dubuffet, had special permission for us to visit there. She hoped Jean Dubuffet might like one of my paintings for his collection.

The lady in charge of the collection was expecting us and showed us into all the rooms. A lot of the work had been done in mental hospitals.

Some of the paintings were so exact, intricate and involved, I wanted to scream, to shout, to push it all away. It didn't really seem to live. A lot of things were stuffed, behind glass cases. Maria was smoking, carefully looking. The lady in charge was explaining some point. There were wooden models of people that moved as machines. Some of the things were animals with great big teeth in enormous jaws.

There was a crocodile, not in a case. Grabbing him I ran to Maria, "Look, look, Maria, Joe—here's Joe! And look there's me!" Pointing to the biggest monster with huge teeth.

"Mary, Mary."

Maria came protectively near. I put the crocodile back on his shelf.

It was all so secluded, "shut off," dead. I wanted to run and shout outside. There were three floors. The lady in charge was following Maria and the elderly lady around, explaining details. I was longing to go. The place had been shut up, they had opened it specially for us. Oh dear, oh dear. I paced about.

Maria called, "Mary come, we go!" Off home, to the house of Maria, by the water and all the stone walls. Again we ate, by candlelight and then off to the ballet.

Crowds of people, it was dark, all the lights and music and shouting with smell of coffee. The theatre was round, as from the sides of a great bowl we looked down to the stage. It was fantastic, all the movement and colour. My head was drowsy, wine, so many happenings, beautiful dreams.

"Mary, you sleep!"

"Oh er, yes, the glasses."

Maria held the opera glasses for me to see the dancers close up.

"Mm, marvellous."

Jean Paul took the glasses. The music swayed and the colours merged. My dreams were mixing with the dancing. It was all a wonderful blur.

"Come—you liked it."

"Oh yes, it was terrific."

In the morning I woke with the light and ran out to Notre Dame. High Mass was just beginning. In the chapel of vocations I prayed for a vocation to Ronnie's work.

Breakfast was more special, black currant juice and apple conserve Maria had made. Jean Paul was ready to take off for the Museum of Modern Art. He brought me a print of the Head of Christ by Georges Rouault, which painting was

in the Gallery, surrounded by an old wood frame. This I
kept running back to, and a huge wall painting by Manes-
sier. Jean Paul left me free to look. Quickly, here, there,
seeing, touching, feeling, taking in gulps what I wanted,
acutely tasting. It was terrific. Lots of space and colour.
You could dart upstairs and down, catching the essence of
a work before it dissolved.

Now out in the air, into a market, branches of almond
blossom and fruit, much riper than in London. Maria knew
that for the opening of my forthcoming exhibition I wanted
to buy a dress in Paris. This was the dress we were to
shop for. We went by the Métro which came out by a big
store.

"Blue, specially would I like blue." Maria took a selection
and we tried them all on. Soon with Maria it was settled,
the dress, the money, the alteration. The lady who helped
Maria at home would stitch up the hem and take in the
waist—on Monday.

Then we bought paints for me, and for herself Maria got
a new brassière, as she said—"to make me a little more."

Maria had said Saturday evening we would spend quietly
together at home. I was sitting smelling the hyacinth, looking
at all the things, touching the table, the sofa, the cushions,
feeling some stones in a bowl, holding a big bird with a
raffia body.

Jean Paul came. "Mary see here, we have some books of
paintings. This I would like to show you, and this."

"Yes, yes."

Three, four books on my lap. Bookcases, high, full to the
ceiling. Maria came.

"Mary, have some music, records, what you like. I like
this. You like it?"

"Yes, yes."

"Soon I read your stories. You show me. Now I make
ready food, to eat. First I do one letter."

Maria didn't waste a minute. So many things, so much
happening. It was marvellous. But how to explain. At home
I painted but it was "separate" not different things at once.
I wanted just to "be," to sit in the little chair, or lie on the
sofa.

It was getting late. Maria told me, "We have to go to a

meeting, just for a little while." Quickly I made for bed. Would Maria come in to say goodnight? Not quick enough. Maria was ready, kissing, hugging me, but I wasn't in bed. "Goodnight, Mary. Sleep well. Tomorrow we go to Chartres."

At Kingsley Hall if I was up Joe always gave me time to get to bed before he came to say goodnight before he left the house.

It was Sunday. Jean Paul who was a journalist had writing to do. Maria and I set out for Chartres.

Leaving Paris by car Maria told me of the pilgrimage on foot that the writer Péguy had made to Chartres for his friend who had wanted to kill himself.

"Maria, Joe's friend Leon feels very bad. I go today specially for him. He has been to Chartres with Joe."

It was a beautiful drive, we speeded along through woods past bushes of hazel catkins, through wide open fields. We were nearly there.

Maria was talking, "I wonder, I don't know if God exists." Suddenly, a loud smash, a shot into the windscreen. The glass splintered out. Dead stop.

"Whatever . . ."

I thought someone had fired a shot at us.

"Mary, it was a stone, up from the road. It can happen, but never before to me. We must go very slow."

Maria got in. As the car moved tiny pieces of shattered glass fell on to us. The stone had bounced on to the windscreen making a tiny hole with lots of radiating lines of damaged glass that got bigger and bigger. It was worrying. St. Michael defend us. My hand was on my Rosary in my pocket. I was praying hard.

"Mary, a garage. We must stop." No, he couldn't do it, but turn off, a few yards ahead, into a village, he told Maria. We got there. The garage was open. He had just the right size of windscreen for Maria's car. "Leave it. Come back in half an hour," he told us.

All was well. We went for a walk, through the village into a wood. It was a soft day, the trees, standing straight close together were swaying at the top. There was green on a wood pile and red on the house tops. Through a vegetable garden we came into a café the back way.

Carrying on to Chartres, we saw the cathedral, across the bare fields, and coming up through narrow cobbled streets to the centre of the town we stopped and drank in the beauty of the stone.

Maria told me, "My father, years ago, brought me here. It was winter, covered in snow." We went inside, into the dim darkness of the years. I touched the stone, the pillars, the walls. The church was pregnant with the past. Deep in our own souls we wandered round.

Outside, Maria suggested, "Let's buy cards, then we eat, then go back inside."

It was a good meal. We had wine. Maria talked about the desert and Father de Foucauld. She spoke very lovingly of The Little Sisters of Jesus. We had both been in the desert and like me, Maria had been in a convent. We seemed to understand each other, to really meet.

Back in the cathedral we saw the sunlight through the glass. The colour was glorious. When we came down from the tower I at last found the altar of St. Joseph. Just time to light a candle, say one last prayer, and hurry to the car.

"Mary, we get back, early, before the traffic. Tomorrow I work, seeing patients at home, at the hospital"—Maria sighed—"it's not like Kingsley Hall, we haven't got that—but you go out—see some paintings—what you like. Tomorrow night we go to dinner with a friend of mine, Zu Zu, a Belgian sculptor."

The next morning I walked by the river, went to the Louvre, and to Mass in the chapel of the Miraculous Medal in the Rue du Bac. Where the Mother of God had appeared in 1832 to St. Catherine Labouré.

In the evening with Maria and Jean Paul I met Zu Zu and his family. He gave me one of his sculptures and I did three finger paintings, a Crucifixion for Zu Zu, trees for Maria, and an abstract conception of the birth of life, for Maria to give to Jean Dubuffet.

The next day, back in London it all seemed another world, and yet it was "with me."

Karen came to my room. We looked at the dress. Beautiful. I was well pleased—most of all for being with Maria.

Chapter Twenty-two

My first exhibition—Peter

Upon my return from Paris at the end of February 1969 I began to prepare for my first one-man exhibition, to be held at the Camden Arts Centre in April. Ronnie and Jesse Watkins came to choose the paintings to be shown. Some of my work was already at the Art Centre, for it had to go before the Chairman, Jeannette Jackson, and the committee of the Hampstead Artists Council.

Ronnie especially liked "The Vine," a crucifixion painting of Christ as the vine. Everything was out. Ian, who lived in the house told me, "Get it all out, show them the lot, they must see it all." Ian had painted and had exhibitions.

The Games Room was full, the Hall was full, some was in Janet's room, lots was in my room. Canvasses over mattresses, spread over chairs, on the floor, my head was full, they mustn't miss anything. Jesse had pencil and paper. "I'll have that. What's this?"

"Oh, an early work, it's not much colour."

"Open it up."

"The Back of the Cross."

"I'll have that. What have you got there? How, how am I going to frame that? Paint on anything, you would. Put it over there. Now let's see, that's eighteen."

"Oh Jesse?"

I had about two hundred works. "Now Mary I have got to think of the look of the whole exhibition."

"Jesse, those small ones?"

"No, you can't put one on top of the other. People like things properly spaced, so you can see each work distinct."

"Oh er?"

"One more, I'll take that, what is it?"

"He shall come as the Sun, with healing in His Rays."

"Mm—'He shall come as the Sun'—don't have the title too long."

"No, all right—this one, Joe likes?"

"Yes, 'Fire,' and that's it."

I was so angry, furious. All those works, everything out and that was all, just twenty works. An exhibition, twenty works! Surely people would like to see a lot. I was getting greedy for showing. "The Way of the Cross," thirty foot long, all those huge hardboards of early works, all those canvasses only half unrolled, those sculptures, the head of Janet.

"Jesse, Jesse."

"Now Mary, some of your works are very big. Gallery space is limited. That's an exhibition."

"Come on upstairs."

Up in the Flat the rest of the community were silently sitting. The air was heavy, taut. I was in all my best clothes, green, purple and orange. Ronnie eased the room. When the house is very tight you sometimes have to be a shoe lift to ease someone in.

The next hour saw me unobtrusively putting some work away. Jesse told me, "You can have a portfolio of un-framed canvasses and oil pastels, and that will all be extra to what we have chosen today. You can show people those." When "Our Lady of Africa" came from Cape Province and "Break Through" arrived from America, Jesse added these to the exhibition, also the Triptych, the panel of which Bill Mason was still putting together.

The next big exciting event before the exhibition was the coming of Richard Broan with his television team. They were making a film for the BBC in which I was to feature. The film, about schizophrenia, was titled, "A True Madness" and it was being produced in association with David, Dr. David Cooper of the Philadelphia Association, whom Richard also interviewed. To make the film, my part in it, Richard came to Kingsley Hall. Some people in the house being rather afraid of TV they came early in the morning, when there was less risk of anyone smashing up the cameras.

I was awake, all ready in my room. Richard put the

microphone thing inside my nightdress. "Wait—don't speak yet—keep it fresh." The cameras squeezed in, almost on top of me. Richard fixed his microphone. He made a sort of snap noise with a board, said, "Take one" and, we were off.

"Mary, can you tell me what happened when you first went mad?"

It was marvellous. Richard told me, "You gave two beautiful examples of double bind."

"Mm, did I?"

"Yes, it was fantastic, really."

The men were roll up flexes. Someone said, "That's sixty pounds worth of film."

"Richard, shall I put on my painting dress now?"

"Yes, love, you do that, we're going to show your paintings in colour, you do some finger painting for us?"

"Oh yes." It was a crucifixion that I painted and the sound man came right up to my hand to take the sound of my fingers on the board.

Then they photographed other paintings, including the "Children of Israel going through the Red Sea" and "Our Lady of Bow," which Richard specially liked, and the last scene, the end of the film, was my third painting of "Spring, the Resurrection." Some weeks later, with David I saw the preview. When the film took us into laboratories and talked all about drugs and pink spots I suddenly got all cold and had to put my coat on. I was relieved to get past all that. Seeing David and my paintings made me feel warm and living again.

Later on I went with Michelle, who had recently come to live with us, to the Black Swan Pub to see myself on TV. Michelle ordered drinks.

"You know Kingsley Hall?" The landlord looked mystified. I tried to help.

"Round the corner—opposite the John Bull."

"Oh, you mean the Mad House!" Now we were home.

"Yes, that's us."

Michelle was horrified. "If they laugh when you come on!"

"Oh, what's the matter? The kids chalk up 'the nut house' outside the front door." A child visitor Adrian, once said to me, "She's a bit of a nut, but I like her" and two little girls with him murmured "Mm, Mm." It was at a time when

I wasn't talking. Now here I was, the other end of four years.

Mr. Sargent, the hardware store man, told me, "You spoke up very nicely."

They said my name, Mary Barnes, on the TV and showed me finger painting. As the film ended a woman put her arm round me, a man was shaking my hand.

Michelle was making for the door.

"Mary, did you hear what he said to me? 'Ere, she's got talent, they should take 'er in 'and.' "

I took Michelle's arm. We hurried home.

Ian told us, "It was a very well composed film. Your paintings were wonderful in colour."

About this time, Ronnie rang me up, would I speak to Brian Inglis of *Vogue?* Oh yes, and Karen asked me, will you see Oliver Gillie of *New Society?* He wrote an article about us all entitled "Freedom Hall." It came out on the 27th March 1969 with a photograph of me in my room taken by Karen Hagen.

Brian Inglis worte of me in his article "Society and Psychiatry" published by *Vogue* on March 15th, 1969. I was delighted things were warming up—the Exhibition was coming!

Make lists of all you want invited to the opening, Joe told me. My dress was ready. Gold shoes to get, and Anne, a friend of mine, was making me a blue cape.

This is what Ronnie wrote to go in the Catalogue:

In her painting, Mary puts outside herself, with the minimum mediation, what is inside her. Paintings are executed with her finger, not because she cannot use a brush, but because she prefers (often) not to. She is not "professionally" proficient in the "art" of composition, not because of a failure to master the means to the end, but because hers is not the end that this is a means towards.

We must take her on her terms, and ask ourselves whether she succeeds in what she attempts.

They are embarrassing. They are too raw for our liking. We are inclined to condescend. To make allowances, to judge by those canons of "art criticism" we can all dredge up, more or less articulately, when the occasion seems to demand.

There is a frenetic silence just before the narcotic of sound. When cry cannot be justified, or mitigated: is unredeemed, and is perhaps consoled, only by being allowed.

We forget it. But a 44 year old woman represents it to us and recalls us to ourselves.

She does not go as far "out" of herself as propriety and artistic convention requires. We cannot meet her, anywhere else than the place in nowhere whence she paints. There, I recognize her, in myself, and am disturbed in myself, by her.

Rilke wrote of "the other side of nature." Mary gives us the "other side" of the flesh.

For want of a better word, we call it the "inside." But it's an inside we are forever on the outside of whenever we try to get inside by means of dissecting instruments. The flesh *pour soi*, where spirit and matter, raped and raping, are capable, sometimes, despite their worst intentions, of a scarcely credible chastity. It has to do with incarnation.

All our words are misleading.

At the Camden Arts Centre, Jesse, with the help of David Bacon and his girl friend Maria, had been getting my canvasses stretched and some paintings framed. Joe had ordered the catalogue and invitations. Bill had finished the Triptych, it was six feet high and beautifully made. I got my fingers into the paint and on to the wood. It smelt good. All thick in my fingers, great globs on the wood. My hands in the tins, a fist full of blue, a splash of red, the painting grew. Eve, the serpent, seven fruits, seven deadly sins. Adam already covering himself. The big middle panel, Joshua leading the Children of Israel into the promised land. They are leaping forth from the desert.

In the green are the twelve stones, to mark the twelve tribes of Israel, across the dried Jordan is the Ark of the Covenant, carried before the people.

Beyond, a smaller panel, came the Annunciation, Mary receiving the good message from the angel as Eve had heard evil from the serpent. From the fall came the redemption.

The next day, the other side; Ruth and Naomi, as trees separate yet intertwined; Mary and Elizabeth, the Visitation and on the centre panel, the Nativity, Mary, Joseph and Baby Jesus alive, to the breast. The dress of Mary spread wide, as a peacock in full feather.

When painting the Triptych I was all bundled up, the weather being cold, and Karen took some photos for the catalogue.

All the invitations were sent out and to my parents, my brother, my sisters. My excitement was immense. Nicola Tyrer came to write an article for *The Guardian,* for which I was photographed before my finger painting "Christ Triumphant" on the dining-room wall. Atticus came from the *Sunday Times.* As he talked to me, John Hodder took shots of me sitting before the "Sun Shining on the Sea," a finger painting I had just done. John called his photographs, "The Artist and Her Art."

Then Joe told me, Felix Mendelson of the underground newspaper, *International Times* would like to interview me. He talked to me about the Catacombs, seemed to really understand my experiences. I showed him something of my book "Writings and Paintings," all about my soul.

Joe also said, "If you don't watch out, all these people coming to see you, you will get a swelled head."*

At last the day came, April 11th. Putting my clothes for the evening in a bag I went off, early in the morning, to the flat of Leon and Liz, where it had been arranged for me to spend the day. Liz was in bed, not too well, expecting a baby, whose life it seemed was in some danger.

"Mary, I'd like to come."

"Leon, surely there will be chairs there, she can sit down, quietly."

"Well, that seems to settle it."

Leon agreed. Liz invited me to have a bath, with her perfume that made the water soft and sweet smelling.

Then I lay on the floor by my painting, "The Red Christ" and slept, until it was nearly time to go.

Fine stockings, gold shoes, gold bag, blue dress of Maria,

*The articles they wrote were: "To Paint it Out" by Nicola Tyrer, *The Guardian,* April 14th, 1969. *"Making the Break"* by Atticus, Philip Oakes, of the *Sunday Times,* April 13th, 1969, photograph by John Hodder. "The Floodgates of My Soul Are Open" by Felix Mendelson in the April issue of *IT.*

rom Paris, blue cape of Anne in London, hair long, scarf
blue and gold. Blue, colour of the Mother of God, my
Mother used to dress me in blue.

Leon came, daffodils, masses of daffodils for Liz, and for
me, and freesias and blue hyacinths for my cape. They smelt
delicious. The phone rang, a press interview. Leon got me a
cab. I was off. How would it be? How would my paintings
look? Marvellous, Jesse was there. "Well, how do you think
we arranged your work?"

"Oh, Jesse, it's wonderful."

"See, got to space them nicely. Have a drink, white or red
wine?"

"Red." It was early. Jesse was giving Vernon and Austin
and the other men of the Gallery a drink.

Father Paulinus arrived, out of his habit. I wasn't sure if it
was him. Ronnie was coming early to be introduced to the
Dominican, who had news of a property near Oxford. Here
was Ronnie. Relief.

"Hullo, Ronnie, er—"

"Paulinus"—he was introducing himself. That was all
right. They went off to talk business, joined later by Hugh
Crawford, secretary of the Philadelphia Association.

Then Joe came, glorious in a huge robe of gold dragons.
The big bear who had caused all the painting. "It's really
wonderful, what you have done for Mary," Mrs. Nix, an old
friend, was saying.

Joe replied, "Oh, Mary teaches me."

Anne arrived and Jessica with daffodils and narcissi. Soon
so many people, all the past, the present, the future seemed
there, together. How I must have changed. Catherine Gins-
berg, an analyst who had known me six years ago, remarked,
"Well, maybe the eyes, the nose, the same—but!" It was
terrific, to sense her knowledge of my change. Brother
Simon was there, in his habit, no mistaking him. Father
Grande came, the Spanish priest who had received me into
the Church. Margaret was there with Cecily, and Wendy
came, also Gerda, links with my past, people who knew my
family.

Cousin Hilary was there, and here was Peter. Looking
strained, stiff, trying to be "right." Terrified, frightened; Joe
shook his hand, saw how he was, stone cold, nearly catatonic.

It was getting very crowded. Joe was calling me. "Mary
I want you to meet these students from Holland." Someon
else was talking, "Tell us all about it."

"Come here, be photographed."

"Where?"

Nicola Tyrer was there reporting, Peter Goodliffe from
Oxford and Barry Roberts were taking photos. Liz was sit
ting down with Vivien and Karen. Joe was moving, dartin
about, piloting me from this group to that.

"Maria, it's wonderful, you came today from Paris?"

"Mary, I'm so happy for you."

"Here's Joe, and Jesse and Ronnie."

John, from home, with Frances, was stalking around
Would he try to have Father Paulinus exorcise the lot o
us? Paul Lawson, who designed the catalogue, and Harry
Trevor, the South African artist who so encouraged me with
my painting, were there.

"Mary," Harry flung his arms around me, "your paintings
your paintings, they so live, they move, the colours, oh the
colour!"

"Harry, Harry, your work, your—"

"Oh oh—my poor efforts."

Harry is a very fine artist.

Maybe lots of people were talking lots of psychiatry
understanding madness. Harry and I were caught—for a mo
ment, completely in paint, lost in the joy, the smell of the
oils.

Jesse told me, "Mary, meet my children, they spoke to
you on the phone and wanted to come." Sheila I knew
Jesse's wife, but lots of people I didn't know. Joe was calling
me. "Meet Michael Dempsey, the publisher."

"It's great to see you. How's the book going?"

Sid hugged me, "Mary, the exhibition! It's come at last!"

Members of the local Council, Jeanette Jackson. The
Mayor was abroad, or he would have come, so Jesse told me

Suddenly, it seemed time to go. The men of the Gallery
were ringing a bell, seeing people out. Goodnight, Vicky
Dodo, Jutta, John Haynes, he had photographed my paint
ings at home, Hugh, Ronnie, Leon, Liz, Harry, Noel, Fay
Father Grande, Anne, Jessica—she was staying with Gerda
the night, Ben Churchill, friend of Sid's, Harry Pincus the

American psychologist from Oxford, Peter Barham from Cambridge, Jean, Hilary, Maria—Maria Boons from Paris—Goodnight, goodnight. It was getting quieter.

Goodnight, Muriel—she was typing the book—see you Pamela—she was from home—glad you could come—Oliver Gillie, of *New Society*, was going, Peter had gone.

Joe was taking off his dragon robe. Goodnight Joe, goodnight Jesse. The Gallery men were closing the doors. Masses of flowers, daffodils, narcissi, the freesias still fresh on my cape.

I put them before the Mother of God, a white sculpture with arms in a bow, her breasts revealed in an open cape.

In the candlelight the walls of my room glowed in colour, the Sacred Heart, a Crucified Christ, the empty tomb, breath of the Spirit, my prayers on the walls—"May I float on the sea of Thy love—as a gull on the waves."

Quiet, utter stillness, not a sound. Alone in my room was I held in the peace of the moment, in the depth of the space.

The whole house seemed together, breathing in a deep sleep. Softly I crept in to Janet, to give her a flower, to say goodnight. Her painting of the Crown of Thorns on the Head of Christ was vividly against the wall.

During the time of my exhibition, April 11th to 25th, I sometimes went to the Gallery. People talked to me, about themselves, as well as about painting. It seemed I really met people. Some had been two or three times to see my pictures.

One lady told me, "I'm on the committee of a large mental hospital. We have a unit where people can regress a bit, but it's not nearly enough. Your experience will help others. It's good to have met you."

Mrs. Coveney came, the ex-warden of my Hall of residence when at Hull University. "Mary, the paintings are so powerful, tell me all about it, how is your brother?"

Mr. Sargent of the hardware store took his wife on Sunday afternoon. A lot of my painting was on his hardboard. The Wednesday afternoon prayer ladies came, Ada, Fra, and the others. Ever since we came to Kingsley Hall they had been praying for us, every Wednesday afternoon at their meeting in the Hall.

Once when I was bad and wandered into the Hall Ada

had hugged me, saying, "Stand there a minute, I'm goin
to pray for you." Ada had told me, "I'm specially remem
bering your brother in my personal prayers. How's Joe?
"Oh look there's Ronnie!" All the prayer ladies looked. I wa
showing them *Vogue* magazine and *New Society* whic
they read with great interest. Lilli remembered me from m
first period in bed, when she had once fed me.

The exhibition occurred in April 1969. It is now the Sprin
of 1970.

Over the past year I have been mainly concerned with
finishing this book, and preparing for another exhibition o
my paintings which took place in Newcastle early in th
year. But the most important event in my life is that m
brother Peter has finally come to live at Kingsley Hall. S
I am going to conclude the book by telling how Peter cam
to Kingsley Hall and what happened since his arrival.

The first time Joe saw Peter was in the Fall of 1967 whe
he took me in his car, an old London taxi with three doors
to see Peter in the mental hospital where he was then stay
ing.

It was Sunday afternoon, my excitement was immense
How would Peter be? Three, four years in the hospital.
had come so far and Peter was still there, stuck in his anger
Would he still walk that terrible shuffling way? If only h
would come away with me and Joe.

We got there early. I had hold of Joe's hand. "Come on
this way." Through the passages, up the stairs, straight intc
the ward. Long lines of beds, half way down Barnes or
the end of one of them. I knew exactly where.

We stopped. "Where is he?" Maybe he's in the day room,
Joe, where? where? "He's coming." Peter had been having
a wash.

"Hullo, Peter, here's Joe."

I kiss Peter, getting hold of Joe. Joe moves back. Pete
asks us, "Would you like a cup of tea?"

Joe said, "Yes, please," and I told Peter I don't have tea,
if you have got some milk, please.

Peter took us to a table and chairs in the day room. He
brought the tea. I chattered. "Peter, when are you coming

out? Joe, couldn't Peter come with us, to live at Kingsley Hall."

"Yes, if he wants to, ask him."

"Peter, come and stay with us at home."

"Well, I want to leave the hospital and get an office job, but Mary, not now, to come to Kingsley Hall."

Joe asked Peter, "Do they teach you typing?"

"There is a typewriter you can use, but no, they don't teach you. We do industrial therapy."

"Joe, Peter packs plasticene in boxes every day—it's not making him better—he's on drugs—can't he come with us?"

"Mary, it's what *Peter* wants—he just told you he doesn't want just now to move to Kingsley Hall."

Oh, God—what can I say? *Make* him come. Peter looks strained, his face is twisting. "Joe, I want to water, I know where it is."

"All right, you go." Relief, I dash outside, pee on the grass, and run to the chapel. Mother of God, Mother of God, *please* save him, save him. Please help Joe. St. Therese of Lisieux, St. Joseph, help us—please, please.

I am at the altar rail, as near to the Blessed Sacrament as I can get. It's quiet, it's warm, it's time to go back. Must see Peter, must try to be quiet, must leave it to Joe.

Peter looks easier, he's speaking with Joe. Then Joe is saying, "I must be getting back. Mary, it's time we were going." Other visitors had come. The day room was filling up, there were other people, talking.

I'm dead, like a machine, we are walking back down the ward, through the long lines of beds, there's one, in the middle, marked Barnes. We pass it, his locker, his bed, completely in line, tidy, not a ruffle, not a stir, dead.

We get to the door. Joe says goodbye. I'm bending up. Peter, Peter my *brother*, he's still there.

"Oh God, oh God, give him a chance, please just one chance." I'm crying, talking aloud.

Peter stands over me. "Mary, I'll come down to the car with you."

Peter is completely calm, immobile. We go down the stairs, I'm so sad. Joe holds my hand. Peter walks beside us. Through the long passages, out to the light, to Joe's car.

"Peter, come for a ride with us, in the taxi."

"No, no, goodbye Mary." We kiss. He is cold, a statue. Joe shakes Peter's hand. "Goodbye, pleased to have met you."

"Goodbye, Joe."

Peter is walking away, back into the hospital, back into that ward.

I'm hopeless, cold as ice, my heart is torn to bits. The car starts. Bent up on the seat I'm crying and crying. Joe drives on. "Joe, can't you do anything? Can't you get him out? Joe, Joe." The car stops. Joe opens the back door, holds me till the panic ends.

We go on to Kingsley Hall. I'm stuck. How to get to my room? Joe takes me. "But Joe, Joe . . ."

"Look, Mary, you know I will see Peter any time he will come to me. He said he wanted to leave the hospital."

Joe is going. The door shuts. I'm alone.

Peter, Peter. If only we could help him—if, if.

Since the second world war Peter had spent most of his life in and out of mental hospitals. He had been over four years in his present hospital. A few weeks after Joe had taken me to see him, Peter wrote to me.

"I am now in the psychiatric ward of a general hospital in London. Next Saturday afternoon at four o'clock I am coming to visit you."

I rang Joe. He was out, I got Leon.

I don't drink tea. Shall I give Peter tea? I haven't got any. Shall I dress? What shall I wear, my blue skirt and blue jumper? What shall I say?

"What, I mustn't try to make him stay if he wants to go."

"Oh, yes, let him feel welcome, but let him go, the moment he wants to."

"All right, Leon, I get tea bags, and a cake each."

At last it was Saturday afternoon. The front door was open. I was watching at my window. Suddenly there was a tap on my door. "Hullo, who is it? Come in." Peter stepped carefully in. I moved on to my bed so he would have room to sit down. No, he didn't want to take his coat off. Gingerly he sat down. He was covered, in hat, coat, gloves, well-creased trousers, shining black shoes. He was contained and controlled. Rather like a robot.

"I got your letter. I'm glad you could come."

Yes, he spoke slowly, deliberately, the words felt separate, chosen, apart.

"I have been moved. I've got my things with me, my cases. The bed has a curtain round it. There's only six beds where I am. There's some drawers."

I wanted to cry. I could hardly believe it. He was really no longer *there* in that chronic ward, one of a long line of beds. He had his things, his own things, his cases with him.

"You don't have to do anything?"

"No, you can rest. You can lie on your bed."

"Oh, Peter, that's wonderful. Rest yourself. Would you like a cup of tea?"

"Well, yes, all right."

Oh God, he hasn't to pack plasticene in boxes any more. Perhaps he will come here. Oh God, get him here.

"Peter, have some sugar."

He sits upright, motionless on my stool.

"You could sit here, against the wall." I'm on the floor. "No." He smiles, shakes his head, that is not for him, a cushion on the floor, he seems to say.

"Have a cake—I got two."

"Er, no—I have a meal when I get back."

We sit in silence. It is a heavy silence. Peter is so clean and neat. He doesn't seem quite real, rather as if he had been packed away and just come out of a box.

I feel somehow I must mention it, the possibility, the hope for Peter. "Do you think, Peter, you might like to come here, say to stay with us a little while, from the hospital, to see how you like it?"

"Mary, you know I want to get a job."

"There's no hurry, you don't have to do anything yet, do you?"

"Oh, no."

"You know you can speak with Joe about it."

Peter looks strained. He turns his head away, screws up his face.

"Peter, would you like to see some photos of my paintings?"

"Yes."

"Here, and that's one of Mother and Father and Ruth and the children. They send you their love."

I knew that Peter had no contact with the rest of the family. His letter to me was the first for over four years. For a long time Peter studied the photos. I didn't want to rush him. He was rather stiff and wooden, moving as if set along a certain way.

He handed the photos back.

"I must be going now."

"Yes, all right." I mustn't detain him. He gave me a big comb for my long hair and some powder for our Mother to take for her arthritis.

"Is there a lavatory?"

"Yes, across the passage."

I went downstairs with Peter.

"Let me know how things go. Come again."

"Yes."

I kiss him goodbye. Peter smiles. He is gone.

I had taken him down the back stairs. I wondered when he arrived, did he come through the Games Room? Perhaps the cat's shit on the floor had put him off wanting to stay with us.

I told Joe. He reminded me. "Peter has been a long time in the hospital. You have to be very patient."

From the General Hospital Peter went to live at a Cheshire Homes hostel in Wimbledon. I went to visit him.

There were three beds in his room. Peter sat on his. I sat on a chair. Peter wound up his clock. He got a little box out of a drawer and turned on some music. It was a wireless.

"Dorothy (our youngest sister) gave me this, it was in my cases."

"Mm, that's nice."

Peter brushes his shoes. He goes to the wash basin and washes his handkerchief.

A man enters the room. He smiles, moves quickly, lies on his bed.

Peter tells me, "He's deaf and dumb, he works in a park."

Peter worked in a factory. I asked, "Do you have to go to work very early?"

"Yes, I get up at half-past six and I get breakfast before I go to work."

"What do you do?"

"I cut up pieces of metal to make coils."

"Oh." I imagined it must be something electrical. Father sed to talk about coils. He did electrical work.

Peter looked at his clock.

"It's time for supper. Will you have some? Mr. Gargon, ne warden, said you could."

I ate with Peter and two other people at a little table 1 the dining-room.

Peter seemed glad to be working. The next time I visited im, he said, "I must give you your fare."

"Oh, thank you, Peter." We were sitting in the Common Room. It was Saturday afternoon. The room felt heavy, solid, lead. It was too much. The air was stifling. At home, in Kingsley Hall, I felt alive, able to breathe. Here I seemed lattened. I was rather whispering to Peter. Two of the men had met before said "Hullo," then concentrated on the elly. It was sport. Father always used to look at and listen o football on Saturday afternoons.

A girl came in. Peter introduced her. "Cathy, how is your vork?" asked Peter.

Cathy replied, "I've left. I had a row with the head girl."

"Oh," said Peter, rather severely, "I thought sewing work vas what you wanted."

"It wasn't nice there. Can I have one of your cigarettes, 'eter?"

"Mary, what's it like where you live?"

I tell Cathy about Kingsley Hall. The tea trolley has come n. Peter is getting me some milk.

I feel it's time to go. "Mary, I will come to the station vith you."

Peter is putting on his hat and coat and scarf and gloves. He dresses slowly, carefully, every movement seems planned, :here is no gust of wind, no sitting in the sun. Peter's weath-er has a regular sameness. He tells me, "I can stay one year at the hostel, then I may get a room."

"Well, don't forget, if you like to come with us you can. Ronnie said there was a place for you—as well as me—in he place he was getting—that's Kingsley Hall."

It was now the late spring of 1968. About once a month, n a Saturday afternoon, throughout the summer Peter came to visit me. Twice he stayed to dinner. Once he nearly staye[d] the night.

"Really, Peter, it's quite all right." We were looking at a[n] empty bed in a room off the Hall. "This used to be the Med[i]tation room. It's where Ronnie slept, when we first g[ot] Kingsley Hall."

"Really, Mary, I think I should get back."

"Yes, all right." Mustn't try to keep Peter a moment longe[r] than he wants. Always let him freely go, that's what Joe to[ld] me.

Mr. Gargon, the warden of Peter's hostel, had been [to] Kingsley Hall to a seminar that Morty had arranged.

Once Morty, when I'd asked him, came to my room to s[it] with Peter and me. It was very silent. I felt Peter was ver[y] frightened and that I must not try to push him in front o[f] therapists. How I longed for him to go to Joe. Ronnie told m[e] "Mary, you can take a horse to the water but you canno[t] force him to drink."

In the autumn of 1968 after nearly nine months at th[e] hostel, Peter got himself a room, with meals provided, i[n] Wimbledon. He was still on tablets, Stelazine and somethin[g] else.

Over Christmas I went to see him. He had a little deco[r]ated tree that someone who visited the hostel people ha[d] brought him.

"Have you got time off for Christmas, Peter?"

"Yes, I have three days."

"Well, if you like to come over to see us—and if you like[,] stay a night, you can."

"No—I get my meals here."

"All right."

I felt Peter seemed rather tired, quite controlled, bu[t] somehow not so alert. He gave me my fare. He sent me [a] Christmas present of five pounds. I cried. He was on drugs[,] in a factory, alone in a room, shut away from himself. N[o] writing, no paintings, no help to live, to get whole. He sti[ll] wasn't going to Joe, to therapy. If only he would come t[o] Kingsley Hall, so far as I could see the only place in th[e] whole world for him to live.

It was so near, and yet so far, I knew the convents a[t] Llandovery and Presteigne were praying very specially fo[r]

eter. Joe, as always, had great hope and patience. Mother
Michael reminded me, put all your trust in God.

Then I got busy, going to Paris, preparing for my exhibi-
on. It was March 1969. Oliver Gillie had been writing about
.ingsley Hall for the magazine *New Society*.

When the article came out I went to see Peter, my brother.
t was a bit early, he was out. "Go and wait in his room,"
he landlady advised. As I opened the door I felt how he
vas. The smell, there was no mistaking it. That's how it was
vhen he first broke down. It was too intrusive to enter.

I sat, rather trying to merge into the wall. Peter came,
urprised, nervous, started to brush his shoes. I waited. He
at down.

"How's things?"

"I've given in my notice." Peter was sitting silent, turned
n.

I longed to help Peter. He was stopping work.

"Well, Peter, I'm not sorry you haven't to go there any
nore."

He hated the factory.

"I shall probably be leaving here too—can't eat meat. I
vant to get somewhere I can get my own food."

"Oh, like to see this? *New Society*, there's an article about
is, page 473." Peter took it, became absorbed.

I was back, twenty-five years ago. That smell, as I had
ome into Peter's room, how he looked, fragile, breaking,
vet wax-like, still. He was going down, drawing in. Oh God—
lon't let him disappear. Many times in the past Peter had
oroken off all connections so that no one knew where he was,
r even whether he was alive or dead.

I started talking, about our childhood, about my madness,
ibout Joe, about therapy. Peter was putting the book away,
carefully, in his cupboard. He was "nice feeling." "Just now,
is you are leaving that job, it seems a good time to see Ron-
uie, I can arrange it for you."

"Er, well—"

"It's quite easy, I just have to ring up Ronnie, then let you
cnow."

"All right."

Peter receded, his eyes were shut. We sat in silence. He
vas going down, in, miles away. Unaware of me, I seemed

to see him, to feel his whole life, the sadness, the burden of the suffering of his being. My tears were coming. Peter didn't see. He was at the door.

"It's time to go down for the meal." I followed. We sat at table. Someone spoke twice, Peter seemed in a daze, not hearing.

The next day I rang Ronnie. Peter was hesitant, he thought he would go to Ronnie. At the time of his appointment I was near the Camden Arts Centre. I went into a church, a modern circular church. You could kneel within inches of the Tabernacle. I put myself with God and Ronnie and Peter. Peter went to Ronnie. He didn't take another job.

For some weeks Peter remained where he was on unemployment pay. Mr. Gargon from the hostel visited him. I felt Peter was in danger. Oh God, don't let him go back to the hospital. What could I do? If only Peter would come to us.

I rang him. "Peter, come and stay with us. I'm moving up to the Flat—come into my room. I'll make it nice for you."

"Is there a bed?"

"Yes, I get you a bed." Peter knew I slept on the floor.

"I shall come Friday afternoon with some things. Then I shall bring the rest and stay on Saturday."

"All right, goodbye."

"Goodbye."

So that was it. Peter was coming. Quickly I sorted myself out, up into the Flat. A bed, the desk, a stool, a chair and a table, no room for any more, in my old room.

Peter came. The paint was still wet on the stool and the table. It got on his coat. I got turps. He got it off. No, he wouldn't stay for tea. He took the table out into the Games Room. "Mary, there's not room for that."

The next day, Saturday, by way of celebrating my exhibition, we were giving a party at Kingsley Hall. It was now well into May.

Aside from coming to the opening of my exhibition, Peter had read with great interest all that had been written in the Press about me and Kingsley Hall. I had sent news cuttings to all our family. Joe thought the exhibition would give my Mother great joy. My sister Dorothy in Australia was delighted, but my parents, and sister Ruth in South Africa, go very angry. It seemed a reference to the unhappiness of my parents' life had caused a great disturbance.

At the time an aunt, my Father's sister, was visiting Ruth. My aunty and Ruth were angry with me because I had upset my parents. I felt my parents were seeing unhappiness as a "state of sin" and so were very grieved that, in their eyes, I was accusing them of wrong doing. Always aware of the sorrow, the suffering of my parents, I could not help but feel hurt that they should think so ill of me.

Their anger still frightened me. Joe helped me through it, telling me, "Their anger cannot kill you, or Peter." My Father had seemed in a panic, telling me, "You leave Peter where he is."

I began to understand, there was much more "in it" than met the conscious eye. Peter had been the sacrifice, the life that was labelled "mad" in order that the rest of the family be considered sane. Peter was set in the way my Father had moulded him. Any change in Peter, the possibility of Peter really coming to himself was sheer disaster to the unconscious pattern of the family in so far as it was still enslaved.

My Father was least free of all, I was reminded. "Just now, with all those paintings, you have the penis, the power of the family. Your Father feels very threatened."

I had the benefit of understanding. How to tell my parents that facts of the unconscious were not conscious accusations. I wanted them to share my joy, to rejoice with me, and they felt hit, smashed, miserable, perhaps ashamed, of mental illness in the family.

I wanted so much to love them, to caress my Mother in so much pain with arthritis and a skin cancer. But it was difficult for my Mother to be loved and she didn't understand about unconscious motives.

Once I told her, "Mother, it seemed to me that I had caused all Peter's illness and all your sickness."

"No, dear." Mother was distressed. "It was not your fault." Feeling happy, enjoying myself, instinctively I would wonder, is Mother ill? As children, when we were being loud and boisterous, a hint of "showing off" was associated with Mother's body. "Calm down, calm down, you'll give me a headache."

The day of the opening of my exhibition Mother was having an operation for removal of a skin cancer. This seemed quite "natural." I was up—so Mother was down. However, now that I was free, this fact had no repercussions on me. I did not punish myself, bury my heart in an armour of deadness, the encapsulation of Mary in guilt.

It was not possible to "tell" my parents. Joe helped me to accept this, to love them, to respect them, yet not to be enveloped, caught, back in my past, and in their anger of the present.

He cautioned me, "Don't show these letters to Peter, he is not free as you are." I wrote to my Mother, pleading to her, please only write kind loving letters to Peter. I felt she would. Mother had said to me, "Mary, Peter has not yet found himself, not found God." She had hoped Peter would go to Joe.

As the storm died down I realized that really I wanted my Mother to live to read my book. Perhaps the feeling that one could only escape condemnation by remaining in a past deceptive state or so-called "ill" would pass.

It's only safe to be dead, in a false state, or hidden away, shut up somewhere, mad Mary. This was my immediate reaction to the anger of my parents. The truth must be concealed, or our barriers might break, was the panic of my parents.

The idea of Peter going the same way, through madness to freedom, stirred the depths of my Father as nothing else could. Peter had been "safe" in a hospital "being looked after." In a place where there was no possibility whatsoever of him ever becoming himself, the person he was meant by God to be as opposed to the Peter his "family had produced." The chronic ward of that hospital was a big insurance against any "risk" of freedom.

The family walls were breaking, the sea was rushing in. Peter would learn to swim, so float, to let himself "be."

When Peter arrived I got him some tea.

"You know, you don't have to come to the party, only if you want to. You can just stay here in your room."

Peter said, he liked Rice Krispies to eat, and carrots, raw carrots.

"Yes, Peter, we have those things here."

I left Peter to sort his things out. People were starting to arrive for the party.

Soon it was evening, the party was in full swing. In the Games Room the red lights glowed, the paintings showed. We were dancing, moving, separately, alone, yet together in lines, moving slowly, in tune with the music, with each other. A visitor from China, a master of movement, was leading us. Ronnie was near me, moving, Frances, David, Vicky. Dodo, everyone was there. Some watching, some dancing. Peter was sitting, I caught a glimpse of him—miserable, isolated. Yet my soul surged—at last Peter had come.

My red dress, my gold shoes, the paintings, the people, and oh God—Peter! At last, at last, he would be helped. Peter, that's what we're all here for—that's what it's all about—to help you—to save you—to give you—your life.

We care—we really care about you. Look at the movement—Ronnie—Joe—close my eyes, the touch, the tune. Peter is here, hope, joy, my heart is full.

The next day, Sunday, was very quiet. People were sleeping after the party.

Monday I was going out with Doris, an American psychiatrist, friend of Morty's. She was taking me to see the frescoes of Florence then being exhibited in the Hayward Gallery in London.

It was early in the morning. Peter was still asleep. I wondered would he go to Dr. Brill for a medical certificate. I had suggested this to him. I put a note under his door—when you go to Dr. Brill for the medical certificate, say you are under Joe—Dr. Berke.

I got back about five p.m. Doris left me at the door. I went upstairs to the Flat. Janet, a girl who lived in the house, came to me. "Peter has gone. He said he looked for you and James. You were both out. He said to say he will write to you. Here's the key of the room."

I felt stunned. Why, why? Did Peter feel so bad—angry, cross, that I had gone out, was not there when he wanted something, that he had gone away?

I rang him up. "Peter, what is it? Couldn't you wait until I came back?"

Peter replied, "It was very noisy, there was too much noise for me."

"But we had a party—and that's not usual. Maybe you are angry because I left you alone."

Peter seemed to listen.

"Why not come back and let's talk about it?"

He was hesitant.

"I can stay here."

"But Peter—it's not secure for you like Kingsley Hall."

"I'm going now, my tea is getting cold."

"Goodbye, Peter."

I was furious. If only I hadn't gone out . . . If only I'd seen him on Sunday. Joe had told me to leave him alone. To think he had *come*. Joe and Ronnie were going to get him better. *They* should have kept him there. Now I was angry with them. It was choking me, my rage.

I rang up Joe. "It's the *end*."

Joe laughed. "No, it's not—it's the beginning. He'll come back."

"Well, tell him you're angry with him for just going off after you got the room nice for him."

It seemed very dangerous to be angry with Peter. I was afraid my anger would smash him. However, I let him know I was cross about the room.

Mother Michael wrote, "Peter is a neat and tidy person who likes things in order. Judging by the newspaper reports (I had sent her all the cuttings) Kingsley Hall is not a tidy, well-ordered place. Peter must have found it very trying. We will pray he returns."

Joe consoled me. "Mother Michael *hasn't* said she doesn't like your room."

Kingsley Hall was my home. It so suited me. I wanted everyone to love everything about it.

I moved back into this, my room, where Peter had been and felt so bad that I went down again. James brought me some food. Joe came over. I got up and went after Peter.

I'd arranged to meet him at the hostel where he used to live. It was a Sunday afternoon. We sat in the kitchen, Mr. Gargon, the warden and his wife, Peter and me. Mr. Gargon was talking.

"What, no job? You're still retired, Peter?"

"Oh," said Peter, referring to his landlady. "She asked me

to do painting for her. I do her shopping and I'm paying seven pounds a week to be there."

Mr. Gargon continued, "You're still in that same room?"

"Yes, but she has people coming to watch the Wimbledon tennis and I have to move out into a chalet in the garden, there's no water."

I intervened. "Oh, Peter, you know we have that room empty now, on the roof, where Gandhi stayed, and also there's a room in the Flat, next to the bathroom, empty. Come over and see what you think, if you would like one of these rooms."

"Mary, I don't know that I—"

Mr. Gargon went to his office. Mrs. Gargon was going out. I got up. "Peter, it's time we were going to Benediction."

"Oh, yes, you wanted to go to the convent chapel."

"That's right, up the hill." We said goodbye to Mr. and Mrs. Gargon. Mr. Gargon checked that he had my phone number.

Back home, I asked James (James Greene, the psychologist then living at Kingsley Hall) if he would see me and Peter together. James agreed, suggesting 4 p.m., adding that he would come before, about 3:30 p.m., to my room.

I rang Peter. "Will you come over to see me and James, to talk about things?"

Peter agreed, yes he would come at 4 p.m. On the appointed afternoon I was lying in bed, ready and waiting. Peter always came a few minutes late. It was 3:30 p.m. I was expecting James. There was a knock on the door.

"Come in."

In walked Peter.

"Hullo."

He said "Hullo," sitting down on my stool. Then there was silence, dead silence. Peter seemed quite stuck. James arrived. He asks Peter, "What sort of community would you like to live in?"

Peter tells us, "Somewhere, something like a monastery I once wanted to join. You get your own food and eat separately, but you have a Common Room and sometimes come together."

I remind Peter, "Sometimes people do that here. Just now I get my own food—and James gets his."

Peter seems inclined to listen, he is rocking himself back and forth on the stool.

I continue, "You know, Peter, therapy isn't magic. You have to be here some time, see how you feel, try to talk to Joe about yourself, then you change, get better. You're not me, you won't necessarily have the same experiences as I had, will he, James?"

James assures us, "No, Peter is a separate person. He has different needs to you."

I'm lying back with my eyes shut.

"You know, Peter, we are from the same womb. You got twisted up, mixed in with me and our Mother—you could get free. Joe got me free. I've changed haven't I?"

"Oh yes," Peter agrees.

"James, Peter could stay in Gandhi's cell, or have the room in the Flat next to the bathroom, couldn't he?"

"Oh yes, if he wants. It's a matter of what Peter wants."

Peter seemed unsure, didn't know.

James mentioned there was one new boy coming.

I reminded Peter, "Let us know if you would like to come."

James went to get tea. Peter followed, brought some milk. The next weekend Peter came to see me. The room in the Flat was locked.

"Peter, I'll get the key, Karen must have taken it when she left, will you come next week to see the room?"

"Yes, all right."

I rang Karen. She was going to a meeting that Leon was holding in his house, if I was there she would give me the key. I went to the meeting. Karen had forgotten the key. Oh God, would Peter ever come?

What's the matter? Jerry was there, Dr. Jerry Liss, a friend of Joe's. I explained. Jerry said he would take one of us on his motor bike to Karen's house for the key.

Karen went. I got home with the key. The next day Peter telephoned. Had I got the key?

"Yes."

"I am coming tomorrow at 3 p.m. to see the room."

Peter saw. He decided.

"I shall move in on Friday."

When Peter arrived with his cases the Flat sitting-room seemed full. John, David, Frances, everyone seemed to be there. I took Peter into his room. There was silence outside. I asked David, "Please is there another bulb for Peter's light? Where's the broom? Peter wants to sweep out his room. Help me with that mattress, Peter likes a hard one."

People started to clear off. I lay downstairs in my bed. I was terrified of the anger of the other people, imagining they would be anticipating another "Mary Barnes" coming in.

However I soon saw the other people realized that Peter was very different to me. They quite accepted him. Peter told me how sad he had been because he had been unable to find a girl to marry him and that he wanted it, so much, a wife and child. He wished his parents had arranged a marriage for him, as was still done in India.

I said, "Yes, me too. I know the feeling for it. But Peter, if you let Joe help you—get free—grow emotionally, then you know a man can marry a younger woman, and have a child."

Peter told me he felt he had "no foundation."

"Yes, that's how I was—but here with help you can get your foundation. That's the first thing to do. Then you will find the rest will just happen."

I very much felt Peter's sorrow. Although I felt sometimes that Peter was my baby and I knew that we had sexual feelings towards each other I really wanted Peter to have his own life, quite separate emotionally from me.

Within a few days of coming to Kingsley Hall Peter went to Dr. Brill. He told me, "I have a medical certificate for a month. I'm not taking any more tablets." Since that day, now ten months ago, Peter has not taken any drugs. He came at the end of June 1969. It is now late March 1970. Two weeks ago Peter stopped smoking.

Just before Christmas, on the 23rd of December, Peter told me, "I've got a room. I've leaving."

"What's the matter, Peter, why?"

"It's too noisy. I can't sleep at night."

"Come with me to look at the downstairs room. It's quiet there." Ian gave us the key. "You see, Peter, it's a big room, you could cook here and be alone and quiet."

"No, I don't think so."

"Why not try it, be quiet over Christmas?"

"H'm?"

"Well keep the key."

"All right. I asked Ronnie and Joe to give me references for the room I'm going to. I've lived in that part of London before."

I felt terrible. "Peter couldn't you go and talk to Joe or Ronnie about it? They see you better than you can know yourself."

Peter twisted his face up, turned away. He told me, "I'm getting a medical certificate before I go."

On Wednesday I went to Joe's. It was early. I called in to see Liz, Leon's wife. Her Mother was there. I started crying because Peter was going. Liz's Mother patted me and gave me hot chocolate. Then I went to Joe's. Roberta, seven months pregnant, gave me orange squash and let me touch her tummy. She was all right, the baby inside her was not injured. (I always imagined my anger killed Peter and her baby felt as Peter to me.) Then I was furious with Joe, bashing and biting him, because Peter was going. "How could I care about books and paintings! when *people* were being *lost*. He's there—he came—you, Ronnie—all the lot of you *therapists*—you *have got to cure him.*" Punch, bite, growling, groaning. My anger was killing me. Bash it out on Joe. I wasn't having IT go in on me. I was angry with him, too, Peter.

Joe reminded me, "Peter is a separate person to you. He must do as he wants. He is more smashed than you were. It's very difficult for him to trust."

Somehow we got through Christmas. I managed to put out the crib and a Christmas tree. Ian cooked the Christmas dinner. It was goose and we had crackers and paper servientes. Peter came to the dinner. It was at mid-day. He sat between David Bell and Michelle. My heart was aching. If only Peter was staying and going to Joe. Last summer since he had asked me to arrange for him to see Joe, he had, at Joe's request been going to ring up Joe.

Friday came. I gave Peter a note, to remind him about going to another general practitioner, and giving the doctor Joe's address and phone number and then going himself to

Joe and telling him who his new doctor was. We said good-bye. Peter told me: "Ian said I can keep the keys and come back when I like for the rest of my things."

I saw the back of Michelle, watching from the balcony window, as Peter must have been leaving the front door. Somehow, I felt the sadness through her back, the way she was watching. No one had wanted Peter to leave. The morning before Ian had come to see me.

"Mary, I got very angry because Peter was leaving because of the noise. I got an axe and chopped up the record player and threw it in the street."

"Ian, that's only a thing—it doesn't matter. It's Peter's insides—why he really takes himself away."

Ian said he was sorry that Peter was going. I said so was I, but we must just accept it and recognize Peter's freedom to do as he chose.

Within hours of leaving, Peter was back. It was midnight, I was asleep, there was a knock on my door.

"Come in—who is it?"

Janet came and sat on my bed.

"Mary, Mary, he's back."

"What?"

"Peter is back—he's upstairs in the Flat kitchen. I just came to tell you." I hugged Janet. She said goodnight and went back to bed.

I got some milk and and went up to Peter. He muttered something about the room not being ready. "Have some milk." He was getting himself something to eat. We said goodnight.

I could hardly believe it, that he was back. "Oh God, please may he stay."

Within a few days it seemed Peter was settling in again. He found a new cupboard for his food. He always kept it locked up, seemed immersed in shopping for food, cooking and eating, at most regular times. He ate three times a day.

He was getting very thin. He always wore a collar and tie and never sat about the place. He was alert, taut, as if moving to some inner command or compulsion. When an American psychiatrist, Jim Gordon, called, Peter came to my room. Jim asked Peter what he would advise about starting a place. Peter told him, "Have plenty of space, so people can have privacy. I like to cook and eat in a separate room to where I sleep. If you have only one kitchen have separate gas rings so everyone can have their own cooking place."

The time Peter was going to leave, he had been going to a bed-sitting-room with a gas ring. I realized Peter had now changed his idea of doing as I usually did at Kingsley Hall, eating and cooking in the same room.

I noticed Peter never ate meat and always had lots of raw carrots. His fruit and cucumber he rinsed in mauve fluid. I thought it must be permanganate of potash. Mother used to have us gargle every night with that, so we wouldn't get sore throats. Peter always regularly cleans his teeth and after any food rinses his mouth out with water.

I so longed for Peter to go to Joe, to feel a need for therapy, as well as food. Often as Peter was parting from me he would say, turning his body away, "I must get something to eat now." With Joe I realized he was having sexual feelings with his food. When I worried a lot about Peter, this was really me worrying about myself. Sometimes when I gave Joe rather a lot of details, he would say, "And how many times has Peter blown his nose today?"

When it was time for me to go to Newcastle for the opening of my exhibition in February 1970, I got very bad, feeling my anger bursting out of me. Joe told me to ring him back in an hour. I was wanting to hit and scream and fall to pieces.

I collapsed in tears on the stairs. Peter came by. He stood over me. How he was, the way he spoke, he seemed just like a robot. He had his hat and coat on, looked so neat, tidy, immaculate, contained.

He was saying, "Mary, get up. Come up to the Flat. Have some hot milk and honey. You will catch cold on those cold stone steps." He was saying each word separate—clipped—disjointed.

"Oh, Oh, Peter, why don't you go to Joe."

"Mary, it's just a matter of accommodation for me."

I was bent up, groaning, groaning. David Page Thomas came by.

"Whatever is the matter? I thought you were quite bouncy about going to Newcastle."

Peter announced, "Mary worries about me. It's not necessary. I'm all right."

"Oh, David, I'm bad. I have to think why I'm so angry and ring Joe back in one hour."

Leon and Liz came by. I screamed. Then went up to the Flat and punched Leon. Peter, now in the kitchen, getting out his food, looked relieved. I was shouting "And there's dog biscuits—they feed the dog and there's nothing for me." Joe rang.

I told him, "I've got to go away. Your baby is being born. I'm being sent away. The baby is coming."

Inside me I felt the whole external situation like my past life. I had been sent away for two weeks to my Granny's for my brother to be born. Joe's wife Roberta was expecting a baby at the end of February. Peter seemed like Joe's baby to me. It was all mixed up and I was in agony about going away.

Also the night before I had been to the pub with Ronnie and the boys. I had really wanted us to sit in the Flat with Peter who I knew didn't go to the pub. I hadn't been for a long time. Somehow that had all made me extra bad, so it seemed.

Joe assured me, "You will be back before the baby is born. The baby won't push you out. I still care for you very much. Going out with the boys last night—feeling you wanted to be a boy like them makes you have guilt. You feel it's wrong to want to be a boy."

A few more phone calls: Joe was still there, alive. My anger hadn't killed him, and I went to Newcastle. Mike Yocum came with me to take photos, as he was helping Leon to make a film about Kingsley Hall.

I was having a bad time with my tummy because of my desire to have a baby. I used to swell up and get wind and inside me all my guts felt twisted up in knots. Before I watered there were bad pains and I was always wanting to water and have shits and when the shits wouldn't come, I would strain and strain. Joe told me:

"That's all the babies you are wanting to have—your shits and water, and all those pains are you pushing babies out because you want to go into labour."

When I got back from Newcastle, Peter was using my old room as his kitchen and dining-room. I had moved downstairs to the room off the Hall. Peter told me,

"Ian said I could have this room so I could have somewhere quiet alone to cook and eat in."

"Oh, Peter, that's nice."

He seemed pleased. When Peter smiled he looked soft and yielding. When he was cross, he snorted, like a little bull. Then turning away he would screw up his face looking twisted, set and torn. He always uses his body, waving his arms and moving towards me, or away, according to whether he is pleased or cross. Sometimes he almost seems to dance, or move like a child in a temper tantrum. When he is more serene he sits twiddling his thumbs. He seems quite uncovered, fragile, true to how he feels.

Since last year, he has got thinner and changed in the way that he shows even more clearly in his whole being exactly how he feels.

Rather than saying it in words, he has very few words, his body, the way he moves, expresses his feeling. I think this is a wonderful change from his more covered hospital state. He is quite convinced he is much better without any tablets.

When I get very angry because Peter doesn't go into therapy with Joe, this is really me wanting to cure myself, to get united with my masculine part, which is a part of me, not Peter. He is not really my masculine part. My getting whole is something that happens between me and Joe, with or without Peter going to Joe. Whether Peter goes to Joe or not doesn't really make any difference to my life. Sometimes, I think when he feels jealous and angry, Peter wants me to live somewhere alone with him, without the rest of the community.

Just now Peter is still very involved with his food. When someone else arrived to take my old room, Peter moved his food to another cupboard, that he cleaned and locked up, in the middle floor kitchen. I hope in time, Peter will come to a realization of his own needs, and will go to Joe for therapy.

At the moment all of us at Kingsley Hall are concerned because we have to move at the end of May. I shall be very sorry to leave the beautiful ground floor room off the Hall that I have just moved into. I'm sure that Joe and Ronnie will come up with something nice.

In the future and with Joe's help I myself look forward to helping people who are very regressed to go through the experience and come up again, as well as to paint and to write.

This book has been through many changes. Two of my Christian stories, "The Cross of Christ and the Shepherd," we haven't room for, nor that story, "Baby Bear," that I wrote for Joe's baby, Joshua Damien, born on March 1st 1970.

This is the title and quotation I got from Joe's Jewish Bible, for the book : *The Treasures of Darkness:*

> I will go before thee, and make the crooked places straight. I will break in pieces the gates of brass, and cut in sunder the bars of iron. And I will give thee the treasures of darkness, and hidden riches of secret places, that thou mayest know that I, the Lord, which call thee by thy name, am the God of Israel.
>
> Isaiah, Chapter 45, Verses 2 and 3.
>
> From the translation of Alexander Harkavy, 1926.

Joe and Michael liked it. (Michael Dempsey our editor and publisher.) But as they said, you couldn't really tell what the book was about from the title and people like to see on the cover what the inside is about. So Joe thought of another title, the one on the cover, which I think is very nice. But my quotation means a lot to me, because Joe who was like God to me, as a Mother is to her baby, often called me by my name, tapping my head, saying:

"Who's there?"

"Mary."

"Mary who?"

"Mary Barnes." —

Epilogue

My gifts from Joe

Christmas 1965: a beautiful hardbound book of Grüne-wald's paintings.

February 9th, 1966: a mug with fish on it, wrapped in Mermaid paper. Two spiders, the first black, on a rubber string, the second white and fluffy.

Easter 1966: beautiful chocolate fish, symbol of Christ, a big one with little chocolate fishes inside.

May 1966: after the death of Joe's mother; a tiny delicate Chinese cup and saucer. It had been forty-five years in Joe's family. I put holy water in it and kept it on my shrine. When in bed, when I threw a plate of food, it accidentally got broken. A great sadness came over me. The shrine was lost. It was the crucifixion of Christ in clay on a wooden cross, before a painting in oils on wood of the Mother of God.

July 1966: a fierce chocolate crocodile—marvellous.

August 1966: Donk, Joe gave me, my dog doll with the hair that brushes up.

Christmas 1966: a beautiful yellow cracker. All the things came out of the cracker, but the cracker remained whole, I still have it. Also a book, very beautiful, about the Crocodile who stole the Sun, and the Bear who got it back. Squeaky, a beautiful mouse.

Spring 1967: a marvellous book, *Where the Wild Things Are*.

Summer 1967: the sweet smelling sandalwood scroll book of Chinese painting.

Winter 1967: a book of glorious colour of the paintings of Marc Chagall. Joe brought this from the Louvre in Paris.

Easter 1968: a beautiful Easter egg in a box, with the Three Bears.

Christmas 1968: The Bald Twit Lion, a marvellous book.

Christmas 1969: a box of beautiful jars of honey from all over the world.

Easter 1970: a beatiful Easter egg in a box with flowers and a golden bow. My Teddy, and Topsy, my black doll, I had from Ronnie in June, 1965. I had asked Ronnie for a doll. The gifts of Joe I didn't ask.

Part 6

Untangling Mary's Knot by Joseph Berke

Chapter Twenty-three

Untangling Mary's Knot

After Mary had finally decided to "come up," our relationship changed considerably. In the first place, our meetings became less frequent. From three hourly sessions per week at Kingsley Hall they progressed to two and then to one per week till mid-1968. Thereafter Mary travelled to my office. What a bonanza it was for me to be able to eliminate the two-hour drive through the centre of London to Kingsley Hall and back in order to spend one hour with Mary. No matter how temperamental Mary might be, London traffic was always worse.

Our meetings also became more structured. They took place at a set time and place each week for the primary purpose of my helping Mary to interpret and piece together the various strands of her past and present experience. This exercise had become possible once Mary had gained the ability to use words, besides deeds, to communicate about her feelings. She no longer had to scream or break a cup or take to bed in order to let me know when she felt bad. Now she could just say so. The added advantage of a multi-dimensional Mary was that if she got in a flap between sessions she could simply ring me up and work out over the telephone whatever was going on. This possibility of instant communication at any time during the day or night was a boon to Mary's growing sense of security. To her it meant that we were never out of touch. Of course, if Mary felt so disturbed that she couldn't talk over the phone, I would travel to the Hall. Monumental crises of this sort rarely happened after we had initiated our essentially psychotherapeutic meetings. At best Mary would think, "What would Joe say?", and then figure things out for herself. At worst, she would lie with her disturbance till IT passed. She knew that IT would go away if she could remain calm for a few hours.

Not so long ago Mary had a dream which illustrates the way that her internalized relationship with "Joe" helps her in times of emotional difficulty. In the dream Mary recalls that she was staying at a convent with Mother Michael. (Mother Michael is a nun to whom Mary is very close and who she often visits.) She felt all twisted up into herself and cried and cried. She screamed at Mother Michael to do something for her. Mother Michael replied, "What would 'Joe' suggest?" Mary thought, " 'Joe' would say, 'Don't worry, try to relax, drink a nice glass of warm milk with honey, and go to sleep.' " Mary followed "Joe's" instructions and sank into a calm, peaceful sleep. When she awoke from the dream she felt warm and good. Her upset had vanished.

Mary has had a number of similar dreams including ones in which "Joe" appears and helps her to put together her jigsawed emotional life. These, like all her dreams, are as brilliant and detailed as her paintings and stories. They are Mary's "reality." Whatever happens in the reality of her waking life is always reflected in her dreams, and vice versa. Therefore, when Mary began to have "healing dreams" like the one I have described, I knew she would find her non-dream life more tolerable, if not positively enjoyable. And so it was.

Mary continues to meet with me once a week. Not all our efforts go into the serious business of psyche analysis. We trade news and views and she solicits my advice about a variety of matters to which I often respond, "Mary, you know I am not you. What do you want?" We also talk about Mary's relationship with people at Kingsley Hall who have entered a psychotic state and to whom Mary has begun to serve as a helper. Having been through the experience herself, Mary is superbly able to establish and maintain a rapport with such individuals.

Catherine was the first person whom Mary tried to guide through the experience of psychosis. Previously Mary's presence had benefited John Woods or Stanley, but only within the context of the day to day activities of the community and not with the specific purpose of helping them.

Although Mary could communicate with Catherine as could nobody else at Kingsley Hall, it seemed that she distorted the relationship by trying to repeat with Catherine what she had gone through with me. I used to emphasize to her, "Mary, it won't help Catherine if you simply repeat with her what we did together. While it may be true that your 'down' and that of Catherine are in some ways similar, it is also obvious from what you tell me about her that her way is quite different from yours. Always remember that you and she are separate people. Pay attention to her needs. Otherwise you will confuse her and you may prolong her 'down,' rather than help her through it."

Gradually the message sank in, and Mary began to allow Catherine some breathing space without herself feeling guilty. Unfortunately Catherine's parents were not as generous. They whisked her away from Kingsley Hall (against her wishes) and gave her life in a locked hospital ward, drugs and electroshock (and later, themselves) in exchange for life in the community. I assume that what happened with Catherine is another example of a child being given "treatment" because of the emotional upset (anxiety, guilt, etc.) experienced in and by someone else, in this case, her parents.

Morty Schatzman deserves a lot of credit for creating the context in which Mary allowed herself to take on the role of helper. Once he joined the community, the internal politics of the place were cleaned up and residents felt more free to minister to each other's needs. Mary, in particular, thrived on Kingsley Hall's new found peace and togetherness. Relieved of the burden of anxiety associated with situations of inter-personal tension, Mary could "look" outside herself and lend a hand to people who were in more distress than she.

Morty has written a fine account of life at Kingsley Hall during the period he was a resident. He shows how the community functioned and what problems it had to face. He relates what other members of the community thought about their stay at Kingsley Hall. In addition, a detailed discussion of the historical development of the psychiatric treatment of the emotionally distressed provides a powerful argument in favour of alternative forms of care, such as Kingsley Hall. Entitled, "Madness and Morals," this work has been published as a chapter in *Counter Culture: The Creation of an Alternative Society.* *

1968 was also the year in which Mary met her parents for the first time since she had "come up." Mary had been looking forward to a reunion with her mother and father because she thought that she could "see" them from an entirely different perspective. She no longer felt "trapped" by her previous relationship with them. This proved to be the case.

Mary responded to her parents with joy, but also with sadness and anger. When I saw her for the first time after the visit, the anger was especially evident. I was glad she did not try to hide it, but was prepared to come to terms with the feeling. I suggested that she try to paint IT. With demonic energy Mary set her fingers, coated with paint, on to long scrolls of paper. Explosive bursts of reds flew out of black gobs splattered furiously against a white backdrop. Reds out of black and blacks out of red reach out and entangle the onlooker in Mary's horrific vision.

At the end of a dozen scrolls Mary felt calm, exhausted and purged of her anger. Concurrently, her abstract imagery demonstrated a high level of symbolic expression and artistic achievement. Mary had "discovered" her hands. From this point on she rarely felt the need to use a brush or palette knife. No matter how rough the surface, all that she required was her hands for coarse strokes and her fingers for delicate lines.

In the course of changing her method of painting, Mary developed an ingenious way of outlining and blending colours into her figures at the same time. She would take a tube of paint and squeeze out a thin blob of paint along the side of a finger. Then she would repeat this procedure with a different colour two, three, up to six times, till both sides of the finger were covered by lines of paint. With a couple of fingers covered in such a way she could quickly detail her figures in one or a combination of colours by a slight twist of her finger(s).

Mary's art of finger painting culminated in the Triptych,

Counter Culture: The Creation of an Alternative Society, edited by Joseph Berke, published in the United Kingdom in 1970 by Peter Owen Ltd. in association with Fire Books.

three six foot panels ablaze with biblical figures which she did especially for her first one-man show at the Camden Arts Centre in London in the spring of 1969. This exhibition, which was a great success, was arranged with the help of Jesse Watkins, who also took on the burden of choosing the paintings and getting them hung.

But it might not have taken place without the enthusiastic assistance of Mary's many friends and acquaintances from the network of people associated with Kingsley Hall. Together they made the catalogue, framed the paintings, and delivered them to an enormous room at the Arts Centre in preparation for hanging.

For Mary, "seventh heaven" had come down to earth. She relished the role of queen bee and played her part very well. No painting was too small to be trotted out for this or that reporter, no story was too long to be retold for the umpteenth time.

Old fears and inhibitions about meeting strangers or mixing in crowds were finally laid to rest. Opening night provided the big test of Mary's social prowess. No problems arose. Mary was completely at ease. She moved from this person to that, greeting and being greeted, with charm and dignity. It was an amazing performance for someone who but a couple of years before refused to leave her room during the day for fear of bumping into someone in the hallway.

Mary used the occasion to bring together many figures from her past as well as her present. Old friends from nursing days, religious associates and relatives still living in England all came either on the day of the opening or during the two weeks of exhibition. Aside from being pleased to see them for their sakes, Mary seemed to welcome them as if they were parts of herself with which she had lost contact but which she wished to bring together again. Among these, the most important person was her brother, Peter.

Peter Barnes is a quiet, pleasant, intelligent, middle-aged man whose main difficulty in life seems to be a lack of self-esteem and self-confidence resulting from being locked up for too many years in mental hospitals. Mary had initially consulted Ronnie for Peter's sake, not her own. Even during her most regressed periods she never lost hope that when

she got better, Peter would come to Kingsley Hall and would
be taken care of there as herself. I think Mary thought that
Peter had gotten stuck in the career of a mental patient and
didn't know how to give it up. Once Mary had found out how
to give up being a "schizophrenic" she intended to impart
this knowledge to Peter in order to liberate him from his
self-destructive life-style.

When Mary discovered that her brother was not eager to
move into Kingsley Hall, she was flabbergasted. How could
Peter turn down such a golden opportunity to "find himself"?
How could he reject all that his sister had done and wanted
to continue to do for him? What would happen to him if he
didn't get "therapy"? Mary raised these and similar questions
countless times as she pleaded with me to help her get Peter
to move to Kingsley Hall.

I pointed out, "Mary, you and your brother are separate
individuals. You can't expect him to want what you want or
do what you do. I'm sure his concerns are quite different
from yours. It isn't easy to break with the regimentation
and routine of the mental hospital. Go easy. Give him time
to do what he wants."

Part of Mary agreed with my advice. As a result Mary
moderated her campaign to bulldoze Peter into the community. She endeavoured to respect his point of view, if not
actually defer to his needs and wishes. The other part paid
no heed to me. It thought I was kidding and that all I had
to do was to bestow my magic on to Peter in order for him
to metamorphose into a new version of Lawrence of Arabia.

"Joe, you can do it. I know Peter would get better if he
came to see you."

"Mary, for Christ's sake, shut up. Let Peter make up his
own mind."

Eventually Peter did decide to move into Kingsley Hall,
right after Mary's London exhibition. He retained a shy, reserved, inner directed presence; in sharp contrast to that of
his ebullient, outgoing, high intensity sister.

Having brought her brother into the community, Mary
insisted that the best thing that could happen would be for
Peter to "go down." She was disconcerted when he showed
no indication of doing so.

I reiterated, "Mary, 'going down' was your way of coping

with your shit, your badness, your disturbance. It may not be Peter's."

Months passed before Mary allowed this message to sink in. She seemed preoccupied with Peter's "need" to repeat her experiences. While concerned for her brother's welfare, Mary obviously wanted Peter to regress and "come up" for her sake as well as for his.

Since Peter was in no hurry to "go down," I asked Mary to think about why it was *so important to her that he regress*. The answer, of course, was intimately connected with the reason for Mary's insistence that Peter come to Kingsley Hall to live.

Mary's associations to my questions about Peter revolved around the issue of guilt. All her life she had been guilty about her brother's hospitalizations, about his being diagnosed mentally ill, about his taking up the career of a "chronic schizophrenic." Mary held herself personally responsible for Peter's damaged emotions. Getting her brother to come to Kingsley Hall in order to go through what she had gone through with me was her way of repairing the damage which she thought she had inflicted on him. It was her way of trying to resolve her enormous burden of guilt. This guilt had to do with the murderous envy and jealousy which Mary had felt towards Peter, even when he was still in their mother's womb. Ronnie had been quite right when he suggested that there might be a link between the ocasion of Mary's regressions in the summer/fall and some key event in Mary's history which had occurred about the same time. That event was the birth of Peter. It had taken place in the early fall.

Mary remembers that she became aware of the impending baby when she noticed that her mummy's tummy had become very big. Her reaction was one of fascination, but more of fear. There weren't enough goodies in her world as it was. What would happen when another being came along to gobble up the love and attention which she considered her own. To defend herself against her growing fear of abandonment, she first imagined that she was her mummy and that the baby was getting bigger inside her, and then imagined that she was the baby which was growing inside her mother.

"It was the only way, imagining myself to be Peter."

What most upset Mary was her being sent away to he grandmother's before Peter arrived. Instead of seeing he identifications fulfilled, and herself vicariously reborn, Mar was terrorized by her angry, murderous fantasies toward both her mother for abandoning her and her brother for re placing her. Later, any interpersonal situation which reminde her of this traumatic experience set off similar feelings c fear and rage together with guilt and a desire for punish ment (appropriate to what her conscience saw as the crime of matricide and fratricide).

Mary's response to the impending birth of my son early i 1970 provides a dramatic confirmation of the phenomeno of emotional recapitulation. She had known that Roberta wa pregnant for several months but tried to mask her anxiet about the pregnancy through the mechanism of denial. Whe this didn't work she would frequently inquire about Roberta' health and of "the baby inside her." Then Mary's anxiet attached itself to Peter. She couldn't do enough for him. Sh continually worried about his health. She closely identifie Peter with my baby.

As the date of delivery approached, Mary had to travel t Newcastle to be present at the opening of her second majo exhibition. This completely unnerved her because she as sociated her going away with being sent away. She began t call me up and complain how bad she felt. She couldn't g to Newcastle, she wanted to "go down," what could I do t help her.

Patiently I went over the parallels between her "present" and her "past." Mary agreed. "Inside me I felt the whole external situation as my past life. I had been sent away fo two weeks to my Granny's for my brother to be born. Joe' wife, Roberta, was expecting a baby at the end of February Peter seemed like Joe's baby to me. It was all mixed up and was in agony about going away." I explained that her worry about Peter reflected her anger towards the forthcoming baby. She thought the baby would replace her as the objec of my love and affection. Mary corroborated this: "I always imagined my anger killed Peter, and her baby felt like Peter to me."

Mary went off to Newcastle where, in spite of all her

ars and anxieties, she enjoyed another successful exhibition.
ly baby was not born till she returned to London, which
efully demonstrated that the reality of her "present" did
t necessarily follow the reality of her "past."

Of course, Mary's suffering was not simply a repetition of
evious emotions. She was exceedingly jealous of my
lationship with Roberta and of the forthcoming baby.
his jealousy was experienced as an explosive, volcanic anger
hich threatened to destroy whomever it touched. Fortu-
ately Mary had become capable of confronting this intense
ger, rather than projecting it (attacks from the external
orld), directing it against herself (ideas of suicide), or
enying it.

Regression ("going down") was the main means by which
lary sought to deny jealous anger and all the guilt attendant
n it. To the extent that Mary gained the ability to accept
ather than reject her anger, she allowed herself to become
ware that "going down" was associated with avoiding jeal-
usy feelings which her conscience considered too dangerous.
 be expressed. That Mary always thought of "going down"
t times of severe emotional stress (such as just before she
ad to go off to Newcastle) indicated that "going down" in
ne service of avoiding painful feelings was one of Mary's
1ost vital intra- and interpersonal defensive manoeuvres.

Along with jealousy, Mary's envy towards Roberta and
ther friends of hers who had or were about to have babies,
recipitated the emotional upset she experienced before her
urney to Newcastle, and at many other times as well.
Iary wanted to have a baby because she wanted to be
he baby, but she couldn't allow herself to make this baby
n the usual way because of the enormous guilt associated
vith violating self-imposed and familial sexual taboos. Con-
equently Mary set out to make babies by turning herself
nto a baby.

We have seen that when Mary played with her shit, she
vas, in fantasy, moulding babies. Similarly, when Mary
overed herself with shit, she had, in fantasy, transformed
erself into a baby. This explains her actions on the several
ccasions when she smeared shit all about herself. Mary was
erribly envious of the real or imagined sexual relationships
he felt were taking place all about her. In response she

strove to emulate baby making activity by using her ow
body and body products as the raw material by which sh
could sculpt a baby, herself, in her own image.

However, Mary's favourite means of coping with he
desire to make babies was by "going down" or regression. I
this way Mary created a functioning one year old, or on
month old, or even one day old, replica of her idea c
babyhood. As far as avoiding envy or jealousy is concerned
"going down" allowed Mary to return to a period befor
these disturbing emotions had made their presence felt.
think Mary thought that tiny babies are not troubled b
sexual sensations. Accordingly she transformed the feedin
situation into a real substitute for her forbidden sexualit
Eating was equated with intercourse, and the end produc
of this intercourse, her excrement, was experienced as magi
babies. No wonder Mary was so fussy about who fed he
When she was "down," the acceptance of a new person t
care for her and feed her had the same importance as th
taking on of a new lover by a mature woman. The intens
guilt Mary suffered at such times (for example, when Noc
and Paul began to feed her) was related to the underlyin
sexual interpretation Mary gave to the act of feeding. An
to take food from too many people was to be promiscuous

When Mary began to "come up," she began to allude t
the sexual content of her regressive experience. As she be
came more able to deal with her sexual thoughts and desire
she confirmed that on many occasions she "went bad" be
cause she had woven me or Peter or someone else into one o
her sexual fantasies. These invariably included getting preg
nant and having a baby. "Going bad," feeling extreme guil
anticipating severe punishment, a sense of doom, was Mary
response to this most taboo side of herself.

Mary continually twisted her strong sexual drive up, ove
and into itself. However, the more she repressed her sexua
interests, the more frustrated she became, and the more sh
attributed sexual intent to anything that happened to her
She was tormented by her own experience and reacted wit
great anger towards anyone or anything which aroused he
emptiness. In this state she could not avoid equating socia
contact with sexual contact, feeding with feeling, and feelin
with sexuality. Death was the only way out, first the death

of the hated others whom she mistakenly blamed for her predicament, and if this failed, then the death of herself. At least, from Mary's point of view, *dead people don't feel*. Fortunately Mary was able to feign death by cutting herself from all feelings without actually having to kill herself.

IT was the term Mary coined to describe her rage when she felt threatened by feelings which were too hot to handle. This same word, IT (DAS ES) was used by the German psychiatrist, Georg Groddeck, to describe the basic sexual energies (life-force) which move all men. Later Sigmund Freud incorporated Groddeck's concept into his panoramic understanding of the psyche. In English translation, IT (DAS ES) became the ID. Clearly Mary referred to the same sexual energies and drive when she used the word, but to energies which had been transformed by guilt from the sphere of creation to that of destruction.

If genital sexuality had been the principal preoccupation of Mary's conscience, then she would have been able to work through her guilt, more or less. But it was not. Deep down, Mary wished to remain a baby in the womb. Whether this ontogenetic primitivism actually stemmed from the period before she was born, or afterwards, is debatable. The important point is that Mary constantly thought about returning to a period in her life before she was born and when she was actually carried inside another person. Consequently she refused to allow a baby to grow inside her, she even refused to allow a man to put his penis inside her. She desperately wanted to be the penis or the baby inside the woman, not the woman into which these objects were put, or grew.

Identification was the psychic trick Mary played on herself in order to achieve her aim of getting back inside another's body. Mary has written about this in relationship to Peter, whom she particularly envied. "Before he came, he was there, in my place, filling out Mummy's tummy." "If only I could have got back inside Mother."

Alternatively Mary tried to manipulate her environment (by regression) so that she was taken care of in a way which could be identified with an intrauterine existence. At Kingsley Hall this precipitated the tube feeding crisis.

When Mary found that the act of identification with Peter

or the intrauterine state did not fulfil her needs, she fell int
the greatest despair. Then she would mentally murder Pete
her mother, or any member of an intrauterine baby-mothe
pair whom she met or thought about. Similarly she murdere
men (and was terrified of them) because they had penise
which could be put into women. As for carrying a bab
herself, this was impossible because Mary would have fel
destroyed by her destructive wishes towards the baby. Thes
murderous sentiments generated the guilt which kept Mar
tied up in an emotional knot.

In my discussion of Mary's sexual and atavistic desire
both here and in previous chapters, I have tried to provid
a coherent picture of the main strands of Mary's tumultuou
emotions. A lot more could be added, especially about th
social context in which she grew up and the spiritual quest
on which she embarked. Mary sees her "going down" an
"return" as a spiritual journey rather than as a sexua
struggle. The two are not incompatible. My emphasizin
the mortifications of the flesh does not detract from th
realization of the soul. Most Christian mystics would agre
with me. However, whichever way one chooses to look a
the life of Mary, and whatever words one uses to describ
what she went through, it is clear that *her history is no
unintelligible*. Mary's actions, which may seem quite bizarr
to the uninformed observer, could be seen to have an inne
logic and outer predictability once one took the trouble to
know Mary, her story, her experience, her circle of friend
and relatives.

I don't think the label "mad" does justice to Mary or, fo
that matter, to any other person who may manifest himsel
in a way that a stranger would consider peculiar. Nothin
that Mary experienced, nothing that she went through is fa
removed from what we all have to cope with in ourselves
That Mary confronted her physical, psychic or spiritua
demons may mean that she was just more in touch wit
them than most people.

Modern man has discovered the atom, but not himself. H
remains as ignorant of *intra*- and *inter*personal relationship
as the medieval alchemist who tried to make gold by mixing
bird shit and beeswax. Most of what goes down as psychiatri
treatment is simply an attempt to perpetuate this ignorance

f the patient is docile, a few sweet words will keep both
ie psychiatrist and his client from uncovering what each
night find disturbing in himself and in the other. If the
atient is recalcitrant, then progressive violence in the form
f tranquillizing drugs, forced hospitalization, electric shock,
r lobotomy, the destruction of part of the brain, will be
sed against him in order to shut him up. Mary almost
uffered the same fate because her message was too painful
or those with whom she came into contact.

Did Kingsley Hall succeed? As one resident put it, "That is
n irrelevant question: it does no harm, it does no 'cure.'
t stands silent, peopled by real ghosts; so silent that, given
uck, they may hear their own hearts beat and elucidate
he rhythm."

Since May 1970 Kingsley Hall has closed its doors. The
ease on the building ran out and the residents reluctantly had
o move away.

Mary has taken a two-room unfurnished apartment near
Hampstead Heath in North London. This is her first home
of her own. Here she paints, writes and provides sage advice
o Kingsley Hall *alumni* and others who have entered a
"down" and who wish to meet her.

In the future Mary would like to see another community
et up, like Kingsley Hall. This new place would serve as a
efuge for people who have entered the state of psychosis.*
Mary intends to live in it and to help others to travel the
oads she so painfully learned to navigate. Mary has writ-
en:**

When I think *now* of a place, I think of people, us
people who are already involved and I think first of our
spiritual needs. Our desires to worship God—the great
need of the soul.

*The Philadelphia Association and others have continued the work
iegun at Kingsley Hall. (The Philadelphia Association, Ltd., 20 Fitzroy
Square, London W.1).

In 1970 the Arbours Housing Association was formed by people who
iad been associated with the Kingsley Hall community, in order to
continue and develop the work begun there. (Arbours Housing Association, Ltd., 50 Courthope Road, London N.W.3).

**Network Newsletter, Redler, L., Ed., Vol. 1, No. 1, London, Sept.
1969.

374

Because we do this in different ways I want in such
a community as ours to see real freedom and respect
towards these different ways of life.

I would like then, for Noel, a Meditation room with
symbols of the Buddhist way of life, decorated according
to Noel's taste. What we believe in our mind affects our
bodies, and so for Noel and others, a vegetarian diet.

Joe is Jewish. For him, the Passover seder, the ritualistic
telling of the exodus from Egypt, is an expression of his
being. I am Christian and have been mad.

My faith and my madness are the two great inseparable
influences of my life.

My madness uncovered more clearly and revealed the
Faith within me.

Going through madness is a purification, it brings me
nearer to God, to myself, helps me to a more conscious
awareness of God, to a fuller participation in the sight of
God.

I desire facilities for "going in" to further purify my
remaining madness to holiness, to wholeness.

Others, my brother Peter, and John Woods, not so long
at Kingsley Hall, have a great need to get fully down
into their madness. Then with the help of skilled therapy
to be brought through it. Their desperate need is to be
understood. The place must have Ronnie, Joe, Leon,
Morty, around, to understand them. The practice of their
faith, the same as mine, the Sacraments—confession, communion—cannot of themselves heal John and Peter. They
need psychotherapy, to trust and love a therapist.

A place grows into the sort of place people want it to be.
It then serves the needs of these people.

Similar people come along, mad people, therapy people, they "fall" for the place, perhaps come in and "wreck"
it—because it's the only place they've ever found that
would stand their feelings.

The place must be strong in the strength of God. Good
enough to take the shit of all its people. It must always
go on getting better—through the people who are already
there, through everyone that ever sets foot in the place.

That's the sort of place I want, something sacred, full
of *love*.